Theology in Stone

Theology in Stone

Church Architecture from
Byzantium to Berkeley

RICHARD KIECKHEFER

UNIVERSITY PRESS

2004

OXFORD
UNIVERSITY PRESS

Oxford   New York
Auckland   Bangkok   Buenos Aires   Cape Town   Chennai
Dar es Salaam   Delhi   Hong Kong   Istanbul   Karachi   Kolkata
Kuala Lumpur   Madrid   Melbourne   Mexico City   Mumbai
Nairobi   São Paulo   Shanghai   Taipei   Tokyo   Toronto

Published by Oxford University Press, Inc.
198 Madison Avenue, New York, New York 10016

www.oup.com

Oxford is a registered trademark of Oxford University Press

Library of Congress Cataloging-in-Publication Data

Kieckhefer, Richard.
   Theology in stone : Church architecture from Byzantium to Berkeley /
Richard Kieckhefer.
      p. cm.
Includes bibliographical references and index.
   ISBN 0-19-515466-5
   1. Church architecture.   2. Liturgy and architecture.   I. Title.
   NA4800 .K53 2003
   726.5—dc21   2002153721

9 8 7 6 5 4 3

Printed in the United States of America
on acid-free paper

To the memory of my mother
Virginia Kelley Kieckhefer
(1917–2002)

Preface

Church architecture is a contentious field of inquiry. Polemics, dogmatism, and caricature abound. It would be unrealistic to think any book could resolve the controversies, but a fresh look at the most basic questions about churches, their meanings and their uses, may prove useful to all sides. The incentive to write this book was mixed: it grew out of historical interest, but also out of an urge to see more clearly what churches have meant and what they can mean for communities that build and use them. It might seem that the first four chapters deal with theological questions, while the extended case studies that follow shift the focus to history—but in fact theology and history are intertwined throughout.

With a book of this sort, readers may have more than the usual degree of curiosity about the author's background and point of view. Suffice it to say that my most extensive experience of worship has been in Roman Catholic, Orthodox, and Anglican churches; that I am old enough to have recited mass responses for many years in Latin and to have learned plainchant in first grade; that over many years I have visited churches extensively in Britain and North America and have had occasion to study them in France, Germany, Spain, Italy, Belgium, the Netherlands, Switzerland, Austria, the Czech Republic, and Greece; that I dream of exploring the churches of Lālibalā—indeed, I literally dream quite often of visiting churches—but have not yet done so; that my academic research has focused mainly on western Europe in the late Middle Ages; that my doctorate is in history but I have taught for decades in a department of religion; that I have done much work on the history of magic, which I see as relevant to the broader study of ritual; that one of my maternal grandmother's uncles was pastor of the first Polish church in Chicago, and some of my information on Saint Stanislas Kostka Church is from an unpublished family history; that I have had considerable experience in a Newman Center designed in the years of experimentation after Vatican II; that I have sung for over a decade in the choir of an Orthodox cathedral; that I have been deeply involved at an Anglo-Catholic church where women are welcomed as priests, where openly gay men and lesbian couples with children occupy positions of lay leadership, and where liturgy and an exceptionally strong music program are balanced by ministry to refugees and others; and that if this book is inspired by any particular theological tradition it is that of liberal Anglo-Catholicism. The last point may seem the most important but cannot be isolated from all the rest.

Three people especially have given me the benefit of their wisdom and learning as I have worked on this project. My wife Barbara Newman shares a passionate interest in liturgy and its setting and has contributed immeasurably to the progress of this book at every stage; when I tell of experiences "we" have had in visiting churches, she is invariably my companion. Frank Burch Brown read and gave exceptionally detailed and insightful comments on an early draft; he is largely responsible for giving my research a series of unexpected turns. And Karl Morrison, who read the book when it was in its longest and untidiest state, challenged me helpfully on many points in his double role as scholar and priest.

Various specialists have shown themselves kind and generous with their expertise: Wolfgang Pehnt gave perceptive comments for the chapter on Rudolf Schwarz; Rosemary Horrax helped with the chapter on Beverley; Father Michael Komechak, O.S.B., has showed kindness on many visits to Saint Procopius Abbey, shared his wisdom on contemporary church design, and provided valuable suggestions on various chapters; and David Van Zanten made clear how my perspective relates to that of an architectural historian. All these individuals have contributed immensely toward my project.

I am deeply indebted also to Benjamin D. Sommer for insight into the conceptions of sacrifice in ancient Israel; to David Collins, S.J., for reactions to an early draft; to Richard Webster for giving me a musician's perspective on the subtleties of church acoustics; to Amelia J. Carr for revealing to me something of an art historian's grasp of churches in the Chicago area; to Adhemar Dellagustina, Jr., for expert help with photographs; to Marian Caudron for sharing with me her experiences in sacred places; to Edward Muir, for the subtitle; to Stuart Baumann and Linda Kelley, Roger Boden, Emily Erwin, Amancio Guedes, Lawrence Haptas, John Kemp, Angela Lorenz, Susan B. Matheson, Kelli Peters, Maria Schwarz, Claudia Swan, and Michael Swartz, for various kindnesses; to parishioners at Saint Luke's in Evanston and to students at Northwestern University and Seabury-Western Theological Seminary, for giving me the invaluable opportunity to learn by teaching; and to Cynthia Read at Oxford University Press for proving the ideal editor for a book of this sort. The interlibrary loan staff at Northwestern University Library have obtained a constant stream of materials to sustain my research habit. Countless people have given me invaluable help on my visits to their churches, including at times the most basic service of providing a key. Unfortunately many of them are nameless to me. I must at least express gratitude to Father Donald Schell and Father Richard Fabian, of Saint Gregory of Nyssa in San Francisco, and Father Johannes Floss and Christa Schinkenmeyer, of Sankt Fronleichnam in Aachen; and Father Duncan Ross, of Saint Paul's Bow Common.

The Northwestern University Research Grants Committee has provided partial support for the publication of this book, and I am grateful for this assistance.

Over the decades, several church communities have informed my sense of how ecclesiastical architecture comes alive in a range of liturgical uses: Saint Thomas More Church in Louisville, where I grew up at a time when the church building was architecturally unambitious but the liturgy was more richly developed than I could then appreciate; Sheil Center in Evanston, which accommodates with equal grace the throngs of Ash Wednesday and the quiet few on weekday afternoons; Holy Trinity Orthodox Cathedral in Chicago, known as the Louis Sullivan church but more importantly a coherent specimen of traditional Russian design; and Saint Luke's Episcopal Church in Evanston, which was begun in the early twentieth century as a classic Anglo-Catholic church and still (like the Church universal) awaits its finishing touches.

Not all these people and communities would agree with what I have to say. But I hope, at least, not to have been blind or deaf to what they cherish and what they have tried to teach me.

This book is dedicated to the memory of my mother, Virginia Kelley Kieckhefer, whose contribution to it was by far the most vital: she first took me to a church for baptism when I was an infant, she took me again when I was a very young child (I looked about and asked where God was, and she said he was all around us), she went with me exploring churches even as her health declined, and now she has passed beyond symbols and metaphors to "that eternal and blessed church" which others prefigure.

A Note on Illustrations

In addition to the plates given in this book, readers may consult the listing of churches on the Emporis Web site, http://www.emporis.com. This site gives a wide selection of images, including many for churches discussed here.

Contents

Theology in Stone

Introduction

Robertson Davies tells of an English country church where the women make a slight curtsy to a blank wall on entering. Why they do so is unclear, until the vicar explains that a statue of the Virgin once stood at precisely that spot, and Cromwell's troops destroyed it in the seventeenth century, yet even these iconoclasts "could not destroy the local habit, as evinced in the women's behaviour."[1] The story is not unique to Davies's novel. Historians speak of a Continental church where it is a wall-painting of the Virgin that is plastered over during the Reformation, venerated nonetheless with reverent bows by generations of villagers, then rediscovered in the course of restoration.[2] Here as elsewhere, the old religion lingers.

The tale lends itself to more than one reading. For Protestant Reformers or rationalist critics it can be a lesson in the lamentable tenacity of folk superstition. Just as plausibly it can show how ordinary folk have deeper memory and keener perception of a sacred presence than iconoclast elites, even if their memory and perception are embodied in gesture and not explicitly articulated. A modern liturgical reformer might see it as a cautionary tale showing how private devotion infiltrates liturgical space, while a traditionalist might brandish it with glee as evidence that liturgy and devotion will go hand in hand whatever the puritans of any age do to keep them apart. But neither the skeptical nor the romantic view of such a story, neither the reformist nor the traditionalist reading, could claim authority without somehow entering into the scene and speaking with the villagers, giving them occasion to articulate what they experience. Do they in fact have some awareness, however vague, of a statue or a painting once on view? Does the experience of entering a church and bowing to a spot on the wall, meaningless as the gesture may seem, help give a sense of sacred place and prepare for richer experience of worship? The story brings into focus several issues in the use of sacred space. In the end, however, it can perhaps best be read as a parable urging everyone—reformist theologians and lay devotees, secular scholars and other outsiders—to become more reflective and articulate about what ritual is meant to do, how it gives expression to faith, and how the space provided for ritual is meant to function. The plaster concealing the image becomes a metaphor for all that blocks full realization of the purposes served in liturgy and promoted by liturgical space.

Interesting as it would be to interview the villagers of Davies's tale, the opportunity is not likely to arise, not least because the tale comes with an eyebrow-raising vagueness about exact location. But anyone who makes use of any church has experience of it as sacred space, and there is no shortage of opportunities to clarify people's perceptions by articulating them, by bringing experience to the level of conception. That, most basically, is the purpose of this book. It is meant to stimulate thinking about churches; to provoke deeper and more broadly informed reflection on the purposes of church architecture, and thus also on the worship carried out in churches; to suggest how one might go about *reading* a church; to provide conceptual tools and vocabulary for articulating experience of sacred space. At a time when church architecture is an intensely controversial matter, one may well raise the fundamental questions often obscured in polemics, and reopen possibilities closed off by dogmatisms.

Responding to Churches

During his travels in 1853 Augustus Hare was disappointed by his companion, "a good-looking, sentimental, would-be poet," whose only comment on Cologne Cathedral was "very pretty," and on Sankt Aposteln "very nice."[3] Even in an age that prized sentiment more than ours, these sentiments must have seemed thin indeed. But where does one go beyond "very nice" and "very pretty"? Would Hare have been any more pleased with a less tepid comment such as "magnificent!" or "awe-inspiring!" that required no greater mental exertion than "very pretty"? One might move to the opposite extreme; Edward Dart said about one of his own churches: "Christianity is not a pretty religion—I will be disappointed if our church is classed as a pretty church."[4] Skirting that issue, one might focus on the historically contextualized particulars of a specific church, and the cultural milieux that led to some phase of construction or renovation. One might relate Cologne Cathedral to its seminal role in the development of German Gothic design, and then to the connection between the Gothic revival and romantic nationalism of the nineteenth century, while

Sankt Aposteln could bring to mind the flowering of Rhenish Romanesque and its modern revival.[5] One might walk through these churches discussing the history and background of each feature, each arcade and window, each altar and shrine—but without serious study of historical contexts this sort of information remains merely anecdotal.

Response to a church are conditioned by culture and by cultural interaction. A writer on African missionary churches noted in 1966 that African people are more sensitive than Europeans realize to "the atmosphere created by a building, especially when the building has a high and dignified interior." Passersby might come off the road, kneel in even an unfinished building, and declare: "Truly this is the House of God."[6] It is hard to say how far such a statement is spontaneous and uncoached, and how far it reflects the missionaries' teaching. But this is a special instance of a broader phenomenon: reactions learned from others often seem more spontaneous than they are.

Response to a church is conditioned by expectations, yet a church can frustrate or exceed expectations, even those grounded in long study of photographs and historical background. I am probably not the only person who has gone to the Fronleichnamskirche in Aachen fearing the worst, expecting it to look something like a prison, only to be transfixed on walking through the door by the flood of pure luminosity, and by the divine stillness that Romano Guardini found in this interior.[7] When Sally Kitt Chappell was planning to visit Hagia Sophia for the first time, she feared her expectations might be too high. "Perhaps after all the years of study and anticipation, the work will turn out to be a disappointment; perhaps one will fail to feel what has moved others so profoundly." When she arrived, she found that her expectations had not been high enough. The dome, supported by the half-dome flanking it, first raised and then fulfilled her expectations. "This is what a masterpiece does, it expands your ideas about what is possible." And the immensity of the light-filled space, she found, works its magic on all: "Masterpieces succeed universally." Her experience was informed by analysis and study of architectural history, yet in the end it was reverential. "In the peace and light of its radiant spaces, faith and knowledge celebrate their divine union, wed in the sanctuary of Hagia Sophia, Holy Wisdom."[8]

Response to a church can depend on whether it is being used liturgically. Both scholars and enthusiasts often find themselves visiting churches when they are not in use: as if anaesthetized, the buildings lend themselves more to examination. Yet even between services a church is not *merely* an inert functional structure or an aesthetic environment without religious meaning. Paul Tillich urged that a church building should elicit a response even apart from its liturgical use, that the space should give people an experience of "the presence of the holy . . . even before anything else happens within this space."[9] Or, as a monk once said of his church, it "prays of itself."[10] Still, the sense of sacrality will not be the same in an empty church and a church enlivened by gathering and movement, music and drama. A church is intended by its build-ers mainly for use by the assembly (which, after all, is what *ekklesia* or "church" means in New Testament Greek). In this respect a church is more like a syn-agogue or mosque than an ancient or Asian temple: it is designed primarily for an assembly and perhaps secondarily for private use, while a temple is built primarily for private encounter with the deity or private meditation and sec-ondarily for communal functions. If one knows well enough what kind of liturgy is celebrated in a church, even an empty building can be imagined in use, but liturgists are sometimes full of surprises in their use of space.

Liturgical use of space can give the lie to artificial distinctions. If one church has an altar in the chancel at the far end, while another church brings the altar down into the center of the assembly, the buildings may seem to declare opposing messages even before services have begun. A distinguished interpreter sees the first sort of church as suggesting that "God is remote and transcendent," while the second intimates that "God is near and immanent."[11] But what if the clergy enter into the nave during the liturgy of the word? What if the community senses keenly that God is present not only in the eucharist but in the scriptures, read and preached in the nave, so the altar alone is not the marker of divine presence? What if the entire assembly moves into the chancel during the eucharist, making it into a place not of exclusion but of inclusion? And what if the passage from nave to chancel makes for a more dynamic, less sedentary worship? The liturgy and the ethos of the place then overturn the simplistic assumptions grounded in an uncontextualized mis-reading of the architecture.

The difficulty is compounded when the building is a pilgrimage chapel specially meant for throngs of devotees but sought out at other times by sight-seers. John Ely Burchard visited Le Corbusier's celebrated chapel of Notre Dame du Haut at Ronchamp and found it in many ways lacking. Yet he con-ceded that the building might show to proper advantage only at the time of pilgrimage, when vested priests and throngs of pilgrims stand before the image of the Virgin for whose veneration they have assembled. His own visit was on a Sunday when the building swarmed with mere tourists. Photographs of it devoid of visitors had revealed a unity, an order, that he found missing when it was packed. "Do you judge it, then, by the repose of the photographs when no people are there? Might it be that way in mid-week? Was it our bad luck to come on a Sunday? Or were the people part of the glory of the edifice? A building for people ought to be able to stand the presence of people, but were these the right people?"[12] The taste for liturgy, the taste for special religious events such as pilgrimages, and the taste for sacred space do not always co-incide, and indeed many people would rather visit and judge a church in con-templative solitude when it is not buzzing with chant and redolent of incense. There are even chapels where private prayer is the main intention, and chapels such as Ronchamp that are meant in the first instance for special devotional

exercises.[13] In these cases the experience of sacrality may be relatively independent of regularly celebrated liturgy. But these are special cases. Normally
the reason for entering a church even for private prayer is that the place has a
sacrality derived from association with public prayer, from discovery of a place
where communal prayer, as T. S. Eliot says, has been valid.

On the day in April when I visited Ronchamp, all the other visitors I
encountered were German tourists, a handful of them, whose interest in the
place seemed more cultural than devotional. There was still snow on moun-
taintops not far away, and inside the chapel one could see puffs of one's own
breath in the air. A quiet rendition of the *Regina coeli* (it was, after all, only a
few days past Easter) proved the acoustics more hollow than resonant. At another time of the year, at another time of day, under other circumstances, the
chapel would surely have presented a different face, but that day in April it
was like a cave in which spirits had not yet roused themselves from hiberna-
tion.[14]

One's reaction to a church may well be conditioned not only by whether
people are present but by how full or sparse the congregation is. In the early
1950s it was possible to speak of a church by Rudolf Schwarz in which "the
greatness of the space is that priest and congregation are spontaneously
brought together in unity," even though the priest was standing fully eleven
steps above the congregation and with his back to the people. When both
sanctuary and nave were packed, clergy and servers and congregation seemed
united in a single assembly, and the priest at the altar could be perceived as
standing out *among* the people, not at all isolated from them.[15] With fewer
people present the same altar in the same position could have fundamentally
different effect.

Response to a church will be conditioned not only by liturgical practice
but also by the ethos of the community. A procession down the center of a
long nave, with a cross borne in the lead, accompanied by candles and perhaps
incense, with clergy in vestments and choir in cassocks and surplices, may
seem to some a meaningless show, a display of clerical grandeur, or a manifestation of difference between those processing and those in the pews on
either side. If in a particular parish the clergy are experienced outside of liturgy
as aloof and magisterial, and if the choir members are paid outsiders with little
interest in the life of the parish, this may be precisely the effect of a procession.
But if the clergy are known to be warm pastors or fiery charismatic leaders, if
the choir members are in general active parishioners who wash dishes in the
parish soup kitchen, if there are once and future choristers and acolytes in the
pews, or people who know they could assume these roles if they wished, and
if meanwhile the congregation joins vigorously with the choir in singing while
the procession takes place—if, in short, the clergy and choir are perceived more
as "us" than as "them"—then the procession is likely to be experienced as a
dramatic manifestation of solidarity, an opportunity for clergy and singers to

move closer to the congregation, and a means for setting a tone of solemnity or of celebration. It is not only the liturgy that will be perceived differently, but the space: the long nave will take on a greater or lesser sense of purpose depending on how its processional use is experienced. What one person experiences as meaningless show, and a second perceives as dazzlingly impressive show, a third will recognize not as show but as drama.

Churches that represent one extreme or another are likely to elicit a strong first impression: buildings that are exceptionally soaring, or luminous, or dark and mysterious, or remarkable for any other unmistakable quality. Lindsay Jones says of the uncommonly ornate churches of Santa María Tonantzintla and San Francisco Acatepec in central Mexico that the first sensation is invariably one of stunned surprise, leading visitors to gasp audibly on entering.[16] The middling church, being neither particularly large nor notably intimate, neither radiant nor dark, neither strikingly ornate nor singularly pure, neither very long nor very broad, may be either the most flexible or the most nondescript of spaces; its effect will depend all the more on how it is used liturgically and how the ethos of the community helps define its character. Yet even churches that do make a striking initial impression may not wear effectively with repeated exposure or lend themselves equally well to all feasts and seasons. Like liturgy itself, liturgical architecture must overcome the numbing effect of familiarity, and it can do so only through the ways it is used and the ethos that is cultivated.

Interested observers sometimes suppose a church will elicit one inevitable response from all who see and use it. In 1933 a commentator noted that a certain architectural plan made for "a more worshipful church interior" and that "with it will come an improvement in the order of worship" because the improved design would discourage carelessly prepared services.[17] Only a few years later, in 1940, Eric Gill urged that moving the altar down into the midst of the congregation would *force* people to take notice of what is done in liturgy and *compel* people to seek and to give instruction on liturgical matters.[18] Even more extravagantly, a minister in the early 1950s exclaimed of his new interior: "It would be difficult to speak or think anything but the truth in such a setting."[19] Yet responses are not so simple and predictable. Architecture does not force people to do anything. Careless services can be held anywhere. A building that guarantees truthfulness could only be sought, one might suppose, in the Heavenly Jerusalem where there is no temple.

The idea of responding to a church takes on different meaning if one imagines the church as speaking first. Edward Sövik in the 1960s entertained a contrast between two churches, one of them large and imposing, the other more modest. The imposing church he imagined as saying: "I am the ruler; when you approach me you must be impressed by me, and I want you to move in certain ways and assume an attitude of awe and subservience in my presence." The second church says, more ingratiatingly: "You are people, and you are the most important thing. I offer you shelter within my powerful structure; but I will not impose my forms upon you or make myself the demanding object of your attention. . . . In this way I will be your servant."[20] But even apart from the strangeness of putting words into the mouth of a building, and apart from one's suspicion that if the first of these churches could speak it would strike a rather different rhetorical tone, there is a problem here of misplaced attribution. If we wanted to sustain the conceit of a church that speaks to people, we would have to note that the same church says different things to different visitors. The church that proclaims itself a ruler to one person and demands homage in response would project to another a message of uplift and inspiration in the presence of holiness, and it might expect in response an expression of awe and gratitude to God. But if the church is uttering such different messages, one quickly suspects that someone is ventriloquizing, and suspicion falls on interpreters such as Sövik, who wish their interpretations to be perceived not as their views projected onto the buildings but as inherent meanings, as if emanating from the very stones.

Response to a church is learned, and the process of learning requires informed reflection. The meanings of a church are seldom obvious. One critic suggests of good architecture generally that it "does not make all its meanings explicit."[21] To be sure, another insists that a church has meaning to communicate, in particular "the meeting of God and man in the bond of love," and ought to communicate this meaning to all: "it is no argument to say that some are insensitive, uncultured, and need first to be educated. This *is* a means of education."[22] People respond spontaneously to ordinary natural and social environments, and they should be able to grasp the significance of a church in much the same way. What this argument disregards is that responses to social environments are not purely spontaneous, and even reactions to nature are not purely natural: in various ways, explicit and subtle, people learn how to perceive the world around them, and in the case of a church the lesson is learned gradually, through experience of liturgy and by life within community, and by absorbing principles of interpretation learned from others.

Some individuals report an exceptionally keen sensitivity to the presence of the holy within sacred space. One acquaintance, an eminently practical individual, handy with a hammer and screwdriver, tells of experiencing physical reactions to this presence. When she visited Westminster Abbey she had a sensation of being drawn upward, as if from her heart. At Benares she was absorbed for nearly an hour in a state of insensate bliss so intense that she was unaware of a goat nibbling on her jacket. In other sacred places she has felt a surge of energy running along her spine and up to the crown of her head. The older the place, and the longer its tradition of worship, the more intense is her experience. And she has little sympathy for sightseers who treat a church as merely an object of curiosity. Her sensitivity is perhaps one form of the mindfulness cultivated in meditation, and it is surely no coincidence that she practices and teaches meditation. But as she relates her experiences it is clear that she perceives them as coming in response to a presence rooted not in her but in the places themselves. For her, more than for most people, the experience of the holy is an experience of reality distinctively present in a particular location. For her, sacrality is not ascribed to a place but discovered.

This degree of sensitivity may seem unusual. But what counts then as usual, and why? *All* ways of responding to a church arise from the particular backgrounds of specific observers, who will see in it what they have been taught to see, what their sensibilities lead them to see, and what the uses and ethos of worshiping communities enable them to see. In the midst of all this variation, then, it is a challenge to find aspects of church architecture so basic that they can usefully guide everyone's perception of any church—to find common ground for discussion, for possible agreement, and even for clearer understanding of the disagreements that will inevitably remain.

Four Ways of Looking at a Church

Two basic questions are relevant to the understanding of any church: how is it used, and what sort of reaction is it meant to elicit? But each of these questions can be divided into two more specific questions. To ask how a church is used is first of all to ask about the *overall configuration of space*: how is it shaped, and how does its design relate to the flow, the dynamics of worship? The question of use is secondly a question about the *central focus of attention*, if any, within the church: what is the visual focus, and how does it make clear what is most important in worship? To inquire about the reaction a church evokes is to ask first about the *immediate impact* it makes on a person walking through the door: what aesthetic qualities come to the fore, and how do they condition the experience of the holy within the church's walls? But the question is also one about the *gradual accumulation of impressions* gained in repeated experience of worship within a church: how does sustained exposure to a building and its markers of sacrality lead to deeper and richer understanding?

One might easily devise thirteen ways of looking at a church, but this book will suggest four, corresponding to these four fundamental questions: the spatial dynamics of a church, its centering focus, its aesthetic impact, and its symbolic resonance.

Specialists in the history of church architecture may hear echoes of Friedrich Wilhelm Deichmann, who in a classic essay on early churches distinguished purpose (*Zweck*), meaning (*Bedeutung*), and form (*architektonische Form*) as the main factors in church-building.[23] The spatial dynamics and centering focus of a church might be said to express its purpose, its symbolic resonance might be taken to express its meaning, and its aesthetic impact could be assimilated to its form. But Deichmann's categories refer mainly to the governing conceptions of the people who planned and built churches, while my concern is not only with the intention of the builders but also with the appropriation of churches by generations that view and respond to them, use them and often refashion them. The question what a church *has meant* and the question what a church *can mean* are related but not identical.

Three Traditions of Church-Building

These four factors are handled differently in different types of church. For heuristic purposes, this book will survey three broad traditions of church design (other forms and hybrids could easily be adduced) and will explore how spatial dynamics, centering focus, aesthetic impact, and symbolic resonance function in each.

The first tradition, that of the *classic sacramental church*, stretches back to the earliest generations of public church-building and claims a rich and venerable history. One of its most familiar forms is sometimes called the basilican plan, a long structure with lower aisles on either side and an apse at the end. Variations can be found in Eastern Orthodox, Roman Catholic, and Anglican parishes, and often in other traditions as well. Its standard features include a longitudinal nave (mainly for the congregation) and chancel (chiefly for the clergy), allowing for processions of various kinds from one end to another. The chancel is traditionally at the east end, the nave at the west. Layout and terminology vary, but one standard arrangement is for the chancel to be subdivided into the sanctuary (with the altar) and the choir (with choir stalls). The focal point of a classic sacramental church is the altar, the place of sacrament to which the longitudinal space leads. If a church of this type is based on a coherent aesthetic vision, it is usually one meant to evoke the immanence of God and the possibility among worshipers for transcendence of ordinary consciousness. Such churches often abound with symbolic forms and decorations, making them rich in symbolic resonance. I will refer in more than one chapter to Santa Maria Maggiore, a basilica of fifth-century Rome, as a classic example of this form of church (fig. 1).

The second tradition, the *classic evangelical church*, is meant chiefly for preaching the gospel. The interior is an auditorium, with the pulpit as its focal point. Its space is often relatively small, encouraging spontaneous interaction between preacher and congregation. The main aesthetic goal is to create a space for edification of individuals and of the congregation. The building itself may be relatively plain; in any case it will usually be less adorned with symbolic decorations than a classic sacramental church. Variations on this form were built by sixteenth-century Huguenots and Dutch reformers. The design was taken over and transformed at the hands of nineteenth-century urban revival preachers, and again by modern evangelicals with the latest technology at their

FIGURE 1. Santa Maria Maggiore, Rome, interior. Engraving from Giovanni Battista Piranesi, *Vedute di Roma*. Reproduction courtesy of The British Library, with permission.

command. I will refer to a seventeenth-century Congregational chapel at Walpole in England as one classic example (fig. 2).

The third tradition, more recent in origin than the others, might be called the *modern communal church*. Built for both Protestant and Catholic congregations, this kind of church is meant to emphasize the importance of gathering people for worship, often around an altar or a pulpit. Such a church is usually built with ample space for social mingling at the entry; the importance of gathering people together is highlighted by this provision of social space. More often than in other designs, the modern communal church is built for a congregation that is not already formed as a community in everyday life and that thus needs to be constituted as a social community en route to the place where it becomes a worshiping community. Seating is often wrapped around three sides of the interior, heightening a sense of group identity. The assembly itself may thus become the main focus of attention. The atmosphere is meant to be warm and inviting, to create a hospitable environment for celebration. And while symbolic resonance is not usually as dense as in a classic sacramental church, symbolic reference is often richer than in a classic evangelical setting.

FIGURE 2. Congregational Chapel, Walpole, Suffolk. From Martin S. Briggs, *Puritan Architecture and Its Future* (London, Redhill: Lutterworth, 1946). Used with permission of Lutterworth Press.

I will make reference to a church of the mid–twentieth century, United Methodist Church at Northfield, Minnesota, as one example of this form of church (fig. 3).

The labels suggested are meant to highlight the factors governing the shape of church buildings. All churches are evangelical, if only in reading and commenting on the gospel and claiming to worship in its spirit. All churches are communal, bringing congregations together for worship. And all churches are sacramental, even if they see the word of God as the truest sacrament and the fountain from which others flow. But there are churches that, following a tradition traceable to relatively early stages of Christian worship, take sacramentality in various senses and on more than one level as a fundamental determinant of church design. Other churches, following a tradition anticipated in the later Middle Ages and worked out explicitly in the sixteenth century, accept evangelical proclamation as the basic determinant of design. Yet others, at least since the rise of the twentieth-century liturgical movement, have seen the gathering of community not simply as a factor in sacramental or evangelical worship but as itself a key determinant in design of the church building. The point, then, is not that certain churches unlike others are sac-

FIGURE 3. United Methodist, Northfield, Minnesota, interior. Photograph by Richard Kieckhefer.

ramental, or evangelical, or communal but that one of these three character-istics underlies the basic form of a church building (see table 1).

From a strictly historical perspective this categorization may appear strangely lopsided, because the "classic sacramental" church includes the vast preponderance of forms churches have taken over the centuries, while the "classic evangelical" church represents a particular development within some (not all) Protestant denominations, and the "modern communal" church is a recent development that might not seem worthy of equal footing with the grand traditions it reacts against. But if we focus more on the range of options avail-able now, the perspective shifts, and the forms that loom so large historically occupy a less significant and more contested place.

It might be tempting to say that these forms of church function differently in worship. But while in some contexts the question "How does this church work?" may be appropriate, for the liturgist the more relevant question about any church is "What would it take to make this space work?" Every church and every sort of church presents a specific combination of opportunities and chal-lenges; every variation in design can bring both gains and losses. A classic sacramental church may function as people expect if the liturgy they celebrate in it is dynamic and conveys a sense of participatory drama, if they use pro-cessional space to bring clergy and congregation into interaction rather than

TABLE 1. Basic Patterns in Church Design

	Classic Sacramental	Classic Evangelical	Modern Communal
Liturgical use			
Spatial dynamism	Longitudinal space for procession and return (kinetic dynamism)	Auditorium space for proclamation and response (verbal dynamism)	Transitional space for movement from gathering to worship areas
Centering focus	Altar for sacrifice	Pulpit for preaching	Multiple and movable
Response elicited			
Aesthetic impact (immediate)	Dramatic setting for interplay of transcendence and immanence	Dignified setting for edification	Hospitable setting for celebration
Symbolic resonance (cumulative)	High	Low	Moderate
Relationship of factors			
	Multiple functions, none of which governs the others	Converging functions, governed largely by centering focus	Converging functions, governed largely by spatial dynamic

keep them distant from each other, and if in general the liturgical ethos is marked by a kind of intensity that pervades and transforms the assembly, an animating vitality that fills the space. This kind of church generally does not lend itself to an understated mode of liturgy, let alone a casual touch. A classic evangelical church may require a balance of charisma and sensitivity on the part of the preacher, and an ethos of responsiveness on the side of the congregation. Modern communal churches can be among the most disappointing environments for worship if those who build them have exaggerated expectations about what the architecture itself will accomplish for worship, in particular how it will foster participation. The opportunities such a church presents seem obvious in principle; the challenges are less so, until candid assessment reveals that this church too requires creative use to function well. Integration of silent prayer with word and music may be needed to define a contemplative dimension to the space. Focused attention to symbolic action may be required to prevent a hospitable environment from becoming too familiar, too casual, even banal. The challenge here is to keep the worship and its setting from becoming merely bland.

The Central Arguments of This Book

This book focuses throughout on the theological meanings and liturgical uses of churches. Matters not related to liturgy and theology, such as structural developments, will not be discussed, and questions of architectural style will be of secondary interest except when they bear on theological meaning. Remarkably, books on church architecture often give only passing notice to the liturgy for which churches are built. A finely nuanced comparative study of sacred architecture will analyze buildings as "microcosmic images of the universe," "codified perceptions of order," "the legitimation of authority," and the like, but even when discussing Christian churches will neglect such themes as the gathering of the assembly, eucharistic sacrifice, communal meal, and preaching of the word—in short, all that defines a space as suitable for Christian worship.[24] A lavishly illustrated book on churches will devote a two-page section to the history and use of labyrinths but give no comparable explanation of the mass.[25] A popular book on the ostensibly ordinary church of Saint Agnes at Rome will give a poetic interpretation of its floorplan; will tell how its altar was erected in 1621 over a new silver reliquary, with a ciborium supported on columns of tooled porphyry; will survey the side chapels, including one to Agnes's "milk sister" Emerentiana, nursed by Agnes in infancy; in short, will give loving attention to all the details of the building, but with almost no attention to the liturgy.[26] One can read detailed accounts of Salisbury Cathedral without learning about its leading role in the enrichment of high medieval liturgy or about the rebuilding and extension of chancels to accommodate that enriched ritual.[27] We are better off in the case of Hagia Sophia in Byzantium, for which we have studies that take pains to show how architecture came alive liturgically; these works represent the exception.[28]

The following chapters, then, will focus on the uses and meanings of different kinds of church. But they will pay special attention to the classic sacramental church, because it is most in need of sustained attention and interpretation. The other forms of church, the classic evangelical church and the modern communal church, are reformers' brainchildren, and they often manifest something of the coherence born of single-mindedness. In the classic evangelical church, designed straightforwardly for preaching the gospel, the elements of design will gather to a single point. The conception of the church interior as an auditorium, the centering of attention on the preacher, an aesthetic of dignity rather than of splendor, and symbolic parsimony—in such a classic evangelical church all these factors will cohere in their support of evangelical proclamation. To be sure, buildings that share all the essential features of the classic evangelical model do often borrow from the stylistic vocabulary of the classic sacramental church, and will often display accommodations to its liturgical arrangement, but without the same theological commitment to those features or the same theological interpretation of them; accommodations remain precisely that. In a modern communal church, the space itself, the furnishings, the aesthetic, and the embellishment are all meant in large measure for one main goal, to create a welcoming space for celebration and hospitality. The classic evangelical and modern communal models, each ultimately grounded in a single and readily appreciated principle, are easily understandable and widely understood. They have the plainness and the familiarity of prose. The classic sacramental church does not have this kind of convergence of purposes, at least in the same way or to the same degree. Rather, in a classic sacramental church one can grasp first one dimension and then another—first the processional organization of space, then the focus on the altar as a place of sacrifice, then the emphasis on the immanence of God and the transcendence of ordinary human experience, then the dense web of sacral associations—and while they are not unrelated to each other, the strands are not tightly woven, the aspects of the church are not corollaries of a single basic principle. A classic sacramental church is not the invention of a reformer with clarity of conviction, and clarity is seldom its most notable virtue. A classic sacramental church works on multiple levels, while for others the levels tend to converge and are more of a piece.

The classic sacramental model is thus more difficult to understand. More than the other forms of church, it requires interpretation, and interpretation on multiple levels, not reduction to simple formulas. Its different aspects may be compatible with each other and even mutually supporting, but they rest on separate principles. To make matters yet harder, each of the principles underlying the classic sacramental church is now countercultural and thus hard to present in easily accepted terms. Forms of church design once taken for granted are now beyond comprehension to most viewers. Such a church is difficult to understand in much the way a dense and highly allusive poem is difficult, a poem that works its tangled allure on more than one level. Its attackers have a simple task; its defenders must appeal for patience and a kind of poetic imagination. The architect Daniel Lee tells about meeting a Christian poet who professed ignorance about architecture: "I really don't know, architecture is such an esoteric art form." Lee observes that "most Christians cannot begin a conversation on architecture" and that contemporary church architecture in particular "is as confused as the tastes, and faith, of building committee members."[29] Understanding church architecture is indeed difficult, but not uniformly so. The purpose of some churches may be easy both to grasp and to articulate; for others this is not so.

Our culture tends to see classic sacramental churches and the liturgy they are built for as formal and therefore artificial; we know too little of the formality that implies heightened drama and focused attention. Does this mean these churches are esoteric and elitist? To the contrary, there is no reason they cannot serve as people's churches. Cultural richness and complexity appeal to a range

of classes, in varying ways and for various reasons; the simplicity of tidy coherence is mainly a concern of elites and ideologues. The classic sacramental
church may for many people have immediately clear meaning on an intuitive
level—even if this meaning resists articulation because it is complex or because
our culture does not provide the needed vocabulary.

In another way the classic sacramental church is paradoxical and resists
easy articulation: it is built for transitions of various kinds, and within its
structure oppositions are brought together in simultaneity. It is built for movement and dynamism but also for rest, for sound and for stillness and for the
reverberation that mediates between the two, and for centering focus that permits a kind of scattering, often also for passage from darkness to light and
from narrow enclosure to open space. At its heart is a sacrificial block represented as a place of death, but of life-giving death, a place of conflict between
death and life. It means to awaken a consciousness of the holy within the
sacred: that is to say, a simple awareness of divine presence within a richly
complex symbolic network, in which narratives from the past and expectations
for the future come into the immediacy of present experience.

My purpose, then, is not so much to advocate or disparage any tradition
of church-building but to explore how each tradition can be coherent and lend
itself to creative and inspired use. But making that argument in the case of the
classic sacramental church requires closer and fuller attention. If this book
reads in part as an apologia for that model—and it will—this is not because
of an animus against other conceptions of church but because they can more
easily look after themselves.

A further theme, then, which will emerge more gradually in the course of
the book, is again central to an understanding of the classic sacramental church
and its relationship to alternatives: the question how "the sacred" and "the
holy" are expressed in church design. For many theorists of religion, sacrality
is a quality achieved or expressed by separation: the sacred is that which is
separate from the profane, and sacred space is space behind barriers meant to
restrict access, or veils meant to restrict visibility.[30] Those critical of this understanding have generally shared its basic premise, and have sought to strip
churches of sacred associations in order to overcome the separation taken to
be the heart of sacrality. In response to both extremes, this book will argue that
a church can be marked by a sacrality not of separation but rather of association: that what makes a building sacred is not its detachment from the profane
(although this may be a secondary effect of sacrality, often mistaken for an
essential factor) but the richness of its symbolic associations, its connectedness
to images and narratives that bear on the deepest questions of human life.
Further, a church differs from other spaces by its making concrete and vivid a
sense of the holy, of the divine presence. It is association and presence that are
most important to church architecture, not separation.

The main arguments of this book, then, are two. First, it will argue for a reconception of the classic sacramental church and its relationship to other forms. Second, it will urge reconception of the question why and how a church should be thought of as sacred space, a place for encounter with the holy. These two arguments are independent yet have bearing on each other. They will be developed first within a systematic survey of themes, then within a very selective range of case studies.

A Note on the Title

Various terms in the title may seem to call for comment, although they should be clear enough in context. The reference to Byzantium and Berkeley is meant simply to indicate something of the book's chronological and geographical scope. The term "theology" may suggest to some readers that I am going to lay out an interpretive scheme, telling how Romanesque and Gothic styles convey different theological messages, or explaining why one form of church is theologically correct and others theologically deficient. For some interpreters the "meaning" of a church or of some feature within a church does depend on a fixed code of symbolism.[31] But this is decidedly *not* my approach. Churches have theological significance, but in fluid and complex rather than fixed and simple ways.

Why theology in *stone?* This is shorthand for all the materials used in constructing churches, including brick and wood, concrete and glass. People have even worshiped in churches made of cardboard, though not for long.[32] Stone may seem not to be a neutral or innocent selection from among these materials, standing as it does for monumentality and traditionalism. Should we really be taking stone as the normative building material for churches at a time when so few churches are actually made of stone, and its significance is open to challenge? We are told: "the construction of buildings in stone has always carried a strong symbolic charge, conveying notions of stability and permanence."[33] Again: "images of divine powers are made of durable materials, and the heavy stone walls of temples, fortresses, and palaces have always served as a suitable metaphor for temporal and spiritual power."[34] One Victorian writer proposed that natural stone should predominate in a church to call to mind the Great Architect who made the stone: "The works of nature remind us of the GOD of nature."[35]

But on this point, as on most, symbolism is not univocal. The question arose when Renzo Piano—hardly a reactionary or a devotee of traditional monumentalism—was asked why his new church at San Giovanni Rotondo in southern Italy was to be built of stone. His first answer was straightforward: "Stone makes it look more like a church. There is an instinctive memory of the church built of stone." But he went on to comment on the way stone gives a sense of relationship to a particular place:

As we looked at the empty site there were rocks coming through to the surface and we thought "What about digging stone locally?" The topography of the site is very interesting. You don't see the landscape in the immediate vicinity, you see the sea beyond, there is a sense of the infinite rather than the local. There are almond trees all around and a sense of calm in the air. This is how we started to build up a sense of place.[36]

While brick and concrete and glass are international materials, and wood does not easily reveal its exact provenance, stone tends to be specific to its region, and with some exceptions it is traditionally quarried not far from where it is used. By one estimate, if medieval stone was transported overland for a distance of twelve miles its price thereby doubled: strong incentive to use local building material, unless waterways were conveniently at hand for transport.[37] And the limestone of Somerset is clearly different from that of Lincoln and of Yorkshire, let alone the sandstone of Cheshire or the granite of Brittany. When Sophia Gray, the first woman architect in South Africa, combined hard local building stones with imported and already carved softer English stone for moldings and capitals, tracery and corbels, she established a practical and symbolic link between the colonizing and colonized lands.[38]

None of this means, of course, that stone is in any way a normative medium for church-building. But it does mean that when a church is of stone its material calls attention to the particularity of a specific building at a given place, in its own environment and community. And therein lies a salutary lesson about the multivalence of meaning: stone may mean permanence and power, but that is not all it means, and more generally churches have meanings and uses beyond those immediately perceived.

Further, there is biblical basis for taking a building of stone as a metaphor for the people who assemble in it: the congregation is a church built of "living stones" (1 Peter 2:5). When the Roman Catholic bishops in America issued their latest document on church architecture, they called it *Built of Living Stones*.[39] The metaphor can work in either direction: many languages use derivatives of the Greek term *ekklesia*, or "assembly," and apply them to the building as well as to the congregation; others begin with the Greek for "house of the Lord" and apply its derivatives (Germanic terms such as *cirice*, *Kirche*, and "church") to the community as well as to the structure.[40] In either case, the building and the community, inert and living stones, have meaning in relationship to each other. That a church building is a structure for an assembly is common knowledge. That the community brings its shared experience and its culture into the act of worship, and that doing so requires a particular kind of building, is equally but less obviously true. And it is true in various and potentially conflicting ways, making church architecture immensely exciting and inescapably controversial.

I

The First Factor:
Spatial Dynamics

Entering a church is a metaphor for entering into a spiritual process:
one of procession and return, or of proclamation and response, or of
gathering in community and returning to the world outside. The
form of sacred architecture will follow largely from the conception
of spiritual process it is meant to suggest and foster, the type of dynamism it aims to promote.

When books on comparative religion come into the hands of architects, they sometimes begin speaking about churches as sites for
such things as "spiritual paths" and "sacred places." One such writer
speaks of "gate," "path," and "place" as critical factors in sacred architecture, marking the beginning of spiritual experience, the journey to transformation, and the culmination of the journey, and he
construes these journeys broadly enough to include the route from
parking lot to church building as well as a passage down the aisle to
an altar, pulpit, or other destination.[1] The architect Thomas Barrie,
in *Spiritual Path, Sacred Place*, distinguishes various types of path
found in churches, temples, and other sacred places.[2] The axial path
leads progressively across increasingly sacred thresholds and spaces,
terminating in the home of the gods, to which only the deities themselves and their priests have access. The split path has diverging
routes, or two routes converging as they move toward the final destination. The radial path has avenues converging from several directions on a central point. The grid path has either no center or several centers, suggesting the presence of God everywhere and
nowhere. The circumambulating path makes its way around the sacred space or itself forms the sacred area. The segmented path has

twists and turns that most fully mirror the decisions and trials along the hero's journey.[3] But for Barrie the spiritual quest "has always centered on the individual," even when individuals have banded together for pragmatic reasons as pilgrims.[4] He makes little distinction between paths within liturgical space, paths on the exterior that might be used liturgically on special occasions, and external paths leading up to the liturgical environment but of no direct liturgical relevance. All are the same for him, as paths trodden by the individual pilgrim. When he proceeds to a sustained analysis of the monastic church at Vézelay, he devotes scant attention to liturgy and gives a somewhat confused sense of how the church was used liturgically.[5]

This book will adopt a different perspective. It will analyze three of the most common ways the shape of a church can be linked to notions of spiritual process enacted specifically in liturgy: the longitudinal space of the classic sacramental church, meant for procession and return; the auditorium space of the classic evangelical church, built for proclamation and response; and a relatively new form of space in the modern communal church, designed for people to gather in community and proceed back out into the workaday world.

Case Study: Santa Maria Maggiore

The basilica of Santa Maria Maggiore is one of the four major basilicas of Rome.[6] Medieval legend tells that one August night the Virgin Mary left footprints in miraculously fallen snow to mark the location for the church, whence the feast of Our Lady of the Snows on August 5 as the festival honoring the church's foundation. (The miracle is traditionally observed by a shower of white rose petals in one of the basilica's chapels.) A church had been founded nearby already in the fourth century, but the grand basilica was begun in the early fifth century and brought to completion by Pope Sixtus III. It was an early manifestation of devotion to Mary in the Western Church, and a manifestation in a densely populated district that the city of Rome was now a Christian city. The provision of a baptistery suggests that from its origins the church was meant to serve the surrounding community. By around 1200 Rome had seventy-two churches dedicated to the Virgin; as in other cities of Italy, the primary Marian church was designated Major, or Maggiore. Earlier basilicas had been built with patronage of the emperor Constantine, but this was a project of the pope alone. In features such as its colonnades, its pilasters, its decorative friezes and stucco work of pilasters, the new basilica recaptured the architectural style of first- and early second-century Rome; Sixtus seems to have sponsored an architectural revival of earlier imperial styles, striving already in the fifth century to recapture the grandeur that had been Rome.[7] The nave is nearly 290 feet long, and the length is accentuated by the long processions of forty marble columns, originally taken from the temple of Juno Lucina,

which separate the nave from the aisles. The eighteenth-century print by Giovanni Battista Piranesi (see fig. 1) gives a dramatic sense of the church's length,
the prominence of the altar, and the rhythmic progression of columns leading
toward the altar, which stands before the emphatically clear vanishing point. As
one observer has noted wryly, the drama is heightened in Piranesi's engraving
by manipulation of the lighting and by peopling the nave with Lilliputian figures to exaggerate the grandeur of the building.[8] Yet this is in fact a church of
considerable prominence in every sense: an imposing structure, connected
with the highest ranks of ecclesiastical authority, and so evocative as to generate
a legend linked with its founding and with the feast of its dedication.

The nave at Santa Maria Maggiore was preserved over the centuries largely
as it was originally built, although both ends were reconfigured: the end with
the high altar was refashioned in the late thirteenth century; the opposite end,
where an atrium originally led into the main entrance, was rebuilt in the mid–
twelfth century. In the mid–seventeenth century both ends were again remodeled, and the nave as well was renewed. Still, much remains that is faithful to
the early design of the interior.

The very term "basilica" means "royal hall," and because the earliest basilicas were built with Constantine's patronage one might well expect these
churches and others of their kind to be monuments celebrating the triumph
of the Church and its alliance with the Empire. Thomas Mathews gives a radically different perception of these buildings. Pagan temples, he reminds us,
had been places where priests entered to offer sacrifice to the gods while ordinary people waited outdoors in the courtyard.

> The Christian church building, on the contrary, was a public assem-
> bly hall. . . . Crowds gathered within it, singing hymns and amen-ing
> the fervent imprecations of the preacher. There were no pews or
> benches to confine the people, and the crowds moved in repeated
> waves through the spacious columned corridors during the liturgy.
> Entries and exits, readings, offertories and communion were all mo-
> ments of public involvement. This democratization of worship re-
> quired a fundamentally different kind of building from the pagan
> temple.

Unlike the temple, Mathews argues, the church actively involved the multi-
tudes, in a space meant to draw them toward the altar and to give a sense of
common orientation in prayer.[9]

How far does this argument apply to Santa Maria Maggiore? It is a longitudinal structure, designed as processional space. It allows and even invites
clergy and laity to pass from one end of the building to the other at different
moments of the mass. The movement is governed chiefly by the altar at the
far end of the nave, which stands as the chief visual focus in the church and
exercises what can be imagined as a kind of magnetic attraction, drawing the

worshiper forward. The columns on either side of the nave mimic the processions of clergy and laity, as if suggesting that the proper response to such an interior is movement from one end to the other. Yet processions were not limited to the obvious processional route down the nave to the high altar: a document of the thirteenth century tells that when a person was buried within the basilica the canons went out in procession from their choir to the grave site after vespers, bearing cross, incense, and holy water, and then they sang a service at the altar nearest the grave. And when relics were installed in shrines, devotees would have moved toward these in veneration. In any event, the building was clearly meant for movement.

Can we speak of it as a place of *popular* ritual? Santa Maria Maggiore was mainly designed for the highest authority in Rome, the pope. It served chiefly as one of the places of papal liturgy, especially for the Nativity and feasts of the Virgin. Medieval sources tell a great deal about the pope's participation in processions to Santa Maria Maggiore.[10] He rode a horse, dismounting on arrival, was greeted by lay dignitaries and taken in through the main entrance, was greeted by canons, proceeded to the far end and performed a ritual of flax-burning as a symbol of the transitoriness of the world. Only the pope or a cardinal explicitly delegated by the pope could celebrate mass at the high altar; when a cardinal celebrated without that authorization, he used a special altar set up in front of the high altar. From the eighth century there is reference to monks who were charged with maintaining liturgy in the basilica, including the canonical hours, and from the mid–twelfth century there was a college of secular canons headed by an archpriest. But these clerics would not have used the high altar; they celebrated daily mass at locations that varied from one era to another. It is possible, therefore, to see the building chiefly as a scene of papal hegemony. The pope's authority was always present, even when he himself was not.

Still, even the grandest papal liturgy had also a popular character. A rich celebration arose for the feast of the Assumption, which marked the reunion in heaven of Mary and her Son: icons of each were brought out from the churches where they were housed, and a nighttime procession, lighted by scores of lamps burning along the route on rooftops, was accompanied by singing in Greek and Latin, including hundreds of Kyries. In the sixteenth century this feast took on dimensions of a folk festival, with popular observances alongside the solemn liturgical celebration. And this is merely one example of liturgy merged with popular observance.

The Kinetic Dynamism of a Longitudinal Church

Whatever its particular use on a given occasion, a church like Santa Maria Maggiore was meant for movement and dynamism going far beyond that of most modern churches. Writers of various persuasions have argued the importance of a sense of dynamism in liturgy, and the need to provide for this in church architecture: "we need to give far more thought to the possibilities of liturgical *movement*"; churches require places "for doing, not just seeing; for moving, not just sitting."[11] Nor would most such writers be content to emphasize the visual dynamism of space, the leading of the eye from one resting-place to the next. Leading the eye is easy enough: a focal point attracts attention; placing arcades or colonnades along either side, or using a patterned design on the wall behind the visual focus, may sustain and heighten the sense of perspective and direction.[12] But those who advocate movement want it for the body, not the eye alone.

The processional space of a longitudinal interior can be used in various ways, yet it is not always used as fully or imaginatively as it might be, and many people have limited experience and therefore limited understanding of its possibilities. Shown the interior of a longitudinal church like Santa Maria Maggiore, some will speak of it as placing distance between clergy and congregation, and as removing the altar to a place where it can be seen only at a distance. They may assume that clergy and congregation occupy fixed positions, or that movement is incidental, a way of arriving at positions proper to congregation or to clergy. They may take longitudinal space as preserving the sacred unapproachability of the altar: when Kenzo Tange designed Saint Mary's Cathedral in Tokyo, he insisted on keeping the altar on a high and wide platform because, as he said, "Fear of God should deter us from passing by the altar."[13] Viewers may suppose the movement within a processional space is imaginary: the congregation stands in marching order, as if moving forward, with the priest at the head, but without actually changing position.[14] If they are conscious at all of a church's processional character, viewers may focus on the secondary phenomenon of specific processions, the entrance procession especially, rather than the shift in use of space that marks the different stages of liturgical action.

Longitudinal space can indeed be distancing, but there is perhaps no better space for inviting movement, for suggesting a sense of passage or of kinetic dynamism. Five main principles govern this dynamism and the architecture that accommodates it. First, processional space permits clergy and congregation to move and thus relate to each other in shifting patterns as worship progresses. Second, the different uses of processional space can mark transitions from one stage to another in the liturgy; rather than serving simply as space for processions, longitudinal space is space in which processions help define the dynamics of the building and of the liturgy. Third, processions can take place within a single, unified space, but they give a sense of heightened sacrality when they involve transition from one type of space to another. Fourth, even before movement occurs, and even if movement forward toward the altar comes late in the service (most obviously at communion), processional space defines the possibilities for movement and serves as alluring invitation to the movement that eventually takes place. But fifth, the historical tendency has been for markers between one area and another to develop into barriers, partially or fully obstructing visibility and passage.

A longitudinal space typically gives not only a processional route but a clear sense of direction to that route. Placement of the main entrance at the end opposite the altar is only the most obvious means toward that goal. In medieval English churches where the customary entrance is through a south porch and the west door is reserved for ceremonial entries, the processional character of the interior is most fully clarified on special occasions, such as episcopal visitations, when the opening of the west door establishes an unambiguous axis from west to east. Iconography can heighten a sense of direction. Mosaics at Sant'Apollinare Nuovo in Ravenna depict processions of saints moving toward the east end of the church and toward Christ and the Virgin.[15] Directionality can be achieved by widening or heightening of the church at the end that is liturgically dominant, so that the sanctuary is more expansive and more dramatic. In the chapel of Notre Dame du Haut at Ronchamp the altar end flares out like a trumpet.[16] But directionality can be equally conveyed by narrowing and lowering the liturgically dominant end, perhaps suggesting a sense of deepening mystery. Not uncommonly in a Gothic church the chancel will be separately roofed at a lower level than the nave. Alvar Aalto's Heilig-Geist Kirche at Wolfsburg is designed with sweeping curves, the roof and its trusses plunging dramatically downward and the side walls tapering inward as they approach the altar, giving a clear sense of direction.[17]

Not all processions follow the linear direction of a traditional processional church. Thus, the modern Anglican church of Saint Paul's, Bow Common, in London, has a processional path marked by a distinct pavement around the periphery of the church, and part of the intention is that processions should help define the nature of the space circumambulated, allowing the space to become an expression of people's incorporation in a body of worshipers. The architects contrast the movement intended in this church with the linear movement in a Gothic church. Here the procession moves inward: from the corner entrance, past the baptismal font, along the peripheral pathway, into the congregational seating in the central area, then further into the sanctuary and the altar.[18] In this alternative plan a procession may still be experienced as movement from one form of sacred space to another, giving a sharp sense of heightened sacrality to those moments when clergy and then congregation make their way toward the altar—or it may instead become merely movement about within a single space. The longitudinal church makes its message more unambiguously.

Rudolf Arnheim discusses with psychological subtlety the ways a church interior suggests movement. The cues need not be overwhelming; "a simple strong color on the end wall of a corridor suffices to transform the static passage into a goal-directed track." More paradoxically, even features that might seem to thwart a sense of dynamism may promote it. "Temporary retardation is known in the arts as a strong incentive toward forward movement," as in the monastic church at Vézelay, where a column in the center of the portal is seconded by a "traffic-stopping post" at the entry from the narthex to the nave, inviting the visitor to pause before an image of Christ and then move forward into the nave "with a new momentum." More complicated is the difference between a church with side aisles and one (such as Alberti designed at Mantua) with side chapels. Aisles contribute to the eastward movement of the interior, guiding the visitor "as strictly as a ball rolling in a groove," but as soon as the aisles are replaced with chapels the visitor is invited to step aside in that movement.[19] And yet one might argue that here too the *succession* of side chapels, like the succession of columns or of windows or of stations of the cross, has ambiguous effect: any station is a stopping-point in a procession, yet a procession can be made of stages without losing its sense of an ultimate destination.

The ebb and flow of liturgical movement echoes the rhythms of spiritual life and the Neoplatonic theme of procession and return: all things flow out from God and return to God; the worshiping soul turns to God in prayer and returns into the world. The entire liturgy echoes this ebb and flow, but specific processions give clear dramatic form to the process. And yet the procession can be effective as symbol only if it is first effective as experienced reality. It serves as a sign of spiritual process only if it rouses worshipers from ordinary consciousness by its sheer dramatic force.

Robert W. Jenson protested in 1967 that longitudinal space, with its implication of access to God through movement in space, invites a false conception of God, as the "God of religion" as opposed to the "God of the gospel."[20] The God of religion is an "absolute and changeless Presence," and such a deity may be conceived and related to in spatial terms: this God is transcendent and immanent in the sense of being somehow "out or up or in there." Designing a church with a focus for seeing, hearing, or approaching is a way of representing the approach to this God of religion. "The God of the gospel" is not a Presence in that sense. "The God of the gospel does not now exist, analogously to things in space; he happens." And he happens as a future event; this God is "the Coming one." The basic argument hinges on the distinction between religion and faith, or religion and gospel, borrowed from Neo-Orthodox Protestant theology and molded by popular theologians of the 1960s.[21] Whether "the God of the gospel" as represented by Jenson can actually be found in the New Testament is problematic; it would be difficult to prove that any New Testament writer thought of God as transcendent specifically in the sense of being a future reality, and easy to find notions of divine absence and presence that borrow from Israelite sources the conception of a divine-human relatedness imaged in spatial terms.[22] More important for my purposes, Jenson makes the mistake of assuming that longitudinal space signals only a process of access

to a transcendent God. The space can be used in various ways. Most fundamentally it can serve to mark the distinct stages in liturgy, and movement
forward is movement from one liturgical moment to the next—not toward
God but toward sacramental communion with God.

Longitudinal churches were meant for processions from the outset, but
particular processions evolved gradually over centuries.[23] When Constantine
ended the threat of martyrdom and Christian worship became public, the most
dramatic processions moved out from churches into the streets or countryside.
In medieval Rome, the bishop went in procession on Sundays and feast days
to the several churches of the city, maintaining a liturgical bond among those
churches, and the processional space at a basilica like Santa Maria Maggiore
would have served most dramatically for ceremonial entrances of the pope with
his retinue. The routine entry procession of ordinary clergy within the church
at the beginning of mass was a later development, of the ninth through twelfth
centuries, inspired partly by adoption of the monastic Asperges, in which the
priest moved out into the nave and sprinkled the congregation with holy water
at the beginning of mass. By the twelfth century, such weekly mass processions
had become common in the West.

In the later Middle Ages, processions in a major church could be far more
than ways for the clergy to reach the altar: they were rituals of coordination by
which the church as a whole was given liturgical significance and the interre-
latedness of its parts acknowledged. The route of a procession could vary
widely, including stations (or stopping points) inside the church, such as altars
and fonts, and stations outside that might include other churches. At each of
these stations the clergy might perform blessings, aspersions, censing, pros-
trations, and other ritual acts. Liturgical manuals specified the order of clergy
and choristers participating in processions, the vestments worn, the music
specific to the occasion, and the objects carried (candles, cross, thuribles,
books, or relics). The accouterments of processions at Salisbury Cathedral,
including banners with the forms of a dragon and a lion, suggest something
of a phantasmagoric display.

Processions have historically played a crucial role in setting a tone for the
ensuing liturgy. In general, a procession may simultaneously strike a tone of
both solemnity and celebration: solemnity, bringing focused attention to a liturgical service that bears on life's deepest concerns and calls to be taken seriously; celebration, leading to joyousness and praise proper to all feasts and
seasons, even in the interstices of mourning. But the emphasis will vary. In
later medieval liturgy it was a procession that sounded the tone of celebration
appropriate for a feast day such as Candlemas, for other major festivals, and
eventually for any Sunday. A festive procession might include celebratory banners in addition to all the other objects carried, while a penitential one might
require a hair-cloth banner and bare feet. A procession could also at times take
on a dramatic character: by around the twelfth century the Palm Sunday pro-

cession at Sarum was a dramatization using the consecrated host to represent Christ, and later in the Middle Ages the same feast was celebrated in Germany with a carved wooden *Palmesel*, or donkey bearing the figure of Christ.

In processions outside the church, clergy were generally accompanied by laypeople. Within the church, during the liturgy, laity participated mainly in two other processions: at the offertory and at communion. (There might be a third at the end of the mass to receive blessed—not consecrated—bread.)

The offertory procession has a complex history.[24] From at least the third century, the laity were expected to make offerings of bread and wine for use at the eucharist. Not only bread and wine but also oil, wax, and candles could be presented, and monetary offerings eventually became common. Yet lay offerings did not necessarily imply a lay offertory procession: they could be collected by the clergy (or in modern times by ushers) rather than brought forward in procession.[25] Still, lay offertory processions did develop, at different times in different regions. They might take place only four or five times yearly, on the greater feasts of the church year, perhaps on the anniversary of a church's dedication or on its patronal feast day. Sometimes the gifts were still of bread and wine; sometimes other gifts were brought. A fourth-century floor mosaic at Aquileia depicts men and women bearing bread and wine, grapes, flowers, and a bird in an offertory procession.[26] In ninth-century Gaul the laymen and then the women, followed by priests and deacons, moved forward to the altar after the Creed in an offertory procession that was compared to the procession at Jerusalem on Palm Sunday. Even when a procession was made with offerings, it did not necessarily occur at the liturgical offertory: in a given region it might take place at the Kyrie, before the gospel, or even at communion time. From the later Middle Ages we hear of processions in which the priest blessed each person making an offering, but elsewhere the clergy went on with the liturgy seemingly oblivious to the laity who processed forward.

The form of the communion procession has also varied.[27] When early Christian congregations first moved away from a conventional dining space to a kind of assembly hall with the altar at one end, people seem to have come forward in procession to receive communion at the altar. In Gaul that custom remained the norm up to the ninth century. In later times people might still form communion processions, but shorter ones, to side altars. Where the congregation was larger it might seem fitting for people to stay in place and for the clergy to deliver the sacrament to them; this was the custom in early medieval Rome. In modern times procession forward to a communion rail or to a space in front of the altar has been the norm in most longitudinal churches.

More fundamental than any particular procession is the coordination of the very structure of the eucharistic liturgy with different uses of sacred space: the *liturgy of the word* may be centered on the west end of the church, with the readers facing the congregation, or in some cases moving into the center of the nave; for the relatively brief *eucharistic prayer* that follows there is a great stretching out, with the priest at the east end and the congregation to the west; then for *communion* the congregation typically moves to the east end. The service thus both contains processions and is structured as a procession. While the altar could be said to draw the congregation forward with something like magnetic force, for much of the liturgy the attraction is one of creative tension, like that of a magnet held at a slight distance from the object it attracts: the force is present, and there is an energy produced by the attraction, even before actual contact. In any case, the altar is meant not to be *seen at* a distance but rather to be *approached from* a distance.

This arrangement of a church allows for reciprocal movement in the liturgy, with clergy moving out into the nave and then congregation moving into the chancel. On this point an interesting and important parallel to synagogue worship has been noted.[28] In both contexts there is reciprocal movement of clergy and laity, in which the clergy first goes out into the congregation and then members of the congregation move into the more sacred space of the sanctuary: in the synagogue it is the Torah scroll that is first brought out into the congregation, after which members of the congregation come forward into the more sacred space near the ark to recite blessings over the scroll. Everything is meant to suggest and facilitate fluidity and transition between distinct but integrated spaces.

If for some interval, perhaps relatively brief, the priest stands at a distance, at the altar, facing perhaps away from or possibly toward the congregation, this is (in many churches) because the priest at that moment has entered into that space in anticipation of communicants' entry, and one of the priest's primary functions is *to invite*. Especially powerful in this liturgical arrangement is the experience of moving forward into a distinct liturgical space for communion, of passing between choir stalls (again, in many churches) as one goes up toward the altar, and as it were of being embraced along the way by the choir—all lending a heightened air of solemnity and momentousness, together with a sense of invitation and welcome. The altar and its environment exert a kind of visual and psychological pull throughout the service; yielding to this attraction marks communion as the culmination of the liturgy.

While the longitudinal form of a church invites processional movement, no one form of procession has been used consistently in the liturgical practice of such churches. We cannot say that the tradition of longitudinal design evolved in response to a fixed concept of processional liturgy; what we can say, rather, is that it remained a dominant form for centuries in large part because of its flexibility, because it gave room for creative innovation in processional liturgies of various kinds.

But people seldom leave longitudinal space alone. They set up rails and screens.[29] The vista from one end of the church to the other will eventually seem too long, or someone will think of a more efficient way to use all that extended space, or distinct groups within the flock will claim their own liturgical pasture and fence it off from the commons, and what was once longitudinal space becomes a corridor of discrete spaces. Still, not all these developments have the same effect. A rail may be closed in the center and understood to exclude the laity from one end of the church, or it may be open and allow passage back and forth by laity as well as clergy. A screen may be simply an open metal frame that does not impede visibility at all; it may be a wooden partition with wainscoting on the bottom and window-like openings on the top, only slightly restricting vision, like a rood screen in a medieval English parish church; it may be a solid wall with icons on it, but with doors in the center and on the sides to allow some vision of what lies beyond and permit the clergy and servers to pass into the nave, like an Orthodox iconostasis; or it may be a wall massive enough to enclose one end of the church as in effect a private chapel, as in many a cathedral. In early Irish Christianity a church might have a solid partition for the sanctuary and another one down the middle of the church segregating men from women.[30]

In general, however, the isolating function of screens has probably been exaggerated. Eamon Duffy argues that rood screens in late medieval English parish churches allowed much greater lay access to the mass than has been realized. Jacqueline Jung goes further, emphasizing that laypeople in the medieval West helped pay for screens, that screens could be used for preaching and for drama and for other activities that brought clergy and laity into contact, that screens were often designed to permit vision from the nave of what was transpiring at the high altar in the sanctuary, and that laypeople actually entered into the choir and approached the altar for communion and at other times, more than people now realize.[31] In short, rails and screens might serve as barriers, but they might instead be meant more as markers: as indications of distinct spaces through which (in some cases) laity as well as clergy could pass.

As already mentioned, many churches have stalls in the architectural choir (the space between chancel and nave) for members of the liturgical choir (the singers). The role of the choir in a processional space is complicated, potentially crucial, and controversial. In 1837–41 the parish church of Saint Peter at Leeds was rebuilt under the vicar Walter Farquhar Hook, an important early example of the Gothic revival that would soon become a dominant force in church architecture, and Hook's friend John Jebb persuaded him to introduce a surpliced choir to sing in the chancel. In a book of his on Anglican choral services, Jebb argued for extension into parishes of the choral tradition of the cathedrals that placed choirs in choir stalls in the chancel.[32] It soon became clear that in parish churches this would require seating lay choristers in those stalls, although some at first disliked the notion that laity should infringe upon the clerical space of the chancel. This breakdown of strict distinction between clerical and lay space was accentuated by a development introduced by George Frederick Bodley in the 1870s, the building of chancel and nave as a single architectural space, without a chancel arch; the chancel was distinguished by low rails and differences in floor level, to demarcate space without obstructing transition between spaces.[33] If there was a screen of any kind, it could be an open one, substantial enough to bear a rood but not so as to constitute a visual barrier between nave and chancel.

To many observers since the mid–twentieth century, this Victorian arrangement has seemed a regrettable extension to the parish church of cathedral usage, particularly in its positioning of the choir. One writer argued in 1962 that the use of a surpliced choir in stalls between the sanctuary and the nave created an inappropriate "intermediate caste, neither clerical nor lay."[34] This creation of a distinct class may or may not be the effect, depending largely on the ethos of a particular community: whether roles in the choir and altar party are open in principle to all, and whether those serving at any particular liturgy are perceived by the congregation more as "we" or as "they." (The elimination of both vested choristers and acolytes can have the effect of a heightened clericalism: when vested laypeople are removed from the liturgy, attention is focused more specifically on the priest who remains.)

A further dimension of processional space is sometimes important: the continuity between procession within the church and procession leading toward the church. At Santa Maria Maggiore and the other greater basilicas of Rome, procession through atrium and narthex, down the nave and toward the apse, was the culmination of a richly contextualized ritual of procession through the city, particularly at times such as Christmas when this basilica was the center of papal liturgy. In a different way, a pilgrimage church acts as the culmination of exterior movement, and often the precinct just outside such a church will be laid out in such a way as to mark clearly the process of final approach or ascent to the shrine, as at Gottfried Böhm's pilgrimage church at Velbert-Neviges.[35] In a pilgrimage church the transition is one from devotional space outside to liturgical space inside, with individual paths of pilgrims converging into the processional path of a worshiping community; in the stational liturgy of Rome there is less distinction between the devotional and the liturgical pathways. In any case, most churches exist for public and communal worship, and most longitudinal churches are built for the dynamism proper to liturgy, devotional use being secondary.

Case Study: Saint Albans Cathedral and the Segmentation of Longitudinal Space

While the cathedrals of France are generally noteworthy for their height, cathedrals and other major churches of England are more often distinguished for their length.[36] The nave itself was generally long; the chancel was often longer than in Continental cathedrals. Many English chancels were rebuilt and extended in the thirteenth century, to allow for the more elaborate ritual of the "use of Sarum" which spread outward through most of England from Salisbury Cathedral. For a solemn feast in the Sarum liturgy there could be as many as seven deacons and subdeacons, multiple thurifers and cross-bearers, choristers, and others all occupying the chancel along with the celebrant, and the smaller chancels of earlier centuries could hardly accommodate all these clerical participants.

The arrangement typical in England was by no means universal in western Europe. In Spanish cathedrals, for example, the choir was not a distinct architectural unit but rather a large structure within the nave, screened off from the space around it on three sides, and open only in the direction facing the sanctuary.[37] In the cathedral at Florence the choir was enclosed within an octagonal screen placed at the crossing, under the dome.[38] But England elongated its greater churches, then proceeded to mark divisions within them.

One of the most important monastic centers in England was Saint Albans (Fig. 4), where the old monastic church has had the rank of a cathedral since 1877. This is not one of the most celebrated of England's cathedrals, but it is replete with features that repay examination. It was already an ancient pilgrimage site before the Norman Conquest. At least by the fifth century there were reports of miraculous cures at the shrine of Saint Alban, England's protomartyr, on the hillside where he had been martyred in the early third century. In the eighth century the Venerable Bede spoke of a "beautiful church" on the site, and later in that century the rule of Saint Benedict was introduced to the monastic community at this church. When the Normans conquered England they quickly set out rebuilding the cathedrals and greater monastic churches all over the land, including Saint Albans. The new church there, begun already in 1077 and consecrated in 1115, was the largest in the kingdom, notable in particular for its length.[39] As one of England's most important abbeys, it had twenty or so monasteries subject to it. At the peak of its eminence it held roughly a hundred monks and approximately three hundred lay members of the community. Successive abbots devoted themselves with varying degrees of energy to extension and rebuilding of the church; in 1323 two piers in the nave collapsed and brought part of the roof with them, which was one cause for rebuilding. When the monastery was dissolved in the English Reformation, the church was taken over for parochial use, but the parish was unable to maintain such an immense structure, and it was only in the nineteenth century that the building underwent a notoriously controversial renovation at the hands of a renovator distinguished more for idiosyncrasy than for historical knowledge.

In its present condition the church retains vestiges of this long and complicated history. Saint Alban's relics are no longer present in their shrine, but a massive oaken watching chamber still stands guard over the place where offerings were once made.[40] A chantry chapel opposite the watching chamber was built for Humphrey, duke of Gloucester, the "virtuous prince, that good

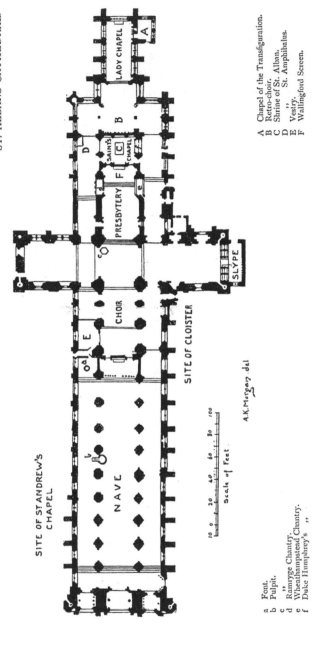

GROUND-PLAN OF
ST. ALBANS CATHEDRAL.

A.K.Morgan, del

Scale of Feet

A Chapel of the Transfiguration.
B Retro-choir.
C Shrine of St. Alban.
D   ,,   St. Amphibalus.
E Vestry.
F Wallingford Screen.

a Font.
b Pulpit.
c Ramryge Chantry.
d Wheathampstead Chantry.
e Duke Humphrey's   ,,

FIGURE 4. Saint Albans Cathedral, Hertfordshire, plan. From Thomas Perkins, *The Cathedral Church of Saint Albans, with an Account of the Fabric and a Short History of the Abbey* (London: Bell, 1910).

Duke Humphrey" of Shakespeare's *Henry VI*, part II, and a lifelong friend of one abbot of Saint Albans from their days as university companions at Oxford. Elsewhere in the building lies a second major shrine, that of Alban's companion Saint Amphibalus (or "Saint Overcoat").[41]

From east end to west, the church was fully 550 feet long. Why was so long a church needed, and how was it used? Four main units served different purposes: the nave came to be used largely for masses attended by the laity; the chancel was the main location of the monks' own liturgy; beyond it in the retrochoir pilgrims would venerate the relics of Saint Alban; yet further east lay the Lady chapel. And over time these units were increasingly set apart. A screen separating the nave from the chancel was built at some point before the collapse of 1323; a new one of around 1360 had doors for processions but still served as a strong visual barrier. A massive screen behind the high altar was built in 1484; the elevated reliquary of the saint in the retrochoir would previously have been visible, but now the chancel and retrochoir were sharply distinguished by the new screen. The retrochoir was further blocked off from the aisle to the north by the watchers' loft overlooking the martyr's shrine. Meanwhile, when reconstruction of the east end was required in 1257 because structural weakening, a Lady chapel was begun, and its construction was finished around 1320. There was further enclosure of space for chapels, including the chantry chapel for Duke Humphrey built in 1447, but the most important elements of the church for its liturgical and devotional use were those lying along the east-west longitudinal axis.

The lay use of the nave is a particularly interesting feature of this building. A series of altars nestled in the nave arcades, beneath the arches, up against the piers. Each of these piers had paintings on its west side, executed in the thirteenth and early fourteenth centuries, to serve as altarpieces, or reredoses for the altars. These altars might have been used by the monks, but there is evidence of laypeople attending mass in the nave, and reason to think secular priests were engaged to celebrate at these nave altars for small lay congregations. Areas within urban monastic churches, or chapels attached to them, often served as parish churches for the laity of the town.[42] In the early twelfth century the new church at Saint Albans had a parochial chapel built at its northwest corner, at the west end, and in following centuries the laity seem to have appropriated much if not most of the nave and the north transept, sometimes establishing guild altars there. Lay piety was reflected not only in the nave altars but also in the shrine of Saint Amphibalus, which by the thirteenth century had been moved to an altar of the Holy Cross, where it was more directly accessible to laypeople.[43]

The history of Saint Albans is, then, a classic example of the progressive enclosure of longitudinal space, and the increasing clarification of that enclosure, partly by means of massive screens. This process of enclosure is the subject of a classic article by Christopher Brooke, who points to a pattern of complexity, simplification, then return to complexity.[44] Continental churches of the ninth and tenth centuries, particularly in Germany, were often subdivided; the ninth-century plan for a monastic church at Saint Gall shows "not only separate altars or groups of altars in the eastern and western apses, but the whole church broken up into boxes" like family box pews. Similar developments can be seen in England. In the late Saxon period, Saint Augustine's Abbey at Canterbury was a classic example of "a great church made up of several chapels loosely strung together," with no greater liturgical space at its center. Canterbury Cathedral was less partitioned, yet before 1066 it too had several altars, with a high altar dedicated to Christ in the eastern apse but major celebrations occurring in a raised chapel in the western apse.[45] The Normans, in their quick rebuilding of England's major churches, brought simplicity out of complexity. They substituted at Canterbury a long building with a vista allowing a clear view of the high altar and of the episcopal throne beyond it. And yet a generation later the cathedral became again less clear in its unity, with shrines of traditional saints restored, then the shrine of Saint Thomas Becket added, making "a jumble of rooms" worse than before. A similar process occurred at Winchester Cathedral, where the late medieval erection of screens around the choir and sanctuary created "a church within a cathedral." Brooke sees the rise of eucharistic devotion as the root of this process: later medieval Christians saw the eucharist as a personal sacrament, and the enclosed sanctuary became a contained structure, a kind of architectural equivalent to the tabernacle. But enclosure of the sanctuary or chancel was only one part of a broader process by which churches in the later Middle Ages became divided and screened off into chapels of various kinds, often for confraternities or for families, in a consummately visible expression of the increasingly complex medieval society, increasingly bent on religious expression of social status.

One might suppose this process of enclosure was limited to the largest and most prominent churches, but it was not. The village of Dunster on the coast of Somerset has a church in which monks and laity coexisted for generations within a single liturgical space. In the fifteenth century, however, conflict between the two groups became intense, in part because their liturgies, no doubt increasingly elaborate on both sides, interfered with each other. Litigation led in 1498 to a formal settlement in which the church was divided into the monks' east end and the lay parishioners' west end. A new chancel had to be defined within the nave by means of a wide screen. What had been a single church became in effect two distinct churches laid end to end. The conduct of processions was the subject for minute specification. For most occasions the parishioners were to conduct their processions in their own part of the interior and in the churchyard, but for thirteen feasts of the liturgical year the monks were to process through an arch in the north transept and on into the parishioners' church, where they merged with the parishioners' procession, headed by cross-bearers from the two communities, who were followed by the parish priest and officials, then the monks, and finally the parishioners. The monastic and parochial communities had in effect been divorced, with elaborate provision for joint custody of their church, and what had been one of the major processional spaces in the region became harder for any procession to navigate.[46]

The segmentation of church interiors did not end with the Reformation but took a different direction, with the creation of box pews and magistrates' lofts reserved for families and for town dignitaries within the context of a preaching space. The habit was carried over and extended in colonial Virginia, where wealthy patrons erected private galleries for their own use, and gentry might compete with each other in construction of "hanging pews" that jutted out at an upper level to provide reserved yet conspicuous seating.[47] It was almost as though the urge to subdivide could not be restrained but needed to find new forms after earlier screens and private chapels had generally been abolished. But box pews, galleries, and hanging pews, as much as they segregated clusters of worshipers from one another, permitted the word of the preacher to carry from his elevated enclosure out to the other enclosures throughout the church. Bodies might be set apart in the post-Reformation church, but the disembodied word could reach them all.

Case Study: Saint Gregory of Nyssa, San Francisco, and the Integration of Longitudinal space

The very notion of longitudinal space has not surprisingly fallen into disfavor, as its segmentation and increasingly sedentary worship have obscured its purpose. Yet the longitudinal church can be creatively reconceived, and Saint Gregory of Nyssa Episcopal Church in San Francisco gives an expanded sense of the possibilities (fig. 5).[48] The rectors, Richard Fabian and Donald Schell, designed the building as a place for a liturgy they had developed over decades, drawing inspiration largely from the historic worship of Eastern Christianity.

This church is built around two clearly distinct spaces. In the elongated space for the liturgy of the word, people sit facing each other in rows of chairs on either side. This area has two main foci: at one end the presider's chair for preaching (a Thai howdah, or elephant saddle); at the other the ambo for scriptural readings (with Ethiopian crosses and cloth streamers behind it). When the liturgy of the word is completed, the entire congregation forms several lines and proceeds in a simple dance step, with song, through a wide passageway behind the ambo into the second space, where the liturgy of the eucharist takes place around a D-shaped altar table under an octagonal dome. The transition is one from linearity to centrality, mediated by a dance that begins in parallel lines and ends in concentric rings around the altar table: in effect, a

FIGURE 5. Saint Gregory of Nyssa, San Francisco, interior. Central space (for liturgy of the eucharist) in foreground, longitudinal space (for liturgy of the word) in background. Photograph by Richard Kieckhefer.

line dance turns into a circle dance. During the liturgy of the eucharist everyone is gathered in close formation around the table. Priests and lay servers (all vested in colorful robes blending West African with tie-dye design) stand immediately about the table, with the rest of the assembly gathered around them. The presiding priest sings the eucharistic prayer, and members of the congregation hum a chord as a vocal drone, thus joining their voices to that of the priest. Later, all those serving at the table raise the consecrated bread and the cups dramatically on high, then move out from the table to administer communion. At the end of the liturgy the entire congregation does a dance around the table, again with hymnody; around the walls, at the base of the dome, saints from various religious traditions are shown with their legs raised in the very dance step the worshipers are dancing.

At each stage in the service clergy and people are together. Each space is meant for the entire assembly. Everyone moves in procession, the procession fully engages all in hymnody and dance, and the movement clearly marks a transition in the liturgy. Neither of the two main spaces is subordinated to the other; each space is clearly visible from the other, and while the liturgy of the word is in progress the table stands in the adjacent space, as if beckoning the assembly onward toward the eucharist. The presiding priest stands neither over against the congregation nor turned away from it; rather, the vested altar party and the congregation form concentric rings around the altar table, and where any individual stands with respect to the presiding priest becomes fundamentally irrelevant.[49]

The main axis of the church extends from the presider's chair to the ambo and on to the centralized altar space under the dome, but another axis cuts across this one: the main entrance to the church leads directly into this altar space, so that immediately on entering one sees the altar table in the center of the room, and beyond it, outdoors, through glass doors, lies the rock with water flowing from it that is used for baptism. The long axis governs each celebration of liturgy. The cross axis governs the broader trajectory of life within the Church, from entry to sharing in communion (which is open to all), and then to the full commitment expressed in baptism (which is meant only for those ready to take that step). The conception of communion as table fellowship is signaled by the use of the altar table precisely as a table: at the end of the liturgy it is cleared of liturgical vessels and used for coffee hour, and then as a place for gathering of the food and other goods to be distributed in the church's ministry. The welcome to this table fellowship is underscored by placing the main entrance in the space for eucharist rather than that for liturgy of the word: the table space is simultaneously the narthex or entry way.

The furnishing and decoration at Saint Gregory of Nyssa are highly eclectic, and it would be easy to misread the eclecticism as arbitrary and capricious. But religious symbolism serves first to contain a richness and depth of meaning, second to express solidarity with broader communities extended in space and time, and the furnishing and decoration of Saint Gregory's do both. A wall painting displays Christ and the soul as the bridegroom and bride, following Gregory of Nyssa's commentary on the Song of Songs, with God as the mother-in-law who leads the pair to their union. Ethiopian crosses with streamers, African and Indian liturgical umbrellas, vestments in the form of West African robes, Tibetan and Japanese bells, a rubbing from a Chinese stele honoring eighth-century missionaries and monks—all this might seem a riot of uncontrolled eclecticism, except for three factors. First, the diversity of symbolism gives an effective setting for celebration. There is such a plenitude of sights and sounds that they blend and fuse into an ensemble of visual and musical color, a reflection of and inducement to exuberance. Second, whatever their provenance, the symbols are contextualized by the rectors' reading of Gregory of Nyssa. Gregory's maxim "The one thing truly worthwhile is becoming God's friend" hovers over the altar table as an inscription around the base of the dome and serves as a reminder of universal fellowship among God's friends. The objects brought together from various sources call to mind friends of God in all branches of Christianity and in non-Christian traditions as well. The extension of solidarity beyond its usual limits is seen also in the paintings of official and unofficial saints beneath the dome: Teresa of Avila and Julian of Norwich, Thomas Merton and Martin Luther, Francis of Assisi with his wolf, a Sufi with his tiger, and many others. Third, an underlying coherence is clear amid the exuberant eclecticism: a coherence in the shape of the liturgy, which is clarified by the use of liturgical space, by the dramatic dancing procession from one kind of space for liturgy of the word to another kind of space for liturgy of the eucharist. Elements of decoration that might otherwise seem merely thrown together and liturgical practices that might seem randomly experimental are fitted into a context that is anything but thrown together or random.

It is the disposition of liturgical space that is of special concern here. The use of space may seem creatively innovative but is grounded in historical precedent, particularly Syriac usage as described in Louis Bouyer's *Liturgy and Architecture*.[50] Bouyer wanted a sense of dynamism restored to the liturgy: the congregation should if possible stand rather than sit, pews and even chairs should ideally be done away with, and the laity should move along with the priest from one focus to another, from the lectern or ambo for the readings to the altar for the eucharist. He traced the evolution of early synagogues, Syrian churches of the early centuries, Roman basilicas, Byzantine churches, and later developments, but of special interest to him were early Syrian churches such as the fourth- and fifth-century churches of the "Dead Cities" in northwest Syria.[51] For the first part of the Syriac liturgy, consisting largely of scriptural readings, clergy and laity alike would cluster about the platform in the center of the church, where the bishop would sit enthroned, and the readings would be done from an ambo. When the eucharistic liturgy then began, clergy and laity alike would move toward the altar. The laity would come forward to the altar both for presentation of their offerings and for communion; for the eucharistic liturgy as a whole, they would be gathered close to the altar. For both parts of the liturgy, then, the bishop presiding at the celebration would be in the midst of his people, facing east along with them, as their leader in liturgical prayer. When Bouyer advocated a keener sense of dynamism in churches, then, what he had in mind was not simply processions as preludes and postludes to liturgical action but changing deployment of liturgical space corresponding to the structure of the liturgy.

Most fundamentally, Bouyer suggested that the reformers should draw more fully on the range of options presented by the history of liturgical architecture, and should take from them inspiration for new forms. Without phrasing the point quite this sharply, he seems to have viewed the liturgical reform being implemented in the church around him as too timid, as restricted to a narrow range of possibilities. The history of church architecture, he insisted, discloses "an astonishing variety of consecrated practice," yielding "both a very wide freedom and an inexhaustible wealth of inspiration," if only the Church can move beyond its limited conception of how churches should be built.

The rectors at Saint Gregory of Nyssa borrowed from many sources in their design and decoration of this church, and in so doing they were faithful to Bouyer's emphasis on freedom in drawing from the wealth of tradition. In two particular ways the imprint of Bouyer is clear: the movement of the entire assembly from one space to another marks the transition from liturgy of the word to liturgy of the eucharist, and in the eucharist the entire assembly gathers with the presiding priest at the altar table. There is nothing timid, nothing casually tinkering or experimental in the liturgical practice here; it is radical in the thoroughness of its conception and in its historical and theological grounding. Even those who disagree with aspects of this liturgical practice cannot dismiss it out of hand but must take account of its coherence, its rationale, and its effect.

Another and fundamentally different way of using processional space can be found at the church of Saint Gervais in Paris, now served by the Monastic Community of Jerusalem. The particular service I have witnessed, vespers and mass on Tuesday evening after Easter, is exceptionally interesting. Monks and nuns gather one by one during the half-hour before vespers, kneel in silent prayer in the middle of the choir, and remain there for vespers and for mass. During mass they come down into the congregation for the exchange of peace and for communion. At the end of the service, when one might expect them to process out through the nave, they continue kneeling as before, until, one by one, they stand to leave. In short, they redefine the processional space of the church, deliberately *not* using it for procession. Dynamism yields to the stability of contemplation. This use of space befits the monastics' self-conception: the role of this community is to model the contemplative life in the heart of the modern city. Thus the liturgy begins, ends, and is grounded in contemplation. In other contexts the longitudinal church may be meant as processional space, but another of its possible meanings here comes to the fore: it is space in which the community modeling contemplation does so in the presence of its guests. While Saint Gregory of Nyssa follows Bouyer's call to free adaptation of tradition in the design of new churches, the Monastic Community of Jerusalem extends this mandate, embracing freedom in the liturgical use of a received and adapted space.

The Central Plan

Some churches are structured around a broad central area, often circular or square, and often surmounted by a dome. This "central plan" is sometimes treated as a distinct type of church design. In its spatial dynamics, however, it is basically a variation on the longitudinal church. When the area under a circular dome serves as a nave, as in the Eastern Orthodox tradition, it stands in much the same relationship to the sanctuary as a longitudinal nave—except that the absence of pews in an Orthodox nave makes it easier for people to gather about the bishop, priest, or reader when the liturgical action moves into the nave. When it is the sanctuary that occupies an area under a dome, and the nave extends outward, as at Saint Peter's in Rome, the continuity with longitudinal design is still closer. The idea of centrality may suggest closeness and ingathering of a worshiping community, but that is by no means the necessary effect, and historically the central plan has its roots not in liturgical democracy but in imperial ceremony and the veneration of saints.

The emperor Constantine and his successors built several churches in their effort to link church with state and to exalt the harmony that binds church with empire, and both church and empire with the universe itself. One of these churches, begun by Constantine in the year 327, the Golden Octagon by the imperial palace at Antioch, was dedicated to the principle of Harmony. Its central octagon was surrounded by a colonnade that led to a surrounding corridor or ambulatory, and above the ground level a gallery echoed harmoniously the colonnaded octagon below. The structure was meant to highlight the majesty of the emperor enthroned in the building, as in the center of the empire and thus of the universe. And this Golden Octagon seems to be the earliest example and perhaps the inspiration for a long succession of imperial churches, including San Vitale in Ravenna and Charlemagne's circular palace chapel at Aachen.[52]

The central plan could also function as a display space for an important relic. Once again one of the most important early examples is in Syria, the monastic church at Qal'at Si'man, built in the fifth century under the patronage of the emperor Zeno. The relic here was the pillar on which Saint Simeon Stylites had perched in the later years of his life. The center of the church, then, was an immensely high structure that allowed throngs of pilgrims access to this relic. Around this core was built a huge cruciform church. The liturgy was presumably relegated to the wings radiating outward from the central relic-shrine.[53] While this arrangement may have been unusual in its precise form and in its size, the idea of building a centrally planned church around relics was anything but unusual. Indeed, many of the earliest churches grew up around *martyria*, the shrines built over places where martyrs had been buried. Saint Peter's in Rome is one of the best-known cases, and here too the new structure erected in the Renaissance has something of the central plan in its design, with the altar at the crossing rather than at the end, over the relics of the Apostle buried beneath it.[54] The tradition is preserved at Justus Dahinden's circular Nmugongo National Shrine Cathedral in Uganda, where the altar is placed on the spot where Joseph Mukasa Balikuddembe was martyred.[55] The prototypical association of the central plan with a burial place was the Church of the Holy Sepulcher in Jerusalem. European churches designed in imitation of that church might have circular naves (as in Cambridge) or chancels (the Temple Church in London), but the relationship between chancel and nave was not fundamentally different from that in a more conventionally rectangular building.[56]

The central plan could be linked to *both* empire and relic-cult, as in the chapel at Aachen. Originally the altar there was placed in a sanctuary on the east side of the circular nave, and the imperial throne was on the opposite side in a gallery; in the high Middle Ages the circular space of the nave became the location for Charlemagne's relics, while other important relics were enshrined in the chancel.[57]

In the Byzantine and Eastern Orthodox world, as well, the central plan is fundamentally a variation on the longitudinal one. The sanctuary (or "altar" in Eastern usage) is at the end, and procession from it into the nave was an essential feature of Byzantine liturgy.[58] The classic case is Hagia Sophia in Constantinople, which gives a sense of central focus under the great dome but has a nave nearly three times as long as it is wide. Further, the semidomes to the east and west serve to elongate the effect of the dome, creating a kind of "spatial ambivalence": whether the interior appears centralized or longitudinal depends largely on where one is standing.[59] Thomas Mathews emphasizes the openness of the early Byzantine church, the use of processional space not simply for movement around within a single space but for transition from one building to another, the passage of clergy and people from the atrium through the narthex and into the nave.[60]

The processions in a later, ordinary Eastern Orthodox church may not be as elaborate as those at a major church such as Hagia Sophia, but still the clergy or reader will come out from the sanctuary and stand in the center at various points in the liturgy: scripture is read from this position, the ceremonial vesting of a bishop occurs here, and in general the liturgy is marked by a sense of spatial fluidity. Mathews emphasizes the difference between the liturgy of Hagia Sophia and that of Middle Byzantine churches: fifth- and sixth-century ceremony entailed much processional movement, but medieval churches were meant more for dramatic moments in which priests emerged from the sanctuary to display a book or the sacrament. Yet even this later development presupposed a fundamentally processional conception of the church, even if the processional path was truncated and its use restricted.[61]

All five of the principles of processional dynamism operate in this kind of central space, and perhaps better than in other processional churches, in part because the use of a dome over the nave gives greater prominence to the space under the dome and more clearly motivates procession outward from the altar to the nave. If there is a clear distinction between the central and longitudinal plans it is not in their spatial dynamics but in their symbolic resonance: the use of the dome in the central plan creates a vertical axis, complementary to the horizontal axis, symbolizing the juncture of heaven and earth. In dynamic effect, the central plan remains a variation on the longitudinal.

The Walpole Chapel and the Verbal Dynamism of an Auditorium Church

The classic sacramental church has a long and complicated history. The alternatives are of more recent origin and present fewer complications, but they too have histories worth exploring, even if more briefly.

The Congregational Chapel at Walpole in Suffolk (fig. 2) is as different from Santa Maria Maggiore in its history as in its form.[62] Its status as a Dissenters' building, used by people who had broken away from the traditional and established Church of England, is signaled already by the term "chapel" rather than "church." The structure appears to have served originally as a cottage, or a pair of adjacent cottages, or perhaps a tannery, before it came to be used for Dissenters' meetings. The congregation was founded during the English Civil War, in the mid–seventeenth century. Its building remained in use as a Congregational chapel after the Restoration of the monarchy and of the established Church, and eventually (perhaps after the Toleration Act of 1689) it was subjected to a radical conversion of the interior and given the form it still has. It is as plain as Santa Maria Maggiore is grand and complex. Even after expansion, its width is only twenty-eight feet. One of the three pillars is reported to have served as a ship's mast. The carpentry is eminently simple.

Whereas Santa Maria Maggiore is a longitudinal structure for processional liturgy, with a high altar at the far end focusing attention and drawing people toward it, and colonnades evoking that forward motion, the chapel at Walpole is an auditorium meant as proclamatory space, for reading of scripture and for preaching. A visitor accustomed to the dynamic liturgy of Santa Maria Maggiore might see the Walpole chapel as a building designed for static worship, with clergy and congregation not moving but rather sitting throughout the service. But to be more precise, both buildings are meant to promote dynamism, of different kinds: kinetic at Santa Maria Maggiore, verbal at Walpole. The point at Walpole is not to provide architectural embodiment for the dynamic of procession and return but to create a space suitable for reading of scriptures, for preaching, for congregational response to preaching, for singing of hymns. The worship is centered on words, said and sung. The visual focus is not an altar but a pulpit. The introduction of pews into such churches, especially the high "box pew" compartments of the seventeenth and eighteenth centuries, and the distinction between a lower floor level and an upper gallery level in the same period, presuppose that people are not meant to move far forward at offertory or communion, that the clergy are not intended to move out into the congregation's space, and that clergy and choir will not be moving dramatically in procession from one sacred space to another. Once people have taken their places they remain in them, with relatively little movement. But the worship of early Congregationalists often involved a lively exchange between preacher and clergy: the preacher might preach the scripture, but laity as well as clergy might engage in more spontaneous "prophesyings" or interpretation of scripture in the course of worship, and in some places the congregation was allowed time to question the preacher on his sermon.[63] The ritual of communion may occur in such a church but is subordinated to verbal worship: the communion table is often placed below the centrally positioned pulpit, as a clear visual clue to this subordination.

Buildings in the classic evangelical tradition tend to be much smaller than longitudinal churches. The Walpole chapel is less than a tenth as wide as Santa Maria Maggiore is long. If the chapel conveys a sense of intimacy, and the basilica a feeling of grandeur, that is in large part because of this immense difference in sheer volume. But processional churches, whether large or small, aspire to something of the grandeur of Santa Maria Maggiore, and auditorium churches, whether modest or ambitious, strive for the intimacy of the Walpole chapel. Even a relatively small church that imitates a Roman basilica in its longitudinal plan and its use of colonnades (or arcades) can give a sense of expansiveness disproportional to its actual size. And even a relatively large church that uses fan-shaped arrangement of seating and brings more people close to the preacher by use of galleries can approximate a sense of intimacy. Frank Lloyd Wright's Unity Temple in Oak Park, Illinois, has seating on ground level and in two galleries, allowing a congregation of four hundred to sit within forty-five feet of the pulpit.[64] Rather different is the solution at Philip Johnson's far larger Crystal Cathedral, in Garden Grove, California, where sound is amplified and an oversized screen allows the image of the preacher to be magnified and seen as if close to the entire congregation: a striking example of an ambitious auditorium space straining for a semblance of intimacy.[65]

If the dynamism of a classic evangelical church is more verbal than kinetic, what are the characteristic features of this verbal dynamism? First, preacher and congregation are ideally positioned in close proximity, not only so the preacher can be heard but so the congregation's response to the preaching can be an effective contribution to the service. Second, the entire space is conceived as an integral whole; the entire interior is called the sanctuary. Third, the size of the sanctuary is as important as its configuration in facilitating interaction between preacher and congregation; but even in an larger sanctuary every effort is made to support that interaction. Fourth, the preacher faces the congregation whenever leading the service, as do others who share that leadership. If there is a choir (in a later adaptation of this architectural form), it is typically installed on the platform behind the preacher, and it joins with the preacher's act of proclamation, ratifying it in song. But fifth, despite all facilities for interaction, the historical tendency has been for the role of the preacher and others facing the congregation to take a dominant role in the service; maintaining a balance of proclamation and response remains a challenge.

Evolution of Classic Evangelical Churches for Protestant Worship

Most churches meant to foster the verbal dynamism of the classic evangelical tradition fit more or less the model just sketched—but the transition from medieval to Protestant church design was not a simple and straightforward one, and classic evangelical churches often maintain links to the classic sacramental tradition. First of all, the design of churches as places suitable for preaching was not an innovation of the Reformers but an extension of late medieval developments. Even in a longitudinal church it was possible to erect a high pulpit with a sounding board at the east end of the nave, and to build relatively simple rectangular churches in which the preacher could claim the attention of all. As preaching became more popular in the fourteenth and fifteenth centuries, churches were increasingly built in this fashion.[66] The insertion of pews (for people to sit during sermons) and the provision of stone or wooden pulpits in parish churches were innovations largely inspired by increasing lay receptivity to—nay, demand for—preaching.[67] The Reformers were heirs to this late medieval process of church design and church furnishing.

Furthermore, the early Reformers adapted existing churches more often than they built new ones, and their greatest ingenuity was often devoted to the reconception of medieval longitudinal space. They often set pulpits midway down one side of the nave, turning long spaces into wide ones. In a church with a distinct chancel, three main possibilities presented themselves. First, the nave could serve as the main worship space, and the chancel could be reserved for other occasions (for smaller services such as weddings). Second, the first part of the service (the liturgy of the word) could be held in the nave, after which the entire congregation could be invited into the chancel for the remainder (the eucharist), with the altar placed either "altar-wise" against the east wall or "table-wise" down the center of the chancel. Third, the chancel could become the space in which privileged individuals or families sat while the service was held in the nave. Along with any of these uses, the chancel could serve also as a space for burials.

Newly built churches allowed more radical measures. When Christopher Wren designed churches conceived as preaching halls, he saw himself as deviating from Catholic tradition, as in some respects he indeed was:

> In our reformed religion, it should seem vain to make a parish
> church larger, than that all who are present can both hear and see.
> The Romanists, indeed, may build larger churches, it is enough if
> they hear the murmur of the mass, and see the elevation of the host,
> but ours are to be fitted for auditories. I can hardly think it practica-

ble to make a single room so capacious, with pews and galleries, as
to hold above 2000 persons, and all to hear the service, and both to
hear distinctly, and see the preacher.[68]

Wren's churches, like other Anglican structures, do still have the table rather
than the pulpit as their central visual focus. But in the parish churches he
designed for the City of London the chancels are as much as possible integrated
into a unified auditorium space, generally with galleries, and his clear conception of parish churches as preaching spaces is expressly linked with the Reformers' theology of worship. Not all Anglican buildings were crafted as clearly
for preaching. Dell Upton has commented that the churches of Colonial Virginia with their axial entrances and clearly defined chancels "created a conspicuous pathway down the center of the church, but a pathway that had no
goal. The act of movement was an end in itself."[69] But Wren's influence worked
in the direction of the centralized preaching hall.

Lutherans often remained in basic continuity with the medieval tradition
of the longitudinal church, while adapting it as much as possible for the needs
of preaching. What I am calling the classic evangelical model is found more
consistently in Calvinist churches. A version of it was also favored by John
Wesley and his followers, whose "preaching-houses" (meant originally to supplement rather than supplant the Anglican churches where people received
the sacraments) were often octagonal structures with a pulpit placed on the
wall across from the main entrance, and sometimes a gallery around seven of
the eight sides.[70] While Protestant church-building has admitted numerous
variations,[71] then, and no absolute distinctions can be drawn between Protestant and Catholic churches, the Reformation, especially in its Calvinist interpretation, led to a form of church design distinct in principle from that of the
processional church. These arrangements may be seen in an early form in the
Walpole chapel, or earlier still in the sixteenth-century Calvinist Temple du
Paradis at Lyon.[72]

In nineteenth-century America, Charles Finney in his Lectures on Revivals
of Religion (1835) laid down the norms for an urban version of revivalism.[73]
Revivalists in Finney's tradition encouraged the introduction of organs into
churches, although traditionalists saw use of musical instruments as a departure from the purity of earlier Calvinist practice. The revivalists used hymns
calculated to heighten an emotional response, as well as a "talking" mode of
preaching, and prayers led by laymen and laywomen. One associate described
Finney's preaching as possessed of a spontaneous eloquence:

For the most part Mr. Finney's manner was simply conversational
and direct, the same variety of intonation and expression as in common intercourse. He came into intimate relations with his hearers.
It was real intercourse. He seemed to be talking with you and to

you, utterly unconscious of any effort at effect or rhetorical art. . . .
Though perfectly simple and natural, [his preaching] was always impressive and often intensely impassioned.[74]

Finney's Broadway Tabernacle in New York unabashedly resembled a theater,
with a broad stage that allowed the preacher to move freely. Influential as
Finney was in American Protestantism, however, his amphitheater-style
church was not widely adopted until the years 1869–1910, which Jeanne Halgren Kilde refers to as the golden era of auditorium churches. Churches of
various shapes but with a fairly consistent interior arrangement then proliferated: the pulpit was centrally placed on a platform, with choir and organ on
the platform behind it, seating at ground level in a fan arrangement facing the
pulpit, and a horseshoe-shaped gallery providing further seating in close proximity to the pulpit.[75] One particularly elegant example of the theater-style
church is Julia Morgan's First Baptist Church in Oakland, California (1906–
7), where the woodwork was inspired by the Arts and Crafts tradition, with
ceiling beams converging on a central octagon and geometrical patterns gracefully worked into the design.[76] From coast to coast, this model of church design
flourished. The pattern of worship implied by such a church was still one of
proclamation and response, although the altar call, bidding converts to move
forward, added an element of kinetic dynamism.

Whether the choir and organ introduced into an auditorium church diminished or heightened the role of the pulpit could depend a great deal on
how the entire complex was handled. The Archer Street Methodist Church in
North Adelaide was built in 1856–67, and an organ was installed in 1887. Pulpit
and organ were made into an ensemble with an elaborately decorative system
of railings that ran across the front of the choir gallery, along the stairs flanking
the platform, and across the platform itself—but all converging on and high-
lighting the pulpit, providing a dramatic framework for preaching.[77]

One or another version of the classic evangelical church has seemed to
many the obvious plan for preaching. And yet a critic writing in 1939 complained: "the erroneous idea persists that the square, octagonal, or circular
auditorium is mandatory for a Protestant church. Actually, for a place of worship and preaching, the rectangular auditorium with a longitudinal axis is
better for [a series of] very practical reasons." Among these reasons were the
acoustical superiority of a longitudinal church, the placement of more people
directly before the preacher and in direct view of the chancel, and the provision
of a natural point of focus.[78] While variations on the classic evangelical plan
remained appealing to many, hybrid forms such as longitudinal space with a
gallery also had appeal. If any generalization is possible, it is perhaps that
Protestants have often held firm convictions about the purpose to be served by
a church but at least as often have shown themselves pragmatic in adopting
means toward those ends.

Case Study: The Westerkerk in Amsterdam and the Transition
to Protestant Design

Reformed architecture flourished for a time in France: several Huguenot temples were built between the Edict of Nantes and its Revocation (1598–1685),
called "temples" to distinguish them from the "churches" of the established
Catholic Church.[79] When newly built they were sometimes major works of
Renaissance design, often drawing inspiration from Sebastiano Serlio's *Quinto
libro d'architettura*. They could be either longitudinal or centralized in plan. The
Temple of Charenton, rebuilt after a fire in 1621 by the court architect Salomon
de Brosse, was the most famous example of a longitudinal Huguenot building.
The Temple du Paradis at Lyon, adapted for worship in 1564, was among the
best known centrally planned houses of worship, but the roughly octagonal
Grand Temple at La Rochelle (opened in 1603) was the greater architectural
achievement, arousing admiration for its construction without interior supports for the massive roof, and described by one source as the "most stylish
and prettiest" building in the world. Whether centrally planned or longitudinal,
what these Calvinist buildings had in common was their use of galleries and
of numerous large windows with clear glass. We know about them, in any case,
chiefly from engravings and from written accounts, because the Revocation
led to their general destruction.

To find early Reformed architecture intact, one must visit a place that was
expanding rapidly in the sixteenth and seventeenth centuries, thus needed to
build new churches, and remained Protestant through the modern era. One
city that answers well to this description is Amsterdam.[80] Yet by a gentle irony,
precisely in a place where Protestants were doing so much building, their
churches are sometimes less decidedly Protestant than one might expect and
show lingering attachment to some of the forms of medieval Catholic design.
Outside of Amsterdam, the Netherlands was among the countries where Protestants experimented with new forms of church design. At Willemstad they
built an octagonal church (1596–1607), with the pulpit placed along one of the
walls. But Amsterdam was less innovative, no doubt in part because its Reformed congregations were driven less by the strong theological conviction of
the preachers and more by the moderate pragmatism of the civic magistrates.[81]
Their spirit of toleration extended de facto to Roman Catholics, who were allowed to worship unmolested in their "hidden churches" so long as they did
not flaunt their religion publicly,[82] while Jews were not only tolerated but allowed to build synagogues of considerable size.[83]

In other respects as well the Protestant churches of Dutch towns could
display remarkable tolerance of medieval traditions, or at least Protestant ad-
aptations of these traditions. When the Dutch remodeled a medieval church
they often left the chancel screen intact or even created a new one, so that what

had been the chancel at the east end of the church could be used as a chapel for smaller events or as a meeting space. In the Nieuwe Kerk at Amsterdam the high altar in the chancel was replaced by a grand monument to one of the most important admirals of the Dutch navy, whose remains were placed under the memorial in a crypt; few could have been unaware that this civic piety mimicked the cult of the saints.[84] Newly designed figural glass was introduced into windows, generally showing persons and events important to the life of the town, or of a nearby town that had donated the window.[85]

The sculptor and architect Hendrick de Keyser designed some of the most important buildings in early seventeenth-century Amsterdam, including the Zuiderkerk, the Noorderkerk, and most importantly, the Westerkerk (fig. 6).[86] The last of these, one of the best preserved, largest, and best-known of early Protestant churches, was, like the earlier Zuiderkerk, in some respects similar to the Catholic buildings that preceded it. One observer says of this Westerkerk that it "represents surprisingly the culmination and conclusion of mediaeval church building," with nave, transepts, and west tower all reminiscent of Gothic design in their basic form and massing.[87] The plan of the church is indeed at first sight traditional: an elongated rectangle, running west to east, with columns separating the center from an aisle on either side. Yet even without minute inspection it becomes clear that the Westerkerk differs in many ways from a classic sacramental church. At ground level, the pillars are slender, and the demarcation of aisles is less pronounced than in most medieval

FIGURE 6. Westerkerk, Amsterdam, interior. Photograph by Richard Kieckhefer.

churches, leaving a clearer sense of a single and unified rectangular space. Further, while the space is a long rectangle, it is used not longitudinally but transversally. At the upper level the design is more complex: the second and fifth bay of each aisle rises higher than the other bays, making for transepts at either end and giving the upper part of the interior visual interest while preserving the relative simplicity of the ground level.

The furnishings of the Westerkerk are typical of contemporary Dutch Reformed arrangements. Everything was planned to make the pulpit a strong focal point. With its prominent sounding board, the pulpit is placed midway down the central space on the north side. Originally it was enclosed by a railing that defined the baptismal space and simultaneously reinforced the centrality of the pulpit itself. (An arrangement of this sort can be seen intact at Amsterdam's Nieuwe Kerk.) The rail had a kind of bulge in front of the pulpit to accommodate a copper lectern. The table for the Lord's Supper stood in front of the pulpit. While there would have been no permanent seating for most of the congregation, box pews for the magistrates were built around the pillars on the south side, facing the pulpit. The pew on the pillar directly across from the pulpit was for the mayor, who had a special side entrance on the wall behind this pew (and a special room with a drinking trough to accommodate his horse). De Keyser did not give the Westerkerk a gallery; one was added at the east end only in 1685, for the children of a nearby orphanage. More radical Protestants might insist on galleries to bring more people close to the pulpit, and the Protestants in Amsterdam whose churches lay on narrower lots (such as the Lutherans) might use them to overcome space limitations, but De Keyser clearly felt no need for them. On the west wall, the Westerkerk has monumental and highly decorated casing for the organ pipes, this being the century in which grand organs were introduced into many of the more prosperous Dutch churches, despite opposition from those who found them a secular intrusion.[88]

Altogether, despite the traditional elements in the plan, it has rightly been said that this is "a purely Protestant house of prayer."[89] The interior is bright and restrained, with white walls offset by exposed structural members of gray stone, and thirty-six large windows with clear glass flooding the space with light. While the side aisles have cross-ribbed stone vaults, a plain wooden barrel vault covers the central space. The building is designed in a Mannerist adaptation of classical style, a departure from the picturesquely ornamented Dutch Renaissance work of De Keyser's early years and foreshadowing the stricter classicism that captured the Netherlands later in the century.

While the Dutch churches of the seventeenth century are noteworthy in their own right, they also figure prominently in the architectural paintings of their day by Pieter Saenredam and his contemporaries.[90] For the most part these show the interiors of churches when worship is not in progress, or from angles that do not highlight the preaching that is being done. Often they are exercises in perspective, using the arcades and the tiled floors of the churches as opportunities to explore the technicalities of perspective painting. Sometimes the churches are inhabited by men digging graves, small boys at play, and dogs. Occasionally there are unexpected touches, as in one of Saenredam's paintings of the medieval ambulatory at Saint Bavo in Haarlem, where the figures emerging into view turn out on close inspection to be the Holy Family, Simeon, and Anna at the presentation of Jesus in the Temple. In the paintings as in the churches, Mies van der Rohe's maxim proves apt: God is in the details. But the details of these paintings have also given rise to suspicion of further Catholic survival in the Netherlands. The churches might be in Protestant hands, but the paintings sometimes show a fondness for details that would have reminded viewers of the medieval heritage.[91]

The Methodist Church at Northfield and the Social Dynamism of a Communal Church

Classic sacramental and classic evangelical churches continued to be built. Since the mid–twentieth century, however, many churches of almost all large denominations have followed a third model, here referred to as the modern communal church. One representative example is United Methodist Church at Northfield, Minnesota (fig. 3), completed in 1966 to a design by Edward Sövik, a Lutheran architect who has referred to his buildings for worship as "non-churches" and who has worked for Roman Catholic as well as Protestant congregations.[92] At Northfield the space for worship is a nearly square room, the walls are of brick partly laid in decorative patterns, simple pews on three sides are turned toward a low platform on the fourth, the communion table and other furnishings are simple and dispersed rather than concentrated, the ceiling is moderately low and not pitched, and a spacious corridor leads into the worship space. Indeed, the worship space is relegated to one corner of the church complex, while the central position in the complex is occupied by the broad north-south corridor that served for years as space for communal gathering.[93]

One of the earliest writers to offer a sustained rationale for such a church was the Belgian Roman Catholic Frédéric Debuyst, in 1966. (Sövik quickly recognized Debuyst as an ideological ally.) Debuyst was willing to accept the view of a church as "a kind of great livingroom, a place where the faithful come together to meet the Lord, and one another in the Lord," so long as it was clear that this meeting took place in the context of a celebration, that the liturgy is fundamentally a festive occasion. A celebration, he went on to say, synthesizes two nearly opposing factors: on the one hand an "aesthetic exaltation" or experience of "splendour, greatness and fullness," and on the other a sense of "graciousness."[94] The appropriate setting for a celebration, in the modern as in the ancient church, is a home, and thus near the beginning of his book Debuyst gives "a short phenomenology of the modern house" as a prelude to understanding what a church might be. This conception of a church quickly became commonplace. In the mid-1970s, the interior of Saint Peter's Lutheran Church in New York was designed as a "paschal living room" that would enable worshipers "to gather around the Table of the Lord," with almost entirely movable furnishings, allowing people to cluster in various patterns around the altar in "an intimate relationship between the one who presides and those who share in the celebration." That churches should be "inviting," "flexible," "meaningful," "sunny and warm" was soon the established rhetoric.[95]

This model resembles the classic evangelical one in some respects, lending surface plausibility to the notion that Roman Catholic churches were becoming Protestantized, but the underlying principles governing the modern communal church are importantly different from those of the classic evangelical model.[96] First, the space is designed mainly to create a sense of bonding among those gathered—within the congregation, as well as between the congregation and the clergy. Second, the space is meant to encourage full participation by the entire assembly: not only is the entire space conceived as an integral whole but visual subdivision of the space is reduced to a minimum. Third, distribution of furnishings in the interior is generally meant to be flexible; in a pure case of the modern communal church even the altar may be moveable. Fourth, the relationship between space for assembly and space for entry becomes crucial: symbolically, the entrance space highlights the process of gathering and of proceeding outward; practically, it provides space for social as well as liturgical gathering. But fifth, while the entire complex is designed to give people a sense of being gathered into a close community, the space can lend itself to focusing attention all the more clearly on the clergy, and the sense of closeness to others can either encourage lively participation or discourage it by making people more self-conscious, all depending on the ethos of the community.

In his survey of twentieth-century church design, Reinhard Gieselmann presents a simple but useful trichotomy of longitudinal, transversal, and centralized disposition of space for worship.[97] (This *centralized* disposition is not to be confused with the more traditional *central* plan.) Longitudinal spaces need not be strictly rectangular, but they are elongated, the seating is more or less in straight ranks, and the altar occupies one end. Transversal spaces are also elongated, with the altar usually along one of the long sides, and with clergy and congregation facing each other at relatively close quarters. In what Gieselmann calls centralized spaces—which may be circular, square, or irregular—the congregation gathers around the altar on three sides or surrounds it on all sides, an arrangement only approximately suggested in liturgical documents coming out of the Second Vatican Council.[98] Roughly speaking, Gieselmann's longitudinal spaces would be expected mostly in what we are calling classic sacramental churches, his transversal spaces are most compatible with the classic evangelical model, and what he calls centralized spaces are typical of modern communal churches.

There has been a wealth of literature promoting the modern communal church. Sövik contributed to the discussion with influential articles and with his book *Architecture for Worship* (1973), which unambiguously emphasizes the role of the assembly: "a house of worship is not a shelter for an altar; it is a shelter for people. It is not the table that makes a sacrament; it is the people and what they do. The things are adjuncts, conveniences, symbols, utensils. The presence of God is not assured by things or by symbols or by buildings, but by Christian people."[99] Sövik reviews ordinary social spaces as analogues to space for worship: people listening to a soapbox orator will gather in a semicircle; people at a family reunion gather in a circle or by a hearth; at a meal they may sit at a round table; in some cases refreshments may be distributed to a scattered assembly; those at a large reception or party will break into smaller groups. On Sövik's interpretation, a space for worship should respect these impulses. It should be a unified space (not divided into chancel and nave), nearly square, or at least no longer than twice its breadth, free of axial character and dominating focus, flexible and perhaps asymmetrical in its arrangement of furnishings, although seating should be in a circle or horseshoe, "not in ranks like strangers in a cinema." The basic values expressed by such architecture are integrity, hospitality, and beauty: an integrity that shuns artificial materials, a hospitality that makes people feel welcomed as if into a family, a beauty that impresses on them "that the ineffable, transcendent, awesome, fascinating mystery of the divine is immanently present."[100] A church, like the Christian community itself, should have "a certain simple, straightforward and unaffected quality," found in sundry aspects of a church building but most evidently in a flat roof, a good and inexpensive feature that gives the most logical way to span a space.[101]

In fundamental sympathy with Sövik and his principles, James F. White and Susan J. White explored the implications of church design in their book *Church Architecture: Building and Renovating for Christian Worship* (first published in 1988), which highlights three basic qualities of church architecture: hospitality, participation, and intimacy. A church "must be inviting in order to welcome all comers and make them feel at home." Hospitality brings people together "so they want to meet, know each other, and act together with a common purpose." Scale is one critical factor in design, because a church that overwhelms with its monumentality makes the beholder into a passive spectator, whereas a sense of intimacy fosters participation.[102]

Scale is decisive for a modern communal church more than for other forms. Maurizio Abeti suggests that the ideal assembly should be one of fifty participants at most, gathered like a family around a common table; when five thousand were gathered with Christ, he had them sit in groups of about fifty (Luke 9:14). Yet Abeti suggests ways small, medium-sized, or large communities can be gathered in square, rectangular, octagonal, or circular patterns, any of which can be centered on an axis defined by the presider's chair, the ambo, the altar, and a recessed baptismal pool.[103] The question in any case is how far a larger space can approximate the ideals of hospitality and intimacy that are more natural to a smaller one, and at what point the challenge becomes so difficult that the attempt is pointless.

To distinguish between a classic sacramental church and a modern communal church is not to suggest that the latter cannot also be an effective setting for administration of sacraments. Indeed, James and Susan White have argued the advantages for sacraments of what we have called here a modern communal structure. The theoretical ideal for them is a concentric space with the community "gathered about a font or an altar-table, where someone reaches out to minister." They distinguish between the needs of sacraments and those of preaching: the human voice can project hundreds of feet even without amplification, but "there is no similar extension of the arm," and it is the arms and hands that are used in the sacraments, for giving bread and wine, for pouring or sprinkling water. "At the heart of sacramental action, then, is a gathering about, a coming within arm's reach—for individuals, if not for the whole community." The sacraments require visibility, proximity, and accessibility. If the congregation as a whole is to participate in the sacraments, the whole congregation must be able to see and be close. And for this purpose, the Whites argue, neither a longitudinal church nor an auditorium church with a gallery is well suited.[104]

Forceful as this argument may seem, it assumes that all those participating in and witnessing a sacrament must have the same kind of proximity to the sacramental action, and that the church must be designed accordingly. But, to take matrimony as an illustrative sacrament, one might suppose that the couple being married should be in a privileged position, that all those present should be close enough to witness the event, which hardly requires being within arm's length, and that a longitudinal nave with its processional space not only maximizes the space for a traditionally festive entrance and conclusion but gives the bridal party the best chance to pass as close as possible to the largest number of witnesses at those particularly festive moments.[105] What a modern communal church gains in visibility, proximity, and accessibility may or may not compensate for what it loses in kinetic dynamism and the festivity that can engender. The Whites do speak of the role of movement as a constituent element in worship: "Literally, Christians worship with their whole bodies, including their feet," and the space inside and outside the church must form "a processional path by which members of the community converge to worship together."[106] But movement for the Whites is a movement of gathering and a movement within a worship space, not the dynamism of a classic sacramental church that entails progression from one type of space to another as a marker of transition in the liturgy. And "movement space" is for them one element in church design, alongside the "gathering space" that leads to worship and "congregational space" that is the main locus for worship; if any of the three is a primary determinant for the form of the church, it is the last.

Sövik and the Whites both emphasize the importance of the entrance space, which Sövik sometimes refers to as a "concourse" and others call a "gathering place." Sövik distinguishes it from a narthex: a traditional narthex is an entry way through which one spends a moment in passing, while a concourse is a gathering space in which members of the community may spend as much time as they please.[107] It is designed to be inviting, as a space that helps to create a sense of community before entry into the worship space. The evident assumption is that people are assembling from different parts of the workaday world, where they may have relatively little contact with each other. They belong to a mobile and highly differentiated society, and when they gather for worship their assembly is not simply the neighborhood or village at prayer. When they meet, they are first constituted socially as a community, then they proceed to the worship space for prayer, then they may move back out into the social space for coffee hour or other informal contact. The gathering space is a critical part of a complex whose dynamic is that of gathering, worshiping, and returning outward. The worship space itself may be fundamentally a scene of stasis; motion within it may be relatively perfunctory, and verbal exchange may be relatively formulaic. But the dynamic interplay of gathering and worshiping is fundamental to the church's role, and to the design of the space created for worship. Particularly well developed is the deliberately low gathering space at Saint Procopius Abbey Church in Lisle, Illinois, which leads onward to a baptismal font, and then to a narrow corridor that opens onto the broad worship space: an entire processional pathway devoted to the passage from the outer world into the place of liturgical assembly.[108]

Theodor Filthaut also emphasized the importance of an entrance hall or forecourt, arguing that theaters, museums, concert halls, even cinemas have such spaces but that buildings, such as churches, which genuinely need them rarely have proper and effective entryways. But for Filthaut the purpose of the forecourt is not (as for Sövik and others) to allow gathering of the community but rather to prepare the worshiper by affording recollection and silence— almost the opposite of the intent in the modern communal church.[109]

Case Study: The Church of the Autostrada

Churches built in the later twentieth century often serve nontraditional communities: not villages or neighborhoods of people who know each other well in their daily lives but subdivisions whose residents are largely unfamiliar to each other, or people who live and work far apart and assemble only or mainly for worship. This liturgical gathering of strangers can be seen in an especially pronounced form at a church on the north side of Florence, Giovanni Michelucci's church of San Giovanni Battista (1960–64), also known as the Chiesa dell'Autostrada from its position alongside one of Europe's most important motorways (fig. 7).[110] The building rises boldly beside the heavily trafficked roadside. Drivers coming from Bologna will have made their way through the Apennines, along twisting routes with tunnels opening onto forested mountainsides. The architect saw the building as a kind of refuge offered to travelers.[111] It is signposted along the highway for the benefit of passersby, and in its design it is meant to resemble a tent inviting voyagers to come in from the motorway and gather under its sheltering roof, and thus further as a symbol of transience for the Christian pilgrim on earth—although this conception emerged in the course of the church's design and was not its point of departure. The church serves also as a memorial to workers who died in the difficult and treacherous work of constructing the mountain road. Its stone walls, offset by concrete on the interior and by a copper roof on the exterior, call to mind the juxtaposition of natural and manufactured materials found all along that stretch of motorway.

Meant to serve travelers with no local ties, the church is unlike a parish church, and it does not highlight those dimensions of church life one might expect to find in a traditional parish. As Giacomo Grasso has pointed out, it is quite unthinkable that the passersby who come in off the motorway to this

FIGURE 7. San Giovanni Battista (Church of the Autostrada), Florence, interior. Photograph by Richard Kieckhefer.

church could form a community.[112] Yet in its plan the Chiesa dell'Autostrada resembles many other modern churches. As people arrive from the motorway, park their cars, and enter the church, the first space they experience is the entrance corridor or vestibule, which could in principle serve as a gathering space. To the left, a series of upright slabs displays boldly executed relief carvings, dramatically lighted by the windows to which they stand perpendicular. The worship space is transversally ordered: the altar is placed along the long side, with no sharp division between its immediate environment and that of the congregation, so that the congregation is gathered close to the altar.

My own experience of this church was an extreme case of fortuitous presence as an anonymous stranger. My wife and I were there on a Sunday in the fall of 2000. Not only were we motorists, but we were delayed on our journey by car trouble and unable to reach the church we had meant to attend that Sunday morning. The Chiesa dell'Autostrada happened to be the closest church, and we arrived just in time for mass. The priest was attended by an elderly gentleman who served little evident function; there was little interaction between either of them and their itinerant congregation. At the end of mass we continued to Bologna and then to Ravenna. That evening we happened on a street performer just beginning his act in Ravenna's Piazza del Popolo. For his equipment he had only a unicycle and a few juggler's balls and clubs, but he handled these with aplomb. He was an expert showman, adept at handling his audience. He had laid out a cord on the pavement to define his performance area, and he invited spectators to gather closely about this space. His ingratiating and teasing patter played as much of a role as his tricks in holding the crowd's attention. On plucking a young boy from the crowd as a "volunteer," he instructed the lad that the first rule of street performance is to keep smiling at the audience; with his own fingers he brought a mock smile to the *ragazzo*'s face. Throughout the performance he found ways of interacting spontaneously both with individuals in the piazza and with the audience as a whole—mostly local people out for an evening stroll, but on this occasion two visiting Americans as well.

Mass at the beginning of the day's travel, and street theater at the end. There might have seemed little connection, but it struck me in a moment of recognition that the positions of the street performer and his audience replicated exactly those of the priest and his congregation. In each case, perhaps one or two hundred strangers who happened to be passing by were gathered closely in front of one individual, in a broad assembly that afforded a sense of proximity rather than intimacy. For the street performer this use of space was ideal: it allowed the rapport with his audience that was essential for his entertainment. But what purpose was served by the identical relationship of priest and congregation at mass? Did this arrangement of liturgical space lend itself to congregational participation? Do those in attendance participate more fully, or feel more deeply engaged, than they would in a different form of space? In fact, their modest participation at the Chiesa dell'Autostrada was scripted and formulaic rather than spontaneous; responses were provided in advance, and the priest was not likely to address individuals in the congregation during the mass or to conscript them as "volunteers" in the manner of a street performer. The audience at Ravenna was far more visibly engaged in the event than the congregation at Florence. Was the priest put in the simple and straightforward position of a leader in prayer for a congregation seeking spiritual refuge and refreshment? If that was the intention one might expect the priest to stand with the congregation, either facing the altar with them, as Louis Bouyer recommended, or gathering with them in a circle, rather than being set before them as the center of their attention. Did this form of liturgical space, then, help to break down a sense of hierarchy or of distinction between clergy and laity? To the contrary, the closer the laity were to the priest, the more clearly they faced the individual on whom all their attention was focused, exactly as in street performance. But while the street performer knew that the success of his act hinged entirely on the power of his personality, few would make this assumption in a liturgical context. A particular priest may indeed convey to the congregation a sense of profound reverence, a consciousness that each liturgical moment has depth and power, or else a mood of intimate and casual familiarity, but relatively few clergy realize either of these possibilities. Yet why else would one wish to design a church that brings the congregation into the same physical relationship with the priest that a street performer can put to such excellent effect?

The dynamics of intimacy differ from those of proximity, and the Chiesa dell'Autostrada may be attempting to do what many modern communal churches attempt, which is to attain a sense of intimacy in a setting that can achieve only proximity. Where six or twelve people are gathered about an altar for worship on a weekday morning, the intimacy of the gathering can generate a kind of energy that is less a function of the presider's personality than that of the group's own dynamics. But in most circumstances a gathering of a hundred or more is unlikely to experience bonding quite so easily or spontaneously. Much more will depend on the use of environmental cues that bring the group to a sense of shared experience focused on a process, an object, or a person presented before it. The greater the proximity of the presider to the congregation, the greater the expectation that the presider will be that focus of attention that gives dynamism to the liturgy. If that is a goal—and in the traditional worship of Catholic churches it is not—it may be realized when the presider has a personality and a manner of expression that encourage a sense of bonding with the congregation. If the presider does not have that capacity, the greater proximity can make the relationship between clergy and congregation all the more poignantly artificial. Proximity creates the expectation of bonding, and places the burden of responsibility on the presider, and if the bonding does not happen the disappointment is all the keener.

The Chiesa dell'Autostrada is not alone of its kind. The later Autobahn-kirche Sankt Christophorus at Baden-Baden, which has perhaps a better claim to resembling a tent, is identified for motorists as a church chiefly by standard signs, posted along the Autobahn and even directly in front of the building, showing the silhouette of a traditional church with its spire, as if to suggest that new forms of church depend for their identity and meaning on the very traditions they consciously set aside. In any case, in serving as liturgical centers for passing strangers these motorway churches are extreme cases of the relatively anonymous congregations that populate many church buildings.[113]

Conclusion

The basic forms of spatial dynamics in churches may be summarized in few words. In a classic sacramental church movement takes place along a processional path, marking the stages in the liturgy. In a classic evangelical church, verbal exchange (largely spontaneous) takes place between a preacher who stands and a congregation that sits in an essentially fixed position. And in a modern communal church people pass from their diverse positions in the world, through a preliminary space of social gathering, into a gathered worshiping assembly where movement occurs within a unified space.

Yet this bare summary abstracts from worlds of qualification and variation. In a classic sacramental church much depends on how the units in the processional space are divided, as they almost always are; on whether the passage is limited mainly to the clergy or involves reciprocal movement of the clergy into the nave and the laity into the chancel; on whether in addition to the clergy and servers there is a vested choir, and if so how that choir relates to the congregation. In a classic evangelical church the dynamics vary with size, sight lines and acoustics, and the presence or absence of a choir to share the platform with the preacher. In a modern communal church the configurations of liturgical furniture and seating are various, and the intimate familiarity of a smaller space can give way to artificiality if the same mood is sought in a larger space. All forms of church can be used to stronger or weaker effect depending on the ethos of the congregation and the qualities of the leaders.

Further models of church design could easily be constructed. A bold architect might devise any number of novel forms for a church, each of which would imply some liturgical use and thus some spiritual process. A design of the 1960s was meant to house five different denominations, each of which would have as its own church one wedge of a circular structure at ground level. A great globe rising up from this base would contain at its center a platform, and ramps spiraling up from the five churches would converge at this center, so that members of the distinct traditions could ascend from their denominational spaces below to a shared one above. This Church of the Encounter was never actually built, but the idea inspiring it, clear from the design, was to promote a process of ecumenical convergence in prayer.[114] A less dramatic but still innovative proposal by another architect called for a church with a communion room built six or eight feet higher than the level for the congregation, but with the communion table placed close enough to the edge that it could be seen by those below. While some in the congregation prepared for communion with hymns and Bible reading, others would rise to the "upper room" in imitation of the disciples at the Last Supper.[115] More extravagantly, one might even imagine a church built as something like a maze; working one's way inward would suggest a process of spiritual exploration and discovery, and somewhat as people make their way through meditation labyrinths, so too they might find their way within complex structures, perhaps questing for the altar.[116]

Captivating as such schemes might be, one crucial point remains: the patterns actually used in church building bear no less of a symbolic charge than these imaginative designs, even if the edge of their symbolism is dulled by familiarity with the forms themselves, and perhaps also by liturgy that makes too little use of their symbolic potential. To ask how a church is used liturgically—how its spatial dynamics reinforce the dynamism of worship—can be a starting point in the recovery of lost meaning. Indeed, it may be the *only* useful starting point in that recovery.

2

The Second Factor:
Centering Focus

Entering a church is a metaphor for centering one's attention and one's life on some particular purpose, usually represented by some object vested with real and symbolic importance in and beyond the act of worship, an object that compels notice and demands response. This object occupies a prominent position in the church, and the action performed at this object gives meaning and purpose to the entire service.

The previous chapter examined the overall configuration of space within a church. The complementary approach is to take a single object within the church, seen as its heart, as the explanation for its existence and its form. Not all sacred buildings hold such objects, and when they do the object may be of various forms: a book or scroll, an image, a relic, even a sacred stone. Secular parallels are rare, and usually they are modeled on sacred precedent. The Lincoln Memorial is centered on the statue of the president within it, an example of civic piety in a structure modeled on a classical temple. For churches, the focal object or heart of the building is often an altar, often a pulpit.

The question to ask is not merely what (if anything) a church takes as its defining center, but how the centering focus functions and how its centrality is signaled. Its position is of obvious importance: traditionally the far end of a longitudinal space, opposite the main entrance, is the most prominent position in the interior, but the literal center of the space can also be defined as the liturgical center. A framing device can accentuate the importance of the focal point: pillars and perhaps a canopy of some kind, something like a classical ciborium, can serve to define the liturgical center—even for a Presbyterian church where pulpit and table are taken jointly as the focus.[1] The overall configuration of interior space can contribute toward this sense of centering: factors such as the slope of the roof can serve to "move" the congregation visually and psychologically toward the liturgical center.[2]

Church designers, like writers, struggle with the conflicting demands of clarity and nuance. They may wish to declare forthrightly that an altar or a pulpit is the heart of a church, but immediately they will qualify that judgment by setting the altar or pulpit in relation to other furnishings, or by using devices that seek to call attention to the focal point but may have the opposite effect. This chapter will examine various ways architects and liturgists deal with this tension.

The Central Paradox: An Unbloodied Altar

Eric Gill puts the point straightforwardly: "The altar is a place of sacrifice, on which something is offered and made holy: this is the Christian idea of a church; where there is an altar there is a church."[3] Gill was no traditionalist in his notions of spatial dynamics. He wanted the altar moved toward the center of the church, and he wanted people literally surrounding the altar as the cross was surrounded by witnesses to the crucifixion. But he was certain it was the altar and nothing else that should give focus to the people's attention, and the altar conceived as sacrificial block. He was voicing a conviction basic to the understanding of a classic sacramental church.

One of the central concerns of liturgical reform in the mid–twentieth century was reviving a clear sense of the centrality of a church's main or high altar: "As Christ is Head of the Church, the altar is the heart of the sacred building."[4] The sacrality and significance of the altar should be marked by its prominent position, its clear presence as the center and heart of the church, isolated from other furnishings, elevated, accessible on all sides, excellent in proportions and material, monumental, and covered by a baldacchino or canopy.[5] At Frederick Gibberd's Metropolitan Cathedral of Christ the King in Liverpool, the high altar was to occupy the literal center of the building, arresting the attention of all, because the building was meant "to enshrine the altar of sacrifice."[6]

At first an altar might seem no more surprising a choice than any other to serve as the core of a sacred structure. Yet the altars found in Christian churches share one feature that should occasion puzzlement and reflection: they are not stained with blood.

It would be instructive to walk into a church as a stranger and inquire with feigned ignorance about that item of furniture on prominent display. "We call that an altar." "But where then are your rams and bullocks?" "Rams? Bullocks?"

"Yes, that is what an altar is meant for, as a block for slaughtering animals and offering them as sacrifice. The Greeks and Romans, the Canaanites and Jews— they all had altars for that purpose. Noah built an altar and made burnt offerings of animals and birds on it. The altar in the Temple was a place of sacrifice. If you are not going to have bloody sacrifice on it, why should you have an altar?" The informant might explain that at this church they think of the altar as a table where a meal is offered, and some people think of it as the tomb where Christ was buried. All well and good, one might say; an altar can indeed have those meanings. But to call it an altar is to identify it as first of all a block for sacrifice. The term for an altar in Biblical Hebrew, *mizbeakh*, means "a place of slaughter." Some might protest, quite rightly, that an altar in antiquity could be used for offering of gifts other than animals, and that the bread and wine offered in Christian worship are analogous to these unbloody sacrifices. But to limit the meaning of Christian offering to this parallel would be to miss levels of meaning that are clearly present in biblical and other early Christian texts.[7]

No doubt most people, faced with this line of inquiry, would remember urgent business elsewhere requiring their attention. Some, with deeper theological insight and keener study in the virtue of patience, might explain that Christ's offering of himself has made all other sacrifice unnecessary, and they might go on to cite the epistle to the Hebrews as their proof text. But the question might still have served the useful purpose of bringing to mind the meaning of the word "altar." The term may now be used in an attenuated sense in some quarters,[8] but Christian traditions that have altars have intended reference to the biblical meaning. If the altar is not in fact used for killing, the paradox is intentional: the altar is meant to sustain a lively sense of what does not occur on it, of what is and what is not present, the bloody sacrifice made present in an unbloody one. The point of calling an altar an altar is to keep alive that sense of absence. An altar is a place where life comes hand to hand with death, but not as a visible act. An altar is traditionally a place of Christ's death: Thomas Aquinas speaks of it as representing the cross.[9] But the paradox on which Christianity feeds is central also to the conception of a church: the place of death is a site of conflict between rival forces of mortality and vitality; the death made present is viewed in sharply paradoxical terms as a source of life; and for those who assemble in a church, this can be the main reason for their gathering. It takes those present out of their immediately present experience and into the presence of an event that is repeatedly fulfilled in liturgy. If a church building has a clear visual focus, it may well be—and for much of Christian tradition has been—a symbol of that conflict, of that presence. And for churches with such a visual focus, this is one of the main sources for depth of symbolic power.

From the sixteenth to the nineteenth century, the high altar in the cathedral at Florence was one carved by Baccio Bandinelli on which an image of the dead Christ lay outstretched as an offering to the Father, who was enthroned above and behind the Son.[10] One might say that Bandinelli and his patrons understood the function of an altar better than most Christians. And yet one might also say the opposite: that an altar with a dead body lying on it is questionable from the perspective of theology as well as that of taste, because it confuses the place of Christ's bloody sacrifice with the place in which worshipers partake of that sacrifice sacramentally.

The theology of sacrifice is a complex matter, but three points are basic. First, in the New Testament narratives of eucharistic institution at the Last Supper, the bread and wine are unmistakably identified as the *sacrificed* body and blood of Christ: the broken body, the blood shed for the remission of sins, a new sacrifice (and a new *kind* of sacrifice) sealing the New Covenant as Moses' sacrifice at the foot of Sinai sealed the Old (Exodus 24:5–8). Second, it is the sacramental partaking in Christ's sacrifice that underlies all other dimensions of the sacrament. Taking Christ's body as food is an act with memorial and social dimensions, but these in themselves do not explain why flesh and blood are consumed. People gathering in remembrance of a loved one do not pretend to eat his body, and the host does not ordinarily become food for the guests. The sacrificial act has also an eschatological dimension, as an anticipation of the messianic banquet with Christ "in the kingdom of God" (Mark 14:25), and as "bread of heaven" it harks back to the manna in the desert, but neither of these themes can explain why flesh and blood are received as food. The element of sacrifice is the only basis for understanding the eating and drinking of Christ's body and blood, and this theme then becomes a foundation on which memorial, social, eschatological, and typological associations are built. Even if the sacrament is symbolic, as some traditions maintain, it is *sacrificial* symbolism that lies at its heart. Third, in ancient Israel sacrifice was sometimes *olah*, a whole offering that ascends in smoke, given entirely to a transcendent deity on high, and sometimes *zébakh*, a joyous communion sacrifice shared by a community and a God thought of as immanent to that gathering.[11] To receive the eucharist as sacrifice is to affirm that the death of Christ was not only olah but also zébakh, not only an offering *for* humankind on the cross but also an offering *to* humankind on the altar, where sacrifice becomes sacrament, an affirmation of and sharing in Christ's life-giving death. In other words, Christ's sacrifice takes place in two acts, the first of which (Christ's olah to the Father) occurred unrepeatably on Calvary, while the second (the zébakh in which the disciples share) takes place at each eucharist.

This cluster of ideas, of the most fundamental importance to the New Testament narrative and to early Christian practice, is not likely to strike modern and postmodern ears as congenial, but then neither was it congenial in first-century Palestine. In the gospel of John it is said that the idea of Christ's flesh and blood as food and drink is a difficult teaching and that after its proclamation "many of his disciples turned back and no longer went about with him" (John 6:60, 66). Why was it so difficult? In large part because human sacrifice was not accepted within the culture. A further stumbling block would have been the insistence on drinking the blood as well as eating the flesh of the sacrificial victim. The Book of Leviticus declares repeatedly that the blood of the sacrificial animal is its life force and cannot be consumed. The eucharist reverses this notion: precisely because Christ's blood is his life force, it must be consumed as part of the second act of sacrifice.[12] The transformations that made it possible to construe Christ's death as a sacrifice would hardly have been acceptable to all. The sheer novelty and complexity of the notion also make it difficult, but no more difficult than the belief—equally novel, equally complex, and equally fundamental to Christianity—in an anointed king who is expected to conquer and reign, instead submits to killing, rises from death but still does not claim an earthly scepter, and is expected to reign in glory on returning at some unpredictable future time.

As early as the second century an alternative emphasis developed: the offering of thanks (*eucharistia*) could be seen as itself the sacrifice at the heart of the eucharistic gathering.[13] Somewhat as Christians by around A.D. 100 had softened and taken the apocalyptic edge off their moral rhetoric, so too they quickly lost the clarity of their early conception of eucharistic sacrifice, substituting for it less difficult and less challenging notions. But the original point, the affirmation of Christ's death as an offering not only for but also to humankind, was never lost, and one of the most powerful reminders is the centering of the eucharist on a sacrificial altar. The presence of an altar, strangely unbloodied, as the focal point in a church is the most potent visible reminder of the sacrificial foundation of eucharist that was of basic importance to the earliest generation of Christians. A further development followed soon after: the offering of bread and wine, if not other tokens of human life and work, became the most clearly visible sacrifice.[14] This was the offering spoken of in the words said to the priest at the offertory: "May the Lord accept this sacrifice at your hands." This development might be taken to imply that God's sacramental offering to humankind was now replaced by a human offering to God. But it was, rather, a joining of human to divine sacrifice: the very bread and wine offered to God were received back as body and blood of Christ. From this perspective, then, a church is in the first instance a place of sacrifice—and more precisely, a place where sacrifice does and does not take place, where there is no bloody offering, no killing, but rather a sharing in what has already been offered.

Reacting against the hazards of superficiality and banality in worship, Kenneth Leech urges a view of liturgy grounded in "the worlds of sacrifice and of myth, of combat, and of death and resurrection"—in what Eugene Masure refers to as the "dark pools where our feet slip in the blood of goats and heifers," the "religious shambles" of ancient rites in which a "Godward movement" can yet be discerned.[15] In roughly the same spirit, C. S. Lewis points to the tragic element in Christian ritual: "Our life as Christians begins by being baptised into a death; our most joyous festivals begin with, and centre upon, the broken body and the shed blood. There is thus a tragic depth in our worship."[16] He would have been among the last to deny that worship has also a celebratory strain, that the death of baptism and of eucharist is also a ritual entry into life. But the tension between the two dimensions is what gives the ritual its force, its mystery, and its depth. Celebration of life by itself, in a spirit of hospitality and fellowship, is a natural human urge. Celebration of life in the face of death is the supreme act of faith in the divine capacity to draw good out of evil.

The eucharistic liturgies of many churches convey in some manner the sacrificial character of the eucharist. The words of institution from the narratives of the Last Supper are included in the Eucharistic Prayers of the various churches, and these already make clear that the bread and wine are taken as the sacrificed body of Christ. But the point becomes more poignantly expressed in certain of the fraction sentences or antiphons said or sung at the fraction or breaking of the eucharistic bread. One fraction sentence proclaims: "We break this bread, Communion in Christ's body once broken."[17] This breaking may seem a simple ritual act, overshadowed by what follows, but it is an act of profound and potentially troubling symbolism, as becomes clear from the fraction anthem (based on John 1:19 and ultimately Isaiah 53:7) known as the Agnus Dei: "Lamb of God, who takest away the sin of the world, have mercy on us." From the fourth century onward, some version of this text was used liturgically in the Eastern Church, and in the late seventh century the Syrian-born Pope Sergius I introduced it to Rome.[18] The lamb in question is dead, or dying—a sacrificial victim. Addressing Christ as the sacrificial lamb and asking for his mercy is to some degree analogous to the Native American ceremonial plea for pardon from a hunted animal. This text, which calls forceful attention to the sacrificial character of the eucharist, has not always been unobjectionable, and indeed was at one point subject matter for a heresy trial,[19] but since the late nineteenth century its use has been widespread in the Anglican as in the Roman communion.[20] If there is any one moment at the eucharistic service in which sacrifice and sacrament, biblical narrative and present ritual come into clear and dramatic focus, it is precisely the fraction, the breaking of the bread. The breaking of the bread symbolizes both the sacrificial breaking of Christ's body on the cross and the unity of those who share sacramentally as beneficiaries of that sacrifice. The fraction is a moment in which the breaking of Christ's body and the sharing of Christ's body come together in one simple act.

This conception of eucharist as sacrifice now often seems problematic. Charles Davis argued already in 1962 against an exaggerated emphasis on the sacrificial notion of the mass: the eucharist re-presents Calvary but also the resurrection and anticipates the heavenly wedding feast.[21] Ten years later the Lutheran Edward Sövik spoke of rescuing the Lord's Supper from "patterns and implications which made it sometimes a kind of exotic ritual in which domestic associations were lost."[22] Sövik also reacted against the sacrificial conception of the altar "because it implies that the essential nature of what happens at the altar is that men offer something to God, and that this is the core of worship"; the eucharist should focus not on offerings brought to God but on "the sacramental gift which God gives His people," not on sacrifice but on sacramental meal.[23] To which the short answer would be, first, that the sacrificial character of the eucharist is fundamental to the New Testament narratives of institution; second, that the central idea of eating Christ's flesh and drinking his blood can only be understood as a transformation of sacrifice, and all the other associations of the eucharist presuppose this foundation; third, that the distinction between sacrifice and meal is false, because the meal itself is clearly a sharing in sacrifice; and fourth, that the basic eucharistic sacrifice is not one offered to God but a sharing in the sacrifice offered by Christ.

But what are the implications of all this for church architecture? Evidently none. An architect might understand what it would mean to design a building meant as a banqueting hall or a theater, and a viewer would probably take the point if told that an interior was meant as a ballroom or a lecture hall; for all these structures there are accepted ways of correlating design with function. But what architect would know what to do if asked to design a building for public assembly that would call to mind an execution chamber? And how would it help the visitor to understand the definition of space if she were told it is meant as a place for the unbloody sequel to bloody sacrifice? A church is a building meant for a purpose served by no building we know. Perhaps in part for that reason, there is often much unclarity about the core on which a church is centered.

Yet the recognition of a church as a place of sacrifice does have implications for the way ecclesiastical space, whatever its precise form, is experienced. In churches where the altar is the focus of attention, the centrality and dignity of the altar may be highlighted by its architectural setting. The gesture of reverencing or bowing toward the altar, even if the sacrament is not reserved there in a tabernacle, bespeaks an attitude toward the church's focal point, an acknowledgment that the sacrifice which took place on the cross here becomes sacramentally efficacious, that the altar is the place where sacrifice becomes sacrament.

The problems of expressing theology in architecture can become clearer when one thinks about alternatives to the familiar arrangements. The architects of the Anglican church of Saint Paul's, Bow Common, in London, were working for a rector who recognized and indeed emphasized the sacrificial character of the eucharist, but even so they attempted to combine two dimensions of eucharist, that of sacrifice and that of mystical banquet, in their design and placement of the altar. The form of the altar combines suggestions of a table's legs with the solidity associated with a sacrificial block. Further, the altar is elevated not on three steps, representing Calvary, but two steps, so that the floor itself becomes the first step, and "priest and people are on the hill together, although still in a hierarchic relationship." If there were no steps at all, the architects reasoned, the altar would signify only a meal; if there were three, it would signify only sacrifice.[24] This may seem a valiant but futile effort to mix metaphors best left apart, but of course the words of the Anglican liturgy combine the theme of sacrifice with that of meal, as do the words of the institution narratives in the New Testament, and the only real question is how the concrete symbols can succeed in conveying the nuances of a complex theology.

Case Study: Dura-Europos and Its Missing Altar

The earliest Christians broke their sacramental bread in the setting of a full meal at a large table. By around the end of the first century they had abandoned this setting and were celebrating their eucharist in a setting that would accommodate larger numbers of people; the ritual remained a symbolic meal, even when it was no longer an actual one. Did those participating still use a table in this ritual? Did they refer to it as a "table" or as an "altar"? The early Christian apologist Minucius Felix is sometimes quoted as having declared: "We have no temples, we have no altars," but what he actually wrote is much less straightforward; whether he was even using the declarative mood is unclear. He probably meant only that Christians did not have temples and altars of the sort pagans used.[25] Christianity had abandoned bloody sacrifice, which may to many have seemed a radical renunciation. And what Minucius was presumably willing to grant his imagined questioner was that he and his coreligionists did not have the temples and altars required for bloody sacrifice. To be sure, early Christians did have a ritual by which they became beneficiaries of a sacrifice, and the table at which they partook of that meal was not surprisingly and not inappropriately likened to an altar, being the vicarious altar for a vicarious offering. And thus, while Minucius Felix may have claimed Christians had no altars, other Christians before and after him did speak of the altar as a feature of Christian worship.[26] Still, to a pagan observer it surely would have seemed obvious that Christians were strange in *not* having temples, altars, and sacrifices.

A recent study by Michael White identifies a series of stages discernible in the early evolution of church architecture. First is the house church, that is to say a building used for Christian assembly while remaining in use primarily as a private residence, and thus indistinguishable in the archeological evidence from other houses. Second is the type now called the *domus ecclesiae* ("house of the assembly"), the private residence remodeled for use specifically as a place of worship. When a local Christian community outgrew such inevitably small accommodations, in some places by the later third century, it might build a new and larger structure specifically as a church, which White refers to as an *aula ecclesiae* ("hall of the assembly"). And finally, with the conversion of Constantine to Christianity in the early fourth century, the public and often monumental basilica was possible. Many such basilicas were patronized by the emperor himself, which represents a novelty of the Constantinian era, but earlier places of worship had also benefited from private patronage, and this seems to be true even for the very earliest place of Christian worship for which we have archeological remains, the domus ecclesiae at Dura-Europos, a town on the Euphrates River in far eastern Syria, destroyed in 257 by the Sassanian Persians.[27]

We know from excavation of the ruins that religious life at Dura was both diverse and syncretic. The oldest and largest temple in town was dedicated to the Greek goddess Artemis but later served also for worship of her Mesopotamian equivalent Nanaia. Other temples showed a jumble of dedications, to Greek or to Semitic deities, or to deities under both Greek and Semitic names, mingled together in this spiritual bazaar of late antiquity. The presence of Roman soldiers in the town would have added to the mix; soldiers were often devotees of the god Mithras, to whom there was a temple at Dura. The Jewish presence in town was marked by a synagogue with extensive wall paintings.[28]

The earliest temple at Dura for which we have evidence, the one dedicated to Artemis, appears to have been founded early in the town's history by its Hellenistic colonists, and it seems to have been laid out in a typical Greek temple plan, with an eastern entrance leading directly to the cult statue of the deity, so that the morning sun would shine upon that sacred image.[29] But in later construction the same temple broke away from these Greek forms. In its later phases, like most temples in Dura, it had affinities not with Greek but rather with Babylonian temple design. Entering through a great gateway at the east, the worshiper would come into an open courtyard containing a large altar; in some of the temples this altar was massive, with steps leading up to it. At the west end of the courtyard lay a shrine complex consisting of the progressively sacred vestibule and inner sanctum with a sacred image of the deity. The inner sanctum would often, perhaps always, be closed to the laity; evidence of barriers has been found in some of the temples.

Certain temples at Dura may have been sites of the frenzied Syrian rituals described by Lucian and Apuleius, in which the priests took knives and lacerated their arms, or scourged each other, to the wild accompaniment of flute and drums. Probably most or all of them were places of procession, in which the cult image was brought out from the inner sanctum into the courtyard and perhaps even out past the gateway. Some may have featured sacred dance and pantomime. But the chief purpose of a temple would be offerings to the deities. A temple was a place of sacrifice. Embedded in the floor of the Mithraic temple were large numbers of bird, sheep, and fish bones, at least partly from sacrifices. The court might contain not only the great altar but multiple further altars erected in it by various devotees, on which they might offer incense or libations, grain or cakes, smaller or larger animals. Generally an altar would be seen in relationship to a cult image, although it was not necessarily placed immediately before the image. While the deity would typically be conceived as present in the image, there could also be vestiges of an archaic notion that the same stone served as both altar and dwelling place for the god.[30]

Many of the temples in Dura were used also for sacred meals. Apart from repasts in which all the temple's devotees might participate, there were further meals within the temple precincts intended for smaller groups. The temples often have small rooms off their courtyards that were surely meant as places for the sacred meals of individuals or groups who established them. They typically had low benches along two or three sides. The men who gathered for sacred feasts would lounge on cushioned benches and eat the sacred food brought to them on platters or in baskets, which would probably be laid on the floor. The Temple of Adonis has nine of these rooms along the east side of its courtyard; one of these was founded and dedicated by a group of eight men, representing seven families, while another was dedicated by a priest. The Temple of Zeus Theos has seven or eight of them.[31]

The building at Dura that concerns us most directly is the house built in 232 and later used for Christian worship.[32] Like other houses, this one was built around a courtyard. A room in the northwest corner, about twenty-one by nine feet, was probably used as a baptistery, with a large niche on one side to house a baptismal font. Paintings on the walls included some of the earliest representations anywhere of Christ: as the Good Shepherd, healing the paralytic, and walking on water. Across the courtyard was a room probably meant for liturgical assemblies. This space was formed by demolition of an interior wall, creating a space about forty-one feet long, with a platform at the eastern end.

An outside observer who knew about the Christian house of worship might have compared it to the synagogue—or else to the Mithraic temple. Like the mystery religions generally, Christianity and Mithraism offered the prospect of salvation, which they represented as an escape from death and the attainment of a blessed immortality. Both religions had spread widely through the Roman Empire in the first two and a half centuries of the Common Era. Perhaps the closest point of similarity between Mithraism and Christianity—indeed, one noted in the second century by Christians—was their ritual practice. Mithraism had emerged from Persian religion, in which one of the central rites was the Yasna ceremony. This was a meal in which the divine Haoma, priest and victim, offered himself in the form of a plant that was crushed to death and released a juice that was the source of immortality. Mithraism adapted this ceremony, substituting wine for the juice of Haoma, along with offerings of bread and water, and it viewed the meal on earth as corresponding to a banquet in heaven. Despite the close correspondence with the eucharist, we cannot say that Christianity borrowed its rituals from Mithraism; the form of Mithraic cult that spread in the Roman world may in fact have arisen after Christianity. But these religions had similar goals and similar ritual vocabulary, and anyone closely familiar with them might naturally have seen them as two examples of the same form of religion: cults intended to bestow salvation through the sacrificial self-offering of a deity, consumed in a sacred meal. The connection would have appeared all the more obvious precisely because at Dura, as at Rome and probably in many other places, Christian and Mithraic buildings were in close physical proximity. Mithraism and Christianity, both providing rituals in which a deity offers himself as sacrifice for human immortality, shared a thirst for the immortality proper to divinity and extended as gift to humans.

In other ways it was the Jews who most resembled Christians. Mithras-worshipers had their communion service, but they also had a bull-sacrifice mimicking their god's own slaying of the cosmic bull, and neither Jews nor Christians had any such ritual. Animals would *not* have been brought in for sacrifice at their rituals, and an observer who watched carefully enough to notice this departure from expected ritual forms might well have been puzzled by this absence. How could you worship a deity properly without offering sacrifice? Jews and Christians both might have answered that their worship did involve a kind of extended or vicarious sacrifice: a sacrifice of prayer, a sacrifice of praise, or an unbloody ritual grounded in Christ's bloody sacrifice on the cross. Michael Swartz observes that Jews and Christians were the only substantial groups in the Mediterranean world who by the second century did not offer sacrifice—yet then he proceeds to ask the key question: "But what is sacrifice?"[33] Synagogue services and eucharists were, in their ways, transposed sacrifices.

Further, among the religious buildings of Dura the Christian house of worship would have been among the exceptional ones that did *not* have the dining facilities familiar to that culture, having deliberately done away with them in the process of conversion to a church. This is, indeed, the feature of the Christian building at Dura most important for the history of liturgical space. The larger part of the room used for Christian assembly had previously been a dining room with a low bench around the periphery, like those found in the chapels of many temples, but at the time it was adapted for worship the floor of that room was filled in to the height of the benches. The Christian community would not have needed to create a dining space, if it had wanted it; that is what it already had but no longer desired. Nor should this transformation seem puzzling, for the religious buildings that did have such dining facilities used them for small and often evidently private clubs, often and perhaps routinely groups of males alone, who would meet regularly for what Jews

called a *chavurah*, a fellowship of men gathering for sacred dinners.[34] The
Christian community at Dura, along with Christians elsewhere, turned *away*
from this model of the sacred private dinner club for men and toward a mixed
assembly in a space that allowed fusion of a highly stylized sacrificial meal
with other forms of ritual.

While in many ways the Christian house of worship might have seemed
similar to the various temples of Dura, it was more specifically designed for
use of the gathered assembly. The temples might contain both altars for individual devotees' sacrifices and also side chambers for the sacred meals of small
groups, but the Christian building was designed precisely for the sacred meal
of the entire Christian community, and that meal itself had a sacrificial dimension to it, there being no offering of sacrifices distinct from the eucharistic
offering. But the meal and the sacrifice were both formalized. No ordinary
feast was eaten, and no blood was shed. Furthermore, while the pagan temples
had multiple altars, large and small, for the offering of everything from animals
to incense, no altar was found in the Christian building; presumably a movable
table was placed on the platform and served as what we would call an altar.[35]
In every key respect the setting for worship at Dura shows a community and
a tradition capable of imaginative transposition: a table could be an altar, a
morsel could be a banquet, and a bloodless offering could be a sacrificial victim.
Early Christians clearly sensed that the most basic purpose of liturgy is to train
the imagination, strengthening and sensitizing it for the perception of reality.

The Christian house at Dura seems extraordinary now because only here
was so much of so early a site preserved amid the ruins, but it is worth reflecting how absolutely ordinary it would have been in its own day. Similar houses
of worship existed all over Rome's far-flung dominion. To find a place where
an early Christian house of worship was nestled amid ordinary houses, just
inside the walls of a remote fortified outpost on the distant borders of the
Roman Empire, perched above the waters of a major river, one might travel to
the deserts of far eastern Syria, to Dura. Or one might go instead to Cologne.
The Christians of that Rhenish outpost had a center for worship at least from
the early fourth century, in a house that was reconstructed more than once and
was presumably given over for liturgical use by a private family, very much as
at Dura. In the early years of the fourth century the complex included a heatable
assembly room fifty by fifty-five feet in size, not a great deal larger than the
assembly hall at Dura. The main difference is that Dura was destroyed in the
third century, leaving the house of worship and everything else buried and
preserved in rubble, and enabling us to see how the complex grew out of an
ordinary residence, while Cologne remained one of the most important places
of northern Europe, and the modest house of worship grew through perceptible
stages of transformation and displacement into the building we now know as
Cologne Cathedral.[36]

Transformations of the Altar

A Christian altar, then, is the place where sacrifice becomes sacrament in the sharing of a meal. But what should an altar look like? While the term "altar" refers to a place of sacrifice, there is no single form easily recognizable as appropriate for that purpose, whether in the temples in ancient Israel, at Rome or Dura-Europos, or in Christianity generally. An altar may be a stone, or a pile of stones, or a kind of pedestal. It may be a table. It may approximate the shape of a sarcophagus. It may or may not have upturned "horns" protruding at its four corners. It may or may not be ornamented. In one Latin American church a modern altar has had the revolutionary form of a barricade with sandbags.[37]

The earliest Christian altars were fairly simple wooden tables. Representations on the walls of the catacombs, like sixth-century mosaics at Ravenna, show them as tables. Even when the association of the ritual of bread and wine had become dissociated from the literal supper, and ordinary tables were displaced by a free-standing and movable table at which the bishop presided, the altar still resembled an ordinary table. A fifth-century stone altar found at Auriol in Southern France is designed as a table supported by a single leg. The altars in the early Byzantine churches of Palestine seem to have been four-legged tables with reliquaries, sometimes in the form of basins, below them. To use a table for an altar is to make clear that it is through a ritual meal that the sacrifice is completed; the table is not an alternative to a place of sacrifice, but is one of the forms that place can assume. The notion that a sacrificial altar could have the form of a table or be spoken of as a kind of table was not an innovation of Christian usage: Malachi 1:7 speaks of the altar in the Temple as "the table of the Lord."

Yet in one respect an altar makes an unexpected choice as visual focus for a church: in itself it is not particularly imposing, and a viewer accustomed to seeing the monumental statuary of an Indian, Egyptian, Greek, or Roman temple might understandably find the flat surface of an unadorned altar disappointing. And so efforts have been made, from as early as the fourth century, to make the altar into a more impressive structure by building one or another superstructure over or around it. Three broad phases in this evolution can be distinguished: from the fourth century to the mid-ninth (roughly from the age of Constantine to that of Charlemagne); from the ninth through the fourteenth century; and from the late fourteenth century into the nineteenth.[38]

1. *Free-standing altar with ciborium and screen (fourth to mid–ninth centuries)*. The first period was a time when the officiating clergy increasingly assumed a position of prominence in the liturgy, increasingly set apart from the lay congregation, while the liturgy itself was to a greater degree seen as action done by the clergy in the presence of the laity, and the altar itself was designed to reflect this distinction. During this time the altar was usually a cubic (some-

times circular and semicircular) structure of wood or stone, and it was left essentially bare. The altar was considered too sacred to bear anything other than the liturgical offerings and vessels, or the gospel book, which was taken as a symbol for Christ himself, enthroned on the altar, and even these objects were placed on the altar only during liturgy.

The dignity of the altar was marked by a "ciborium" above it (a canopy erected on four columns) and a screen in front of it. To the ciborium a cross, lights, flowers, crowns, and other decorations might be attached. Constantine's churches of the early fourth century provide examples of the ciborium, in particular a famously ornate one with a massive silver roof in the Lateran basilica at Rome.[39] For Santa Maria Maggiore, Pope Sixtus III provided a monumental silver altar and a combination of lamps, candles to light both it and the nave, and a wealth of silver and gold liturgical vessels; later there was a low screen and an icon beam in front of the high altar, and later still a ciborium. A ciborium might be supplemented with veils that could be drawn over the altar in the course of the liturgy, although it is difficult to say exactly how or when these veils were drawn, and doubtless there was much local variation on this point. During the era of Constantine a kind of screen developed that had marble wainscoting up to five or so feet in height, porphyry columns above the wainscoting, and a marble beam across the top.

A further innovation of this period is the substitution of stone for wood as the material for an altar. For centuries the standard material for making an altar was wood, sometimes known as "God's board" or "Christ's board." That at least the top of an altar must be of stone is a requirement found only in Western Christianity. The first legislation requiring a stone altar probably came in a Gallican synod of 517,[40] but in some churches wooden altars were known as late as the fifteenth century. Even when the altar was of stone, and looked nothing like an ordinary table, the horizontal slab on top was still known as the *mensa* or table.

It was also during this period that the conception of the altar as a chest or box resembling a sepulcher became firmly established in the West. The notion took its origin from the practice of celebrating mass on the tombs of martyrs; in the fourth century churches were built at Rome and elsewhere with their altars placed over the tombs of Peter, Paul, and other martyrs. The early preference was for placement of a church over the martyr's original burial place— as one historian puts it, "the church was brought to the martyr, not the martyr to the church"[41]—but already in the fourth century, at Milan, Ambrose moved the relics of Saints Gervasius and Protavius to a new resting place in a basilica.[42] Elsewhere cloths or other objects that had touched a martyr's tomb might be placed in an altar, making it a sort of fictive place of burial. By the seventh and eighth century bodies of saints were more often dismembered, so that fragments could be encased in altars when the altars were consecrated.[43] This does not mean that all altars had the relics of saints in them; even in the early sixteenth century many did not. But increasingly the enclosure of relics within an altar was the norm.

2. *Elongated altar for the eucharistic miracle (mid–ninth to fourteenth centuries)*. The second phase was a period when the theology of the real presence of Christ in the consecrated bread and wine (long taken for granted) was being debated and defined,[44] the doctrine of transubstantiation (a specific way of conceiving the real presence) was becoming formulated, the elevation of the consecrated host and of the chalice became established in the Western liturgy, and the altar was mainly the place for the miracle of transubstantiation. The altar came to be a long rectangular structure, pushed up against or very near the east wall of the church, and serving as a permanent and temporary platform for many sorts of objects. Already by the late eighth century there was evidence for the placement of relics not below but on the altar, or in shrines positioned with one end resting on the altar and the other supported behind it. In time the ciborium fell into disuse, and all the decorations previously attached to it came to be placed directly on the altar. Beginning in the twelfth century, a cross and candlesticks were set on the altar during liturgy, but not outside of liturgy. (An *ordo* of 1502 instructed the server that two candles should be lighted on the altar for low mass but returned to the sacristy afterward.) In some countries, particularly England and France, the ciborium was replaced by a wooden tester or decorated ceiling over the altar, and a set of four riddel-posts with rods between them for curtains.

The lengthening of altars to twelve or more feet came around the fourteenth century; one from this period in the Lady Chapel at Ely Cathedral was over sixteen feet long. This lengthening made all the more sense when the altar was placed directly against a screen or in close proximity to a wall. And the longer altar allowed all the more space for ornaments. That the cloth on the altar came to be not simply a covering but an item for display, a silk frontal or antependium with colors coordinated with the liturgical seasons.[45] Alternatively, the front of the altar could be adorned with metalwork, as at Sant'Ambrogio in Milan with its plates of embossed gold.

3. *Altar as platform for retable and tabernacle (late fourteenth to nineteenth centuries)*. In the third phase, the altar became largely a platform for display, both during and outside of the liturgy: the retable or altarpiece behind the altar came to be a major artistic diplay, the consecrated host could be displayed in a monstrance placed on the altar apart from mass, relics and liturgical vessels of various kinds could be exhibited there as well, and routinely the tabernacle for reservation of the consecrated host was on display as the most precious and sacred site in the church.

The feature that now dominated the altar was the great altarpiece, the "retable" or "reredos," an increasingly large backdrop—painted, sculpted, or both—placed on or behind the altar and visually dominating the altar itself. Before the development of the retable it had been possible to see beyond the altar to the relics sometimes placed on platforms behind the altar. But all view of what lay beyond was now obstructed—or, when an altar with its retable was placed all the way against the east wall of the chancel, the presence of the retable compensated for the fact that nothing at all lay beyond. The earliest examples of such a retable or reredos come from the twelfth century,[46] but it was from the later fourteenth century onward that the retable came into its own. English retables for high altars in parish churches tended on the whole to be modest in size, because the altars were placed at or near large east windows and there was little desire to block that source of illumination. But in greater churches, where the high altar might be further west in any event, massive screens came to be placed behind the altar, as at Saint Albans. In the fifteenth and following centuries the superstructure sometimes overwhelmed the altar it was meant to dignify. The elaborate retables of the late Gothic, Renaissance, and Baroque Italy and Spain became dominating displays of art.

The function of the altar was significantly shifted when a tabernacle was introduced onto it for reservation of the consecrated hosts. In popular piety the presence of a tabernacle changed the altar from the site of a sacrifice to a platform for the container of a sacred object. The altar was now hallowed not so much by an event as by an object. The tabernacle came into common use only in the late sixteenth century. Early Christians had reserved the consecrated bread for the benefit of sick and dying members who could not come to church to receive the eucharist, but they had not kept it on the altar. In the high and late Middle Ages it had been common to reserve the consecrated hosts in a cabinet, in a pyx (sometimes but by no means always in the shape of a dove) suspended over the altar, or (in northern Europe) in a "sacrament house" on the north side of the sanctuary.

In most Protestant traditions the altar was reconceived as a table for the Lord's Supper. It might be placed (as at the Walpole Congregational chapel) below the pulpit, or it might be set up temporarily when the sacrament was administered. In either case it was no longer the centering focus of the church. In the Reformed churches of the Netherlands the table was traditionally used precisely as a table, with people seated around it for the Lord's Supper. A long table was sometimes set up lengthwise in the old chancel for communion, but eventually the preference in most places was to integrate communion into the cluster of activities occurring within the orbit of the pulpit, so a long table would be placed in the nave. Wherever it was put, the table would have benches on either side so that groups of communicants could take turns sitting at it; the sacrament was decidedly not a sacrifice but a commemorative meal, and the furniture was designed to make this point. The Immanuëlkerk, a modern Reformed church in Delft, has a forty-five-foot-long table that seats seventy, placed in a recessed space all along one side of the interior, under a lower roof than the main space.[47] The practice is found also in Dissenters' churches in England: one communion table, in a nonconformist chapel at Bunyan in Bedfordshire, was twelve feet long.[48] Scottish Presbyterians also followed this model, but in the early nineteenth century they began administering communion in the pews, evidently because the traditional table could not easily accommodate the large congregations flocking to hear popular preachers.[49]

Anglican usage in this respect, as in others, represented a compromise. In general, the Anglican reformers expected communicants to move from the nave into the chancel and remain there to the end of the service, gathered about the wooden table (the Prayer Book of 1552 called it that, not an altar), which was placed in the middle of the chancel. Similar arrangements prevailed later in the century under Elizabeth, although the table was moveable enough that it could be moved around as required, in a manner sometimes similar to the use of the tables in Reformed churches. Horton Davies has suggested that this arrangement carried two main advantages: "moving to the chancel for the Communion service seemed to give the Sacrament a special sacredness," and the chancel screen (often preserved even when deprived of its rood) "helped to separate the liturgy of the catechumens from the liturgy of the faithful, thus imparting to the climax of worship a sense of deep mystery." But the return to tradition associated with Archbishop William Laud in the seventeenth century, and the Anglo-Catholic movement begun in the nineteenth, restored a more traditional altar to Anglican churches.[50]

Case Study: Saint-Jacques at Perpignan and the Multiplication of Altars

As early as the sixth century some churches had more than one altar. The Lateran basilica at Rome even in antiquity had seven subsidiary altars in addition to the high altar, evidently as places for offerings to be deposited. By the eighth or ninth century, devotion to saints and distribution of their fragmented relics made multiple altars desirable and possible in larger churches.[51] A church dedicated to one saint could have subsidiary altars in chapels honoring the relics of other saints. Sixth-century Roman churches incorporated within their walls oratories dedicated to the martyrs that had previously been dispersed outside of churches. Toward the end of that century the bishop of Saintes built a church with thirteen altars. The early ninth-century design for a new church at the monastery of Saint Gall includes a high altar, an altar in the apse at each end, an altar for laity in the nave, eight in the side aisles, two in the transepts, two at the crossing steps, two in the towers, and one in the baptistery.[52] In France the eastern end of a larger church eventually became a segmented *chevet* with chapels radiating off an ambulatory; at Tours this development came already in the early tenth century.

The link between multiplication of relics and multiplication of altars can be seen at Santa Maria Maggiore in Rome. This basilica may have had a "confessio" for veneration of relics beneath its high altar as early as around 700, although relics are not specifically mentioned as present there until the late eleventh century, at which point the bones of the apostle Matthias may have been placed either in the confessio or nearby. The basilica also claimed hairs, milk, and fragments of clothing from the Virgin among the relics placed in a side altar as early as the eleventh century. Relics of the crib and grotto from the nativity of Christ were brought to Santa Maria Maggiore perhaps in the seventh century, after the Arab conquest of Palestine; the fragments of the crib were housed in one of the side altars, while those of the grotto were enshrined in a tiny chapel that was built around the early eighth century and was probably meant to recall the grotto of the Nativity at Bethlehem.[53]

Multiplication of altars has further been seen as an attempt to built an allegory of the heavenly church, with relics of the saints sharing in the power and the glory of the saints' souls in heaven. It has also been viewed as an imitation of the spiritual landscape of Rome, with multiple altars inside a single church corresponding to the many churches of Rome, and like those churches serving as stations for processions.[54] But by the thirteenth century another factor became more important: each priest was now expected to say mass daily, so in churches with multiple priests altars were added in transepts or aisles to provide places for these masses. It became more common in the West around the twelfth century for monks to be ordained as priests, so that numerous altars were needed in monastic churches. The same circumstances could obtain in a cathedral, with its canons and vicars, or even a larger parish church, which might have not only the rector or vicar but one or more chaplains.

In the late Middle Ages increasing endowment of chantry chapels further motivated multiplication of altars, as did the establishment of separate chapels for trade guilds and devotional confraternities. A wealthy cleric or layperson would endow a chantry to provide masses after death, as a way of shortening time in Purgatory and speeding the soul on its way toward Heaven.[55] For those who could not afford their own chantries, a confraternity or guild served much the same function, among others; apart from its services to the living, a confraternity was often a kind of collective chantry that guaranteed masses for the souls of its deceased members. Neither a chantry nor a confraternity strictly required its own altar or chapel, but if funding was sufficient these were provided. This development coincided with and reinforced a burgeoning of devotionalism, with its trend toward the particularizing of religious practice: toward the establishment of particular altars and chapels to individual saints and to the Virgin.[56] Along with all the earlier factors leading to multiplication of altars, this one brought the development to its climax. During this period a church with thirty altars was not unthinkable, and one with as many as forty-five altars was not unknown.[57]

The effects of this multiplication of altars could vary, depending largely on how visible and how accessible the various altars are. The Mexican cathedrals built in the late sixteenth and seventeenth centuries followed the Spanish plan: the choir was a large box-like structure placed within the nave, open toward the sanctuary, and occupying much of what would otherwise be the laity's space in the nave. This arrangement thrust the side chapels into far greater prominence than they would otherwise have had. Those laypeople who attended the cathedrals were forced out not only from the east end of the church but also from the center of the nave, which was claimed for the clerical establishment. The effect was to highlight "the visual ambivalence between side and center, between subordinate but accessible altars and major but inaccessible high altar."[58]

In principle, every altar in a church is dedicated to Christ, or to the sacramental fulfillment of Christ's sacrifice, but some altars may in fact be used less often for liturgical than for devotional purposes, and for those the secondary character of an altar becomes paramount. The dedications of the altars can at times be complex and confusing. When the Portuguese arrived in the Congo, the first church they built had three altars said to be in honor of the Trinity. One of the three was also spoken of as the high altar, so if they were assigned to the persons of the Trinity the implications would be not only tritheist but subordinationist.[59] But the builders presumably did not intend each altar for a particular person of the Trinity.

The church of Saint-Jacques at Perpignan in far southern France affords a classic study in the multiplication and ornamentation of altars, particularly in the fourteenth through nineteenth centuries (the third phase in evolution of the altar).[60] We can see clearly here the link between this multiplication of altars and the diversification of devotions and of devout societies. Saint-Jacques was the second parish church in Perpignan, founded in the thirteenth century. One of the high points in the furnishing of the church was the construction of an elaborate carved wooden retable for the high altar in 1450, when a coalition of parish members commissioned this work from a local sculptor. The commission specified how the patron saint and various prophets and angels were to be represented—but all that survives of the elaborate monument is the central statue of Saint James. A new retable was made for the high altar in 1769, again placing the patronal saint in a central position, in a niche between Saint Peter and Saint John the Evangelist.

Like many churches of Spain and southern France, Saint-Jacques has chapels built along the north and south sides of its nave between its internal buttresses. These spaces were outfitted in the course of the fourteenth century, sometimes as funereal chapels for prominent parishioners or families, at other times as devotional centers for confraternities, or simply as loci of devotion. One of the chapels on the north side, for example, has a small retable of Saint Liborius, who was invoked by those suffering afflictions of the liver and the bladder; his statue shows him holding a book, on which three stones were often placed as signs of his specialty in healing.

The history of Saint-Jacques is inseparable from that of its confraternities. In the early fifteenth century two new confraternities arose, one of which, dedicated to Nostra Senyora dels Desemparats, provided aid for travelers and had its own chapel in the church. More prestigious was the confraternity devoted to the blood of Christ, whose members held evocative nocturnal procession on Maundy Thursday; and when a criminal was being executed they ministered to him before his death, then buried his remains. Early in its history this confraternity had its own chapel; in the eighteenth century it built a new one, attached to the west end of the church, and after the French Revolution the wall between the chapel and the nave was removed, uniting the worship space for this confraternity with the general liturgical space of the parish and giving the confraternity even greater prominence. On the retable for this confraternity's chapel, cherubs emerge from puffs of clouds, surrounded by rays of sunlight, while dramatically poised angels display the Crown of Thorns and the veil of Veronica.

The weavers of Perpignan had a chapel at Saint-Jacques dedicated to Saint Barthélémy but also to "Our Lady of Expectation," honoring the Virgin not in her usual mode as the mother of the newly born Christ or as the sorrowing mother in the pietà but rather as a pregnant queen. Originally under construction in 1396, this chapel was remodeled toward the end of the fifteenth century, probably in part with funding from a wealthy merchant of the town. The main acquisition in this remodeling was a sort of retable popular especially in Germany, the Low Countries, and the Iberian Peninsula in the late fifteenth century: a sculpted wooden one large enough to fill the east wall of the chapel. Apart from the central figure of the pregnant Virgin, crowned and enthroned under a Gothic canopy, the retable featured her coronation, scenes from her life on the sides, a pietà, Moses, prophets, and apostles (fig. 8).

The devotional complexion of the parish was much enriched during the Revolution, when religious houses were secularized and their furnishings made available to parishes; Saint-Jacques obtained much of this booty. The Dominican friary, dissolved in 1791, yielded a grand Baroque retable commissioned in 1643 by the Confraternity of the Rosary, which had been centered in the friary church. Along with a central figure of the Madonna, this altarpiece had panels depicting each of the fifteen mysteries of the rosary. And Saint-Jacques provided a new home for other altars from other dissolved institutions.

In more recent times this phenomenon has seemed deeply problematic to reformers. Seeking to focus attention more clearly on the high altar, the German bishops already in the 1940s urged that side altars, Stations of the Cross, and other distractions be removed: "Everything really superfluous should be eliminated, and such details as are indispensable should be placed as inconspicuously as possible, perhaps in a lower chapel";[61] the point was ratified in instructions that came out of the Second Vatican Council.[62]

The proliferation of altars might seem to turn the church into something

FIGURE 8. Saint-Jacques, Perpignan, France, chapel of Our Lady of Expectation. Photograph by Richard Kieckhefer.

like a Hindu temple, with diffusion of focus away from any central point and tension among multiple shrines. The analogy of the Hindu temple seems particularly apt because the subsidiary altars would have been used for special devotion to a favorite saint, as a shrine in a temple would be used for devotional offerings and prayers to a particular Hindu deity. In each case the force of devotion is centrifugal, focusing on the mediators of spiritual power rather than on its source: on saints rather than on God, on particular deities rather than the *brahman* that underlies all reality. And in the case of a church such as Saint-Jacques, the centrifugal pull is social as well as theological: the subsidiary altars are foci for confraternities or other subgroups within the parish. The argument in defense of this piety is that on both levels, theological and social, a dialectic between centripetal and centrifugal poles can strengthen both: devotion to the saints need not distract or detract from devotion to Christ, and may serve as one mode of bonding to a life and a culture in which Christ's centrality is taken for granted; attachment to a confraternity need not compete with commitment to the broader parish community but may become one mode of entry into and affiliation with that community.[63]

Traditions such as Hinduism and traditional Roman Catholicism operate as spiritual prisms, refracting the light of divinity to make it manifest in the spectrum of sacred forms; traditions such as Islam and strict Protestantism work more like magnifying glasses, focusing the light of divinity to a single intense point. Neither denies the ultimate unity of God, but they differ in the emphasis they place on God's multiple manifestations and effects.

The Pulpit as Focus

In a classic sacramental church one expects the centrally placed altar to remind people that the eucharistic sacrifice is the core of worship; on any particular occasion there may or may not be a sermon. In a classic evangelical church one expects the centrally positioned pulpit to signal that preaching of the gospel lies at the heart of worship; on a specific day there may or may not be a communion service. But of course there are always complicating factors: most churches have both altars and pulpits, sometimes they are complementary rather than hierarchical in their ordering, and sometimes the furnishings alone may belie the community's conception of worship.

The history of the pulpit is linked with that of the ambo or lectern.[64] An elevated platform, used in early churches primarily for reading the scriptures, the ambo probably grew out of the raised bema used for scriptural readings in synagogues. Usually they were placed in close proximity to the congregation. In the early custom of some Eastern churches the ambo was placed at the center point of the nave and linked to the sanctuary by a kind of walkway.[65]

The churches of Ravenna contain sixth-century ambos, and several Roman churches have later ones. When two ambos stood on either side of the choir, as at San Clemente in Rome, the subdeacon would read the epistle from one and the deacon would read the gospel from the other. But the ambo could also be used for sermons. John Chrysostom preached from an ambo because he could be understood better than if he spoke from the cathedra or throne at the far end of the church; Ambrose of Milan and others also adopted this practice, and in the eighth century the pope was preaching from an ambo at Santa Maria Maggiore. There was thus no clear distinction in early years between the ambo and the pulpit, and even in the high Middle Ages they could be the same. Major churches might also have a *pulpitum* or raised platform separating the choir from the nave, and it could serve for preaching as for other purposes. But a pulpit in the more familiar sense—an furnishing of stone or wood, distinct from the ambo, meant specifically for preaching, placed in the nave, and consisting of a platform with a railing and a desk on which a prepared text can be placed—was a relatively late development. Around the twelfth century, the relatively small ambo can sometimes be distinguished from the more massive and often elaborately carved pulpit. The Abruzzi has an exceptional wealth of richly carved pulpits dating from as early as the mid–twelfth century, with ornamental zones, symbols of the evangelists, scenes from the lives of Saint George or Saint Onuphrius, and narrative scenes from the Old Testament.[66]

Pulpits became more common in the thirteenth and following centuries, when preaching was increasingly important and laypeople grew intent on having regular sermons by effective preachers. A pulpit of the early thirteenth century at Wechselburg in Saxony, probably connected originally with the rood loft of that church, is decorated with relief carvings of Christ as teacher, of allegorical symbols for error, of the sacrifices of Abel and Abraham, and other themes. Giovanni Pisano's marble pulpit at Pisa, commissioned in 1302 and completed after nine years of work, displays scenes from the lives of Christ and John the Baptist, Isaiah and other prophets, lions and other beasts, and personifications of virtues.[67] In Florence, early pulpits often took the form of balconies projecting from walls, again elaborately carved.

We know from documentary evidence that some English churches had pulpits as early as the twelfth century, but examples survive only from around 1340, and far more come from the fifteenth century. About a hundred medieval pulpits made of wood are known, and about sixty of stone. Typical of the fifteenth century are "wineglass" pulpits with splayed stems and polygonal drums on which the four evangelists or the Latin doctors of the church may be carved. The pulpit might be placed near the southeast corner of the nave, where there would be greater sunlight, or near the northeast corner in front of the gospel side of the altar. When a church had a pulpit, it served not only for preaching but also for reading of intercessions, for marriage banns, and for announcements of all sorts, religious and secular.[68] But by no means all parish churches had pulpits; perhaps as few as a quarter of the parishes had them in pre-Reformation England.[69]

In countries affected by the Reformation, where the sermon became the heart of worship, pulpits were correspondingly important and grand. In the later sixteenth century, earlier pulpits in North German churches were often replaced by significantly larger ones, carved with themes such as the Law and the Gospel, or the evangelists and prophets, or scenes from the life of Christ.[70] Scriptural verses were often carved on early Lutheran pulpits; one of the most famous was 1 Peter 1:25 (based on Isaiah 40:8), "The word of the Lord abides forever," which could be given in German ("Gottes Word bleibt in Ewigkeit") or Latin ("Verbum Domini manet in aeternum," sometimes reduced to "VDMA")—a verse sometimes found even on secular objects in Lutheran lands after the first edition of Luther's Bible in 1534.[71]

In 1547 and 1559, royal injunctions in England specified that each parish should obtain a pulpit, and over the ensuing generations English parishes were important in the evolution of what we might call pulpit technology. In the seventeenth and eighteenth centuries pulpits were combined with reading desks for leading much of the service, resulting in the double-decker pulpit. The parish clerk's desk, which the clerk used in leading hymns (or for conducting the service in the absence of clergy), might be added to form the triple-decker pulpit. Polygonal sounding boards were often added over pulpits to direct the sound of the preacher's voice. Pulpits were also commonly equipped with hourglasses; one church in Suffolk preserves four of these, each measuring a different duration. In the eighteenth century the pulpit was often placed not at the east end of the nave but halfway along one side, with seats arranged to face it, as in a Reformed church.[72]

In Reformed or Calvinist churches the pulpit was even more clearly the central feature: the Lord's Supper was relatively infrequent, and so the pulpit tended to become the sole permanent focus. Instead of a fixed altar, the Reformed church could be content with a table set up on those occasions when the Lord's Supper was to be administered.[73] Often placed along the long north or south wall, the pulpit might have a reader's desk in front of it, an iron bracket attached to its side to support a baptismal basin, and a paneled enclosure around it.[74] The enclosure was where baptisms were performed, in the sight of the entire assembly. The pulpit itself was given a sounding board and paneled backboard; in some cases the woodwork was carved with elaborate decoration. The reader's desk provided a place for the lay reader who might lead prayers, read from the Bible, and lead hymns in the absence of an ordained minister, a circumstance that arose often. The pulpit was thus not only the most prominent furnishing in the church, centrally placed along a long wall, elevated, sometimes adorned with decorative carvings, and in any case highlighted with a prominent sounding board, but also the magnet that drew other furnishings and thus other acts of worship toward itself. If there was fixed seating, in early years this would be provided by individuals and groups for their own convenience; ordinary layfolk would usually bring chairs or stand until such time as seating could be provided for them.

The liturgical focus is not necessarily the visual focus. At the Westerkerk in Amsterdam, the organ installed in the 1680s is a more imposing structure than the pulpit; although it is placed at the west end of the church it draws attention to itself more forcefully than the pulpit for the casual visitor to the building, and the priority of the pulpit would become clarified mainly by its use during a service.[75] At the First Baptist Church in Columbus, Indiana, the congregation faces a wall that is pierced with rectangular openings and constitutes a forceful grid of vertical and horizontal lines; the church has been criticized for precisely that reason, the wall being visually so strong as to overpower the pulpit and table.[76] But embedded in that wall, and occupying a central position within that visually compelling surface, is a cross that serves de facto as the focus of the interior, suggesting subordination of both pulpit and table, both word and sacraments, to the cross. Even when the pulpit did become the main visual focus in a church, replacing the altar in this capacity, it did not exactly take the same place the altar had occupied. It was not in the same sense a center of cultic activity. The pulpit itself became a practical aid to a function, and it could even be dispensed with in the interest of that function: Charles Finney's Broadway Tabernacle had a theatrical stage with no pulpit. Still, the general rule in Protestant traditions was for the pulpit to assume a prominent place, sometimes in conjunction with the table, sometimes independently, sometimes clearly subordinating the table and everything else to itself.

It was not only in Protestant countries that pulpits came to be larger and more ornate; the Jesuits and others placed a strong emphasis on preaching and on the pulpit in Roman Catholic churches as well, and pulpits became particularly elaborate in the Baroque period. At Sainte Gudule in Brussels the expulsion of Adam and Eve is shown in carving below the pulpit, while on the sounding board the Virgin appears as a warrior and dragon-slayer. In one church at Cracow the pulpit takes the form of a ship, with mast and rigging and sails, and with sea monsters beneath it.[77] But in the Roman tradition the sermon remained secondary to the eucharist, and thus the altar remained the primary focal point of the church no matter how imposing the pulpit (along with side altars and other foci) became.

Case Study: The Castle Chapel at Torgau

In Germany, as in many places, the first generations of Protestants devoted more energy to refitting old churches than to building new ones. Reform-minded German princes did, however, at times build new chapels in their castles, and these are among the most important models of liturgical design in the early years of the German Reformation. The chapel in Torgau Castle, designed by Nickel Gromann with influence from both Martin Luther and Lucas Cranach, built in 1540–44 and dedicated by Luther himself, was the first of these new churches in Saxony, and thus the first opportunity to work out Luther's ideas about worship in an architectural setting (fig. 9).[78]

On the exterior of the Torgau chapel there is nothing to suggest a sacred structure except for the carvings on the window frames and doorway. The windows have relief carvings of angels. On the doorway a prominent band of relief carving depicts the implements of the Passion displayed by angels; above the door, a further relief carving shows the lamentation of Christ. The interior is a simple rectangle, with galleries at two levels on all four sides. Entering from the courtyard, one faces the pulpit, elevated near the center of the opposite wall, at roughly the height of the lower gallery. While the position of the pulpit is similar to that of pulpits in the much larger late Gothic hall churches, its

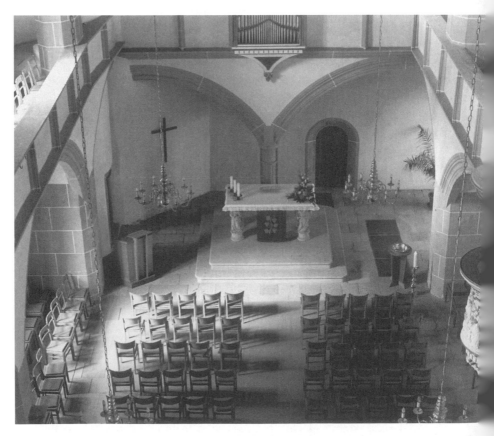

FIGURE 9. Torgau Schloβkapelle, Germany. Photograph by Richard Kieckhefer.

use here in a smaller space (as in other castle chapels) is reminiscent more of the pulpits found in the refectories of medieval religious houses. Relief carvings on the drum of the pulpit at Torgau depict Jesus with the woman taken in adultery, Jesus as a boy teaching in the Temple, and Jesus cleansing the Temple—scenes that may be correlated with the key Lutheran principles of *sola gratia* (justification by grace alone), *sola scriptura* (revelation through scripture alone), and *sola fide* (justification through faith alone, in response to God's grace). The altar, placed at one end, consists of a plain sandstone slab taken from an earlier church and supported now on legs in the shape of carved angels. Behind this altar, a single pillar accentuates the symmetry of the two sides in this longitudinal space. Seating for the prince and his court was on one of the galleries, at the opposite end of the space from the altar, in an arrangement reminiscent of Charlemagne's palatine chapel at Aachen. It is not clear that there was seating for those gathered on the ground level; it would have been difficult to arrange it for proper viewing of both altar and pulpit, and in all likelihood the congregation at this level stood throughout the service, unless there was some sort of moveable seating. As in the chapels at Stettin and the Augustusberg, the Torgau chapel had an organ, installed to encourage congregational singing.

The form of the space at Torgau was dictated in part by the surrounding structures of the castle into which it was fitted. The two galleries served in part as a means for passage at the upper floors from one side of the castle to the other; the prince's residence was in that part of the castle adjacent to the balcony in which he and his court sat at worship, and he could pass from his residence through the chapel gallery into other parts of the castle. A similar arrangement with one gallery had been used already in chapels for Wolmirstedt Castle (1480) and the castle of the bishop of Brandenburg at Ziesar in der Altmark (1478). As late as the seventeenth century, other chapels built for Lutheran princes were modeled after the one at Torgau. Yet the influence of Torgau was not limited to these castle chapels. Lutheran churches were newly built for new communities, such as silver-mining settlemts, as early as 1534–40 at Joachimstal in Bohemia; such churches might follow the late medieval hall-church design, but even in these ordinary parish churches the influence of Torgau can be seen.[79]

While Luther clearly found this form of altar and this arrangement of furnishings congenial, he was nondogmatic on such matters, and alternatives are found. A similar but more elaborately ornamented table altar at Memmingen, probably from around 1530, also reflects the influence of the early Reformers, but not many early altars of this simple table form survive. Luther's basic conviction that "Our altar is Christ—where he is, there is our altar" was consonant with the traditional maxim *Altare est Christus* ("The altar is Christ"), but with shifted emphasis: rather than emphasizing the sacrality of the altar by making it a privileged symbol of Christ himself, he deemphasized it by taking Christ alone as the ultimately true altar. One implication was that a church should have only one altar, or if side altars were left in place they were deprived of liturgical significance. In his German Missal of 1526, Luther took the table form of altar as the best form, and he preferred to have the clergy standing behind it facing the people. Nevertheless, showing his characteristic willingness to make at least temporary accommodations, he was willing to tolerate other arrangements, in particular the use of a retable on the altar that made celebration *versus populum* impossible.[80]

The chapel at Torgau had a retable placed on it, brought to Torgau from Dresden, between 1662 and 1945, and there is evidence for an earlier retable, possibly placed on the altar as early as 1545. The retable altar done by Lucus Cranach's workshop for the church of Wittenberg clearly reflected Luther's theological views.[81] Before long, altars in the typically medieval chest or box form became widespread in Lutheran churches, while later there were variations such as a combined altar and pulpit in which the pulpit loomed over the altar. In short, one cannot speak of any one typical form of altar—or any single relationship between altar and pulpit—even in the early generations of the Lutheran Reformation.

When the chapel at Torgau was dedicated in 1544, the sermon that Luther preached made clear his conception of worship and of space for worship.[82] In lieu of the traditional aspergillum and censer for sprinkling holy water and dispersing the fragrance of incense at a consecration, Luther urged his hearers to help him in sprinkling the new chapel "with the true holy water of God's Word" and to take up with him the censer of prayer, so that the place would remain pure and be used only for speaking of the Word and responding to it with prayer and praise. Thus the building would be properly consecrated, "not like the papists' churches with their bishop's chrism and censing, but according to God's command and will." Just as the sabbath is a day fittingly set aside for the gathering of the community in prayer, but not a binding custom, so too it is appropriate to have a building for worship in Christian freedom, "for those who dwell here in this castle and court or any others who desire to come in." Yet the emphasis lies not on the building but on the community gathered there. "We know that we need not build any special church or temple at great cost or burden and that we are not necessarily bound to any place or time, but have been granted liberty to do this whenever, wherever, and as often as we are able and are agreed together." The prophets, says Luther, had little use for the Temple or its priesthood, but the psalmist did take delight (Psalm 42:4) in going in procession with the throng "with glad shouts and songs of thanksgiving, a multitude keeping festival."

In short, both in his reordering of churches and in his thinking about church design Luther was more concerned to avoid dogmatic insistence on any one conviction than to articulate his own preferences. Yet his basic inclinations are clear: he did not insist on redefining the altar as a communion table, or institute a table at which communicants could actually sit, as the Calvinist tradition did; he did not advocate clear subordination of the altar to the pulpit; yet he wanted the pulpit to be effectively placed for proclamation of the word, and he preferred a simple table-like altar that allowed the pastor to stand facing the congregation.

The Baptistery

While the relative significance and placement of the altar and the pulpit have usually been in the forefront of debate, there have also been diverse opinions about the role and position of the baptistery. The altar can be placed in front or in the middle of the congregation, and the pulpit is almost always placed in front, but the baptismal font can be in widely varying places, and interpreters have long been eager to explain the meaning of each option. Thus, in the words of one writer,

> emphasis on purification prefers a baptistery and font separated
> from the church; emphasis on incorporation into the body of Christ
> prompts a baptistery-font located at the entrance to the church; em-
> phasis on participation in the death and resurrection of Christ has
> led to the baptistery-font being joined to the ambo.[83]

On this interpretation, a detached baptistery outside the church is rather like the purifying font in the courtyard of a mosque, a place where the worshiper can be cleansed before daring to enter into the sacred building; while the purification of baptism occurs only once and not on each entry into the church, the position of the baptistery is a constant reminder of the need for cleansing prior to prayer. When a baptism is being performed in such a detached baptistery, those witnessing the event will all need to leave the church for that purpose and process from church to baptistery and back, unless the baptistery itself has an altar and is the place for a special mass at the time of a baptism. (The integration of liturgical furnishings into a detached baptistery was common at an early date in Italy; the baptistery at Pisa provides a particularly good example of how this space can be fully equipped for liturgical celebration.) A baptismal font or pool placed at the entry to a church symbolizes the role of baptism as the rite of entry into the Church; those passing the baptistery are reminded that they originally became members of the Church through this sacrament. At the time of a baptism, the congregation (if there is one present) may simply turn around to witness the event or may proceed to the entrance. If the font or pool is located in front of the congregation, the symbolism again shifts, and now the emphasis is on the integration of baptism into the full liturgical life of the community, the correlation of the font or pool with the other liturgical furnishings, and the induction of the person baptized into the mysteries of Christ's life and death that are preached and celebrated in worship. This position affords the easiest congregational participation: without leaving the positions they occupy for the rest of the liturgy, people can be witnesses to the baptism and perhaps participate by joining in the renewal of baptismal vows.

Historically, detached baptisteries have been seen as places for ritual death and rebirth, and their shape has mimicked that of a mausoleum, round or octagonal in structure. Saint Ambrose explained that the octagonal baptistery at Milan symbolized salvation and new life. The number eight stands for the eighth day (the day of Christ's resurrection, after the seventh day of the week), the eighth age of the world (that of eternity, after the traditional seven ages), and the eighth age of human life (that of eternal life). An octagon is thus fitting for both a mausoleum and a baptistery.[84] The use of a detached baptistery may also convey a message about community. Such baptisteries are found most notably at Italian cathedrals—Florence and Ravenna provide well-known examples—and they were built to serve as the place of baptism for the entire city. The separation of the baptistery from the cathedral indicates that it is a place to which not only those attached to a particular church but all those in the broader community resort for baptism.

Even when the baptistery is not detached, symbolism of death and rebirth may be expressed in the act of going down into the water and then rising from it. Most fonts are elevated rather than depressed, but at Marcel Breuer and Herbert Beckhard's church of Saint Francis de Sales in Muskegon, Michigan, the font is set in the floor of the narthex, one descends into it by a short flight of stairs, and similarly recessed fonts have been introduced elsewhere.[85]

In some traditions the baptismal font has been placed in a separate chapel within the church but distinct from the main worship space, in the expectation that those witnessing it would be not an entire liturgical community but only a small group of family and friends. And in the earliest place of Christian worship for which we have archaeological evidence, the one at Dura-Europos, the baptistery was almost certainly the room in the northwest corner of the complex, across the courtyard from the assembly hall used for the eucharist: an arrangement that might be taken to undercut any hierarchical subordination of one sacrament to another, any notion of baptism as simply a prelude to eucharist. While the baptistery at Dura-Europos was smaller than the eucharistic assembly hall, it was richly decorated, and the balancing of the two main sacramental spaces on opposite sides of the complex would presumably have served as a statement about the importance of baptism in the community's sacramental life.

Aelred Tegels has emphasized two basic principles: that the baptistery should be placed where the entire congregation can participate and should be located and designed to make the dignity of baptism clear. But often either communal participation or symbolic meaning is slighted: having the baptistery in a small chapel by the entrance or in the narthex is symbolically effective but does not encourage a large congregation to participate; placement in or near the sanctuary promotes participation but does not clarify the meaning of baptism as incorporation into the body of Christ. Ideally, Tegels suggests, the baptistery should be within the body of the church but at the back.[86] A striking application of this principle is at Saint Benedict the African Church in Chicago, where the baptismal pool is twenty-four feet wide and three feet deep and is placed at the main entrance to the worship space. On entering the church, the worshiper walks along a curving ramp that passes alongside the baptismal pool as it descends into the worship area. One visitor to the church observed parishioners gazing down at the water in the pool as they passed by, feeling the stones on the low wall between the ramp and the pool, and talking about recent or upcoming baptisms—all suggesting that the pool functioned effectively as a reminder of the sacrament.[87]

Multiple Foci, No Focus

The notion that a church must have a centering focus, and that this must be single and unambiguous, should perhaps not seem obvious. What other buildings create such an expectation? The classic sacramental church centers on the altar, and the classic evangelical church centers on the pulpit, but need there be a single visual focus for worship? Would it not be possible for liturgy to center on more than one focal point, or to conceive a church with no clear focus of any sort?

The altar, or the pulpit, or the altar and pulpit together, have rarely been the only furnishings important to the liturgy: ambos, sedilia for the altar party to sit on at certain moments, Easter Sepulchers for sequestration of the host on Good Friday, communion rails, and other furnishings have had important roles at various times in Catholic tradition.

Even when there are only two liturgical and visual foci, the altar and the pulpit, their relationship to each other can be the subject for much reflection and disagreement. Otto Bartning, one of the foremost Protestant architects of twentieth-century Germany, spoke of the balanced coordination of altar and pulpit as characterizing the Protestant tradition but emphasized that the possibile relationships between them have always been many and none has ever become definitive. Bartning confessed that at one point he found the challenge of balance so daunting that he was inclined to suggest total separation of preaching-churches from celebration-churches, but on further reflection he recognized this as an evasion of the critical challenge of establishing balance or equilibrium.[88] But in the same collection of essays Bartning's contemporary Martin Elsässer went further and emphasized in a particularly forceful way that for Lutherans it is the *act* of preaching itself that is central, and all foci within the church, even the pulpit, are desacralized. To be sure, both pulpit and altar are used in the worship service, but without the sacral character they possess in a Roman Catholic church. For Elsässer, then, the ideal of a Lutheran church is a central plan without a pronounced axial character, without an apse or choir for a high altar that compels vision and gives a sense of direction. The interior space as such is what is important, and not any of the furnishings within it.[89]

In other Protestant traditions as well, the pulpit has often taken its place in an ensemble of furnishings. To consider one modern case, Eero Saarinen's design for North Christian Church at Columbus, Indiana, is a classic example of two liturgical foci in combination. The plan of the worship space is an elongated hexagon, with the pulpit at one end and seating along the sides. Attention is drawn to the pulpit by two backdrops: a bright silk hanging that stands out within the interior, and behind that a set of organ pipes designed to reinforce rather than compete with the visual centrality of the pulpit. But in the center of the church, with seating on either side, is the table for the Lord's Supper, which is celebrated weekly in this church and occupies a central position literally as well as figuratively.[90]

Proponents of the twentieth-century liturgical movement in the Dutch Reformed Church, seeking keener recognition of the sacraments, often brought table and font (sometimes also ambo) alongside the pulpit in a cluster of furnishings in front of the congregation, with much variation in the ordering of these items: a centrally positioned table might be flanked by pulpit and font, a centrally placed pulpit might have a complex table with font in front of it, and so forth.[91] Even in Roman Catholic circles, by around 1960 the unrivaled centrality of the altar was no longer absolute. Partly in response to ecumenical concerns, a new generation of reformers recommended a balance of altar and ambo, corresponding to an equilibrium of sacrament and word. In 1962 Charles Davis urged a keener sense of the link between word and sacrament, reflected in the correlation of ambo and altar, and he maintained that the seat of the priest should take its place as "the third essential feature of any balanced sanctuary." Just as the bishop in the early church presided over the assembly from a chair in the apse, so too the priest should lead the prayers from the presidential seat.[92] Within a few years it was possible to say flatly that "mass no longer rotates around the single pole of the altar, but has three clearly differentiated poles: the altar, the celebrant's chair and the ambo."[93]

One development that has elicited some enthusiasm is the elliptical plan, with ambo and altar as complementary foci, and with the congregation on either side of the elliptical space (in "antiphonal choir" arrangement). One German writer comments that this plan differs from a circle with a single center, allowing for not only the ambo and altar but for a multiplicity of focal points within the space for liturgical action that stretches between these two points; the free space at the heart of the assembly allows for an openness to transcendence experienced in and through the assembly.[94] The Church of Saint Julie Billiart in Tinley Park, Illinois, has seating for the congregation flanking an oblong central liturgical space in which the altar is placed toward one end and the ambo toward the other, neither markedly more prominent than the other.[95] The design is essentially bifocal, and the sense of liturgical space elliptical. The explanatory literature provided by the parish specifies that "the centrality of the altar and the ambo strongly emphasize that the primary reason we come together is to share the Lord in Word and Eucharist," and the ambo is even given a shape suggesting that it, like the altar, "is a 'table' at which the Word of God is shared."[96]

One might expect a modern communal church, with its strong emphasis on the gathered assembly, to move away from a clear sense of focus on either altar or pulpit, to keep both modest in scale, and in general to conceive and display them as instrumental rather than as possessed of sacrality. And indeed altar and pulpit in such churches often are relatively modest and unimposing, arranged so as to avoid any clear suggestion that they should dominate the room. Edward Sövik notes that we tend to assume a large room should be symmetrically organized, with "some dominating feature about which the room comes to focus," this being the safe and easy approach that amateur designers almost always take. But "if we declare that *people* are really the focus of what happens in the liturgy," and if we see that the people move from one function to another, we conclude that no one focus should dominate consistently: the pulpit should serve as focus during preaching, the table during the eucharist, the choir when it sings special music, the baptistery during a baptism, and the community as a whole for actions such as hymn-singing.[97]

The deemphasis on all furnishings can be grounded in a conviction that the assembly itself should be the focus, or in a preference for a fluid and dynamic service that is not bound to any focal point. Both themes arise in Sövik's statement regarding his United Methodist Church at Northfield, Minnesota: "the most important things in a church are not the communion table, the font, the cross, or the pulpit, but the people; and God's presence is associated not with any part of the building but with the service and the proclamation of His Word." Churches may often "imply by their architecture that God is locatable, that one part of the church is a uniquely holy place, or that God's presence is related to an object instead of to His people and what they do," but not so this church.

> The space will not focus on any one thing. But as the service is followed its progress will move the focus from one place to another and sometimes the whole body of believers will be the real center of attention. And we hope that this will remind them that the kingdom of God is not here or there but among them, as Jesus said.[98]

And this detachment from any centering focus is also detachment from hieratic formality. The church is meant not as a place of disciplined focus but as a site of welcome and familiarity.

This use of multiple foci in a modern communal church might have the same scattering effect as the proliferation of altars in a classic sacramental church. If it does not, that is partly because modern communal churches are relatively small and simple in their design, and the multiple foci are often clustered together rather than widely separated. From Sövik's perspective, however, the crucial point would be that demotion of the furnishings leads not to scattering but to a subordination of all objects to the assembly itself.

Conclusion

A visitor entering a church for the first time and attempting to see how it is disposed will want to know what the church takes as its centering focus, if indeed it has such a focus at all. More complicated is determining *how* exactly that focus is established. The altar may be given an imposing visual frame, which may then overwhelm the altar itself. The visual focus may or may not coincide with the liturgical focus. Competing foci may diminish the impact of the main one, or a multiplicity of foci may instead enrich the interior by supplementing the main focal point. Devotional foci such as saints' shrines may compete with the liturgical focus or supplement it.[99] The focus may be placed at more than one point within the church. And still more difficult is the matter of how the focus is used, how in a particular cultural context it is seen as functioning.

Lindsay Jones tells of a mass in the cathedral of Cuernavaca, Mexico, at which he observed a little Mexican boy. Amid the processions, the incense, the mariachi music, and everything else, the boy focused his attention on a three-foot-high stone carving of an angel. This was an object to which he could relate, "precisely his size, receptive to his touching, and somehow approachable by its familiarity," and rather than attending to the mass the boy "paced in front of the angelic image, put his hands all over the angel's carved face, interrogated it and listened impatiently for its response."[100] For this child, the cathedral had a centering focus entirely different from the high altar. The clergy might be more tolerant toward such behavior in a child than in an adult. From a woman or man they might expect closer attention to the altar and the liturgy celebrated there. But it is not enough for clergy or for architect to say that the altar—or the pulpit—should be the centering focus of a church. They must also show that it is. With line and with light and with color they must make clear where they want the eye and the mind to come to rest, if that is what they intend. And how (or whether) they do so effectively is one of the most important questions about any church.

3

The Third Factor:
Aesthetic Impact

Entering a church is a metaphor for entering into the presence of
the holy. A church is sometimes called a house of God, or *domus
Dei*. This is not to suppose God is limited to a particular place, as if
a church could place objective boundaries on the divine. Rather, to
speak of a house of God is to recognize community and its culture
as means of allurement toward God—to recognize that the house
made by the community is an apt setting for the people to assemble
in the alluring presence of the divine. In the prophet's formulation,
God says of Israel, "behold, I will allure her, and will lead her into
the wilderness, and speak tenderly to her" (Hosea 2:14). The image
of encounter with God in a starkly natural setting, a world untouched
by human culture, finds its complement in the theme of being allured by God also within a kind of house, a work of people formed
by a particular culture and linked in common effort, and thus within
community and its works. Cultural creations and activities that
might distract from the life of the spirit are here specifically designed for recalling attention to that life. Entering into a church is a
metaphor for recognizing that prayer—being allured by God—is
possible not only in solitude and in nature but also in community
and in culture. And essential to that allurement are a church's aesthetic qualities.

Writers on church architecture are in broad agreement that a
church's aesthetic character is central to its purpose: that beauty is
"the only symbol we humans can devise that illuminates the transcendent";[1] that the climate of liturgy is "one of awe, mystery, wonder, reverence, thanksgiving and praise," requiring nothing less than

"the *beautiful* in its environment and all its artifacts, movements, and appeals to the senses."[2] Even Paul Tillich, who proposed that the term "beauty" be replaced by "expressive power" because of the "complete collapse of the meaning of the word *beautiful*," did not mean to dispute the importance of ecclesiastical aesthetics.[3] The aesthetic impact of a church is the dimension that impresses itself most forcefully at once on entry. Leon Battista Alberti thus viewed a church as a place built and adorned to inspire in its visitor an awestruck exclamation that the place is "worthy of God."[4] To be sure, a critic of the mid-twentieth century might protest that a church is meant first of all not to provide a "worship experience" or "an æsthetic *frisson*" but rather to shelter the liturgical assembly.[5] Yet most church-builders have striven—and been expected to strive—for aesthetic as well as utilitarian effect. If they have sometimes worked with limited finance, they have still agreed in principle that even a simple church can and should, in Ninian Comper's words, "became glorious by beautiful workmanship within."[6]

Horst Wenzel unfolds the experience a medieval Christian was meant to have in a church, taken in ideal terms as a place for manifestation of God to each of the senses: to the eyes, in its dazzling artwork and in the ritual acts performed; to the ears, through both word and music; to the nose, in "divine fragrance" of incense and flowers; to the taste, in the eucharist, said to give a foretaste of God's sweetness; to the touch, in the kiss of peace and the kissing of various sacred objects, and especially in extraliturgical contact with relics. The participation of the senses comes vividly to the fore in the account of a church in the *Gandersheimer Reimchronik* of around 1216: the building is decked out with masterfully wrought tapestries; it is radiant with glass, silver, and glistening gold; the fragrance of incense and myrrh raises the senses to God; readings, chant, and the sounding of bells redound to God's honor. If everyday life is perhaps gray and filled with workaday cacophony, the church is meant as a place where one can experience the beautiful as an emanation of divine beauty.[7] The force of this ideal may seem less clear in an age when the secular world also offers refuges from environmental blight, but in this respect churches were long exceptional.

For whose sake is the church designed as an aesthetic work? With or without a theology of merit, it can be represented as an offering to God, an expression of response to grace. Ralph Adams Cram suggested as much in his characteristically florid description of medieval Gothic churches where every detail shimmered with sacrality—

> where [people] were surrounded by the dim shadows of mysterious
> aisles, where lofty piers of stone softened high overhead into sweep-
> ing arches and shadowy vaults, where golden light struck down
> through storied windows, painted with the benignant faces of saints
> and angels; where the eye rested at every turn on a painted and

carven Bible, manifesting itself through the senses to the imagination; where every wall, every foot of floor, bore its silent memorial to the dead, its thank-offering to God; where was always the faint odor of old incense, the still atmosphere of prayer and praise.[8]

More often writers speak of the aesthetic impact of a church on human sensibilities, and they tend usually to speak of the impact on isolated individuals visiting the church alone. They will speak about the atmosphere of a church as conducive to private devotion; they may praise a church for producing "an atmosphere of dignity and serenity appropriate for the individual exercise of worship."[9] Only rarely will they speak of aesthetic impact on an assembly. Yet communities become communities by what they see together, by shared perception of objects and events that engage the senses as well as the mind and are richly charged with symbolic value. A secular community may be constituted by the common experience of sports events, political spectacles, the deaths of celebrities, and other objects of collective consciousness. A sacred community is ideally formed by the common experience of reverent attention to the divine, and by shared perception of a transcendent and quickening beauty. Liturgical worship is more than merely a moment in the life of a sacred community; it is the defining moment, without which there is no such community. Worship may also energize the group and give it direction for work in the world—but inevitably for diverse tasks, whereas the common experience of transcendent beauty and holiness in worship is what people with different ministries share in common, and what keeps the members focused on a shared symbolic vision.

The effort required is itself a means of engagement. It may often seem easier to experience God in prayerful solitude, in nature, outside the artificiality of a built environment. If people can think of God on their beds, meditating in the watches of a sleepless night, why should they seek out a setting less congenial to meditation? The challenge of a church building for such people is that of integration, of bringing personal experience into harmony with life in community, of fusing immediacy with tradition, and of discovering also in works of craft and art the presence of the holy as it is sensed perhaps more spontaneously in nature.

Art in a religious setting can serve as a sacrament of grace, and the capacity to see oneself as worthy of beauty is one dimension of recognizing oneself as *by* grace made worthy *for* grace—the sole condition for beginning to receive it. That it is the product of artists working within a spiritual tradition makes it a symbol of the synergy in which inspiration and creation are inextricable, especially when the artist's spiritual tradition construes creation itself as a spiritual discipline, as in the case of Eastern Orthodox iconography. That it arises within and for a community makes it a symbol for the corporate experience of grace. The bond is close between saying that God is worthy of praise, that humans are worthy to praise God, and that humans are worthy of the experience of holiness transmitted in the beauty of praise. The claims are distinguishable yet inseparable.

A church is a work of art meant not only for the benefit of those who worship in it but for the sake of the environment in which it is planted. It was not always so. In the early Byzantine era the embellishment of a church tended to be almost all concentrated inside the building. The interior might be densely packed with floor and wall mosaics, wall paintings, ornamented capitals, and marble work, while the façade remained utterly plain. This disparity can be found in the early Byzantine churches of Palestine,[10] and it can be observed as well in the Byzantine churches of Ravenna. But at least since the rise of Romanesque style, aesthetically ambitious churches have commonly been designed for strong impact on the exterior as well, which one might have thought less relevant to their basic liturgical functions. The development of the ornamental facade meant that a church was to be an enlivening presence for the community. "A liturgical building enters into a dialogue with the city, and even with the territory, in a way that corresponds to the proper relationship between Church and world."[11] Perhaps today nowhere more than in Italy is greater care given to the impact of a church on an otherwise depressed environment, the need to integrate the church proper into the community by means of careful planning of architectural complex and grounds, most generally the role of the church in city planning.[12] But any building, or even monumental sculpture, could contribute toward the ambience of its setting; a church is usually expected to give on the outside an anticipation of and invitation to the liturgy inside.

Aesthetic Impact and the Holy

"The experience of the presence of the holy by the kind of space the architect has created is what must be intended, even before anything else happens within this space."[13]

The psalmist, thirsting for God in the dry and weary landscape of the desert, enters the sanctuary of the Temple to be refreshed by the sight of God's power and glory, posing a model for the experience of sacred space elsewhere. Attaining and departing from the presence of an all-present God is one way of imaging the moments of a contemplative disposition, sometimes keener and sometimes duller. The image might just as well be reversed; one could speak of God entering and departing from the soul as from a house, and imagery of this sort does occur in mystical theology. Caesarius of Arles manages to combine the two motifs: "Just as you enter this church, so God wants to enter your soul."[14] But the more general Christian image is of God at rest and humans in pilgrimage, perhaps in part out of a Platonic sense of the timeless divine

immutability and out of a consciousness of human vicissitude. Equally important in the image of entering into the presence of God is the social dimension
of the entry, the recognition of all members of a community congregating in
the divine presence, and that theme is lost if the image is reversed and the
visit is one of a pilgrim God making the rounds of human houses. Meeting
with God is the common act of a community of worshipers, a community
constituted by its common entry, becoming the Church by entering a church
together.

If the accent is placed on this theme of entering the presence of God, the
building itself may be simple, as God is simple and as contemplation is simple.
Like Mies van der Rohe's chapel at the Illinois Institute of Technology, it may
be inspired by a Thomist sense of contemplation as the simple intuition of
truth, the *simplex intuitus veritatis*. But few churches even in a modern idiom
are simple to that degree, and the relationship between the simplicity of the
divine and the complexity and ornamentation of the architecture serves as
commentary on the relationship between simplicity and plenitude in religion,
between the one and the many, between the holy and the sacred.

Like the apparatus of liturgy, its verbal formulas, the vestments and the
music, the incense and the gestures, so too the architectural setting is meant
as a means for cultivating the disposition of reverence, construed as a virtue.
One is drawn toward the holy in awe and wonder, and one responds to the
holy in reverence. This cultivation of reverence becomes the affective purpose
for the entire liturgical exercise. The ethical assumption is that a holy manner
of life, one made attentive to the presence of the holy through experience of
the sacred, is more worth living than a merely good life. Reverence is not itself
a particular mood; it may by turns be festive or solemn, effusive or restrained,
linked with a sense of fellowship or turned more toward inwardness. If it is a
virtue, it is such in the sense of a habit of disposition and behavior, in which
neither the disposition nor the behavior is dominant but the two go hand in
hand. One does not first learn to feel reverent inwardly and then act reverently
with genuflections or other gestures, or the reverse; reverence is an orientation
of both dispositon and behavior, both learned simultaneously. Most important
to this way of viewing matters, reverence remains constantly open toward a
fitting object. One is not merely in a state of reverence. "Revere" is a transitive
verb, requiring an object, someone or something to be revered. But what? The
obvious answer for the theist is: God. But the transcendent God is not visible,
and reverence in a church is directed in the first place toward objects and
occurrences that can be seen, even if there remains something provisional
about that reverence and its choice of object. One is reverent and seeking a
due object for reverence, directing it toward objects that point toward the final
and truly fitting object, directing it toward the sacred in anticipation of the holy.

But beyond these generalities there is much room for differences in the
purpose, the character, and the means for pursuing beauty within churches.

And the differences correspond in broad outline to the three traditions of church building I have been considering: at least as a starting point for discussion, a classic sacramental church can be seen as a dramatic space for a subtle interplay of transcendence and immanence; a classic evangelical church as a dignified environment for edification; and a modern communal church as a hospitable setting for celebration.

A Church as a Dramatic Setting for the Interplay of Transcendence and Immanence

A church cannot serve directly as a sign of divine transcendence, but only of varying modes of divine immanence.[15] Transcendence is what remains unmanifested when all manifestation has reached its limits. But a church can be meant as a means for human transcendence, or for the transcending of ordinary experience and ordinary consciousness. The transcendent is not only that which exceeds one's capacity for participation but that which expands one's capacities through participation. Within a church, at least in the classic sacramental tradition, the ascending curve of human self-transcendence and the descending curve of divine immanence intersect. This is the direct, immediate impact that a church building can be meant to have—not to arouse a sense of insignificance and dread[16] but on the contrary to give assurance of presence of and to the divine. The aesthetic character of a church, whether simply or elaborately conceived, economically or lavishly executed, will determine its capacity to evoke a sense of this interplay of transcendence and immanence; indeed, the main reason for conceiving a classic sacramental church as a work of art, as a dramatic environment for the enactment of drama, is precisely to foster this consciousness, not simply within individuals but as a factor in bonding the congregation, giving it a sense of collectively experienced and collectively valued encounter with the divine.

Reverence and awe are both relational: they are not simply states of consciousness but modes of relationship to someone or something within one's consciousness. Both, one might say, are responses to the transcendent-made-immanent, but awe is a response to what we experience directly, and reverence is a response to what we intimate, or experience indirectly. If we experienced God directly our response would presumably be one of awe, and imagining that experience and that response is a mode of contemplative prayer. But normally the objects of awe are creaturely, because it is the created world that we experience immediately and directly: a canyon, a mountain, a cathedral or any other church stands open to view, bringing vividly to mind the sense of the transcendent-made-immanent. If we recognize the canyon or cathedral as giving intimations of the divine, this sense of awe inspires a response of reverence for the divinity experienced indirectly within what we see as awesome. And this experience of awe before the seen and reverence for the unseen underlies an entire tradition of church-building.

Fundamental to the aesthetic of the classic sacramental church is a sense of participation in a reality greater than any individual and greater than any particular community—a dramatic evocation of a sense of being caught up in something greater than oneself, and greater than the experience of any one place or time, requiring a keenness of presence and conviction. But more specifically, the classic sacramental church is characteristically marked by a sense of aspiration, of mystery, and of timelessness. Among the means used to convey these qualities, the most important are height, light, and acoustics: height chiefly to convey a spirit of aspiration, light to evoke a sense of mystery, and acoustics to suggest timelessness. These factors shape not only the feel of a church, the emotional response it elicits, but also the way it orients attention.

These aspects of architecture could be considered from a formalist perspective: church architecture makes use of conventions that call attention to themselves and mark a church as a distinctive kind of building. The handling of volume in a classic sacramental church is, more often than not, deliberately extravagant: the building need not be as high as it is.[17] The light is typically not of the usual sort: it is colored by passing through colored glass, or its source is indirect, or it is Milton's "dim religious light." Nor is the sound the same as in an ordinary secular building: the classic sacramental church is likely to have distinctive acoustics, with longer than usual reverberation time. While the sheer facticity of the building, its structure and material, is not denied, it is the dynamics of space, illumination, and reverberation that come more vividly to one's attention than usual. But of course the point is not simply for volume, light, and sound to call attention to themselves but for them to serve effectively as evocative symbols of something beyond themselves, to serve the anagogic or sacramental function of pointing to the immanence of the transcendent.

There is a partial parallel in the formalist conception of literature, especially poetry, as the use of formal devices to estrange or defamiliarize language, to force the reader into dramatic consciousness of the language used, to renew the blunted edge of consciousness, to arouse a vivid awareness of the world contained in literary language.[18] The parallel with church architecture is, however, limited: while classic sacramental churches may be designed to call attention to volume, light, and sound and to arouse fresh perception of liturgical space, this is not an end in itself but a way of setting the environment for the drama of liturgy, which in turn is meant to evoke real events and spiritual realities not limited to the particular liturgical occasion.

When a Benedictine community was preparing to build a new church the monks looked at other recent designs and found them lacking in "that character of aspiration which traditionally a church should have"; in the words of their prior, "A church should soar upwards!"[19] Aspiration is inspiration. The theme is lyrically sounded by a mid-nineteenth-century enthusiast of the

Gothic revival, for whom God is only to be rendered in the monuments of Christianity by loftiness of structure. . . .

> The tendency of the structure must be continually upwards . . . leading the mind to the infinite above, which conveys the idea of the presence of God, not only beyond the limits of the building, but beyond the limits of space appreciable to the physical sense.[20]

Oskar Söhngen speaks of a church's loftiness as the most appropriate and effective means of representing the sacred—"in earlier times." A space in which believers lose themselves or feel overwhelmed is a fitting reflection of creatures' relationship to the wholly Other, although the sense created may range from one of simple strength to one of pompous and blustering gesture, and the message about God will vary accordingly.[21]

Romano Guardini spoke of this anagogic function of a church, contrasting it with reactions to the natural environment. On crossing the threshold one lifts one's eyes, surveys the expanse of the interior, and experiences "an inward expansion and enlargement." The church's volume has "an analogy to infinity and eternity"; a church is a likeness of God's heavenly abode. Granted, mountains are higher and the sky immeasurably wider. But space outside a building is "unconfined and formless," while the space marked out by church "has been formed, fashioned, designed at every point with God in view."[22] Objects and spaces in the natural order may also be signs of the transcendent, but a work of architecture is a sign that engages human participation in a wider range of modes, not only as viewers but also as planners and builders, and this participation itself is one element in the human transcendence of ordinariness.

If height is a sign of aspiration, it has also been an invitation to the disaster, as the builders of Babel learned at notorious cost. In France, where one town might vie with another in the height of its cathedral, the 1284 collapse of the choir at Beauvais showed the hazards of overextension; structural engineers still ponder precisely where the strain led to breakdown, but the ambitious height of the building was the obvious condition for failure. In England, where even major churches were not as tall as their French counterparts, the crossing towers built over the juncture of chancel, nave, and transepts were still precarious. They were constructed not over solid masonry but on arches put up from floor level on each of the four corners: over air, in effect. And their collapse meant disaster, because a falling tower could bring much of the church with it to the ground. The ambition of twelfth-century builders often exceeded their skill as they went about knocking down and replacing the cathedrals and monastic churches of their Saxon predecessors. They guessed at how much support their towers would require, but they often guessed badly, and their towers often collapsed.[23] In later centuries the towers themselves tended to be more stable, yet the spires placed atop the towers as needle points extending up into the sky were always vulnerable.[24]

Given these hazards, why should high churches and towers be built in the first place? As monuments to the builders' ambition, no doubt. More fundamentally, a high interior demarcates and thus emphasizes space that cannot normally be attained by the person left standing below, the person who might only imagine floating upward into that space, who surveys its dimensions and perhaps its decoration from below, noting continuities and discontinuities between what is literally at hand and what can only be touched by the eye, and noting that even what is inaccessible still contributes to the experience of the setting precisely by offering itself to vision. The volume of a spacious interior calls to mind that one is present in—and in relationship to—far more than one's immediate surroundings, the small corner of the world one could turn toward and touch. As for a tower, it served the practical function of allowing a place for bells to be hung where they would be heard more widely. It served further not only as an object to be seen but also as a place for seeing. The God of the Bible is imagined as a sky deity not only because he is transcendent but also because height allows total simultaneous view of an entire community, a world of interlinked experience. Those at the foot of a tower do not share this perspective, but gazing upward reminds them of its possibility.

Height of construction has rarely been limited to sacred architecture; palaces and hotel lobbies also display aspiration—which, of course, does not make aspiration specifically secular, and does not diminish the capacity of expansive space to express spiritual aspiration in a religious context. Still, both high ceilings and the sense of aspiration they are taken to express have likewise been called into question. Mario Salvadori argued in 1956 that modern construction techniques make possible structures that are broad but not high, so the modern ideal becomes that of the horizontal rather than vertical cathedral.[25] Edward Sövik, whose "non-churches" have the simplest of decoration and relatively low ceilings, argued further that Christianity, unlike other religions, cannot be grounded in human aspiration:

> Its core and essence is not human aspiration but divine condescension. And this is why people like Dietrich Bonhoeffer have said that Christianity is not religious, it is fundamentally different. It is not based on man's search and God's response, but on God's search and man's response. And man's response does not take the form of aspiration but of service.[26]

The theological premise here is doubtful. Alongside the theme of divine condescension, the New Testament does ascribe fundamental value to human aspiration. The classic maxim that God shared our humanity so we might share in divinity is solidly grounded in biblical ideals of participating in divine life or divine nature, and the desire for that sharing is clearly a form of aspiration.[27] Indeed, it would be difficult to imagine why any religion would exclude all sense of aspiration, or how it could hold much appeal if it did so. Most important, "every Godward aspiration of the soul" presupposes a dialectic of human aspiration and divine condescension, and the critique of aspiration that takes it as an independent striving mistakes the theology—and the architecture that gives it expression and context.[28]

A church with a roof or a tower higher than any other structure in the vicinity becomes a defining point for the community, with houses nestling in the shadow of their highest building. To grasp the effect, one must imagine away the skyscrapers made possible by constructional developments of the later nineteenth century and project oneself into a world in which the only competition for height came usually from military fortifications, and a world in which churches often served a defensive function and thus became assimilated to military architecture, with battlements that served to conceal the drainage but also turned churches into sacred fortresses. In many places the external height of a church has lost its religious significance; it is on the interior that an expansive church can retain religious meaning—not because there are no comparable secular interiors but because the meaning of the space is molded by its liturgical use. When a voluminous interior resonates with richly celebratory liturgy, the experience of worship comes from the interaction of the space and its use.

Jacob Needleman tells of an exchange he had with a prominent Orthodox bishop regarding the merits of Gothic and Romanesque architecture. Needleman himself, on visiting Gothic cathedrals, had a "sense of being drawn upward within a vast cosmic scale filled with light," and the quality of that light, along with the "immense vertical spaces" and other dimensions of the cathedrals, transmitted to him "the sense of a greatness and mystery." The bishop's reactions were entirely different: "I have always been revolted by Gothic. . . . All that aspiring, aspiring upward—yet not all the way." The Romanesque, he said, is inspired by an entirely different principle: "In Romanesque something has already come down to man: love."[29] But other interpretations are equally possible. Thus, Ronald Goetz tells us that a Romanesque church such as the eleventh-century Saint-Etienne in Nevers, with its thickness and mass, its severity, its "radically downward verticality," allows the eye to move upward only to drive it immediately back down, conveying a theology of profound finitude, of fallen and helpless humanity bound to the earth, whereas the thirteenth-century Gothic cathedral of Amiens leads the eye upward without forcing it back down, height and slender columns collaborating with other elements to create a dizzying effect, all conveying a belief in the possibility of union with God and a "new confidence in human reason."[30] But whichever style they prefer, those who formulate such distinctions typically make the mistake of interpreting the earlier in light of the later: those who have seen the fully developed Gothic may perceive a Romanesque church as massive and earthbound, but those who lived when Romanesque architecture was in full flower would have seen the more ambitious specimens of that style as straining heavenward with all the grandeur that construction techniques then made possible, and the earliest Gothic churches were not in fact remarkably high by comparison.[31] It would thus be a misreading of either Romanesque or Gothic to take the one as expressing divine immanence and the other human self-transcendence. Rather, they both give expression, using different technical and aesthetic vocabulary, precisely to the intersection of the descending and the ascending curve.

While greater height than surrounding structures is a classic sign of aspiration, manipulation of light is a classic way to create an aura of mystery. "Architecture," one writer has observed, "begins with the organization of light. A sacred space is the purest form of architectural experience. Its function is to communicate transcendental reality."[32] Thus, Ninian Comper saw the atmosphere of a church as a quality attained through use of color and lighting, which in a particular case might actually be so closely connected that one can speak of them as a single factor. Comper spoke of his own experience of working throughout the day decorating a church with gold and color, evidently to no avail, when "suddenly, with the evening light, what before had seemed so hopeless became beautiful," calling to mind Milton's "storied windows richly dight/ casting a dim religious light," neither darkness nor even light but rather light like that of early morning or evening, "when the Lord God walks in the garden."[33] Rafael Moneo has been called "an expert at setting traps for sunlight," but the light he traps at the cathedral in Los Angeles is not natural but transformed by passing through sheets of alabaster.[34] In various ways, light calls attention to itself and to a presence beyond itself.

That a church should be a chamber of light is a medieval notion. Far more ancient, indeed archaic, is the conception of a church as a chamber of shadows, a place of entry into the mysteries of the earth, a cave, a tomb. "The Lord has set the sun in the heavens, but has said that he would dwell in thick darkness."[35] Christianity has never quite foresworn the sacrality of chthonic dark. Caves were perhaps among the earliest cultic places in human culture, and in various ways caves and grottoes have exercised a compelling sacrality. Churches can still be reminiscent of these archaic sites of ritual. In early Spanish shrines with images of the Virgin Mary, the images were often said to have been discovered in caves, and legends sometimes tell how after the discovery the image miraculously returned to its place of origin, in effect identifying the Virgin as an Earth Mother who shared by her miraculous childbearing something of the Earth's fertility.[36] Christ was thought in early tradition to have been born in a cave and then buried in a cave, and like the god Mithras he is often venerated in cavelike structures.[37] The ideal of airy, luminous churches was an innovation of later medieval Europe, and for centuries churches had been otherwise. Even in the twentieth century, the Episcopal Church of Saint Clement in Alexandria, Virginia,[38] concentrates attention on liturgical action by having no windows at all, the ceiling painted black, and just enough artificial lighting for reading and for focused attention to the chancel, altar, and baptistery. "Our desire was to create a sense of spaciousness and grandeur," the rector explained:

> It could have been oppressive, but we achieved a sense of mystery. We look up into the darkness that reminds us of the vastness of the over-brooding presence of God as does the night sky, and all variations of light and darkness, heat and cold, wind, rain, snow and sound are shut out as much as is humanly possible.[39]

Dennis McNally makes the point more generally:

> Darkness is akin to silence in that it creates an environment in which the spirit may attend to itself. Here it must be said that the dark must be qualified enough to be awesome, not enough to be frightening. This means that dark in high recesses or far from this very place of the pilgrim would be unthreatening though awesome. Absolute dark is hardly what is sought but that soft light which can be penetrated by candles. . . . In that context, when there is so much light that a candle is insignificant, then, the atmosphere of light may destroy the archetype of light.[40]

When Abbot Suger consecrated his newly constructed east end of the church of Saint Denis in Paris, he was introducing to the world one of the earliest works of the new Gothic architecture—a mode of design that, over succeeding generations, would impress its viewers with the ever broader expanse of its windows, especially when the glass in them was bright in color. The verses Suger wrote for the occasion celebrated in particular the luminous brilliance of this new work, attached as it still was to a much earlier and previously much darker interior. The light afforded by the new chevet illumined the church as a whole: with the new east end added to what had previously been built, the entire building shone with a new brightness. "For bright is that which is brightly coupled with the bright." The light that Suger speaks of here and elsewhere is not exclusively the light that comes through windows. The metalwork of the west doors, the jeweled ornaments of the altar, indeed in principle anything that reflected light and called attention to the divine source of all light was itself a "light" and an apt subject for admiring meditation. Erwin Panofsky has suggested that what lay behind this fascination for Suger was the theology of the Christian Neoplatonist Dionysius the Areopagite, long identified with Saint Denis the missionary to France. And in the theology of Dionysius, any object at all, not only glass and gems but a piece of stone or of wood, can serve as a light that transmits the light of God to beholders, enlightening them by leading them beyond itself to the higher source of all light. Whether Suger's theology was specifically Dionysian remains a debated question, but in any case Neoplatonic light symbolism opens a strikingly evocative way to articulate the experience of luminosity made possible by the increasingly tall and wide windows that the pointed Gothic arch allowed.[41]

Within decades of Saint Denis, church-builders throughout western and central Europe were captivated by the new technology and the aesthetic that accompanied it. One enthusiast writing in the mid–twentieth century contrasted the "dark world of outer barbarism" found in pre-Gothic architecture with the "bright and open world" that followed in succeeding generations as more and more light flooded the churches, the "surest index of the movement of the times." By the thirteenth century, a building such as the Sainte-Chapelle in Paris showed how sacred space could be marked by a richness of colored light, in which reds and blues mingled and the proportions shifted as the direction of sunlight altered through the day, so that the worshiper might seem to be praising God from within a kaleidoscope.[42] Like other "glass houses" of similar design, Sainte-Chapelle was meant to house a relic, and the building itself was in effect a grand multicolored reliquary.[43] The effect changed as the windows grew larger and the preference was for white or lighter colors.

Partisans of brightness will sneer at those brooding Romanesque churches where the "sombre gloom of cave-dwelling and cave-worship" lingers, and where "midnight must have reigned at noon."[44] They will wag their fingers at those Spanish architects who learned from their French colleagues how to construct properly luminous Gothic churches but then, when the French had packed their bags and left, blocked up the clerestory windows, preferring "a religious but Romanesque gloom."[45] But the brightness of Gothic churches should not be exaggerated. The immediate impression on entering the cathedral of Chartres is one of sudden darkness, until one's eyes adjust to the dark and the light from the windows comes fully into play, and then it is not darkness but color that claims attention. If the medieval glass were restored to Gothic churches in which it has been sacrificed to war or to iconoclasm, in place of the plain modern glass that has often replaced the loss, these would appear far dimmer than they now do but a great deal more colorful. Indeed, if all the medieval colors were restored to many Gothic churches—the wall paintings, the polychrome on wooden furnishings—they would afford a variegated display of color upon color rather than a wash of pure luminosity. At Matisse's chapel in Vence the simple color combinations in the windows play conspicuously on the white walls, but when the colors are more diffuse and the walls are darker the effect is subtler.

Whether a church presents itself as a chamber of light or a chamber of shadows, it is in any case a chamber, an enclosed space, and this seemingly obvious fact bears reflection. Both light and darkness could just as well be experienced outdoors. The demarcation of fixed space has the obvious advantage of giving shelter from the elements, more important perhaps in some climates than in others, but it furthermore gives concrete and particular form to the interplay of light and darkness. The way the sunlight enters through a series of windows, and the way the arcades or other features produce a play of shadows—these factors, specific to a given building, serve as reminders that the universal is always experienced within the particular. Grace is never simply grace in general; it is mediated by particular individuals, circumstances, and experiences. The holy is rarely experienced directly; it too is mediated by sacred forms. Within a church, darkness and light are perceived not simply as conditions of nature but as natural phenomena mediated by human constructs and constructions, not merely symbolizing but concretely exemplifying the capacity of culture to give specific form and manifestation to nature, the capacity of particular sacred forms to manifest the holy.[46]

If height evokes aspiration, and light mystery, the live acoustics of a highly reverberant church can be the most important element in creating a sense of timelessness.[47] The acoustical qualities of a space can be sensed even from the sound of footsteps, but they are more fully revealed by music, the role of which is profoundly important to a classic sacramental church. Music transforms ordinary action into ritual action. People may move from one end of the church to another without doing so in procession; one of the ways simple passage is transformed into procession is by musical accompaniment.[48] The traditional design of a major church in this tradition—with its high ceiling, its multiplicity of aisles and other subsidiary spaces making for a proliferation of parallel and perpendicular surfaces to reflect sound, and its avoidance of soft surfaces to absorb sound waves—creates what one thinks of as a "churchly sound," or perhaps rather a "cathedral sound," with a long reverberation time, or the suspension of sound in the building after it has been sung or played. Even a relatively confined space with a complex vaulted ceiling can produce a richer than usual tone, as one can easily show by chanting in, say, a vaulted chapter house: the sound returns quickly but is reflected off multiple surfaces, at varying angles, and thus at different intervals. When the space is larger, the reverberation time is longer and the sound is all the richer.

Live or highly reverberant acoustics can have multiple effects. Practically, the reverberation can make it easier for individuals to hear each other and thus reinforce a sense of community in the worshiping assembly. Children from one confirmation class, taken to a massive Gothic revival church, responded with astonishment when their own voices filled the space and "sounded like community."[49] A live acoustic contributes toward a sense of energy. It calls attention to the connectedness of liturgical action and liturgical environment: it makes more clearly noticeable the effect of environment on sound. The building itself is clearly experienced as participating in the creation of a distinctive sound, one not often experienced in secular environments, and is thus easier to identify as sacred; the building is perceived as a kind of extended organ for the production of sacred sound. The sense of sound lingering in the air is evocative of a spiritual presence, the presence of the numinous, or perhaps of past generations that have worshiped in this space. A relatively long reverberation time is particularly appropriate for chant, in which there is no counterpoint to be muddled: it enhances the fluidity, the spontaneity, and the rhythmic unpredictability of sound, in a manner associated mostly but not exclusively with chant.[50] But for a classic sacramental church the most important symbolic function of live acoustics is the evocation of timelessness, the creation of echoes that sustain each note beyond the measured time in which it is sounded, the overlapping of moments in music that suggests a release from the linearity of time.

Ninian Comper's formulation captures something of this ideal: "The note of a church should be, not that of novelty, but of eternity. Like the Liturgy celebrated within it, the measure of its greatness will be the measure in which it succeeds in eliminating time and producing the atmosphere of the heavenly worship."[51] And yet the term "timeless" can be misleading, suggesting a disregard for history and human experience, a flight into detachment; it might be more accurate to speak of freedom from linear and particular time, from fixity to present experience, or to emphasize the perduring presence of each moment within time.[52]

Factors other than height, light, and acoustics are, of course, relevant to a church's aesthetic impact. The materials used are obviously of crucial importance: the subtle texture of most stone provides more warmth than concrete, and generally wears more gracefully;[53] brick and wood can both contribute to an atmosphere of graceful simplicity. Juxtaposition of colors is just as strong a factor: at All Saints, Margaret Street, in London, the colors are so varied and so lavish that the ensemble as such becomes a feast for beholding and a setting for high celebration even before particular details are singled out for examination.[54] The complexity of the interior is crucial for creating an alluring sense that there is always something further than what is immediately seen: that chancel, transepts, and perhaps tower open out into spaces present and partly visible but extending beyond one's view. From the nave of a church such as York Minster one can see that the tower opens vertically and that light from that opening falls onto the crossing, that the transepts open horizontally, that the nave aisles lead into the aisled chancel lying beyond the pulpitum, in short that in each of several directions there lies something more than what is directly at hand. This intimation can itself be a sign of transcendence, of a presence not limited to the immediately present. Further, sheer multiplicity of forms—whether structural or decorative, representational or abstract—affects the quality of the interior, and the classic sacramental tradition more than alternative traditions favors a profusion of forms. (A church marked by pure and stark simplicity can evoke a spirit of simple and collected meditation—but a church filled with a plenitude of forms fusing into a single whole can also elicit this simple response, more readily than one that compromises and calls attention to one discrete image and then another.) Articulating what many viewers have no doubt sensed, Dennis McNally has argued that profusion is a desirable quality in church design, "an expression in material form of the infinity of things," involving repetition of architectural or decorative forms to communicate a sense of infinity, presumably the infinite variety of the created order seen as exemplary of the divine creation.[55] One might further take the profusion of forms in a classic sacramental church as corresponding to the profusion and repetition of classical liturgical language, which, as in many of the Psalms, establishes a tone of earnestness and urgency.

In general, careful plotting of transitions is essential to church design, and a subject of careful study particularly in the classic sacramental tradition. What has been said of the Norwegian stave churches might be said of many others as well, that their genius lies not in one quality or another but in the transitions, the movement from profane to sacred, from lowness to towering height, "from the concrete and present to the exalted and distant," and from light to darkness, but then to a different experience of light: "after a time the forms, ornamentation, liturgical objects become apparent through the darkness of the interior."[56] This emphasis on transitions was important to Rudolph Otto, who found the numinous not simply in darkness, silence, and emptiness but in the contrast between these qualities and their opposites. "The darkness must be such as is enhanced and made all the more perceptible by contrast with some last vestige of brightness, which it is, as it were, on the point of extinguishing; hence the 'mystical' effect begins with semi-darkness."[57] Building on this perception, one observer emphasizes "the transition of oppositional forces" as critical to the atmosphere of a church. Elements contributing to this atmosphere work not in stasis but through the "spiritual energy" engendered by dynamic tension of "light becoming darkness, or noise dimming to silence, or profusion becoming emptiness, or monumentality becoming humility."[58]

But is all this evocation of aspiration, mystery, and timelessness, all this plotting of transitions and of alluring spaces just out of sight, ultimately artificial and illusionist? Is the manipulation of aesthetic effect a manipulation of the viewer? Oskar Söhngen proposes that the attempt to create a sacred effect with the artificial means of stimulus-psychology will result in a pseudosacrality at best.[59] Karla Kowalski and Michael Szyszkowitz specialize in using what they refer to as "the tricks of our job" to create an atmosphere that has been called magical, sometimes sinister, rich in dramatic diagonal lines and "skyward shooting glazing," meant "to produce psychological effects and provoke ideas," as in their church at Graz-Ragnity, for which Söhngen would presumably have little patience.[60] Again, in churches such as Eliel Saarinen's or Edward Dart's,[61] an atmosphere of mystery is accomplished through indirect natural or artificial light from concealed sources. Even apart from special cases of this sort, is any evocation of aspiration, mystery, and timelessness a kind of architectural priestcraft meant to suggest the presence of something that is not in fact there?

Edward Sövik writes disparagingly of churches that make a display of the mysterious with their indirect lighting and their illusionist effects. Whereas true mystery entails unresolvable wonder, the mysterious can be resolved, like a detective story: the source of indirect light can be discovered. "The expression of the mysterious depends upon artifice, the expression of the mystery upon art."[62] This way of phrasing the matter serves to sharpen the debate, but it assumes that the use of devices such as indirect lighting is meant as a sort of puzzle (as if viewers are meant to scratch their heads and wonder where the light is coming from, until they discover the hidden window) and that true mystery cannot validly be symbolized by a device that is not itself true mystery. The source of light is known but not seen. While knowing that grace comes from God, one may not reflect consciously on the divine source until it is called to one's attention. Indirect light also evokes reflection on inwardness and outwardness: entering a church is an occasion for turning inward in prayer, but with the achievements and concerns of the outer world still present, even if subtly and indirectly. More generally, subdued and indirect lighting sets a mood of reflective calmness.

If the objection is that the architecture of a classic sacramental church points to a presence that is not there, the worshiper can in the last analysis only respond that the presence suggested *is* there, and that the sacramental evocation of self-transcendence and of divine immanence is anything but an illusion. Within this tradition a church building is perceived as sacramental not only because it shares in some generic beauty but because light, volume, and sound are presented in a way that calls attention to them, suggesting that they are meant to be out of the ordinary, and raising the question what they are meant to signify. That God is both immanent and transcendent, present in and with humankind yet not limited to any particular place, time, or form of presence, is a given in classical theology. To speak of divine transcendence is to characterize God not as remote but as radically unlimited, as bound to no particular place, time, or mode of action. God is immanent to every place and time but limited to none. Human sharing in that quality also means freedom from limitation. And a church, sacramentally understood, suggests a presence not limited to the immediately present. Ritual is traditionally seen as an occasion for making the transcendent God more fully immanent in the community's life, or more properly for making God's presence more fully manifest and efficacious. But worship can also serve as an opportunity for the community to transcend its constricted perceptions and experiences. Liturgy itself thus becomes a point of intersection between descent and ascent, between God's becoming immanent to the assembly and the assembly's aspiration toward contact with God. A church of notable height can be experienced as a sign of humankind aspiring for transcendence of the ordinary and simultaneously as space for a transcendent divinity aspiring to manifestation in the world of human experience. If the pointed arch of the Gothic church expresses transcendence, this is presumably not the transcendence of God but that of the human beholders, the transcending of their ordinary life and consciousness by being (in Needleman's words) "drawn upward within a vast cosmic scale filled with light," in a state of *ekstasis* that does not preclude but rather requires consciousness of divine immanence, of God present and made manifest.

Ultimately each of the chief aesthetic marks of the classic sacramental church must be grasped within a complex relationship between transcendence and immanence. Human aspiration is never independent of divine condescension, and the volume of a classic sacramental church can be seen as expressing both. Mystery is never independent of presence, and the lighting in a classic sacramental church can be taken as a sacrament of holiness or divinity present in human experience, either in clear abundance (as suggested by a bright and open interior) or in suggestive intimations (as symbolized by dim and indirect light that partially relieves the darkness). And timelessness is never simply a flight from time or from ordinary experience but is a manifestation of the holy or the eternal present within the world of human experience.

Case Study: Hagia Sophia as Epitome of Transcendence-in-Immanence

Soon after his deportation from Russia in 1922, Sergei Bulgakov made his way to Constantinople and stood in Hagia Sophia, which served then as a mosque. He was inspired—then terrified—then finally won over by a grand messianic vision of this building as once again a center of the universal Church, as a nexus between earth and heaven. In the wake of his experience he penned an account of the building's impact:

> Yesterday for the first time in my life I had the happiness of seeing Hagia Sophia. God bestowed this favour upon me and has not let me die without a vision of St Sophia, and I thank my God for this. I experienced such heavenly bliss that it submerged—if only for a moment—all my present sorrows and troubles and made them insignificant. . . .
>
> Human tongue cannot express the lightness, the clarity, the simplicity, the wonderful harmony which completely dispels all sense of heaviness—the heaviness of the cupola and the walls. A sea of light pours from above and dominates all this space, enclosed and yet free. The grace of the columns and the beauty of their marble lace, the royal dignity—not luxury, but regality—of the golden walls and the marvellous ornamentation: it captivates and melts the heart, subdues and convinces. It creates a sense of inner transparency; the weightiness and limitations of the small and suffering self disappear; the self is gone, the soul is healed of it, losing itself in these arches

and merging into them. It becomes the world: I am in the world
and the world is in me. And this sense of the weight of one's heart
melting away, of liberation from the pull of gravity, of being like a
bird in the blue of the sky, gives one not happiness nor even joy, but
bliss. It is the bliss of some final knowledge of the all in all and of
all in oneself, of infinite fullness in multiplicity, of the world in
unity.[63]

Bulgakov's encomium for Hagia Sophia stands within a tradition of *ek-phraseis*, or rhetorically polished descriptions of churches, extending back to Eusebius's fourth-century ekphrasis of the church at Tyre. A classical ekphrasis of a building or any artwork was meant to convey a vivid sense that the object was present before the reader's eyes. With subtly crafted loose ends, the ekphrasis suggested the many possible perspectives for viewing. With awestruck accounts of the building's construction, it reinforced the sense that the work was a marvel to behold.[64] An ekphrasis might be embedded in a chronicle or even a homily. One of the most eloquent specimens of the genre is found in a homily by the ninth-century patriarch Photios that speaks of entry into a church as something like unexpected passage through a hidden door into an enchanted kingdom:

when, having torn oneself away from the atrium, one looks into the
church itself, with how much joy and trembling and astonishment
is one filled! It is as if one were stepping into heaven itself with no
one standing in the way at any point; one is illuminated and struck
by the various beauties that shine forth like stars all around. Then
everything else seems to be in ecstasy and the church itself seems to
whirl around; for the viewer, with his twistings and turnings in every-
direction and his constant movements that the variety of the spectacle imposes on him, imagines that his personal experience is transferred to the church.[65]

The earliest ekphraseis for Hagia Sophia are by two courtiers who served under the Justinian, the emperor of the early sixth century for whom the church was built. The historian Procopius, who wrote *On the Buildings* honoring Justinian's architectural accomplishments, said of Hagia Sophia that "the visitor's mind is lifted up to God and floats aloft, thinking that He cannot be far away, but must love to dwell in this place which He himself has chosen." Paul the Silentiary, the second of these courtiers, composed a lengthy poem in Homeric verse describing Hagia Sophia in enthusiastic detail.[66] Another famous account, if not exactly a full-fledged ekphrasis, is given in the tenth-century *Russian Primary Chronicle*: envoys sent out by Prince Vladimir of Kiev went to Constantinople and reported back to the prince in breathless terms about their experience of liturgy in Hagia Sophia: "We know only that God dwells there among men."[67] In the twelfth century the deacon Michael of Thessalonica wrote an ekphrasis noteworthy mostly for its cosmological interpretation: the hemisphere of the dome, combined with the quadrispheres of the semidomes to the east and west, add up to a sphere, which represents the outer heaven, while elsewhere Michael finds enough further components to serve for the inner or visible heaven.[68] A century or so after the conquest of Constantinople by the Turks in 1453, when Hagia Sophia had been made a mosque, Evliyá Efendí (or Çelebi) continued the series of encomia in his travel writings, declaring that "this mosque, which has no equal on earth, can only be compared to the tabernacle of the seventh heaven, and its dome to the cupola of the ninth. All these who see it, remain lost in astonishment on contemplating its beauties; it is the place where heavenly inspiration descends into the minds of the devout, and which gives a foretaste even here below of the garden of Eden."[69]

These accounts reveal subtle but important shifts in perspective. While Bulgakov's poetic prose meditation tells how the building overwhelms the beholder and dissolves the ego, wrenching the soul out of its ordinary consciousness, the Russian envoys were overwhelmed rather with a sense of the divine presence, and Procopius captured the sense of a dialectic in which the mind is raised aloft to a God who comes down to this place on earth. Yet, most important, the two sides of this dialectic are finally inseparable, because consciousness of divine immanence is the transformation that releases mind and soul from ordinariness.

Even the longest of the ekphraseis break down in exclamations of the church's indescribability. Transferring the conventions of apophatic theology to architecture, Paul the Silentiary and especially Procopius are fond of exclaiming how the church surpasses description and even belief. The building as a whole "is distinguished by indescribable beauty," and to those who hear of it the account is incredible. The gold, silver, and gems cannot possibly be described. The ciborium is "a tower indescribable." No words can convey the effect of the nighttime illumination. "Seeing the art which appears everywhere, men contract their eyebrows as they look at each part, and are unable to comprehend such workmanship, but always depart thence, stupefied, through their incapacity." If the church and its features transcend both comprehension and expression, the holiest of these features, the altar, is so holy that even to tell what could be told of it is to transgress. Paul begins to tell how the golden mensa stands on golden legs and foundations, all aglitter with a variety of stones. But he catches himself disclosing the undisclosable, and cries out, "Whither am I carried? whither tends my unbridled speech? Let my voice be silent, and not lay bare what is not meet for the eyes of the people to see."

Echoing the Psalmist's praise of Solomon's Temple, Paul says that anyone who sets foot in this temple would gladly live there forever, "and his eyes well with tears of joy." Procopius remarks: "The entire ceiling is covered with pure gold, which adds to its glory, though the reflections of the gold upon the marble surpass it in beauty." But both emphasize the sheer luminosity of the building, by day and night. Procopius says, "The church is singularly full of light and sunshine; you would declare that the place is not lighted by the sun from without, but that the rays are produced within itself, such an abundance of light is poured into this church." To which Paul the Silentiary adds: "through the spaces of the great church come rays of light, expelling clouds of care, and filling the mind with joy." So brilliant is the artificial lighting that "the night seems to flout the light of day, and be itself as rosy as the dawn." Whoever sees the illumination of the church "feels his heart warmed with joy," while the sight of some other feature causes all care to vanish.

More than one writer has seen the architects' goal at Hagia Sophia as dematerializing the structure, giving it the appearance of an ethereal and weightless beauty. Thus, the dome appeared to be suspended by a chain from heaven (as Procopius says) rather than supported structurally from below, because the church was meant to convey a sense of immaterial splendor, and the solidity of its structural members was understated. The vaults were covered with literally acres of gold mosaic, to the floors and walls they added colored marble, and even the piers were highly embellished, to conceal weight-bearing structures and hard surfaces beneath a dazzling filligree.[70]

Yet Paul the Silentiary describes the church not so much in ethereal as in naturalistic terms, as a place where the beauties of the natural world are gathered and exhibited. He does not single out the geometry of the building, which elsewhere is cause for particular amazement. Nor does he highlight the symbolic significance of the figurative art, which he mentions only on occasion. He does not even dwell on the liturgical use of the building. No doubt his ultimate purpose is to suggest the spiritual meaning of the church, but what he cannot keep from praising is the capacity of the building to suggest the world beyond its walls, not in the first instance as a paean to the Creator but as a display of the concrete magnificence of stones and metals that seem naturalistic replicas of the natural order. Procopius too, commenting on the marble, exclaimed: "One would think that one had come upon a meadow full of flowers in bloom!" But the theme is far more fully developed in Paul's Homeric verse. The church calls to mind "flower-bordered streams of Thessaly, and budding corn, and woods thick with trees; leaping flocks too and twining olive-trees, and the vine with green tendrils, or the deep blue peace of summer sea, broken by the plashing oars of spray-girt ship." This is not an account of mosaics or paintings but of the patterns to be seen in the marble, which he refers to elsewhere as "marble pastures." He does admire the naturalism of carvings on capitals and elsewhere, but the naturalism spills over to features where it might not be expected. The lights at nighttime could make viewers suppose they were beholding the constellations. And an entire lengthy section of the poem describes the ambo in minute detail, beginning with the conceit that this item of furniture, positioned in the midst of the church, is a magnificent island buffeted by waves of faithful worshipers.

> And as an island rises amidst the swelling billows, bright with pat-
> terns of cornfields, and vineyards, and blossoming meadows, and
> wooded heights, while sailors, as they steer by it, are gladdened, and
> the troubles and anxieties of the sea are beguiled; so in the middle
> space of the boundless temple rises upright the tower-like ambo of
> stone, with its marble pastures like meadows, cunningly wrought
> with the beauty of the craftsman's art.

He immediately pauses to reflect that the solea or walkway connecting the ambo to the sanctuary makes it not an island but a peninsula, yet the analogy with its extraordinary naturalism remains essentially intact. He tells how sailors at night are guided by light from inside the church, which inspires him to remark that the building "also shows the way to the living God." But this touch of anagogy is more the exception than the norm in a poet who delights most evidently in the effect of surfaces on the senses and the imagination. Paul's naturalism is punctuated by flights of personification in which the natural world offers up its riches to adorn the church. The Lybian sun nurtures the glittering golden stone found "in the deep-bosomed clefts of the hills of the Moors." The hills of Proconnesus have "bent their backs to necessity" and provided marble for the floors. Pangaeus and Sunium, too, have "opened all their silver veins." Where one might expect to find creation paying homage to its Creator, we find instead images of a purely natural order manifesting a gracious generosity.

It is Procopius who gives the fuller statement on the anagogic function of the church, but even here the emphasis is not so much on transport to an ethereal realm as on the beauty of the created and built environment in which God delights to partake:

> Whoever enters there to worship perceives at once that it is not by
> any human strength or skill, but by the favour of God, that this
> work has been perfected; the mind rises sublime to commune with
> God, feeling that He cannot be far off, but must especially love to
> dwell in the place which He has chosen; and this is felt not only
> when a man sees it for the first time, but it always makes the same
> impression upon him, as though he had never beheld it before. No
> one ever became weary of this spectacle, but those who are in the
> church delight in what they see, and, when they leave, magnify it in
> their talk.

The wording here suggests, perhaps, that if Paradise is meant as prototype for Hagia Sophia it may indeed be the celestial Paradise, but, just as important, it is the earthly one where God came down and walked in verdant meadows among his creatures. The uplifting of mind and soul is inspired by the indwelling of a God who delights in beauty on earth and calls worshipers to share that delight.[71]

For those who think of churches as places meant to emphasize the transcendence of God, these accounts of Hagia Sophia make a vitally important point: precisely the church that might have been thought most deeply imbued with a sense of transcendence was in fact conceived in subtler terms. The interplay of human self-transcendence and divine immanence—the presence of God here below, in a church whose beauties very much reflected those of the material order—was of fundamental importance to the earliest encomiasts.

A Church as a Dignified Setting for Edification

Protestant statements on church architecture often betray a degree of ambivalence regarding the notion of churches as houses of God or as holy places. Thus, the Second Helvetic Confession of 1566 says that God does not dwell in temples made by human hands, yet spaces dedicated to God and to God's worship are not secular but sacred (*non profana sed sacra*), so that those present must act reverently, being "in a holy place, before the sight of God and his holy angels."[72] In general, Protestant traditions tend to be more cautious about such language than Eastern Orthodox or Roman Catholic sources.

James White has observed that "Protestants expect to be edified in worship, Catholics to be sanctified,"[73] and the emphasis on edification is fundamental to the classic evangelical tradition in church-building. In some cases, such as the Unitarian Church built at Baltimore in 1817, the influence of the Enlightenment is manifested in "the austere beauty of pure geometrical forms," in simple cubes or cylinders, alluding to the divinely created order in nature.[74] Perhaps more often, church-builders in this tradition will incorporate stylistic and symbolic vocabulary familiar in the classic sacramental tradition (steeples, Gothic arches, and the like), but even when they do so the building up of faith and the cultivation of a proper response to grace—in short, edification—remains the central concern.

When Paul Tillich reflected on the character of specifically Protestant churches, he began disarmingly by noting: "the great periods of Christian art and architecture from which we draw our tradition have been, without exception, the great periods of Roman Catholic art and architecture." And to the extent that Protestant architecture has been willing to borrow from the aesthetic vocabulary of Catholic design, even while interpreting this design differently and adhering to it with less ideological conviction, Tillich is surely right. Nonetheless, he proceeded to set out at least fundamental principles to govern the design of a Protestant church: Protestantism being "a religion of the ear and not of the eye," the word should dominate over the sacrament and the congregation over the liturgical leader.[75]

The Dutch architect Karel L. Sijmons attempted in 1946 to define the proper atmosphere for Protestant church architecture.[76] Just as the paintings of Vermeer and other old masters cultivate an atmosphere of inwardness, of spiritual concentration, of stillness, so too the monuments of Dutch Protestant architecture are marked by "the same devout stillness," a stillness in which everything is bound together in perfect harmony. The purpose of a Protestant church is to bring the individual directly before God, and the atmosphere of stillness within a church is meant for that end. While Sijmons admits that atmosphere does not lend itself to tidy formulas, he finds it manifested chiefly in the qualities of color and form. He grants the aptness of Oswald Spengler's notion "Protestant brown," which works in combination with white, and a range of grays and ochers in between.[77] The brown color comes largely from the wooden furnishings that play so prominent a role in setting tone. The white comes largely from the painted plaster, and Sijmons emphasizes that white by itself, however widely it is taken as a symbol of Calvinist puritanism, is a noncolor that functions properly only in conjunction with color. Still, the churches in which he finds the proper atmosphere have a great deal of white, and he had little sympathy for the practice of scraping plaster from church walls and piers to expose the natural stone. "Protestantism is spiritual," Sijmons declared, and plaster dematerializes the stone walls, making the interior properly spiritual. Alongside color, form is a prime determinant of atmosphere, and the goal is harmony, balance, monumentality. Light too plays a role, and here Sijmons is at one with Ninian Comper in seeking neither the "mystical half-light" of Roman Catholic churches nor the brightness of daylight found in secular assembly halls but rather the same balanced evenness that in color and form produces an atmosphere of inwardness and calm.

A classic evangelical church may sometimes borrow its most basic aesthetic vocabulary—its forms of height, light, and sound—from the classic sacramental tradition, even if with suggestions of ambivalence.[78] Penuel Bowen, a Congregational minister in South Carolina, confessed in 1786 that the "superb and grand" churches of Charleston appealed to him in ways he evidently found discomfiting: "these things have and always had an agreeable effect on the sensitive, nay the feeling part of Devotion in me. You will lampoon the idea if you please and beat it out of me if you can please." But even when the vocabulary is the same, the classic evangelical tradition tends to interpret it differently.

James White calls attention to the importance of lofty interiors in church architecture and notes that on the question of height there is fair agreement, however divided taste and opinion may be on other points:

Bright or dim light, soothing or brilliant colors, rough or fine tex-
tures, all these and many more find their proponents. Indeed, about
the only real constant seems to be a demand for extra height. With
remarkable unanimity people seem to associate an unusually high
interior with worship and to reject low ceilings or roofs as not conducive to worship.[79]

For another observer "an upward or heavenward tendency" is essential to all
church design and "should impress itself on the visitor the moment he enters
the church, and preferably he should be aware of it even before he enters."[80]
But in the evangelical tradition the effects sought are more psychological than
sacramental: the height of a church is more an aid to edification than a sacrament of the immanent transcendent. Evangelical churches will also make
use of colored glass: Paul Tillich contrasted the rationality of ordinary daylight
with the broken or mystical light filtered through tinted windows, and he saw
the latter as fitting for a sacred building, so long as the colored glass was not
representational.[81] But few theologians in the evangelical tradition would interpret light in terms of a Neoplatonist metaphysic of divine manifestation.

   Classic evangelical churches may make use of indirect lighting and colored
glass, but more in keeping with the quest for edification is clear glass and plain
light, even the sheer luminosity of a modern church such as Bruce Goff's
Crystal Chapel or Phillip Johnson's Crystal Cathedral.[82] The clear windows and
light colors in Boston's Old North Church (1723) have aptly been said to reflect
an Enlightenment demand for clarity,[83] but well before the Enlightenment reformers were covering wall paintings with whitewash, even paintings of biblical
themes, in an effort to create a simpler, more sober environment for edification.
Oskar Söhngen goes so far as to say that the God of Christian faith is no longer
the *Deus absconditus* but the God revealed in Christ, and Protestants are
therefore disinclined toward a mystical half-darkness: indeed, the rediscovery
of the gospel in the Reformation was also, for Söhngen, a victory of bright over
dark within churches.[84]

   It is true, as James White has emphasized, that Protestant churches have
by no means always or straightforwardly exercised the restraint associated with
"plain style."[85] The pulpit at the Nieuwe Kerk in Amsterdam is rich in decorative carvings, depicting the works of charity, the virtues, the evangelists, the
Last Judgment, classicizing fruit and foliage, and putti playing with the carved
simulation of rope. In the same church, the monument to the fallen naval hero
Michiel de Ruyter is rich in classical ornament, and seventeenth-century glass
in the transept windows is rich in civic themes.[86] Paradoxically, the Protestant
furnishings are more ornamented than what remains of the medieval structure, and each item stands out against a relatively restrained background, serving as a focus for instruction, for edification. The effect is *not* that of an en-

semble of ornament blending into a richly articulated edifice and presenting a fully developed and integrated dramatic array.

The acoustical quality of a building is as much an issue in the classic evangelical as in the classic sacramental tradition, but again the goals are different. The live acoustics often found in a classic sacramental church will favor music over spoken word in proportion to the length of the reverberation time. If there is a preference in a classic evangelical church, it is typically for spoken word over music, and a relatively long reverberation time may complicate the articulation of speech—a problem that is alleviated but not entirely solved by sounding boards, by bringing the congregation closer to the preacher, and in a later age by electronic amplification. Before the rise of modern scientific acoustical engineering, the most important single factor in making a classic evangelical church favorable for the spoken word was the simple one of size, and it is no accident that churches in this tradition are generally smaller than those in the classic sacramental mold.

Case Study: Christ Church Lutheran, Minneapolis, and the Aesthetics of Grace

Eliel Saarinen's Christ Church Lutheran in Minneapolis (1950) may at first seem exquisitely simple on both exterior and interior: essentially a plain brick box (fig. 10).[87] A closer look, however, begins to reveal something of the subtlety of the building's design, and study of the plan and its evolution discloses the careful coordination of aesthetic effect with liturgical purpose.

The minimalism of modern design fuses here with a theological emphasis on simplicity. The pastor who recruited Saarinen as architect spoke of a "search for honest building": "Our Gospel is as honest as it is simple, and we felt that the building should express these qualities." The materials used in the interior are all simple, mainly brick and wood, and the colors muted. The starkly simple cross of brushed aluminum stands out on the chancel wall. But here, as anywhere else, the intent must be judged in terms of the building's intended use, and at least part of the purpose of the subdued liturgical environment was to allow the rich colors of the vestments and altar cloths to stand out more sharply in contrast. Having decided that only modern architectural idiom could support the project of making the Christian message relevant to his day, the pastor nonetheless emphasized that while the superstructure is contemporary, the plan is traditional. "Church design," he said, "must always have very firm roots in the past; otherwise it is merely an aberration."[88]

The subtlety of the lighting quickly becomes clear. The white brick wall of the chancel is flooded with light from a window on its south side that extends from floor to ceiling, but the source is concealed by a wooden screen. The only other sources of natural light are windows in the aisles; the nave itself is with-

FIGURE 10. Christ Church Lutheran, Minneapolis, interior. Photograph by Richard Kieckhefer.

out windows. Yet the interior walls are light enough in color that that the illumination reflected from the chancel gives a soft light even to the upper walls of the nave.

Indirect lighting of this sort can suggest a sense of inwardness, an invitation to meditation. Five years before designing Christ Church, Saarinen had been engaged for a chapel at a college in Missouri, and the president of that institution had asked for a building with mysterious lighting, descending from above, so that the students could find "a quiet and private moment of spiritual comfort," and the world outside would seem remote. "Even if the chapel were full, each occupant should feel alone."[89] This building was never executed, but some features of the design are found at Christ Church, where the indirect and subdued lighting could be experienced as inducing a similarly contemplative frame of mind.

In its early years Christ Church was celebrated particularly for its exceptional acoustics, which provided for clarity of music and effective projection of even the unamplified spoken word. What appears at first sight a rectangular box is in fact subtly slanted to avoid the parallel surfaces that would otherwise create acoustical flutter. The north wall of the church splays outward from the chancel to the rear end of the church, and the roof is canted. Acoustical tile on the ceiling is supplemented by a rippled acoustical wall, in which more sound-absorbing material is covered by bricks laid in an open-jointed pattern.[90]

According to an often quoted report, an unbeliever who visited this church soon after its completion exclaimed, "I am not a Christian. But if I have ever felt like getting down on my knees, it has been here." One is reminded of J. L. Pearson's declaration that his business was "to think what will bring people soonest to their knees."[91] But then Pearson worked within the established forms of Gothic revival, whose vocabulary anyone would have recognized as whispering a summons to reverence. Saarinen's accomplishment was to achieve a similar effect without the conventions of recognized sacred architecture, engendering a spirit of reverence with what might have seemed—and in the hands of another architect might well have been—the desacralized vocabulary of a modern aesthetic.

A Church as a Hospitable Setting for Celebration

From the 1960s onward, what I am calling the modern communal tradition in church design opted for a break with the emphasis on aspiration, mystery, and timelessness—a break more radical than that of the classic evangelical tradition. One of the early voices for this movement, the Belgian Roman Catholic writer Frédéric Debuyst, was content to view a church as a sort of living-room for celebration marked by aesthetic exaltation and graciousness, which raised questions about the tone or atmosphere wanted in a church. For him the ideal was an atmosphere of hospitality, of invitation to a celebration, and everything in the church—its proportions, the arrangement of its furnishings, and its decorations—is designed with this hospitality and this celebration in mind.[92] He would have been pleased at the account of a Presbyterian church in Oregon designed to "produce an intimate and inviting atmosphere," suggesting "a small friendly church where people know one another, and work together to do God's will," or by the suggestion that a simple, friendly, informal worship space "helps to create an atmosphere of directness and honesty" or that a multicolored curtain fosters an atmosphere of "well-mannered gaiety."[93] Debuyst justified using art in a place of worship by citing its ability to enhance an air of hospitality, to create "an atmosphere favouring a calm, recollected and transparent celebration."[94]

The quest for greater lay participation accords with an emphasis on hospitality, graciousness, and even comfort: "liturgy flourishes in a climate of hospitality: a situation in which people are comfortable with one another."[95] The handshake of peace is now taken for granted in many churches. Coffee hour and other activities after worship claim much attention. When the architecture is meant to generate a sense of hospitality and comfort, this can mean an ambiance of domesticity. "The feeling is comfortable and warm. . . . Welcome to the ultimate, intimate, 'user friendly' church of the nineties."[96] Those who prefer a more intimate worship environment may find a larger structure over-whelming. Artistic embellishment of a church may seem to make it all the more grand, imposing, and thus uninviting. Informality and comfort are widely prized in our age, while formality is seen as artificial and sterile. We have reversed the values of nineteenth-century society, which might see an element of formality as a sign of careful attentiveness and concern.

In his survey of recent church-building, Debuyst distinguished between the "analytic" churches from the first half of the twentieth century and the "organic" ones built after 1950. The analytical style assumes an abstract con-ception of architecture as of humanity, remains independent of particular lo-cale, makes rational use of materials, remains simple in line and in volume, and in particular displays "an accent on pure, universal proportions." The or-ganic style, by contrast, expresses a more organic and totalizing view of hu-mankind, and its churches are often lyrical, making use of folded planes and curves, so that "walls, ceilings, floors, become part of each other," and "conti-nuity is everywhere." The goal for Debuyst is a synthesis of the extremes, a form of church design "which is neither purely organic, nor really analytic, but which tries to find its way between those two extremes, and to combine, as coherently as possible, the analytic and the organic vision."[97] But this urge for synthesis is subordinate in his work to the dominant theme of hospitality.

Edward Sövik began designing churches and formulating his theory of church design before reading Debuyst, but on discovering the Belgian's work was delighted to find a kindred soul. For American reflection on the aesthetic of the modern communal church, Sövik is the obvious starting point. And one of the most curiously important articles on liturgy and liturgical architecture from the 1960s was a contribution of his with the title "Tea and Sincerity."[98] In 1965 Sövik visited Japan, where he found the tea house a useful model of a structure combining the domestic with the spiritual. The tea house helped Sövik in his effort to crystalize an explicit aesthetic for the modern communal church. In the tea ceremony, he noted, the host invites four or so guests for the drinking of tea. "But the tea and the ritual which surrounds its preparation and distribution is the hinge on which turns a most serious human interaction, the establishment of community, the sharing of minds and feelings, and the reflective response to the mystery of beauty." The tea house is modest, usually about a hundred square feet. The host places a flower arrangement or some other object of beauty in an alcove, but it is the gathering of people and not this object that is the focus of attention. A garden path leads to the entrance porch; passage along this path is deemed important to the ceremony. The building is made of bamboo and other ordinary materials to convey an air of what one authority has called "refined poverty," but the artistry and craftsman-ship are of the highest quality. "I have wondered whether there is a better symbol of incarnation and redemption than this—that one cherishes the earthy and natural things enough to invest to the limit in them and thus to transform them into something superlative, without ever changing them into something synthetic or exotic." While a Japanese shrine or temple is axially symmetrical, a tea house is asymmetrical, combining a sense of both tension and serenity. "This asymmetric composition has nothing of chaos; it is simply a different kind of order from the stable classic and geometric."

Sövik suggested that the Last Supper had "at least as much in common with the tea ceremony as with the twentieth century Christian Eucharist or communion service," with flexibility of ritual, direct and unceremonious participation of the disciples, and intense discussion of immediately present and future events. "The skeleton of form was not inhibiting but apparently catalytic as in the tea ceremony." And Christian liturgy, which may often be quite different, might well follow this model. While taking the tea ceremony, then, as a paradigm of worship, Sövik also recommends many of the qualities of the tea house as appropriate to Christian architecture: not the sense of fragility, perhaps, but the humble earthiness, the asymmetry, the clarity and refinement.

Height, lighting, and acoustics are thus all adjusted to meet the demands of the modern communal church. The ceiling is flat and relatively low. The lighting does not call attention to itself as in a classic sacramental church. And ideally the acoustics are suited to congregational participation. One recent writer notes that discussion of church acoustics tends to focus on the requirements of the organ, the choir, and the spoken word, with no mention whatever of what the congregation needs to support its singing.[99] The acoustics of congregational singing are complicated by factors that rarely come to mind: untrained singers tend to project their voices downward rather than out, they sing directly into the sound-absorbing clothes of those in front of them, they hear other voices at very close range that does not allow the efflorescence of sound, and they hear music from other people standing on the same level without the acoustical advantage of differential height, and thus they perceive the music they and fellow worshipers produce as dry in contrast to the choir's singing.[100] The ideal modern communal church would be one that takes these factors into account to maximize the conditions for group involvement. To approach the matter schematically, we could say that a classic sacramental church tends to be most effective for choral singing with or without organ accompaniment, that a classic evangelical church is designed acoustically for the spoken word, and that a modern communal church places choir and congregation close enough that the choir has no acoustical advantage over the congregation.

The modern communal church shows a straightforward correspondence between theory and practice, making it less necessary to clarify or to test the theory in the light of a case study. Instead, we may turn to further dimensions of church aesthetics: the effect of articulation and the relationship between a church and the natural environment.

Case Study: Julia Morgan and the Aesthetics of Articulation

The concept of architectural articulation plays a central role in the reflections of Christian Norberg-Schulz, who defines articulation basically as the expression of a form's structural skeleton.[101] The rhythmic succession of a church's bays, columns, buttresses, pilaster strips, blind arcades, or roof beams, is not fundamentally decorative, but neither is it exclusively structural. Rather, structural elements are presented in a way that contributes to the aesthetic effect of the building. Supports are laid open to view as integral constituents of both structure and form. Elements that might be taken as ornamental articulate the way the building is constructed. They may actually be exposed structural members, or (in cases such as pilaster strips or blind arcades) they allude to other structures that have structural importance. They form complexes of elements subordinated one to another. They are repetitive and often redundant. Early Christian architecture was not highly articulated, but over succeeding centuries churches not only became technically more sophisticated but expressed that sophistication more overtly in exposed members. Because most churches are regular in their design, most often rectangular in plan, the structural members exposed along the length of the building will create a rhythmic articulation through their repetition. The psychological effect is to suggest unity within multiplicity by giving a sense of direction; the rhythmic succession of bays, of columns, of buttresses, or of exposed beams leads the eye and in some circumstances directs the body along the length of the building toward a terminus, and in so doing suggests that each of the units along the way is part of a single progression.

Without grandness of scale, without lavish ornament, and without expensive materials, a church can still convey a sense of richness through careful articulation of structure, through the repetitive use of exposed beams and other members to make the building into a unified ensemble of intricately distinguished parts. One example of a church noteworthy for harmonious integration of elements is a church that was built on a tightly restricted budget, Saint John's Presbyterian in Berkeley, designed by Julia Morgan (fig. 11):

> Like the music of Bach, the building reveals a play of repetition and variation. The angles of the roof and bargeboards, the timbers beneath the clerestory windows, and the gable over the main entrance parallel the modified Tudor form of the main church doorway and of the Sunday school roofs and window. The horizontality of the upper cross members of the window frames is carried across the face of church and Sunday school. Verticals also play a role in this harmony: narrow sections of wall punctuate the clerestory windows, which have a modified Gothic form that reinforces the subdued verticality.

FIGURE 11. Saint John's Presbyterian, Berkeley, California, interior. Early photograph, courtesy of the Berkeley Architectural Heritage Association.

> This verticality is continued by the bands of long, narrow windows below. The rich complexity evolving from such simple forms is powerful testimony to the architect's geometric imagination. . . . The ingenious play between the inside and outside and the relation of details to the whole at Saint John's have rarely been equaled in American urban architecture.[102]

The "rich complexity" of this economically constructed church might be taken as a neutral fact but could also be seen as in itself a positive quality—which would be expected more in the classic sacramental tradition than in others.

Morgan has been referred to as "America's greatest woman architect—and probably the world's," the equivalent in architecture of Mary Cassatt in American painting and Edith Wharton in literature. Yet she emulated the anonymity of the medieval builders, avoided publicity, generally did not have her designs published, declined interviews, and had her files burned at the end of her career, all of which had the intended effect of making her less well known.[103] Her mentor and friend Bernard Maybeck sent her to study at the École des Beaux-Arts at Paris at the turn of the twentieth century, and when she returned she was patronized by the Hearsts and other wealthy families in Northern California. Her oeuvre combines two forms of eclecticism, serial and

simultaneous. Like many Roman Catholic architects of her era she could replicate any of various revival styles; three churches of hers done in 1923–24 are
all in "Mediterranean" style, with white walls and red tile roofs, and she designed a Roman Catholic church in a form of Spanish Colonial or "Mission"
style. But if she was capable of moving from one style to another and practicing
each one coherently, her most interesting work shows the simultaneous use
of more than one style. In this she imitated Maybeck, whose work is more
exuberant than hers in its simultaneous eclecticism. For Saint John's Presbyterian at Berkeley she produced a longitudinal design combining Romanesque,
Tudor, and Arts and Crafts elements. Her Chapel of the Chimes combines
Romanesque and Gothic, and when she went to Florence to seek out artwork
for it she located a Della Robbia piece, a Byzantine-style font, and a great deal
else with no concern for stylistic coherence.

Saint John's Presbyterian was the second church Morgan built for the
same congregation, and each time the funding was severely limited, so her
designs were of necessity economical, and "stunningly pure." Each time she
produced a church in the Craftsman style then prevalent in California. The
building erected in 1908 was a simple one of exposed redwood, with no ornament other than lighting fixtures. In 1910, when a larger church was needed,
she built in the less expensive Douglas fir, with a reddish stain on the interior.
A Celtic cross in the window at the east end was the only religious symbolism,
although a cross was later added on the roof. The roof tresses were simplified
by elimination of vertical supports. Wooden chandeliers in the form of wheels
served for lighting. The building has been compared with Maybeck's more
famous First Church of Christ Scientist nearby: "While Maybeck's church reveals his genius for combining disparate styles with an innovative use of modern, industrial materials, Miss Morgan's is a single-minded, straightforward
expression in one material, much like a perfect barn."[104]

Morgan's churches illustrate a principle with broader application: harmony is more interesting and engaging than mere unity. Not all churches are
meant to share this ideal of harmony, and especially those built or modified
over centuries are likely to be marked by other qualities. Mexican cathedrals,
for example, were large and complex structures that did not lend themselves
to "the cohesive coördination dear to the Late Baroque"; instead they remain
"fascinating, if uncoördinated, documents of vital changes of taste over as
many as three centuries."[105] Saint Augustine's at Kilburn in London, designed
by J. L. Pearson, represents an opposite case, celebrated for its harmonious
integration.[106] But this harmony in Pearson's design is a harmony of intricate
articulation: as in many southern French and Spanish churches, internal buttresses divide the aisles into distinct spaces;[107] the gallery and the molding give
horizontal counterthrust to the church's clearly defined verticality; distinct elements of the interior are brought into visual harmony partly through Pearson's use of vaulting, which was not common for parish churches in either

medieval or Victorian design but allows greater coherence of lines and forms throughout the interior; most important, the bays of the chancel are consistent in design with those of the nave, and the chancel is defined chiefly by a rood screen that is open enough to allow clear view from the western to the eastern end of the church.

While Morgan's work comes out of an American version of the Arts and Crafts tradition, at Saint John's Presbyterian it is craft more than art, in the sense of applied decoration, that prevails. The other end of the spectrum is seen in the memorial chapel Mary Watts designed in 1896 at Compton in Surrey for her husband, the painter George Frederick Watts. Almost every square inch of the interior is covered with gesso patterns of Art Nouveau angels and interlace, which Watts herself described modestly as "glorified wall-paper." As the leading commentator on this chapel has noted, architecture can arouse admiration or awe, derision or depression or amusement, but for "straightforward astonishment" one need go no further than Compton.[108]

Case Study: Thorncrown Chapel and the Integration of Structure with Environment

In a survey taken in 1991, the American Institute of Architects designated E. Fay Jones's Thorncrown Chapel (1980) near Eureka Springs, Arkansas, as the best work of American architecture from the decade (fig. 12).[109] One observer has commented eloquently on this building:

> Thorncrown Chapel is elemental—a man-made temple married to the woodland. It rises with the authority of nature in the Arkansas forest from a stone foundation to wood columns and layered branches to folded roof. In plan no more than a single room, in form no more than a gabled shed, the small building draws visitors with the magnetic, irresistible force of truth.[110]

It is a pilgrimage chapel, not mainly (like Notre Dame du Haut at Ronchamp) for a seasonal gathering of pilgrims, but rather for meditation, as "a little chapel . . . to provide wayfarers a place for relaxation," but capable of gathering three hundred for services, and in certain seasons attracting over two thousand visitors daily. One of the defining features of this chapel is its openness to the forest around it. The walls and particularly the roof are elaborate and famously inspiring in their design, but they provide essentially a frame for glass that opens onto the natural environment. The structure delineates in artful outline a space within the natural world, declaring and clarifying its sacrality; the shape of the building acknowledges and honors a sacrality already present in the forest beyond the walls. "The old myth that Gothic vaulting was an imitation of the forest comes to mind," Dell Upton says of Thorncrown, "and the asso-

FIGURE 12. Thorncrown Chapel, Eureka Springs, Arkansas, exterior. Photograph courtesy of The Arkansas Historic Preservation Program.

ciation is strengthened by the immaculately clean, nearly invisible glazed walls that make the roof timbering appear to be part of the natural canopy of trees that envelops the chapel."[111]

Already in 1915 Julia Morgan had provided a glass wall behind the altar for her chapel at Asilomar, so that worshipers could see the pine trees, beach, and ocean.[112] Occasional churches of the 1930s took advantage of their natural setting with broad windows behind the altar affording views of mountain ranges: the Church of the Good Shepherd at Tekapo in New Zealand, where Lake Tekapo and the highest of New Zealand's mountains lie outside,[113] and Saint Philip's in the Hills Episcopal Church at Tucson, which opens onto a desert landscape with mountains in the distance.[114] The Marilyn Moyer Meditation Chapel at Portland, Oregon, is built on a 130-foot cliff, from which it offers a panoramic view of forested mountains.[115] Giovanni Michelucci's church at Longarone has an amphitheater on top from which the congregation can behold nature in a new way: "in the divine presence, after all, nature is God's thought."[116] When a new building was needed in the early 1990s for Metropolitan Community Church in Washington, D.C., the pastor had in mind a dark interior with stained glass and controlled lighting, but the architect, Suzane Reatig, persuaded her client to accept a very different church: a broad expanse of glass opens above a low stone wall, allowing "an atmosphere of lightness, clarity, awareness of the passing sun . . . and of the panorama of sky, clouds, trees, and flying birds in view from every seat."[117] But the classic case of openness to the natural setting is Lloyd Wright's chapel at Palos Verdes, California,[118] a spiritual greenhouse with worship on the inside and a grove of trees beside the Pacific Ocean on the exterior.

Unlike Lloyd Wright's building, Fay Jones's is also a modern adaptation of the Gothic aesthetic. The Gothic element may be clearer in later work by Jones,[119] where the straight roof beams of Thorncrown are replaced with beams bent to form Gothic arches, or the plan is cruciform. More important, Thorncrown Chapel is an experiment in the interaction of form and light. It is not remarkable for its loftiness, standing forty-eight feet tall. But the repetitive complexity of the beams replicates the complexity of a vaulted Gothic church. The emphasis on the roof calls attention not only to the upper portions of the structure but to the interaction between this patterned structure and the sky that serves as its background. And the complexity of the framework combined with the expanse of window space makes for a constantly shifting play of light and shadows that makes emphatically clear the relationship between interior and exterior sacred space.

If any one Gothic building serves as precedent, it is Sainte Chapelle in Paris, the chapel Louis IX built to enshrine the Crown of Thorns—whence the name Thorncrown.[120] Jones refers to the "proportioning" and "ascendancy" of Sainte Chapelle as a source of inspiration, and he uses the tension of interior crossbracing as a reversal of the compression of exterior buttressing used in the Gothic prototype: a system Jones refers to as his "operative opposite." The apparent irony here is that a building so clearly integrated to its environment is held together with an intricate network of internal rather than external members that call attention forcefully to the interior structure. But the irony is only apparent: the complex system of crossbracing creates a highly stylized version within the building of the forest canopy outside, reinforcing rather than undercutting the harmony between structure and environment. And further correspondence to Sainte Chapelle shows even in the integration of structure with environment: the "kaleidoscope of leaves and sky, seen through tall clear walls and overhead skylights, suggest Sainte Chapelle's stained lancet windows," allowing nature itself to provide the color produced elsewhere by art.[121]

Conclusion

If one basic purpose of church design is to call attention to the holy present in the context of sacred space and sacred symbols, there are various ways to achieve this goal. It may seem plausible that the different visions of ecclesial aesthetics are correlated with differing notions of God: that a cathedral of impressive dimensions and design, with intricately articulated space and with a dazzling array of symbolic ornament, will speak of a God known chiefly through works of culture; that a refined and dignified space with white walls and broad uncolored windows suggests a God revealed mainly through the reading and preaching of scripture; that a relatively small and low, comfortably domestic environment invites an awareness of God as present within the gathered assembly; that a yet smaller space, with interior walls of unconcealed brick and with dim and indirect lighting, will serve best as a place for private meditation on an inwardly present God. Yet these are only the most obvious possibilities. There is no reason why the cathedral cannot be a place for meditation or for communal interaction, or why the domestic church cannot be a place for the manifestation of the holy through sacred art.

Much depends on the way the church is used. Even more important is how people are sensitized to perceive it. The way a church is experienced—particularly those factors that make it resonate *as a church*—will always be colored by factors beyond the way it is built. When construction of the building is completed, construction of the church can begin.

4

The Fourth Factor: Symbolic Resonance

Entering into a church is a metaphor for entering into a shared world of symbolic narratives and meanings, somewhat like entering into a story and discovering the richness and internal coherence of its structure. The symbolic associations of a church's structure, furnishings, and decoration evoke a sense of the sacred, as its aesthetic qualities elicit a sense of the holy. Both the holy and the sacred are experienced as inexhaustible, but in opposite ways: the holy in its sheer simplicity, immediately and intuitively grasped; the sacred in the depth and richness of its symbolic resonance, gradually recognized over time.

Symbolic Resonance and the Sacred

The power of any ritual depends in large measure on the richness and depth of the associations it evokes. A baptism can call to mind one's own baptism, other baptisms, the gospel narratives of Christ's baptism in the Jordan, representations of that scene in art, the terror of drowning and the baptismal symbolism of death and rebirth, even the Israelites' passage through the Red Sea taken as a type of baptism (1 Corinthians 10:1–2). A funeral brings to mind the life of the deceased, other funerals one has witnessed, images of death and of life after death, and intimations of one's own mortality. In any ritual, the richness of associations is enhanced through music, through liturgical texts, and through the embellishment of the architectural surroundings.

Three principles govern the resonance of liturgy and its environment: the grounding of worship in memory, the widening of vision in worship, and the engagement of experienced concreteness with historical concreteness.

First, the grounding of worship in memory. Like any culture, liturgical culture rests on memory, on the capacity to relate what is said and done in one's present experience to what has been said and done in a remembered past. The fuller and more vivid the memory, the richer the culture. The numbing of memory, or the failure to discipline memory in ways that most traditional cultures do, makes it harder to understand the associations presupposed in liturgy. The earliest of liturgies, and indeed the New Testament itself, abound in references to earlier material that the reader or hearer is expected to know, and failure to remember and to connect can lead to a loss of resonance, often a loss of meaning. The habit of reading a book, seeing a performance, hearing a poem or a lecture, or attending a liturgical service as a transient event unrelated to other events is a source of impoverished experience, of thin and diminished liturgy.

Second, the widening of vision in worship. Any time a person experiences a church, but especially at moments of special enlivening or vulnerability—times of celebration and mourning, moments of inspiration or of spiritual and emotional dryness—the place itself becomes charged with meaning as the setting for the experience. One may not consciously call it to mind, thinking "This is the place where my first child was baptized, where my aunt's funeral was held, where sunlight flooded the altar last Easter morning, where I once sat for the greater part of an hour trying to pray and suddenly realized that the effort itself was prayer." Even without such a review, the place acquires resonance. Shared experience of a community builds shared resonance. Hearing stories about the experiences another generation of people had in a place extends the resonance yet further. And symbols, if they are effective, are ways of opening the field of resonance indefinitely: they bring past and future into connection with the present, they call to witness members of a far broader community, and they goad people into reflection about sacred narratives, about "things unseen" and their relevance to what is seen, and seen in a particular place. Events that occurred elsewhere, commemorated and celebrated here, come into connection with events that happened here. The role of symbols is to extend associations beyond immediate and directly remembered experience of acts, places, persons, and objects, and thus give present experience deeper resonance.

Third, the engagement of experienced concreteness with historical concreteness. Rudolf Arnheim proposes that successful architecture "rarely limits symbolism to arbitrary convention, but rather seeks to ally it with features of more basic, spontaneous expression." Thus, the perception of morning light shining through sanctuary windows onto an altar "carries with strong immediacy a sense of enlightenment and blessing"—it works as a valid symbol—precisely because morning sunlight falling through windows when shades are raised is spontaneously "received as a gift of life." The interpretation of illumination in specific philosophical terms, including Suger's appeal to Neoplatonic metaphysics, is secondary. "Sensory symbolism reveals the general in the particular and thereby raises the latter to a higher level of relevance." For Arnheim, then, the limitation of a symbol to a particular ecclesiastical meaning is a restriction of its possible meanings. Ideally, the cross might symbolize "the conjunction of opposites, the action of centrifugal or centripetal forces, the spreading of life or fire, crossroads, the relation of vertical striving to horizontal stability, and so on." But within a Christian church a single meaning becomes privileged.[1] No doubt this is all true, but the limitation Arnheim speaks of is also a gain, because it means a movement away from abstraction and toward the vividness of the concrete. The focus in liturgical symbolism is on the connectedness of historical particularity with the particularities of present experience: the relevance of a sacrificial death on a day in ancient Palestine to the concrete particulars of life here and now.

One might expect to find a wealth of imagery and symbolism in a medieval church, where it could function as Gregory the Great supposed it could, as the Bible of the illiterate. But a modern church can equally invite visitors to a higher level of biblical literacy, despite the modernist preference for minimalism of decoration. Thus, Friedrich Zwingmann's Autobahnkirche St. Christophorus at Baden-Baden is a treasure-house of symbols. Meant for passing motorists, it could leave some visitors baffled, but for those who take the trouble to examine the building and the interpretive literature it is a structural catechesis, bearing symbolic meaning even in its form, which evokes the image both of a pyramid and of a tent, the most and the least enduring of structures. Its windows surround the interior with images from the Gospels and the Book of Revelation. The floor plan is based on the upright cross (the "master-cross"); the main structural beams present the diagonal Saint Andrew's cross (the "disciple-cross"). Massive concrete towers outside the building—the Noah tower to the east, the Moses tower to the south, the Elijah tower to the north, the John the Baptist tower to the west—integrate biblical history with contemporary images such as a head on the great Flood Giant in the form an automobile.[2]

For individuals and for communities, liturgy is a means of integration. Liturgical formulas and the environments provided for them can seem to present a jumble of unrelated images and notions: a man hanging on a cross, a woman standing at a table, angels hovering below the ceiling, recollection of friends and family now deceased, decorative trefoils and triangles, intercessions for those sick or traveling, cans of food heaped in boxes, spontaneous exclamations of joy, ritual expressions of grief. Lectures and discussions might trace connections linking all this and more. A network of symbols presupposes their connectedness. Liturgy and liturgical space are effective to the extent that they give scope for experiencing and expressing the connections.

But this way of viewing church architecture lends itself to a telling critique, particularly at times when both art and liturgy move toward minimalism: associations arise either out of personal experience or out of explicit instruction, and when churches are filled with symbols grounded in tradition rather than in the immediate experience of worshipers they give rise either to esotericism or to didacticism. It is all well and good to saturate a church with sacred symbols, but how do they function for a community that has not been told their meanings, and what point is there in constantly having to instruct and remind people about symbols whose meanings are not obvious? In recent time a church or chapel could be praised for being "completely devoid of conventional symbols of creed,"[3] and if symbolism is thought of as inevitably empty, one could see why its absence would be cause for celebration.

The loss of symbolic meaning concerned Paul Tillich, who spoke eloquently on the matter in his writings on church architecture and elsewhere. For Tillich, "much of what previously had symbolic power has become meaningless," including the eastward disposition or orientation of churches, the basic plan of a church, the relationship of altar and chancel, and other matters both basic and minute. In most cases, Tillich continues, an "esoteric and archaic knowledge" of such symbolism cannot now be communicated, and occasional sermons on such matters do not help. "Symbols must be able to attest to themselves, and the one great symbol of the church building is the building itself."[4] The symbols that retain clear meaning are often those asserting ethical values, and these symbols can at times be powerfully conceived. One thinks, perhaps, of Cândido Portinari's murals of Saint Francis of Assisi as the friend of birds, beasts, and children, and of Christ as friend of the sick, the sinners, and the poor, in Oscar Niemeyer's church of São Francisco at Pampulha in Brazil, where the images of the afflicted have something of the tortured quality found in Picasso's *Guernica*, and where one supposes no one could miss the point.[5]

As shared meanings fade, the meanings ascribed to a symbol may well seem arbitrary. The very form of a church may remind some of a ship, others of a bird in flight, or even "a bird sheltering all the various church activities with its wings."[6] Any particular symbol may come to mean anything or nothing. If traditional symbolism often seems to have lost any clear meaning, experiments in new symbolism carry risks of their own: if they seem capricious, they may convey little sense of solidarity with a broader community extended in space and time; if they express transparent and agreeable meanings, they can have the flatness that comes from the avoidance of difficult or problematic meanings. In 1962 Peter Hammond protested the "whimsical symbolism" of churches built "to 'express' this and to 'symbolize' that," an approach that he disdained as having nothing to do with serious architecture: "we have churches which look like hands folded in prayer; churches which symbolize aspiration or the anchor of the industrial pilgrim's life; churches which express the kingship of Christ; churches shaped like fishes, flames, and passion-flowers."[7] Does it help if the images employed are in some Jungian or quasi-Jungian sense archetypal? A chapel in the Orkney Islands designed by William Richard Lethaby, one of the leading proponents of universal symbolism in architecture, uses images of water, sun, moon, and cross.[8] And Imre Makovecz's Lutheran and Catholic churches in Hungary display mythic motifs and forms of animals and birds, trees and plants, drawing on Magyar folk tradition, Scythian antiquity, and Celtic lore, all in an effort "to tap into the underlying spirit of European culture; the 'collective unconscious' described by Jung."[9] Evocations of the cosmos are no doubt fitting in churches; being religious means daring to look at the heart of the universe and call it holy. But little is gained if the archetypes are randomly applied, as if sprinkled from some great archetype-dispenser that gives a bit of "sacred tree" in one place and a touch of "sacred water" in another, without connection either to actual experience or to liturgical use.[10] Frank Lloyd Wright designed the First Unitarian Society of Madison, Wisconsin, with a triangular facade that usually evokes the image of a ship's prow, but for Wright himself the geometrical form was also of fundamental importance: "As the square has always signified integrity and the sphere universality, the triangle stands for aspiration. . . . Here is a church where the whole edifice is in the attitude of prayer." A curious statement; traditionally a triangle has entirely different meaning in Christian symbolism, but for a Unitarian structure that meaning must be set aside and new meaning discovered.[11] Of another church we are told that it "celebrates opposites and expresses their reconciliation": "opposites" such as "brick and glass, light and dark, indoors and outdoors, horizontal and vertical, circle and square, earth and wind, fire and water,"[12] as if the opposition between brick and glass were a matter weighing heavily on people's souls, or the conflict between squares and circles were on the verge of flaring into crisis.

Yet it is probably misleading to take a lachrymose approach to ecclesiological symbolism, pining for some golden day when the meanings of church buildings were clear to all. The assignment of meanings for church buildings and their parts has always been something of an esoteric art. A Syriac text of the sixth century described in highly symbolic terms the cathedral of Edessa in Asia Minor:

> Its ceiling is stretched like the heavens—without columns, vaulted
> and closed—and furthermore, it is adorned with golden mosaic as
> the firmament is with shining stars. Its high dome is comparable to

the heaven of heavens . . . Its great, splendid arches represent the four sides of the world; they also resemble by virtue of their variegated colors, the glorious rainbow of the clouds.[13]

It is difficult to believe that this sort of meaning would have been intuitively clear to clergy and laity alike in the absence of clear markers, such as stars painted on the insides of domes.

Allegorical interpretation of a church building received systematic exposition by the thirteenth-century bishop and theologian William Durandus in his *Rationale divinorum officiorum*,[14] and such interpretation has undergone many revivals over the centuries. Anthony Sparrow's *Rationale upon the Book of Common Prayer of the Church of England* is a seventeenth-century classic of the genre. Following longstanding tradition, Sparrow takes the nave (from the Latin *navis* for "ship") as a symbol of the ship that carries worshipers through the raging sea of life to the haven of paradise. In a less familiar interpretation, he says the doors stand for the stone rolled away from the tomb of Christ to allow the women entry, but the pulpit represents the same stone as that on which the angel sat to preach the gospel of Christ's resurrection to the women. More generally:

> The whole church is a type of heaven . . . the nave represents the visible or lowest heaven or paradise; the lights shining aloft, represent the bright stars; the circling roof, the firmament . . . Thus the whole church typifies heaven, but the chancel, parted and separated from the nave or body of the church, so as that it cannot be seen into by those that are there, typifies the invisible heaven, or things above the heaven, not to be seen by the eye of flesh.[15]

For others, allegory was found in such details as the tilting of chancels away from the east-west axis of the nave; for Victorian ecclesiologists, these chancels represented the head of Christ inclined to one side on the cross.[16] The Trinity was symbolized by the nave and two aisles; by the clerestory, the triforium, and the piers; and by nave, choir, and sanctuary. The north side of the church, under the sway of the Prince of the Power of the Air, was on that account sinister.[17] And deeply rooted in the interpretation of churches is the notion of the church building as a city, an earthly image of the Heavenly Jerusalem, and at times the facade is given functionally unnecessary towers to convey the image of a city gate.[18]

This sort of symbolism may now seem artificial, detached from any immediate experience of the architecture. Rather than extending experience outward into broader spheres, it condenses experience into a set of abstractions. But even in its heyday, this was not a way of perceiving churches that would have seemed obvious to everyone; it was an exegetical exercise for cognoscenti that might or might not reach a broader audience.

For those who did take such symbolism seriously, it represented in any event merely a further level of meaning in a church that was richly meaningful at all levels: the buildings were meant as feasts for the eyes and the worship in them as feasts for all the senses as well as for the mind and the soul. The church interiors Augustus Pugin and his followers designed were dedicated to reviving all the splendor of a fully decorated and painted medieval interior. Pugin certainly was enthusiastic regarding symbolism; each particular of a church interior might symbolize "some holy mystery." But the cognitive meanings of these symbols could not be dissociated from the appeal they made to the senses, the allure of the symbol suggesting a deeper allure of the mysteries symbolized. For Pugin the Gothic was indeed part of a broader symbolic world, and his ideological commitment to that world was profound. For him, a church was meant to declare the three doctrines of redemption, Trinity, and resurrection: redemption through the symbolism of the cross, found in the cruciform plan of a church and also in the crosses terminating spires and gables and imprinted on the altar; the Trinity in the triangular arches and in the subdivision of a church into sanctuary, choir, and nave; and resurrection of the dead in the height of a church and in its vertical lines, evocative of rising upward from the earth. Images of the martyrs and of the heavenly host, portals showing the Last Judgment, the majestic arcades and lateral chapels, the lights and images, the richly ornamented high altar, the candles, all draw the viewer into a state of awe.

> It is, indeed, a sacred place; the modulated light, the gleaming tapers, the tombs of the faithful, the various altars, the venerable images of the just,—all conspire to fill the mind with veneration, and to impress it with the sublimity of Christian worship. And when the deep intonations of the bells from the lofty campaniles, which summon the people to the house of prayer, have ceased, the solemn chant of the choir swells through the vast edifice,—cold, indeed, must be the heart of that man who does not cry out with the Psalmist, *Domine dilexi decorem domus tuae, et locum habitationis gloriae tuae* [Psalm 26:8, "O Lord, I have loved the beauty of your house, and the place where your glory dwells"].[19]

This passage suggests a close link between the meaning and the aesthetic impact of a church: decorative touches are never merely decorative, and symbolism is never merely cognitive. In the later nineteenth century the emblematic notion of symbolism as code was supplanted or at least supplemented by further developments in conception. Ruskin saw buildings as having a kind of poetic metaphorical value, while others took a church as a form of sacrament standing both within and outside of time, reflecting within history the timeless paradigms of church architecture.[20] Yet already in Pugin and his contemporaries the meanings of a church were inextricably enmeshed with its aesthetic impact.

Robert W. Jenson argues that the structure of a church by itself cannot establish what story it is that is dramatized in worship—that only the representations in sculptures, paintings, glass, mosaic, and other forms can be specific on this point. He allows that the purging of "cheap and irrelevant decoration" may have been necessary in the 1960s, but "a bare church is too undetermined as to which God is to be worshiped."[21] This instructional conception of art may be the only one clearly supportable in a classic evangelical environment. Yet it may seem to beg the question why that specificity has to be provided visually at all: like all didactic arguments for iconography, this one is weakened by the possibility of nonvisual pedagogy. Not surprisingly, the pedagogical argument by itself has historically been less effective in support of liturgical art than the devotional approach to imagery found in the classic sacramental churches of Eastern Orthodoxy and traditional Catholicism, the view of images not only as tools for education but also as foci for veneration. But even apart from Protestant fears of idolatry, this use of art again raises the question whether the means is necessary: some may find it useful to pray before a statue or an icon, but others do not, and the usage is perhaps waning. A third argument is used by Frédéric Debuyst in his description of what we have called the modern communal church:

> the real successes of modern religious art have as their starting point a much more modest and human aim: that of contributing to the hospitality of the church building, to an atmosphere favouring a calm, recollected and transparent celebration. . . . In the churches of which we are speaking, the image is indeed present, but no longer seeks to dominate, or even to 'teach': its gift to the Christian community is above all one of depth, of poetic transparency . . . But the ultimate source of the image is found at a still deeper level: in a sort of creative participation in the celebration itself.[22]

In principle this may seem a useful conception, but if the selection of art is guided by the desire to create a spirit of hospitality and celebration, then butterfly banners may be preferred over art of the Passion, art may become casual adornment rather than being integrally connected to the liturgical space, and its connection to narrative and belief may be thin. The most basic and most effective argument for liturgical art, then, may be a fourth: that it serves as a reminder of connectedness between the present liturgy and the network of symbols and narratives in which that liturgy is grounded.

The most fundamental reason for having representations in churches, whether narrative or iconic, is neither for education nor for devotion, and indeed many of the paintings and carvings in churches are placed so high that they serve neither of these purposes very effectively. They are there, rather, most basically as reminders of the religious culture from which they derive, as witnesses to a history that could in principle be known. One need not consult the guide book to determine which angel is represented on a window or in a statue suspended high above the chancel to know that the angels and saints hovering all about in the building relate the liturgical action to a broader narrative, to a sacred culture, to a process extending well beyond the present time and place. The effect is something like that of going to a friend's house and discovering a wall devoted to framed photographs of family members from several generations. Images and symbols may become so numerous, so profuse, that there is little hope of identifying them all; they fuse into a totality, a community of images, perceived only as a symbolic world of identities and meanings entered into easily but known only gradually and perhaps never fully. Without needing to know the story or even the identity of each subject, one may recognize the ensemble as testimony to rootedness in family history. Knowing all the particulars is less important than knowing what might be known.

Tradition is constituted by consciousness of standing within tradition. It does not require detailed and intimate knowledge of all that has been passed down. It does not require uniform appropriation, experience, or integration of what is passed down. It does require perceiving oneself as member of a family and thus as heir. Sharing of cultural goods is then as much a consequence as a source of this self-perception.

In general it is safe to say that classic sacramental churches are likely to have richer artistic programs, likely to invest church buildings themselves with richer symbolic meaning, and likely to integrate art with liturgy more fully than other sorts of church. Classic evangelical churches may not be totally devoid of symbols, but their use of symbolism tends to be relatively sparing: they will use crosses rather than crucifixes to avoid any suggestion of idolatry, and they will rely more on word than on visual symbol as the chief bearer of meaning. Modern communal churches are less predictable but often represent a compromise, making use of religious art in discrete units rather than in integrated programs, and ascribing occasional rather than systematic symbolism to the church buildings. Between the plea for richness and the argument for plainness lies the urge toward a minimalism that concentrates meaning on a few subtle touches, perhaps so discreet they must be sought out carefully. Suzane Reatig's design for the Metropolitan Community Church in Washington, D.C., has almost no decoration, but there is one focal point, utterly unobvious: a simple cross on the exterior that is discernible through the clear glass behind the altar.[23]

Case Study: Santa Maria Novella and
Modes of Symbolic Reference

Surface decoration has given symbolic resonance to churches since the third
century, when at least the baptistery at Dura-Europos was given its extensive
wall paintings. By the 430s a program of mosaics in Santa Maria Maggiore
combined narrative action with theological reference: the Virgin at the Annunciation, clad in the diadem and robe worn by women of imperial families, spins
a scarlet thread that foreshadows the shedding of Christ's blood; at the flight
into Egypt, Christ is met by an imperial figure and a philosopher, probably
signifying his mission to extending salvation to all peoples.[24]

Religious art is said to use "narrative" and "iconic" modes of depiction.[25]
In a narrative scene the characters are shown in action and mainly in relationship to each other, gazing at each other, gesturing or moving toward each other.
In an iconic representation, the characters are static and mainly in relationship
to the viewer: they stand or sit in fixed and often hieratic posture, gazing out
at the viewer and inviting a return of that gaze, in a Christian equivalent to the
Indian act of *darshan*, seeing and being seen by a sacred personage. Narrative
scenes are meant chiefly for education, while an iconic work is intended more
as a focus for devotion. Painting and statuary alike may be either narrative or
iconic, but statues are more often iconic in form and meant to arouse a sense
of devout contact with the person represented. Yet the distinction is not absolute, and even the most common iconic work can be taken as a frozen moment
abstracted from an assumed narrative: the crucifixion or the crucifix concentrates the passion narrative into a single scene, usually the time just after the
death of Christ; the Virgin and Child emerge from the adoration of the magi,
and the devout viewer is invited to venerate the child on his mother's lap as
the magi did.

Medieval artistic programs on church walls are now often mere fragments
of what once met the eye, but sometimes an ensemble survives or has been
restored. In the Collegiate Church at San Gimignano the walls were painted
in the later fourteenth century by Taddeo di Bartolo, Bartolo di Fredi, and
others, with gospel scenes on the south wall and scenes from the Old Testament on the north wall with vernacular labels that a literate guide could use
for instructing children: "How God created the world," "How God created the
first man," "How God gave Adam dominion of the earthly Paradise," and so
forth. More space is devoted to Job than to any other figure of the Old Testament, reflecting the prominence of Job in an age well familiar with sickness
and affliction.[26] At the end of the cycle Job appears as a type of the Man of
Sorrows, facing the scenes of Christ's passion on the opposite wall.[27]

One might suppose such an exuberant artistic display could only have been
carried out in a wealthy town or a monastery, but a visit to a place such as

Lanslevillard, high in the mountains of Savoy, gives a fuller sense of how widely this culture was diffused. A tiny chapel there, dedicated to Saint Sebastian, is unprepossessing on the outside but fully painted inside with mural cyles, probably from the fifteenth century, juxtaposing the life, passion, and posthumous cult of the martyr with the more familiar life and passion of Christ. The scale is smaller than at San Gimignano, but the urge to surround the devout with Christian narrative in all its ordered detail is palpable here as well.[28]

The church of Santa Maria Novella in Florence holds examples of the various ways painted images could integrate past and present. There was a small church on the site at an early date, but the building was given to the Dominican order in the thirteenth century and fundamentally remodeled. In the later Middle Ages the church was divided most basically into a nave (for masses and sermons attended by the laity) and a chancel (meant specifically for the friars), and the screen dividing the two spaces was a massive construction, extending upward to fourteen feet, and more than twenty-six feet deep.[29] (A similar arrangement survives in the Dominican church at Guebwiller in Alsace, with extensive unrestored wall paintings.)[30] In the fourteenth century Andrea di Bonaiuto painted the walls of the chapter house (later called the Spanish Chapel): a panorama of the crucifixion graces the north wall, Saint Thomas Aquinas sits enthroned on the west wall, scenes from the life and miracles of Saint Peter Martyr adorn the south wall, and a complex of scenes on the east wall brings the Dominican order into connection with the broader history of the Church. Also in the fourteenth century Nardo di Cione and Giovanni del Biondo executed frescoes in the Strozzi Chapel, while Orcagna provided an altarpiece for that chapel. Then in the following century Ghirlandaio painted scenes from the life of the Virgin and the life of John the Baptist in the choir, while Filippino Lippi depicted the lives of Saint Philip and Saint John the Evangelist, and in the nave Masaccio painted his well-known mural of the Trinity. In the same century Leone Battista Alberti redesigned the decorative facade of the church.

The paintings on the four walls of the chapter house indicate how art could be used for meditation, for intercessory prayer, for veneration, and for a sense of group identity.[31] The panoramic view of Christ's crucifixion serves as an aid to meditation on the events of Christ's passion and death. The formal, hieratic scene of Thomas Aquinas, enthroned amid allegorical and biblical figures as the master of all learning, depicts the saint gazing forward at the viewer who invites prayer for intercession: a preacher might have prayed to Thomas here for inspiration in preaching, and a theology student might have sought his aid in his studies. The south wall shows Saint Peter Martyr, the Dominican who was famous for his preaching here at Santa Maria Novella and elsewhere, was assassinated by the heretics he opposed, and was noteworthy for miracles at his tomb; the scenes from his life and miracles could instruct, but even more they could encourage pious veneration. Finally, the east wall gives a composite

scene in which specifically Dominican themes are woven together with motifs
from the history of the Church and of salvation: Christ seated as the judge on
the last day, holding the book and key that symbolize the Dominicans' tasks
of learning and of saving souls; the cathedral of Florence, still under construction; black and white dogs, the order's *Domini canes*, attacking heretical wolves;
Saint Peter Martyr preaching against heretics; Saint Thomas Aquinas holding
the book in which he writes against heretics, causing some of them to submit
to his authority while another stops up his ears; Saint Dominic pointing toward
the gate of Paradise. If the other walls elicited meditation on the Passion, pleas
for Thomas Aquinas's intercessory prayer, and veneration of Peter Martyr, the
east wall gave its Dominican viewers a sense of their role in the Church's
work.[32] And these paintings not only alluded to individuals and events from
the past, and not only pointed toward modes of response, but also echoed
previous representations of the same themes. The panoramic view of Christ's
crucifixion was done in a manner that had become popular among Tuscan
painters earlier in the fourteenth century. The enthroned Thomas Aquinas
recalls an earlier painting of Thomas in Pisa. It also brings to mind much
earlier representations of ecumenical councils in which the heretics they condemned are shown lying defeated before the council fathers. The miracles at
the tomb of Saint Peter Martyr are largely the ones shown in artwork at the
tomb itself. Even the scenes on the east wall were in part modeled after parallels
in the art of other religious orders.

　　Viewers would have recognized the facade of the building, too, as alluding
to prototypes despite the abstract geometrical character of its marble decoration
(fig. 13). The lower sections were largely in place well before the fifteenth century and were modeled on local Florentine precedent at San Miniato al Monte
and at the cathedral baptistry. Decorative marble revetment was a local trademark, found on several churches in Florence. But in the fifteenth century,
Alberti reconfigured the lower level of Santa Maria Novella's facade, turning it
into one of the primary monuments of early Renaissance architecture. He
made the central door significantly wider and grander than it had been, he
superimposed classical elements over the marble panels, and he added further
classical motifs in the upper levels. The lower level received an engaged column
and pilaster at each end, a classical pediment crowned the facade, and curved
or scroll-like "volutes" on its shoulders provided a graceful link between upper
and lower levels. For most of these details Alberti could find precedent not in
Florence but in Rome, perhaps in the Arch of Septimus Severus, the Basilica
Aemilia, and the Pantheon.[33] By the time he was done, while the interior of
the church was reminding people of the Trinity, the saints, and the living and
the deceased of Florence itself, the exterior was declaring affiliation first with
other churches of the vicinity and second with traditions of architecture from
Roman antiquity.

　　The best-known chapel at Santa Maria Novella, the Strozzi Chapel, was

FIGURE 13. Santa Maria Novella, Florence, exterior. Photograph by Richard Kieckhefer.

the burial place for one of Florence's prominent families over several generations, and successive members of the family participated in the building and decoration of the space, which was in one sense specifically theirs and in another belonged to the broader community, and, being dedicated formally to Saint Thomas Aquinas, served as another link to the Angelic Doctor. This chapel was painted with scenes of the Last Judgment, Heaven, and Hell, and these frescoes make frequent allusion to Dante's *Divine Comedy;* laypeople in the church could be expected to know Dante's work, and the painters evidently trusted their audience to grasp these allusions. More exceptional was the Chapel of the Pura, established (according to tradition) when a young boy playing in the churchyard one day in 1472 heard a voice beckoning him and found that an image of the Virgin was asking to have an accumulation of dust and cobwebs cleared away from her. The site of the miracle was honored by having the chapel built around it, to which a confraternity then became attached.[34]

Masaccio's fresco of the Trinity, in the nave, was of a type that conflated the timeless eternity of the divine persons with the historical realities of salvation. An old man for the Father and a dove for the Spirit accompany the crucified Son, and the Virgin looks out at the viewer and points to the cross, while John the Evangelist wrings his hands in grief. Below is a skeleton with the famous inscription "What you are now I once was, and what I am you too will be," a fitting theme for one who encounters this complex image on entering the church through the door opposite it—the door leading from the churchyard.[35]

Those who framed the symbolism of a church need not be forced to a choice between the universal and the particular, because the universal manifested itself in the particular, because architectural and artistic motifs in broader circulation become adapted to the requirements of a particular church, and because devotion to Christ's passion or to a widely venerated saint will become concretized in a chapel intimately associated with a particular patron, a specific family, a confraternity. Masaccio's Trinity has been seen as linking the timelessness of the divine with the concrete particularity of history, with the Trinity entering via the crucifixion into history and then into the community of living donors and of the deceased represented below. But that linkage of historical particularity with themes taken sometimes to be eternal and at other times to be part of the general tradition of the Church is nothing exceptional: it is the very stuff of which religious art is routinely made.

Integration of Past, Present, and Future

The symbolic associations presented by a church building are on the whole more elusive than those of the artwork found within its walls. As a point of departure it may be helpful to say that a church is a place of conjunction in four senses—integrating the past and the future with the present experience of the worshiping community, relating the liturgy experienced within the church to an idealized liturgy imaged as celestial worship, connecting the living with the dead, and bringing the particular church into association with other churches, and by intention with the Church universal.

Religion is, in part, a way of entering into and reliving sacred narrative. Myth and ritual tell and enact the stories of a sacred past; the telling of myths brings them to life and activates their spiritual power. Christian worship is also, in more than one way, a ritualization of memory: a memorial and making-present of the Last Supper, a bringing to completion of the sacrifice on Calvary, a plotting of Christ's life upon the grid of the liturgical calendar, and a recollection of Christian history in the commemorations of significant individuals noted in the church year. But worship also points toward an eschatological future and makes repeated reference to the coming of a messianic kingdom. And this knitting together of faith in the past and hope for the future with expression of charity in the present is a primary source of resonance in Christian ritual.

Approximate parallels abound. When we see a film, the settings we view take on a quality they would not have if we passed through them in our everyday lives. Even apart from the cinematographer's art, the simple fact that a place is registered in a film gives the expectation that it will be the scene of action, the setting for a plot, for the unfolding of character. It is as though a voice were saying: *Look at this room, this landscape, observe it carefully, because it is preparing you for what will follow.* It is the opposite of visiting a battlefield or the scene of any other known historical event, where the challenge is to recreate mentally and emotionally the carnage or the accomplishment of which the scene is perhaps distantly reminiscent. Different yet again is a place for ritual reenactment, where with regularity both past events and future expectations are symbolically set forth. If entering into a church is a moment for pausing, for entering into a different frame of mind—a moment that in some cultures might be marked by removing one's shoes, by lying prostrate, or at least by bowing or signing oneself with holy water, all stalling maneuvers to break one's rush forward, to heighten one's consciousness of being on ground laden with meanings—this is largely as reminder that the place is one of both recollection and anticipation. Entering into a church carries with it something of the sense of being in a historic place, and something of the feel of coming upon a place where action is about to unfold.

This linkage of past, present, and future is explicit in virtually every eucharistic prayer used in the liturgical traditions of Christianity. The eucharistic prayer brings past, present, and future into a single focus, most sharply in the memorial proclamation or "anamnesis" that proclaims "Christ has died, Christ is risen, Christ will come again," where Christ's death is proclaimed as past event, his resurrection as present reality, and his return as future expectation. But this linkage is implied also in the theology of the eucharist as sacrament. The eucharist as sacrifice brings the sacrifice of the cross into present experience, but it is simultaneously anticipation of the messianic banquet Christ announces: "I shall not drink again of the fruit of the vine until that day when I drink it new in the kingdom of God" (Mark 14:25). It is not as though the eucharist could be seen either as sacrifice or as eschatological banquet. Rather, the partaking in sacrifice is taken as the means for sharing in the memory and presence of Christ until the eschaton (1 Corinthians 11:26). In John's gospel the eucharist points backward as well to the bread come down from heaven, which is to identify it as antitype of the manna of the Israelites in the desert (John 6:25–58), a variation on John's basic conception of Jesus himself as the Word come down from heaven. Thus communion, like the eucharistic prayer, is a symbolic nexus bringing past and future into connection with the present.

The historical reference most expected within a church is to biblical narrative, and second to the lives of the saints, but on occasion even the history of the particular worshiping community is memorialized in art and thus by implication integrated into broader patterns of biblical and historical narrative. At Eibingen, on the site of the abbey of Saint Hildegard of Bingen, paintings show scenes of the foundress's life.[36] Among the windows at Saint Mary's

Cathedral in Sydney is an ensemble with eight scenes telling the history of Catholicism in Sydney, from the mass celebrated in a kitchen by a convict priest in 1803 through the presentation of balance sheets for building of the cathedral and on to its consecration.[37] Differently reflecting the experience of the community, paintings at a Ukrainian church in Canada include the faces of Hitler, Lenin, Stalin, and Khrushchev among the souls in Hell.[38]

Integration of Ideal with Experienced Liturgy

Equally important in various traditional conceptions of liturgy, and perhaps more directly relevant to traditional conception of a church building, is the idea of worship as a participation in the celestial worship rendered to God in eternity. One recent writer harks to this theme and links it to an emphasis on the priority of divine action: "Our liturgy is holy because it is the liturgy of heaven on earth, because in this event God acts upon us and makes us holy, so that we can react to what he does."[39] Traditional prefaces to the Sanctus invite those in the church to join their voices with those of celestial worshipers before the divine throne, and the Sanctus itself joins the hymn of the seraphim (from Isaiah 6) with the praise of human worshipers from Palm Sunday (from Matthew 21:9 and parallel passages). The Cherubikon in the Eastern Orthodox liturgy, a hymn of the sixth century that probably pertained in the first instance to the deacons, is one of the best-known ways the theme is expressed in the Orthodox tradition: "Let us who mystically represent the Cherubim, and who sing the thrice-holy hymn to the life-giving Trinity, now lay aside all earthly cares," followed by the exclamation "that we may receive the King of All, who comes invisibly upborne by the angelic hosts."[40] From this perspective the traditional Byzantine exposition of a church building as a point of junction between heaven and earth—symbolized by the round expanse of the dome, sometimes adorned with stars, and the square nave on which it rests, standing for the earth with its four corners—suggests one way of articulating in architecture a conception of the worship that occurs within the church walls.

> Those who visit Orthodox churches are often struck by their light and their warmth, by a certain intimacy, a familiarity with heaven. Even when no service is going on, every spot in the very walls is alive with presences to which the icons bear witness, presences which create a communion between our humankind and those who have gone before: angels, prophets, apostles, martyrs, saints. Humanity, unbidden, has an immediate, a natural sense of visiting with God, surrounded by God's friends.[41]

Lest this conception seem forbiddingly hieratic, Romano Guardini tempered its solemnity by dealing with it under the heading of the "playfulness" of liturgy: Ezechiel's vision of cherubim flashing about with great rushing wings in the divine presence, a "living image of the liturgy," seemed to him a picture of consciously purposeless activity, a "mystic diversion."[42]

But if the church is allegorized as heaven, the reverse is also possible: Caesarius of Arles speaks of heaven as "that eternal and blessed church," and a fifteenth-century manuscript illumination in the Hours of Etienne Chevalier shows the coronation of the Virgin taking place in a heaven laid out very much like a medieval church, with Christ and the Virgin in the sanctuary, saints seated as if in choir stalls, and the throngs of the blessed occupying the nave.[43] Among Anglo-Catholic writers from the first half of the twentieth century, the Book of Revelation served as a classic witness to the liturgical practice of early Christianity, seen as an earthly reflection of heavenly liturgy: the throne of Christ in Revelation recalls the bishop's throne, flanked by the seats of elders or assistant priests, the altar placed before the throne for the Lamb that is slain the offering of incense and the burning of lamps: "This is indeed a picture of heaven, but it is in terms of primitive Christian worship. The Church and the Eucharist on earth are mystically one with the scene in heavenly places."[44]

At the end of Augustine's *City of God*, the state of the blessed is envisaged as a great liturgical act of collective contemplation and praise: "For there in resting we shall see, in seeing we shall love, and in loving we shall give praise." Augustine conceives paradise as a place of contemplative beholding but not of individual contemplation: it is a city, a community in heaven, as the Church is on earth. Humans are made to live as community, not to endure social life on earth as a prelude to asocial bliss in eternity. When Augustine uses the first person plural—"we shall behold," "we shall love," "we shall give praise"—he speaks not about individuals but about the saints as a society joined in the action of contemplation.[45] Notions of heaven are never exclusively about life after death: they also reflect ideals to be approximated on earth. And when the churches imagine the eternal praise of God in paradise, imaging liturgy here below in its light and vice versa, and representing church buildings as types of a celestial antitype, the message is one about the present as well as the future.

Integration of the Dead and the Living

My most vivid experience of a link to the past came at Mystra, a Byzantine mountainside town in the Peloponnese where several small churches stand in varying degrees of preservation, some with wall paintings remarkably intact. We went there on the feast of the Dormition of the Virgin. When the rising sun brought chanting and other sounds of liturgy through the window of our hotel room, we proceeded straight to the modern church in the new town, only to find it locked. Where, then, was this liturgy taking place? Perhaps in one of the churches in the historic town along the mountain slope. Yet there too the sounds of liturgy could be heard everywhere but the actual celebration seen nowhere. We inquired, and people gestured vaguely to churches in one direction or other. We could hear a sermon being preached, babies crying, and cantor singing, but all was mysteriously disembodied. Could it all have come from a radio somewhere? Not even that was anywhere to be found. We never solved the mystery, but for a romantic sensibility the liturgy of Byzantine Mystra seemed mystically alive, echoing on the ancient site, where the very stones seemed still to resound with the chant of the founding worshipers. We had come to a place where the communication of dead generations was tongued with fire "beyond the language of the living."[46]

Americans may on the whole have a less lively sense than Europeans of churches as places of association between the living and the dead. If one's ancestors for several generations are buried in the churchyard, perhaps even within the church, the site plays a role generally assumed in America by outlying cemeteries. The presence of the dead may be more keenly felt in churches with columbaria for the ashes of those cremated; at the Metropolitan Community Church in Washington, D.C., a church with a high proportion of AIDS victims, the architect Suzane Reatig placed the columbarium along the back of the sanctuary "to have deceased members of the congregation take part in services."[47]

Even in the Old World, the earliest graves are often unmarked, and over centuries bones have customarily been exhumed and taken to the charnel house to make room for new burials. A tiny eleventh-century church at Epfig in Alsace, which began as a mortuary chapel, is more blunt in its message: hundred of skulls are displayed openly in a kind of cage on the north exterior wall of the little church. For the more affluent—aristocrats, patricians, and relatively wealthy merchants and artisans—burial within the church itself was an option, especially from the thirteenth century onward. It was from that period, for example, that burials proliferated inside Santa Maria Maggiore. The burial could be marked with a brass set in the floor; a fifteenth-century wool merchant thus memorialized might be shown with his feet resting on bags of wool, and with family members at his side.[48] A table tomb with an effigy of the deceased, carved perhaps in alabaster, could be set over the actual site of burial; a knight might be buried in a chantry chapel, might be depicted recumbent in his suit of armor, and could have masses said for his soul at an altar there in the chapel. In the parish church at West Tanfield in Yorkshire, memorials of the Marmion family include an item used in the actual funeral ceremony, a reminder of the event that marked the passage of these people from time to eternity: a framework fitted over one of the Marmion tombs is a wrought-iron hearse that would have served originally as a support for the pall on which the bodies were laid out at the funeral, and attached to the hearse are iron sconces for candles.[49] When the deceased was wealthy, late medieval funerals were occasions for conspicuous expenditure, and one form of this was the burning of candles, for which elaborate provision might be made in wills.[50] What we have at West Tanfield, then, goes beyond the usual survivals of the deceased. Tombstones, burial slabs, inscribed plaques, chest tombs with sculpted images of the deceased, tombs with the deceased shown as rotting corpses ("transi tombs")—all these are in varying degrees routine in European churches. What we do not find so frequently are concrete links between burial as site and burial as event.[51]

Burial places could be perhaps the most overtly political of all church spaces. It has been suggested, for example, that when the condottiere Barto- lomeo Colleoni commissioned his own funerary chapel at Bergamo in the 1470s he deliberately planned it to stand in the main public square, conspic- uously positioned before a civic church governed by a lay confraternity, to make a political point: that virtuous individuals such as himself, not an oligarchy like the one that ruled the church, should govern the city.[52] Yet such political mean- ings are inherently unstable, unmistakable to one generation but unintelligible to another when historical personages and their claims fall into oblivion.[53] Churches can be in many ways politicized, and in the short run a church or chapel can be all ablaze with propaganda value for its founder, but the me- morial will have little meaning to those who learn of the memorialized only from guide books. When one looks at the monuments and inscriptions at Westminster Abbey, many of the names are famous and the lives well enough known, but even in a nineteenth-century church the names may be only names to all but a handful of antiquarians. As Leonardo Bruni observed, "What is viler than to have one's tomb remembered, one's life forgotten?"[54]

The memorials in any case serve the living rather than the dead, and for the living they can evoke a recognition of community over time even if the particulars of this wool merchant's or that countess's life are little known. The presence of the dead amid the liturgy of the living more effectively evokes the community of living and dead than it perpetuates the memory of any individ- ual.

The Universal and the Particular: Orientation and Legends of Foundation

One key theme in the work of Mircea Eliade is the relationship of the particular and the universal. From his Platonic perspective, every religious person, place, or object is a particular manifestation of a universal archetype and is experi- enced as a manifestation of something beyond itself: "Any local goddess tends to become *the* Great Goddess; any village anywhere *is* the 'Center of the World,' and any wizard whatever pretends, at the height of his ritual, to be the Universal Sovereign."[55] But if the particular tends to become assimilated to the universal, the universal manifests itself in particularity. In churches that grow out of the Catholic tradition, the Virgin Mary is a universal patroness: the mother of all believers; in courtly terms, Our Lady; patroness of all monasteries of the Cistercians, who did much to diffuse her patronage and her devotion. But she is also intimately linked to particular places. She is not simply Our Lady, but Our Lady of Guadalupe, Our Lady of Czestochowa, Our Lady of Fatima, and the special patroness of countless lesser cultic sites. Images of the Virgin are said to have been discovered in Spanish caves and moved to nearby churches but miraculously returned to the caves where they were discovered, so closely are the images—and the Virgin they represent—connected with a particular location, a specific topographic feature.[56]

This connectedness of the universal and the particular can be seen also in the concept of the Church itself. The Greek term *ekklesia*, or "assembly," refers first to the Church universal, second to the local congregation, and third to the building designed for the congregation's assembly as a worshiping community. The local congregation is taken for a local manifestation of the Church universal; even traditions with congregational polity and a strong sense of local autonomy still see each local group as linked to others through the bonding of divine guidance.[57] And in various ways church buildings have traditionally been taken to symbolize not only the local community but also its relatedness to a broader collectivity.

One sign of this relatedness is the orientation of a church building: its placement with the altar at the east end. From at least the third century, and probably earlier, Christians were accustomed to face east while praying, although different reasons have at various times been assigned for the practice. East was recognized as the location of the garden of Eden where humankind began, as the direction from which Christ would come at the Last Judgment, and most obviously as the direction of sunrise. In Constantine's churches of the early fourth century, and for some time afterward in Rome, this focus on facing east in prayer resulted in basilicas being designed with the apse to the west, so the bishop seated on his throne would face east while the congregation faced west. Before long, the reverse arrangement was generally adopted, in which the apse and the altar were to the east and the congregation with the clergy faced east. The crucial factor was perhaps that the priest had to face east while celebrating. Whether this meant facing the people or facing away from them was a secondary factor: when the church was built with the sanctuary to the west the priest faced the people, but when the sanctuary was to the east the priest faced east along with the people.[58] Be all this as it may—and Josef Jungmann argued to the contrary that the position of the priest facing the same direction as the congregation was determined more by the conception of the mass as a joint act of sacrificial oblation—placement of altar and sanctuary to the east eventually became the norm in most regions of Christendom.[59]

Different regions and different churches have emphasized the importance of this "orientation" of church buildings in varying degrees; medieval English churches are almost always approximately oriented, as are Orthodox churches, while in some other places the tendency is less rigorously observed.[60] It may well be that the stronger emphasis on orientation in England stems from the early English sense of living on the periphery of Christendom. In the early eighth century, the Venerable Bede protested vigorously that the English Church must recognize the authority of Roman tradition, but then Bede was an enthusiast for unity within the English Church and for unity of England with what he took to be the mainstream of Christianity.[61] The orientation of churches did not so much bring them into explicit relationship with a common geographical center: the oriented apse did not point to Jerusalem, as the *mihrab* in each mosque points it toward Mecca. Yet orientation was a kind of alignment, and common alignment could itself be a form of bonding among churches.

Complementing this emphasis on bonding within the universal Church is a focus on the distinctness of a particular church and the sacrality of a particular building, a specific location. Among the ways of emphasizing the sacred quality of a place, perhaps the most dramatic is the foundation legend. The legend of the miraculous snow defining the site for Santa Maria Maggiore is a classic case. Some of the most important shrines of the Virgin are places of Marian apparitions; in other instances a church may be linked with a saint or with the posthumous deposition of a saint's relics. Saint Denis may have been beheaded at Montmartre, but he then picked up his own head and carried it two miles, accompanied by an angelic choir, to his burial at what becomes the basilica of St-Denis.[62] No doubt such legends had entertainment value, perhaps intended. But they were also ways of articulating a perception few would have taken lightly: that not all sacred places were defined as such by mere human convention, and that at least some are rendered sacred by supernatural ordination.

Brittany is rife with such traditions.[63] The church of Notre Dame at Le Folgoët, built in 1422–60, is said to occupy the place where a holy fool had his chapel. He lived in the open air, disciplined himself by sitting naked in the chill waters of a spring, sang Breton tunes honoring the Virgin, and repeated the words "Ave Maria" as a mantra. A lily was found on his grave with those same Latin words miraculously imprinted on its petals, and when his tomb was reopened a flower was seen growing from the hermit's mouth. But a legend of this sort must be seen in the context of a distinctive devotional culture. Few areas of northern Europe can rival Brittany in its proliferation of devotional shrines, many of them centers of living veneration and foci of annual pilgrimage. Many of these shrines are not parish churches but chapels. They are surviving witnesses to a phenomenon once more widespread: the extension of piety to realms outside the strict control of the parish, or in some cases on the edges of parish life and related in complex ways to the quotidian regimen of the parish church.[64] Often the origin of the shrine is enveloped in legend. Sainte-Anne-d'Auray is a pilgrimage site that was founded in 1624 when a white lady appeared to a ploughman and told him where to build a chapel; in the process he dug up a wooden statue that was said to date from the eighth century, and was forthwith redone in an accepted and acceptable contemporary idiom. At Josselin a statue of the Virgin was found in a bramble bush and would not be removed, so a church was built to honor the location. The church at Locronan lies where the Irishman Ronan settled when he came to Brittany and had to confront the antipathy of a local witch. Elsewhere an unfinished chapel was begun with the aid of fairies, who abandoned the project when they saw a magpie on the road and deemed it an ill omen.

The rock-hewn churches at Lâlibalâ in Ethiopia are among most extraordinary in all Christendom, carved downward into the rock rather than built up from ground level.[65] They are ascribed to a twelfth-century founder, the brother of the reigning king, who had visions instructing him that he was to assume the throne. In one vision he was transported to heaven, shown a series of rock-hewn churches, and instructed to replicate these back on Earth. In this case the local church is sacred not simply by virtue of its linkage to other churches in the Church universal, or by virtue of a spiritual presence resident and revealed in a special and particular location, but rather by its status as an earthly reflection of a celestial archetype. What has been seen above in the sky is reflected below in the ground.

To grasp the significance of these legends one might begin by looking closely at the particularities of each site and seeing how they are grounded in a complex of folklore and historical circumstance. The traditions of Lâlibalâ can be linked with the fortunes of royal dynasties that grounded their political claims in a mystique of sacred legitimacy borrowed from Jerusalem, perhaps from Edessa, and from Heaven itself. But whatever the specific factors in its origins, a legend of this sort expresses a connectedness of churches with both the historical and the natural as well as the supernatural order. Any other church or chapel may be recognized as a site of artificial sacrality and arbitrary location: it is constructed and then consecrated, made holy in a way determined by culture and authority. However much a miraculous shrine is absorbed into the institutional sacred topography of a region, its legends of origin tell their hearers that the place is sacred not primarily by virtue of official consecration but rather by dint of miraculous or at least marvelous events that make the site sacred even before the church is designed. Popular lore takes as specifically Celtic the notion of "thin" places where the sacred is unusually accessible; it would be truer to say that in any place where people feel they come in close contact with the sacred they sense the approach as reciprocal, and that if legends of foundation ring at all true it is because they give narrative form to this experience.

The Universal and the Particular: Ceremonies of Dedication

Normally the planning and execution of a church building is recognized as a human undertaking, and its sacrality is bestowed in a ritual act of dedication or consecration. This ceremony declares a particular place sacred, but the common form of the ritual also proclaims each place as integrated into a network of places recognized as sacred by a broader community.[66] As late as the sixth century consecration was done chiefly or exclusively by celebrating mass in a new church and, when they were available, placing relics of the saints in its altar, but by the ninth century the ceremony had become far richer and—what is particularly important for my present purposes—more clearly linked with biblical precedent, with other rituals, and with the ongoing liturgical life of a parish or diocese.

The Church has traditionally sought precedent for these rites in scripture. The earliest biblical precedent for consecration of a sacred place is the story of Jacob at Bethel (Genesis 28:16–18): after exclaiming in awe that "surely the Lord is in this place," Jacob took the stone on which he had reclined his head, set it up as a pillar for a house of God, and poured oil on it. More extended— and of the utmost importance for theology of sacred architecture—is the dedication of Solomon's Temple (1 Kings 8).[67] Standing before the altar, Solomon raised a fundamental question and answered it with a petition:

> But will God indeed dwell on the earth? Behold, heaven and the
> highest heaven cannot contain thee; how much less this house
> which I have built! Yet have regard to the prayer of your servant and
> to his supplication, O Lord my God, hearkening to the cry and to
> the prayer which thy servant prays before thee this day, that thy eyes
> may be open night and day toward this house, the place of which
> thou hast said, "My name shall be there," that thou mayest hearken
> to the prayer which thy servant offers toward this place.

The king asked that prayer for all purposes—for remission of offenses, for release from captivity, for relief from drought and famine, for the welfare of a foreigner, for victory in battle—should be effective in this place. He prayed, in short, that this should be a place where prayer might be valid, as T. S. Eliot said of Little Gidding. Then Solomon sealed his litany of petitions by sacrificing 22,000 oxen and 120,000 sheep. But ultimately, according to the biblical account, it was God who consecrated the Temple and who appeared to Solomon, saying, "I have heard your prayer and your plea, which you made before me; I have consecrated this house that you have built, and put my name there for ever; my eyes and my heart will be there for all time"—unless Israel turned aside from the divine will, in which case the Temple would become "a heap of ruins" (1 Kings 9:1–8 [RSV]). For a theology that emphasizes the priority of divine action in grace, the divine consecration of the Temple becomes an application of this broader principle. But for one that recognizes synergy or collaboration between human and divine effort, it is not irrelevant that the divine consecration comes in response to a petition for a building already constructed, and that the consecration's efficacy is conditioned by Israel's adherence to the covenant.[68]

The ceremony for consecrating (or dedicating) a church that developed in Western Christendom in the early Middle Ages was among the most complex of rituals. Ceremonially vested, the bishop processed three times around the exterior of the church, sprinkling it with holy water on three levels. (Yves of Chartres interpreted this aspersion as a parallel to the triple immersion of baptism, when the soul is consecrated as a temple of God.) Each time, on arriving at the church door, he struck the door with his crosier and proclaimed: "Lift up your gates, ye princes, and be ye lifted up, ye everlasting doors, and the King of Glory shall come in." The deacon positioned on the other side of the door replied: "Who is this King of Glory?" to which the bishop's answer (the first two times) was: "The Lord, strong and mighty, the Lord mighty in battle." (At this point, therefore, the church was imaged as a kind of fortress that God was storming and on the verge of taking under his command.) The bishop and his attendants then entered the church, while the clergy and people remained outdoors. Taking his crosier, the hierarch traced the Greek alphabet diagonally across the nave in ashes spread on the floor, then the Latin alphabet crossing over the Greek. (According to Gregory the Great and Egbert of York, this ritual symbolized the instruction given to baptized Christians.) He then undertook an elaborate ritual of sprinkling on and around the door a special holy water (whose ingredients were variously allegorized). At this point, accompanied by clergy and people in procession, the bishop brought into the church the relics meant to be placed in the altar. All these steps were preparatory to the two main acts of consecration. The first was the formal consecration of a fixed altar in the church, usually the main altar, culminating in the sealing of relics within the mensa, or top of the altar. The second was the anointing of the twelve consecration crosses that were painted or attached to the interior walls; with the anointing of each cross, the bishop's words began: "Let this temple be sanctified and consecrated . . ." When all this ritual had been completed, the bishop or a priest celebrated mass, and in later centuries an indulgence was published. From then on, the anniversary of the church's consecration might be observed annually; if the church thus dedicated was a cathedral, the anniversary might be observed throughout the diocese.

The symbolic network was yet more dense: the ritual presupposed for all further rituals in the church carried overtones of specific rituals that governed the beginning and end of human life. Because the placement of saints' relics in the altar was integral to the consecration ceremony, the event as it was observed in the Roman tradition had much of the character of a funeral, with the sacred remains solemnly sealed in their new tomb and a mass celebrated on the site. Liturgists in Gaul, however, developed a consecration ceremony that borrowed more from the ritual of baptism and confirmation. The altar and church were sprinkled with water and anointed with chrism; in one liturgical source the altar was expressly said to be baptized and confirmed.[69] What gradually emerged in the West was a composite ceremony of consecration that combined features of the Roman and Gallican usage. For an even more deeply layered ritual, a ceremonial exorcism was introduced to purge the newly constructed church of all untoward influences; in one version of the rite, the exorcism was dramatized by having a cleric play the role of the demon, fleeing afar when the doors burst open and the bishop claimed possession of the building.[70]

Reforms of the later twentieth century, in the Roman Catholic and other churches, brought much simplification to this exceptionally intricate ritual, with many of its associations still preserved but perhaps less dramatically enacted. In the Roman Catholic *Dedication of a Church and an Altar* of 1977, the dedication proper comes during a mass, just after the homily, which is the same place a baptism, marriage, or ordination would occur. The wording of the ceremony repeatedly makes clear that the Church is primarily the collectivity of people, a "spiritual temple," and that the building serves the purposes of the community.[71] Elsewhere one finds the suggestion that a rite of dedication or consecration should now be understood not as changing the nature of the building but as declaring its function, acknowledging explicitly its relationship to God.[72]

While the ceremony of consecration or dedication does not always occupy a significant place in the consciousness of later generations of worshipers, a related factor does indeed tend to remain prominent: the dedication of the church to a particular saint (Saint Luke, Saint Nicholas, Saint Mary the Virgin, in some cases All Saints), to an event (the Annunciation, the Dormition), or to a credally affirmed reality (the Holy Trinity, the Light of Christ). The main reason for the custom of giving a church such a specific dedication is the very early conflation of churches with martyria or shrines of martyrs: a church would be dedicated to Saint Lawrence not simply at random but because it was built over the tomb of that martyr or (in a later stage) had relics of the saint translated to it. In rare cases a church might have more than one dedication: the Lateran Basilica, the pope's cathedral, proclaimed as "head and mother" of all churches everywhere, with a consecration feast celebrated throughout the Roman Church, was originally known at the time of Constantine simply as the "Basilica of the Savior," but in 904 Saint John the Baptist and in 1104 Saint John the Evangelist were added as patrons. There are also special cases in which the title marks something exceptional to a particular place; an extreme case is the Chapel of the Snows at McMurdo Station in Antarctica.[73] For most churches, a single patron suffices as both a particularizing factor (distinguishing this church from other churches) and a universalizing one (because the patron is shared and venerated by the broader Church).

Case Study: The "Cathedral of Huts" at Maciene and the Symbolic Value of Indigenization

The relationship between the universal and the particular may take on a special range of meanings in a place where traditional architectural form is linked with colonialism, but modern international design is prized as a sign of modernization, and use of indigenous architecture may fall into a cultural limbo.

In 1972 an impoverished parish in the bush country at Maciene in Mozambique needed a new church building that could be economically designed. So the architect Amancio ("Pancho") Guedes provided for the villagers an extraordinary design called the "Cathedral of Huts" (fig. 14). In the tradition of vernacular architecture from south and central Africa, the church was to resemble a kraal, a village with huts gathered inside a kind of stockade. The enclosing wall was designed to bend around the cluster of huts, zigzaging in a succession of thirty-six right angles, tracing a jagged Greek cross with gateways at the four equal extensions. The parishioners themselves would construct the church, as they did their own homes. The entire community would collaborate in building a large hut in the center to shelter the altar; individual families would build for themselves smaller huts around it, something like box pews. The grouping of huts, the outer walls, the pathways, and the water channels would all form crosses.[74]

Local labor and use of local materials are often among the hallmarks of church building in Third World settings, for reasons of economy but also perhaps to convey a sense that the religious tradition imported from abroad has become rooted in local soil.[75] At several places in Africa local building types have been embraced for church design, as in the round chapel at Douvangar in the Cameroons.[76] And yet Guedes's exercise in use of indigenous architecture is, not surprisingly, the invention of a Western architect in Africa. In the early 1970s Manfred Ludes set out to build a church following African prototypes at Makuukuulu in Uganda and found that the clients were not in a position to read and interpret Western architectural plans;[77] Guedes's hope of using not only indigenous design but traditional methods of construction could be judged more thoroughgoing and consistent. An American priest and architect, Terrence M. Curry, has noted that Nigerian architects preferred Western forms of design and gained credibility by using them. A Nigerian architect told Curry that he as an outsider might "get away with using traditional Nigerian forms" but an African could not. Curry himself designed a church with an entrance in the tradition of the Oba palace of Lagos, a pyramidal assembly

FIGURE 14. "A Cathedral of Huts," at Maciene, Mozambique, isometric drawing. Reproduced with permission of Amancio Guedes.

room inspired by "the work of the ancient African architect Imhotep," and a tower "inspired by the great bronzes of Ife and by the custom of *obi* and the shrines to Oluron."[78] Thus, while Guedes's design for Maciene is grounded in a coherent adaptation of vernacular design from the region where the church was to be built, Curry's is an eclectic mix of monumental motifs various in their provenance. Again, Swiss architects in the 1960s designed prototype mission churches that blended modern design principles with use of economical local materials and adaptation to local climate, sometimes to striking effect.[79] African motifs are integrated with modern design at Justus Dahinden's Nmugongo National Shrine Cathedral and Mityana Pilgrims Shrine in Uganda, at Saint Anne's Cathedral in Brazzaville, at George G. Pace's cathedral at Ibadan, and on a more modest scale in Bulawayo Pentecostal Church, but each of these buildings is modern in conception and construction, and the African character is usually a matter of relatively incidental allusion.[80] African motifs could also at times be used in America for African-American congregations: Calvary Baptist Church in Milwaukee was inspired by the architecture of a village in the Cameroons,[81] while a new building for Martin Luther King's Ebenezer Baptist Church in Atlanta takes the form of an African meeting house, with a roof suggesting grass thatch, African-style crosses on the interior, African textile patterns, and African motifs on the communion table.[82] It may be a more significant step toward indigenization when not only African design but also African practice is envisaged—as when space is provided before the altar for traditional dance in a liturgical context, although this measure requires only arrangement of furnishings.[83] In any case, Guedes's design for Maciene is exceptionally thoroughgoing, with its use not only of African design but of local materials and labor.

One might object that neither Guedes's design nor Curry's was grounded in specifically African understanding of what makes a building sacred; their interest was in the Africanness of the structure but not in the ways a particular African people related to a particular kind of design. Instructive in this respect is the work of an Italian missionary in Madagascar, Cesare Giraudo, who found that the churches built by his predecessors were treated casually by the local populace precisely because they were not grounded in local conceptions of sacrality: they were not oriented, for example, and the altars were either simple wooden tables or artful stonework imported from outside the region (in one case from as far away as Carrara). Giraudo discovered that the altars used in the ancestral religion had sacred dignity (*hàsina*) because they were stone slabs found locally, "forged by the hand of the Creator." And so for a new church he was building he went about seeking an appropriate flat stone of sufficient size. His people soon began to call him *Mompèra mirèmby vàto*, or "The Father who seeks the stone." Eventually he succeeded in building the new church, with an altar and other furnishings, all designed with *hàsina*. The grafting of local notions of sacrality onto Christian liturgical usage made for an immediate transformation in people's attitudes toward their places of worship, which now gained the respect of not only the women and children but even the men of the village.

To return, however, to the Cathedral of Huts. The architect, Amancio Guedes, was born in Lisbon and spent much of his youth and received most of his education in colonial southern Africa. He practiced as an architect in Mozambique from 1950 until the political upheavals of 1974, training and employing Africans as draughtsmen, as sculptors, and in other roles. After 1974 he practiced and taught architecture in South Africa. Along with secular buildings of various kinds, he designed more than one church in southern Africa. His Church of the Twelve Apostles at Gala Massala was designed for a sizeable Anglican parish as a large round mud hut formed with twelve segments; a ring of posts bears most of the weight of the roof, and the altar is placed in the center, under a skylight. Saint James the Great at Nyamandhlovo in Rhodesia, "a rough and strong church," Guedes says, was "put up easily and for very little money, without being bare and stingy." Noting that people usually came to church in crowds at times of celebration and mourning, Guedes designed the space to welcome crowds and allow them to pass easily through seven doors. To accommodate also the individual who came for prayer, he included a chapel. Whenever he needed to save on expenses, Guedes inclined toward vernacular African construction, with buildings made of sticks and reeds, mud and grass, but this initiative was rarely accepted. His clients "always wanted a 'Casa do Branco,' a white man's house, instead. They were ashamed of their own wonderful, most suitable and economical grass houses."

And so the Cathedral of Huts was ultimately never built. Special interest often attaches to churches that were planned but never executed. One wants to know why they were not built. Sometimes the reason is not hard to imagine, as with the inspiration of the 1960s for a chapel to be built on the moon.[84] Often the problem is simply lack of funds. In other cases the design provokes a reaction that may help clarify what is novel and challenging in the architect's proposal. In the case of the Cathedral of Huts, the local bishop preferred a more traditional form of building; indeed, Guedes says rather blithely, the Cathedral of Huts was "summarily dismissed by the Bishop as unsuitable," nor does the architect seem to have been greatly surprised.

One must know something more about the architect's spirit, his eclecticism, his indebtedness to Art Nouveau and the Surrealists, his conception of architecture (in the words of one commentator) "not as a profession . . . but rather as a total artistic immersion, in which clients, builders and staff are manipulated and overwhelmed."[85] In a short essay with the long title "Architects as Magicians, Conjurors, Dealers in Magic Goods, Promises, Potions, Spells—Myself as a Witchdoctor," Guedes reveals a vision of himself and his profession that helps clarify the fluid boundary between his actual projects and his purely visionary fancies. Complaining of the "mechanical and abstract rigours" of current architecture, Guedes describes a "hunger for buildings as symbols, messages, memorials, chambers of ideas and feelings," a hunger so strong that the very need recharges signs and ideas that have lost their original power. Architects must become "technicians of the emotions, makers of smiles, tear-jerkers, exaggerators, spokesmen of dreams, performers of miracles, messengers," inventing "raw, bold, vigorous and intense buildings without taste, absurd and chaotic . . . artificial organisms, mechanical dolls and monsters, purring and puffing, blowing and whistling, containing chambers with the muffled roaring of sea-shells, black rooms, lascivious passages, halls of infinitesimal multiplications, visceral houses turned inside out." The vision was a populist one: "buildings shall yet belong to the people, architecture shall yet become real and alive and beauty shall yet be warm and convulsive."[86] Scarcely calculated to curry the favor of bishops, and worthy of an Italo Calvino, this statement expresses a romantic vision nourished by the indigenous culture of Africa, and seeking (often in vain) to affirm values in that culture to which modern Africans may be ambivalent.

Conclusion

Any religious structure is likely to *have* a wealth of symbolic associations, but not all *display* these associations with equal force. An outsider visiting a Hindu temple might be struck by the richness of symbolism both in the structure itself and in its representations, and on witnessing the ceremonies might grow ever more conscious of the temple's connectedness to the cycles of the seasons, to the stages of life, to the myths of ancient India, and to roles ascribed to individuals and families in accordance with caste and gender. Indeed, this intricate web of associations might become obvious even before the visitor learned the exact meanings of specific symbols. Entering the temple is entering a world of meanings that are never exhausted, and one could know something of their complexity even without knowing precisely what those meanings might be. So too, a visitor to a church might sense something of its symbolic function as a place charged with meanings. Yet more important, even a member of the church might retain that sense of being surrounded by symbols always awaiting fuller articulation, deeper comprehension. A church designed according to a puritan theology and aesthetic is not likely to convey the same richness of meaning, and for its richness of association may depend on verbal rather than on visual and otherwise sensory communication. If it has neither, its fascination will quickly pall. The difference between a church to grow into and a church to grow out of is a difference closely connected with richness or poverty of symbolic association.

When a church is marked by a high degree of symbolic resonance, drawing not so much on a personal vision of the architect but on a culture shared among the living and between them and the dead, what sort of culture is it that such a church enshrines? On the face of it, one might say its culture is a traditional one, but "traditional" can have more than one meaning, and a certain type of traditional culture is not in question here: that culture which is primarily oral in its transmission, with narratives and values preserved in oral recounting and accounting, with the meaning even of its artistic expression either left implicit or explicated orally. In this form of traditional culture, particular themes and narratives can be preserved over long periods. When change occurs, there is little disposition to recognize it explicitly as change. To take only one example of such traditional culture, grassroots devotion to a saint and to a saint's shrine can endure for centuries, even in the face of official disapproval. This is not the sort of culture primarily fostered in the symbolic world of a church. But neither is its opposite, the commercial culture sometimes called "popular," which has a vested interest in obsolescence, with cultural goods meant to be consumed and discarded rather than retained, with information given in place of knowledge, and with interest in traditional sources chiefly so far as they can be recast and represented as newsworthy.

One might speak, rather, of a third form of culture: developmental culture, transmitted more in writing and in written commentary on nonwritten as well as written expression. Such culture may be elitist, but it may also be a means for accommodating, disseminating, and preserving cultural goods of the disempowered that would otherwise be quickly lost. An apocryphal narrative of Christ's life may find its way into a medieval meditation, into the work of an anonymous village artist, into a modern novel or poem. While such culture may not easily acknowledge change, in fact it changes often, preserves the traces of its own revisions, and sometimes reflects on these changes in later commentary on earlier expression.

To be sure, churches also contain elements of traditional and commercial culture. But to the extent that buildings, furnishings, and decorations are grounded in an evolving heritage that refers back to earlier sources and honors and critiques them, giving constant commentary on them, they are expressions of a developmental culture. And it is by keeping symbols alive in this way that churches become vested with symbolic resonance.

5

Late Medieval Beverley

Traditional Churches in a Traditional Culture

That a church of our time could have the complexity of meanings, the intimate and intricate connectedness to people's lives, or the symbolic resonance routinely seen in a late medieval church is virtually unthinkable. A church of the fourteenth or fifteenth century was often a riot of representation: an image of Saint Christopher on the wall opposite the main entrance, guarding its viewers from sudden harm; angels hovering overhead on roof beams; saints peering from panels of the rood screen; biblical scenes and devoutly kneeling patrons shimmering in glass; knights translated into alabaster images on their sarcophagi, lying in full armor, hands folded and feet supported by obliging lions; merchants and their families on brass memorials, beseeching the prayers of passersby; carved monkeys and bears sporting on choir stalls. The clerical establishment or monastic community might rub shoulders with the members of trade guilds, chaplains paid to say mass for local families, or pilgrims making their way with offerings to the bones of saints. Within a church lines were blurred between professional guilds and religious confraternities, between care for the indigent and exaltation of wealthy patrons, between critique and hallowing of social institutions. Far from being out of touch with the world, detached from the needs of the people it was meant to serve, a church would typically be saturated with intimate and jumbled links to society. A critic might see the complex strands linking private life, family life, social life, celebration and mourning as an accumulation of cobwebs, well swept away by the Reformers. But even after the Reformers did their work, the saturation of ordinary life and social convention with pious associations can still be read in the design and furnishing of late medieval churches.

Like the church itself, the liturgy would be enmeshed with social convention. Virginia Reinberg has also argued persuasively that in the late medieval parish the laity would have had a lively experience of the mass different from and parallel to that of the clergy.[1] The priest with his missal might have a keen sense of the mass as sacrifice and sacrament; for the laity it would have revolved more around communal rituals of greeting and sharing, giving and receiving, and peace-making, all richly resonant within the context of the society.

> Any congregant present and awake could not have failed to recognize in the gestures accompanying the Gospel reading—standing, hat doffing, saluting—elements of seigneurial rites of justice and administration, that is, the peace-keeping functions of the community. The offertory procession closely resembles not only almsgiving ceremonies, but also obligatory donations by tenants to seigneurs. In the distribution of *pain bénit* we see shadows of seigneurial and communal distributions of wine, cakes, and other gifts. In its entirety, the greeting, peace-making, and gift exchange of the mass might replicate communal oaths taken by urban and rural communities. . . . In this sense the late medieval liturgy can be viewed as the establishment of social and spiritual solidarity among God, the Church, and the lay community.

Churches were in dialogue with their environments. Some churches were hemmed into the tight quarters of a crowded medieval city and thus integrated into the cityscape. Those major English churches that have expansive grounds, famously the cathedral close at Salisbury, convey a greater sense of detachment that has sometimes been seen as a mark of the monastic influence on English cathedrals. Any major church is likely to have dominated its surroundings when it was built, and even if it now seems out of place in the city that has grown around it, like a guest who has stayed behind after last week's party, it will sometimes provide a touch of relief to an otherwise overbuilt cityscape. In the countryside a church may dominate its village, but sometimes a village church will be harder to locate than an urban one. One may search back and forth through even a small village, frustrated in the search for a church, only to find it sequestered at the end of Church Road or Vicarage Lane. While churches in towns might be prominent, they often rivaled each other for influence and attention, and within a town it is often not a single church but the ensemble of church architecture that repays analysis.

Intertwined with layers of religious and social meaning, late medieval churches were rich in symbolic resonance, and when resources sufficed they could also be sumptuous works of architectural and applied art. But did their strength in aesthetic impact and symbolic resonance come at a liturgical price?

Did the focus on these factors come at the expense of clear spatial dynamism and centering focus? To grasp both the strengths and the perils of church-building in this era we must take a close and careful look at how churches were built, how they were used, and what meaning they had in a specific representative setting.

Saint John of Beverley and Beverley Minster

The town of Beverley in southeastern Yorkshire gives ample evidence of the meanings a church could have in a particular religious and social milieu.[2] It developed as a place of pilgrimage centered on the relics of Saint John of Beverley.[3] The Venerable Bede speaks of Saint John at some length in his *Ecclesiastical History*, telling, for example, how he once blessed some holy water for the consecration of a church and then used it to heal the wife of the local aristocrat for whom the church had been built.[4] Schooled under the abbess Hilda of Whitby, he became bishop of Hexham, then in 706 of York.[5] While he was at York he used a spot in the woods as a place of retreat, and when he resigned his episcopacy around 714 he withdrew thither as monk. Before long his place of burial was sought after by pilgrims, and it was probably around this site that the town of Beverley grew, with Beverley Minster (or the church of Saint John at Beverley) (figs. 15–16) as its primary attraction.[6]

Tradition claims that Saint John's monastery was destroyed by Vikings in 866, only to be refounded in the tenth century with a college of secular canons, but it is at least as likely that the house enjoyed continuous undocumented survival.[7] Legend further tells that King Athelstan, who unified northern with southern England, was on his way to battle against the Scots around 937 when he heard the report of pilgrims who told him of the wondrous power of the relics at Beverley. He thus went to visit the church, lifted its banner and carried it with him, and then returned with the banner after securing victory at Brunanburgh. He bestowed mighty privileges and liberties on this foundation, wishing the Minster to be "as free as heart can think or eye can see."[8] Even if little in the legend is historical, the cult of the saint and the association with the king were crucial to development of both the Minster and the town.[9] Medieval clerics knew well the power of a good legend.

By the twelfth century the cult of Saint John of Beverley was growing in importance, with miracles recorded at his tomb for pilgrims who came not only from Yorkshire but from other parts of England, Scotland, and Ireland.[10] The cult was focused on two places within the Minster: the saint's tomb (at the east end of the nave) and a shrine (at the high altar, possibly on some kind of platform above the reredos). There was some vaccilation between these locations, particularly when the collapse of the tower required rebuilding of the entire east end of the church and a temporary high altar was placed over the

FIGURE 15. Beverley Minster, Beverley, Yorkshire, exterior. Photograph by Richard Kieckhefer.

tomb. The shrine regained its position of prominence in the late thirteenth and early fourteenth centuries with the provision of a new reliquary and silver-paneled casing that could be raised for display by a system of pulleys. Pilgrims coming to the Minster on feast days could approach the shrine not by going directly from the nave up into the chancel but by going around and behind the chancel, approaching the saint's relics through the retrochoir, and this was the chief interest of pilgrims. But the tomb was never entirely neglected, even when the relics had been removed from it, and pilgrims' offerings continued to be made to both sites.[11]

The feast of Saint John of Beverley was on May 7, while the feast of his translation (commemorating the removal of his relics from the tomb to a shrine at the time of his canonization in 1037) was October 25, a sort of calendrical double-dipping that was not uncommon. More important than either of these days, however, was Rogation Monday, when the relics were borne in procession out of the Minster and through the town, pausing at various chapels before returning to the Minster three days later on the Ascension. This was the occasion for the greatest influx of pilgrims and for the grandest public display in Beverley. Members of the local craft guilds donned their finery to watch the procession from wooden platforms called "castles." The honor of carrying the reliquary went to eight hereditary bearers who underwent a process of purification before undertaking this responsibility.[12]

FIGURE 16. Beverley Minster, Beverley, Yorkshire, interior. Photograph by Richard Kieckhefer.

From a national perspective, the dignity of the Minster was bound up with the banner of Saint John of Beverley, which troops under the archbishop of York took into successful battle against the Scots in 1138 and which Edward I, Edward II, and Edward III later borrowed. The victory of Henry V at Agincourt on the feast of Saint John's translation added further to the saint's renown as a military patron.[13] Indeed, the military significance of the saint was so great that when troops were levied for the royal army the representative from Beverley was a cleric to bear Saint John's banner.[14]

In one crucial respect, again associated with the privileges given by Athelstan, the sacred geography of medieval Beverley was exceptionally clear and distinctive. There were concentric circles, marked with stone crosses, extending outward from a special object located at the Minster, and this object was neither an altar nor a relic but a chair: the *frith stol*, or "peace chair." Anyone charged with criminal misconduct could make his way to the Minster for the protection of sanctuary. If he made his way to the outermost ring, he was in principle safe, and anyone molesting him was subject to a legal penalty. If the fugitive progressed further toward the frith stol, the penalties for violation of sanctuary were more severe, and after passing five of these boundaries the criminal could hope to proceed all the way to the chair, where the protection was greatest. Enjoying "the peace and freedom of Saint John of Beverley," he swore obedience to the clergy, told in detail of his misconduct, and for thirty days was entitled to remain at the Minster. The canons were expected to do what they could to reconcile him with his pursuers; if they failed, they were to assure safe conduct out of the region. Eventually the criminal might enter permanently into the service of the Minster. This system was perhaps the best prospect for rehabilitation in a society that otherwise did little to rehabilitate criminals. Nor was it a rare occurrence for a miscreant to seek refuge here. A register for the years 1478–99 lists 132 fugitives from Yorkshire and beyond who claimed sanctuary,[15] and over the next forty years there were 337 more.

The privilege of sanctuary at Beverley was hardly unique, nor was the focusing of that privilege on a stone chair, a "chair of peace" or throne: York Minster once had such a chair, and one survives at Hexham.[16] Jacobus de Voragine listed as one of the reasons for consecrating a church the guarantee that those who fled to it for sanctuary would be spared: "The lords of the land grant this privilege to some churches after they are consecrated, to protect those fleeing to them from pursuit."[17] It has been estimated that in the churches of England at any one time there might be altogether a thousand individuals claiming the right of sanctuary. But the privilege at Beverley was more elaborate and more effective than the sanctuary provided by most other churches.[18] Because the privilege at Beverley applied not only to the church building but to a surrounding district of roughly a mile and a half, fugitives could more easily settle and work in the town, as they did, sometimes causing friction and resentment. It may have been one of these men, identified as a servant of the chapter, who went out of control one day on the busy streets of Beverley, forced a priest against a wall, stuck the point of his sword against the priest's chest, and threatened with a curse that if he uttered a word he would pin the hapless cleric to the wall.[19]

King Athelstan was said, then, to have founded a special shrine, given it exceptional protection for fugitives, and established a college of canons to tend it, and popular belief in these traditions, as much as the privileges themselves, gave Beverley and its Minster a distinctive place in the sacred and cultural geography of late medieval England.

Beverley Minster as an Institution

The term *minster* is one worth examining. Its use is various. It is or has been used for York Minster, which is a cathedral; for the major churches at Ripon and Southwell, much later made cathedrals; for Westminster Abbey, which throughout the Middle Ages was a monastery and served briefly in the sixteenth century as a cathedral; and for Beverley and Howden minsters, which may have arisen out of earlier monastic foundations but in their later form were neither cathedrals nor monasteries; and even for such lesser churches as those at Stonegrave and Kirkdale. Not surprisingly, the word gives rise to confusion. It comes from the Latin *monasterium*, for monastery, and in its earliest usage that was its meaning. But during the Saxon era there was a great deal of fluidity in the status of a particular institution: a place might be founded as a monastery and be changed to a nonmonastic house with canons attached to it, or it might be founded as a church without monks and later be reestablished as a monastery. By the tenth and eleventh centuries, "minster" often had the broad meaning of "superior church," a church of higher status than an ordinary parish church, often but not always an older one, often but not invariably a house with canons attached to it, in any case a place with more than one priest serving it, and a center that might provide for the religious needs not only of a locality but of a region. But the boundaries remained fluid; as one historian has said, some minsters "may have passed in and out of monastic phases, according to the whims or inclinations of individual rulers."[20] Major churches designated as minsters are more common in Yorkshire than in other parts of England. They are perhaps best seen as survivals of an early medieval system in which a church with several priests would serve not only a town or village but an entire district; in the tenth through twelfth centuries they were largely displaced by the local parish churches built in most parts of England, but in Yorkshire many of them survived and retained something of their original function. Along with the churches of Ripon and Southwell, Beverley Minster even served as something of a subcathedral, with its clergy organized along lines similar to those of York Minster.[21] These were all major ecclesiastical institutions, which meant they were also liturgical and cultural centers: in a society that knew almost no other publicly accessible art, a church and especially a minster provided ceremonial solemnity and aesthetic grandeur rarely experienced elsewhere.

The clergy making up the chapter or ruling body of the Minster were its nine canons, many of whom had spent time in the king's service.[22] They met in an octagonal chapter house (no longer extant, although the ceremonial entryway to it may still be seen in the north chancel aisle). Canons were assigned to specific altars in the Minster, and each was responsible for a parish in or near Beverley.[23] The division of this responsibility was not even: the canon assigned to the altar of Saint Martin—which for some time was located in an oratory just outside the Minster, over the charnel house—had charge of the greater part of the town. Five of the canons appear to have been assigned to serve parishioners in the town of Beverley, and three others served the surrounding countryside. The layfolk under the care of each of the canons would come for the sacraments to the altar assigned to that canon. If they were housebound, the vicar attached to that altar would take them communion.[24]

But this arrangement was mostly theoretical, because the canons' positions were largely sinecures; they might spend little time in residence at Beverley, and they hired vicars to attend to the cure of souls in the parishes to which they were assigned.[25] For the actual round of services they hired seven individuals who would elsewhere have been called vicars choral, but here they went by the strange name of berefellarii, possibly meaning "bare skins."[26] Apart from the canons, their vicars, and the berefellarii there were numerous other members of the Minster staff. When Archbishop Thomas Arundel set forth ordinances in 1391 regulating the clergy of the Minster, the list included a precentor, a chancellor, a sacrist, a precentor's clerk, a clerk of the charnel, clerks of the berefellarii, two thurifers, eight choristers, two sacrist's clerks, and two men who served as vergers and bell-ringers. Arundel allowed the canons to maintain their private houses outside the Minster but required their vicars to share common residence and meals, an arrangement that seems to have been impossible to enforce with full rigor.[27] In addition the Minster had chantry priests serving it: nine in 1444, and fifteen by the time of the Dissolution under Henry VIII.[28] At every level, membership in this clerical establishment might be either a vocation or a career, and for those who saw it in the latter light the commitment to celibacy might be less than fervent; sexual irregularity was a frequent subject for correction at visitations, one of which led a minor cleric to admit that he had transgressed with no fewer than five women.[29]

The canons lost little affection on the archbishop of York, who technically was a member of the chapter but was expected to leave the other canons to their own business, and normally did so. In 1381 the exceptionally zealous Archbishop Alexander Neville set out to subject the Minster to his authority with a formal visitation. He sought at least an opportunistic alliance with the wealthier townspeople of Beverley in opposition to the canons of the Minster, at a time when the lay population of Beverley was eager to establish a power base distinct from the Minster. Faced with this coalition challenging their customary independence, the canons went for some time into self-imposed exile from their own church. The archbishop was greeted by only a handful of clergy, most of the canons and vicars having absented themselves, requiring the archbishop to bring vicars choral from York itself to celebrate services. This *cause célèbre* was hardly typical of relations yet did bring into public view tensions that at other times might be managed more discreetly.[30]

The archbishop of York was the temporal lord of Beverley, and Edward the Confessor granted him the right to hold an annual fair, which was one reason for the town's expansion.[31] The archbishop collected rents in the town, received dues, and levied tolls on merchandise sold in the market.[32] But while the archbishop was lord of the greater part of the town and its surrounding territory, the Minster also held property in various parts of Beverley, and these holdings could always lead to friction. Thus, there were conflicts over rights to pasture livestock on Swine Moor. The Minster's sanctuary privileges could also lead to uneasy relations, because some unwelcome fugitives settled in the town; they were forbidden to carry weapons, and in 1460 they were prevented from becoming burgesses of the community.[33]

Perception of churches is always influenced by people's experience of churchmen (and in much more recent times churchwomen), but even within a particular community such as Beverley these churchmen were so diverse and related to laity in such varied ways that to speak of "the Church" and its role in society is meaningless. "The Church" existed as a theological construct, but what townspeople would have experienced firsthand was a diversity of clerics with diverse and often conflicting roles and interests.

Beverley Minster as a Church Building

As Rosemary Horrox has observed, "for much of the middle ages worship at the Minster, as in many medieval churches, was carried out on the edge of a building site." When a medieval church was expanded, the old walls were typically left standing until the new ones had been completed, then the old ones were removed or refashioned into arcades, and in the meantime liturgy could be continued in the existing space. Sometimes compromises had to be made: for example, because construction was in process on the nave in 1313 at Beverley Minster, the schoolmaster had to celebrate the feast of Saint Nicholas not at that saint's altar but at Saint Blaise's.[34] And because construction could take decades, medieval worshipers had to take such inconveniences in stride.[35]

By the end of the Middle Ages the old Saxon church built by Saint John of Beverley had been more than once rebuilt. The Saxon archbishop of York,

Ealdred, still in office at the time of the Norman Conquest, was a major benefactor of the Minster and responsible for the building of a new sanctuary there, which may have been built already in the latest Continental style—the first significant rebuilding of which we know.[36] The church was largely rebuilt around 1170 in the English Romanesque or "Norman" style—the second major rebuilding. Throughout England, the Normans set about quickly rebuilding cathedrals and other major churches, with the result that almost nothing of pre-Norman work survives in these larger structures, although in its parish churches England is still uncommonly well endowed with early medieval architecture.[37] At the end of the Norman phase of architecture, a fire in 1188 required repair to the Minster's nave. Then around 1213 the tower collapsed, bringing much of the church to ruin, as the fall of a tower so often did, and necessitating the third rebuilding, which took place in spurts. Reconstruction at the east end was done by about 1250, in the newly fashionable Early English phase of the Gothic. The thirteenth-century builders ensured an uncluttered clerestory by using iron tie-bars within the church instead of flying buttresses on the exterior to restrain the outward thrust from the weight of the vaults.[38] In the early fourteenth century the work of rebuilding continued westward to the nave, but the architect chose to remain faithful to the Early English style even though it was now out of fashion. As in many other places, work was interrupted in the mid–fourteenth century at the time of the Black Death.[39] The late fourteenth and early fifteenth centuries brought rebuilding of the rest of the nave, and now the builders took advantage of their opportunity to work in the latest Perpendicular Gothic style.

The result of this long process of construction and reconstruction was a much-celebrated edifice. Beverley Minster has elicited its share of superlatives, as from the late nineteenth-century antiquary Arthur Francis Leach. "There is no more beautiful building in England than Beverley Minster," Leach opined. Seen across the plain, it "dominates the landscape with an impressiveness of grandeur that the mother-church of York cannot surpass," while from nearby it "may well claim to be the lovelier daughter of a lovely mother," with perfect proportions and exquisite detail. Leach's own first sight of the Minster came on a damp November evening, and at first he saw the parish church of Saint Mary and pondered disconsolately whether this could be the famous Minster. Then the drizzle ended, the fog cleared, the moon appeared, and he made his way through the town to the Minster he had expected. "Sir Walter Scott warns us to visit Melrose Abbey by moonlight; but what, even by moonlight, is that mangled fragment of a second-rate church, with its mean surroundings, compared with the vision of Beverley Minster in its entire and perfect beauty?"[40] Leach was one Victorian who knew how to go beyond "very nice" and "very pretty."

The pilgrim or fugitive who made his way to Beverley Minster might well have been astonished on passing through its doors to discover that his place of devotion and of refuge was also a place of sumptuous architecture exceeding anything he had seen before. At 333 feet in length, it was among the largest churches in northern England. And tricks of perspective could give the visitor a sense of even greater length: the bosses in the choir vault are smaller toward the east end than toward the west, giving the illusion of a longer choir to a pilgrim viewing it from the nave.[41] The use of the Early English style of the thirteenth century even after it had gone out of fashion gave the interior a greater sense of coherence than many English churches could claim. Indeed, John Leland in the mid–sixteenth century singled out the "fair uniform making" of the Minster as one of its salient qualities.[42] The vertical thrust of the high arcades was continued upward into the triforium with its trefoil arches and then the windows of the clerestory. The light magnesian limestone from nearby quarries contrasts with the Purbeck marble shafts used in the clerestory—and at the east end also in the triforium—accentuating the play of light and shade and giving an effect of dignified and harmonious splendor.[43] The glass now seen in the nave windows is of the nineteenth century, but the great window at the east end, beyond the high altar, is from the fifteenth and gives a sense of the spectacle awaiting the fugitive, the pilgrim, or any other visitor. (English churches of the thirteenth and following centuries almost always have rectangular east ends with great windows, allowing the light of the morning sun to flood that end, while French churches with their ambulatories and radiating chapels commonly had more darkened chancels.) The retrochoir, or area behind the high altar, now a Lady Chapel, in the later Middle Ages housed the shrine of Saint John of Beverley to which pilgrims would make their way, just as at Canterbury they would have found the shrine of Saint Thomas Becket and at Saint Albans that of the patron martyr in the retrochoir.

Particular items within the church might well have impressed the visitor as dazzlingly ornate, notably the tomb of the fourteenth century sculpted for a woman of the Percy family. As one writer says of this Percy tomb, "Clusters of luscious fruits and foliage, hosts of little angels hovering everywhere, armoured knights squeezed into spandrels, and a serene statue of Christ holding the Virgin's soul in a napkin, invest it with charm and vitality."[44] For the rest, the impression would have been rather one of orderly and majestic harmony befitting a church of national stature. The words of a modern guide convey precisely what the architects no doubt intended: "Beverley Minster . . . had to convey to the beholder something of the character of the Master of the house— that is, of God. Thus we see a building of serene majesty, in which every tiny detail is carefully executed, just as Almighty God is concerned for the smallest details of His creation."[45]

Apart from the tomb and shrine of Saint John of Beverley, the Minster had other shrines and chapels serving as devotional foci and objects for donation. By far the most important of these was a statue sometimes referred to as the "glorious Virgin," possibly referring to its adornment, but perhaps to attributes connected with the Assumption or Coronation.[46] Apart from the high altar there were at least sixteen further altars in the late medieval Minster and in the adjacent charnel house. As at many if not most late medieval churches, lay experience of the mass would have come more from nave altars than from mass at the high altar.[47] Some of these altars were assigned to the nine canons, and most of these served as the parish altars for laity in and around Beverley. There were altars dedicated to the Holy Trinity, Saint Anne, Saint Thomas of Canterbury, Saint William, Saint Blaise, Saint Nicholas, and Saint Christopher. Many of them served for perpetual chantries. Some also served the liturgical needs of craft guilds; the altar of Saint Christopher, for example, was used both by the porters' guild (after all, Saint Christopher was best known for carrying the Christ Child) and by that of the painters and goldsmiths.[48] The Corpus Christi guild, which organized the annual procession on the feast of Corpus Christi, used the Saint Nicholas altar in the charnel for its liturgical functions; while the guild served in part as an association for the town's lesser clergy, laymen could also be members.[49]

The principle that wealth breeds wealth applies to churches as much as to any other institution. The Minster was the third wealthiest ecclesiastical foundation in Yorkshire, below only York Minster and Saint Mary's Abbey.[50] And its dignity made it an attractive object for bequests. Testators wishing to be commemorated publicly in the Minster might specify a particular and notable object for their bequests, as when one of the canons left £40 in 1416 for the grand east window.[51] The wealthy donated embroidered bedclothes to be recycled as liturgical hangings. Clergy gave vestments to the Minster or to particular chapels in it: one, for example, bequeathed to the chapel of Saint Katherine a set of vestments made of gold cloth on silk.[52]

But for financing of construction, particularly of major rebuilding campaigns, the Minster relied on the standard method of selling indulgences. The archbishop granted a forty-day indulgence in 1290, for example, in anticipation of work on the nave. In the early sixteenth century a printed flysheet assured patrons of the Minster that they would be the beneficiaries of intercession from thirty priests who prayed every day in the church, that they would be enrolled in a kind of benefactors' fraternity founded already by Saint John of Beverley, and that among the indulgences they would gain was one dating from the tenth-century pope John XII. (In other circumstances those offering indulgences sometimes made the even more implausible claim that they had been established by Saint Peter.) Already in the early fourteenth century there were unauthorized collectors taking funds ostensibly for the Minster but in fact pocketing the proceeds. By the fifteenth century the sale was farmed out to a collector who paid £10 annually to the Minster and retained as profit anything he collected above that sum from pious donors.[53]

The Minster and the Parish Church of Saint Mary

By 1377 Beverley was the second largest town in Yorkshire, a town with a not inconsiderable accumulation of wealth and a place that could support a variety of ecclesiastical institutions. Centrally important as it was, the Minster was not in fact in the center of Beverley; it was and is at the south end of town, and if we wish to understand the complexities of sacred topography we must know something of the churches and religious houses other than the Minster. In the first half of the twelfth century the town was expanding to the north, and it was at this time that the chapel of Saint Mary seems to have been founded, at some distance north of the Minster (fig. 17).[54] While Saint Mary's never gained the national prominence of its more powerful neighbor, a resident of Beverley might well think of the ecclesiastical life of the town in terms of an ellipse with two focal points, the Minster to the south and Saint Mary's to the north.

Founded as a chapel of ease attached to the Minster—or, more precisely, to the altar of Saint Martin in the Minster—Saint Mary's was made into a vicarage in 1325.[55] Technically the vicar remained under the authority of the Minster's canon attached to the altar of Saint Martin, but in fact he was largely independent. The clergy of Saint Mary's did have responsibilities at the Minster. They were required, for example, to participate in the Minster's processions, and in 1304 they were reminded to do so and threatened with excommunication if they neglected this duty. In the following year they were admonished not to withhold offerings of wax and candles they were supposed to pass along to the Minster,[56] and before long they were reminded that their clergy must be examined and approved by the Minster chapter and swear obedience to it. "All this," W. C. B. Smith points out, "must have been irritating to a church which by this time was conscious of its own independence and its popularity in the town."[57] Already in the early years of Saint Mary's the increasingly wealthy and independent townspeople were evidently choosing it as their own church and lavishing money on it, often in preference to the Minster. It was quickly adopted as a center by various of the town guilds; fully thirty-eight guilds are said to have maintained their "guild lights" at altars in Saint Mary's. Unlike the Minster, which was governed by outsiders in the chapter and trampled by outsiders coming as pilgrims and fugitives, Saint Mary's was the townspeople's own church.[58] By the early fifteenth century there was a self-governing parish guild, established with royal license, which ran an almshouse and seems to have had a role in the upkeep of the church's fabric, presumably taking responsibility for the nave in particular. When the tower collapsed in 1520, a new tower and nave were constructed, attached to a chancel of late thirteenth- and early fourteenth-century construction. Major patrons of the new construction are memorialized in carvings above the north arcade, and their benefac-

FIGURE 17. Beverley St Mary's, Beverley, Yorkshire, interior. Photograph by Richard Kieckhefer.

tions are there recorded: one, for example, had provided two and a half piers for the arcade.

These two churches are typically English in the monastic influence they display in their design. The difference here between England and the Continent is relative, but the role of monks as missionaries in England, and more immediately the influence of many English cathedrals that served also as monastic houses, may be seen as contributing factors to the design even of parish churches. There was no reason in principle why a parish church, like a monastic one, had to be cruciform in design, or had to have a fully developed choir with the elaborate choir stalls seen even at Saint Mary's, but many English parish churches do mimic monastic churches in these ways.[59] The second typically English characteristic is a rigorous insistence on orientation. Granted, both the Minster and Saint Mary's tilt a bit north of a perfect east-west axis, but in both cases it is not only the high altar but the altars in lateral chapels as well that are placed toward the east. This was the tendency on the Continent as well, but not all countries were as insistent on orientation as England.

Taking their opposing positions in the external geography of Beverley, at the north and south ends of the main axis running through the town, these two churches are interestingly comparable in their internal geography. The first point here is that they exemplify in different ways the tendency of later medieval churches toward compartmentalization. In the late Middle Ages the churches of England often became carved into distinct spaces, each of them often the preserve of a particular guild or even a family, whose members would profit after death from masses said in their chantry chapels.[60] Saint Mary's has a chapel of Saint Michael in the north chancel aisle, one dedicated to Saint Katharine in the south chancel aisle, and a chapel of the Holy Trinity east of the north transept, and chapels were created within the Minster as well. The canon Richard de Ravenser was a leading founder of perpetual chantries, meant to ensure that masses would be said for his soul after his death until Gabriel's trumpet summoned him from his tomb—or rather, at best, until the Reformers dissolved these chantries in the sixteenth century. But for the most part these chapels at Beverley were not for the exclusive use of any guild or family; rather, a chapel might serve as the location for several chantries, endowed for the souls of several individuals. The earliest of the chantries at Saint Mary's, founded in 1388, was established at the preexisting altar of Saint Katherine rather than in a private chapel. Thus, compartmentalization did not always mean privatization, or if chapels were private preserves it was often for multiple individuals and groups. It is further worth noting that the partitioned spaces were in all these cases lateral: they were in aisles, to the north or south of either the chancel or the nave. Thus the division of a church interior may seem to us uncontrolled, but it did generally follow certain basic rules, the most important being that the church's central east-west axis remained immune from appropriation.

Each of these churches at Beverley exemplifies the fully developed cruciform plan. Symbolically, the plan stood for the cross of Christ. Practically, it provided space for a multiplicity of chapels, particuarly along the east sides of the transepts. Aesthetically, it gave the opportunity for an intricately articulated ensemble; the visitor in either church has a clear sense of the progression from west to east, from the nave through the choir and on to the sanctuary, yet the pattern is made more complex and more interesting by its opening out into the subsidiary spaces of aisles and transepts. The Minster has an aisled chancel with transepts, a crossing surmounted by a low tower and flanked by aisled transepts, and an aisled nave of ten bays; Saint Mary's has an aisled five-bay chancel, a crossing with a central tower over it, transepts with aisles to the east, an exceptionally large Trinity chapel (used by the merchant or mercers guild) to the north of the chancel; a chapel of Saint Katherine to the south; and an aisled nave of six bays.[61] The Minster has not only the expected transepts extending from the crossing, for the transverse bar of the cross, but a second set of transepts further east, on either side of the chancel, yielding the double cross of Lorraine, with a second transverse bar (corresponding to the bar on the cross with Pilate's inscription "I.N.R.I.").

Both churches are marked by an aesthetic of ordered complexity. They both display an element of eclecticism, but more than many English churches they maintained coherence and harmony through the phases of their construction. The Minster combines thirteenth- with fifteenth-century styles, and close inspection of Saint Mary's reveals work of every century from the twelfth to the sixteenth. Eclecticism is certainly known on the Continent as well, but English builders on the whole had more tolerance for it. Very often English churches are works of bricolage, with Norman fabric of the twelfth century embedded in later work in the various Gothic styles of the thirteenth through early sixteenth centuries. An originally unaisled nave might have a north aisle added in the Early English style of the thirteenth century, then a south aisle in the Decorated style of the early fourteenth, then a south porch and west tower in the Perpendicular style in the fifteenth. Apart from additions there were replacements or enlargements: the chancel was often rebuilt on a grander scale in the thirteenth century to accommodate the more elaborate liturgy then expected, and the nave might need to be rebuilt in whole or in part if a crossing tower collapsed, as happened in both of the churches at Beverley. But in these churches at Beverley more than in many the new construction was sympathetic addition to the existing fabric. At Saint Mary's, for example, the spandrels in the new nave arcade (i.e., the spaces between the arches) are decorated with quatrefoil carvings that echo those found in the chancel, and the fifteenth-century window that largely fills the west end is echoed by one inserted in the east end. If one examined the stonework closely one could discover traces of work from the twelfth century—patches of Norman zigzag ornament in the stonework, for example—but these are only incidental exceptions to a general effort at architectural coherence.

As I have shown, one of the main tendencies in a longitudinal church is toward segmentation. In this respect, these churches at Beverley are apparently alike but actually quite different. Abstracting from the retrochoir at the Minster, each church has the standard elements extending from east to west: the sanctuary and the choir (together constituting the chancel), whose upkeep in English canon law was in principle the responsibility of the clergy; then the nave, which was the responsibility of the lay parishioners. But the Minster, being a collegiate establishment, had a chancel that was more fully closed off. As in a monastery or in many cathedrals, the chancel was essentially a chapel for the clerical establishment, and the nave was in effect an independent church for such laypeople as would frequent the place. At Saint Mary's there would have been a rood screen, surmounted by the cross (or "rood") and the figures of Saint Mary and Saint John; the screen now in place is a nineteenth-century restoration with some recycled late medieval materials. But the rood screen would have permitted laypeople in the nave at least some view of the mass being celebrated at the high altar; it was a partial barrier to two spaces that could both be used for a single liturgy. The screen might itself have been furnished on its lower register with paintings with carefully selected images of saints that would further enrich the network of associations, something like an Eastern Orthodox iconostasis.[62] At the Minster, on the other hand, the choir stalls were built up at the west end and would have obstructed view, and there might further have been a screen analogous to the massive pulpitum in a cathedral; at present there is an organ screen. In short, the Minster is more sharply segmented than Saint Mary's, with the chancel more clearly marked off as space for the clerical establishment.

While these were churches thickly layered with symbolism, their resonance would have come mainly from their bold display of the sainted and unsainted dead. Emphasis on veneration saints was marked in particular by the pilgrimage to Saint John of Beverley, but also by the dedication of guilds to patron saints, and of course the celebration almost daily of saints' feast days. Mass and prayers were offered routinely for deceased members of the community, especially those for whom living guild members, family members, and chantry priests were responsible. Even on the ceiling of Saint Mary's there were painted images of English monarchs, symbols of national identity and pride, but also reminders of linkage with the Church either suffering or triumphant. Everywhere the eye rested it would find symbolic reminders of connectedness to saints in heaven and souls in purgatory.

The wealthier among the local deceased had their memorials within the church walls, and their location was a posthumous mark of the social standing they occupied during life.[63] As a rule, only the high born, the clergy, and the wealthier merchants or artisans could expect burial within the church, and among these it was a mark of distinction to be buried in the chancel near the altar. A major monument such as the Percy tomb at Beverley Minster was a reminder of the family's dignity. Off the north chancel aisle is a chapel built around 1490 for the burial of Henry Percy, earl of Northumberland, and there were other Percy tombs in the church as well. Indeed, the entire east end of the north choir aisle served as a mausoleum chapel for the Percys, with members of the family buried there amid not only funereal sculpture but commemorative glass: one window showed scenes of one of the earls in prayer with his family, mourning relatives preparing his body for burial, and coats of arms.[64] Lesser dignitaries of the later Middle Ages might be memorialized by brasses embedded in the floors, but the churches at Beverley are not rich in these. Still, at least twenty-two individuals are known from their wills to have requested burial in Beverley Minster between 1382 and 1493, including a precentor of that church, a rector of a church at Houghton, a residentiary canon of York, and several laypeople, burgesses and merchants of Beverley, and at least twenty-nine asked for burial in Saint Mary's during the years 1343–1497.[65] John Brompton in his will of 1446 bequeathed his soul to God, to Saint Mary, to Saints Michael, Alban, John of Beverley, Ursula and her companions, all the virgin saints, and sundry others, and his body to the collegiate church for burial near his wife.[66] Beneath the Trinity Chapel at Saint Mary's was a crypt; elsewhere a crypt might be most importantly the place for the shrine of a saint, but crypts could serve as places of ordinary burial, and here at Saint Mary's the crypt was constructed in the late thirteenth century as a charnel house for bones exhumed from the churchyard to make way for new burials.

These churches celebrated the living as well as the dead in their art. In particular, the churches of Beverley shared a fascination with musicians. The interior of the Minster was decorated at the west end with stone carvings of numerous figures, mostly either grotesques or musicians of various sorts. And at Saint Mary's one of the piers in the north nave arcade is surmounted with a carving of five minstrels, while other musicians appear carved in wood on bench ends, depicted on windows and on ceiling bosses, and elsewhere. Indeed, it has been claimed that these two churches taken together contain the world's most extensive carvings of medieval instruments—the tabor, the cittern and viol, the bombarde and hautboy, the bagpipe and many others, altogether approximately 140.

J. G. Davies's work on the secular use of churches has heightened readers' awareness of the ways sacred space could be used for what we might consider profane activities: business meetings, church ales, and the like.[67] The lines of distinction between sacred and profane were not altogether erased, to be sure; the chancel was usually reserved for liturgy—and for the clergy.[68] Yet the nave could be put to all sorts of uses. At Beverley, the Minster was the site for celebrations other than strictly liturgical ones, including banquets and the dispensing of drinks for various groups such as the deacons, the choristers, and carolers. Most of these no doubt seemed harmless entertainments, but the more boisterous festivities could fall victim to the axe of a reformer who was not amused, as when Archbishop Arundel set out to eradicate the "ancient custom, or rather corruption, of the King of Fools."[69]

Beverley also claims distinction for its surviving misericords, the wooden seats in the choir stalls—often with fanciful carvings on their undersides—that enabled clergy in the choir to prop themselves up during long services.[70] Saint Mary's has twenty-eight choir stalls made at Ripon in 1445, although they may have been brought to this church (presumably replacing earlier ones) at the dissolution of a nearby monastery in the sixteenth century. In any case, the carvings include common themes such as Reynard the Fox dressed up as a preaching friar, as well as an elephant with realistically carved feet (unlike the frequent medieval depiction of elephants with horses' hooves). The choir stalls at the Minster were made by a later generation of Ripon carvers, in 1520, and the sixty-eight stalls that survive with their misericords are said to represent the largest collection in England. The preaching fox appears here too, and an ape who steals from the pack of a sleeping pedlar, and a cat playing with a mouse, and a wife who grabs her husband by his hair as he carries her along in a wheelbarrow, along with much else. At Saint Mary's this interest in secular themes extends to a famous stone carving of a pilgrim rabbit beside the sacristy door, a product of around 1325 that tradition claims and suspended disbelief accepts as the source for the image of Lewis Carroll's White Rabbit.

Why were medieval Christians so keen on sealing off monuments of distinctly sacred architecture, only to blur the distinction between the sacred and the profane by filling them with these secular motifs? The question rests in part on a false premise, that the sacred was meant to be sealed off from the profane. The drolleries on misericords and other features of the church interiors—jesters on bench ends, labyrinths on roof bosses, and a thousand further concessions to whimsy—might be compared with the grotesqueries on church exteriors, particularly the gargoyles. But when gargoyles are grotesque (and they are not always so) there is the excuse that, being perched high on the church walls, they serve the apotropaic function of warding off evil influences, and that hardly seems the point when Reynard the Fox makes his way onto a misericord or a bench end. Part of the answer is that medieval Christians did in fact use their churches for secular as well as sacred activities, for parish ales and other social functions, and for public business transactions, despite the complaints of scrupulous reformers. A church was spacious enough for such use, as few other buildings were. But most of these activities were confined to the nave. Why, then, the intrusion of secular representations even into the chancel itself where the choir stalls are placed? Reynard the Fox may seem merely frivolous, as will to some minds the wild man or the occasional amphisbaena or hoopoe that shows up on a misericord; elsewhere are themes that the puritan will find in dubious taste, such as the misericord at Bristol Cathedral showing a woman eating an oversize phallus.[71] One can only suppose that the late medieval canons who sat on these misericords took a broadly tolerant approach to such matters, and that the more pious among them were willing to see in this mingling of the sacred and the secular a coincidence of opposites that did not dilute the sacred but made it richer and more piquant.

Dell Upton argues that the blending of the holy and the profane in churches of colonial Virginia was an animating factor that helped keep these churches alive for their parishioners.[72] The analogy is not precise: we are speaking here of clergy, not lay gentry, and the drolleries found on misericords are not points of continuity with their ordinary domestic life. Still, in any event it may be useful to keep in mind that for them, as for most worshipers, the sacred was constituted as such not so much by separation from other areas of life but by a richness of association. The association might most often be with sacred narrative and sacred act, but it might also be enriched by what we would define as the secular or the fantastic. In any case, it would be futile to construct a single medieval mentality regarding these matters; on this as on other points, we may be sure, "Diverse folk diversely they demed."

Other Religious Institutions in Late Medieval Beverley

If the sacred geography of late medieval Beverley was an ellipse defined by two foci, it embraced a great deal else as well, and for some of its citizens the other religious institutions of the town would have been at least as important as these two. While the Minster and Saint Mary's lay at the southern and northern ends of the main thoroughfare that passed through the town, the religious houses of the Dominicans, the Franciscans, and the Knights Hospitallers lay to the east and west of the north-south axis, and either at or beyond the edge of town. The Franciscans are known to have been present at least by 1267, in first one location and then another west of town, and at their second location they rebuilt their friary in the 1350s, just after the first onslaught of the Black Death. In 1380 an Agnes Kyler requested burial in the Franciscans' cloister, and twenty years later a chantry in their church was founded for a Thomas de Kelk and his son John, who were buried in the churchyard at Saint Mary's. So the followers of the Poor Man of Assisi were not lacking in support among the rich folk of Beverley.[73]

It should hardly be surprising that the orders built their institutions off to the side of the main thoroughfare; all three needed complexes of buildings that linked dormitories, refectories, and other facilities with their churches, and the land for such developments would be unavailable or unaffordable along the main street of town. We know rather little about the Knights Hospitallers' Preceptory at Beverley, only a fifth of a mile northeast of the Minster, although as early as 1201 a member of the Percy family was showing generosity to the Hospitallers, and at the time of the order's dissolution in 1540 this house was one of the wealthiest of its establishments in England.[74] There was in addition another parish church, the suburban one of Saint Nicholas, located approximately half a mile east of the Minster.[75] A chapel roughly the same distance west of the Minster was dedicated to Saint Thomas of Canterbury.[76] And other chapels lay further from town.

We are well informed about the Dominicans in Beverley, who probably arrived by 1240 and by 1310 had forty-two members. Of the religious houses, theirs was the one closest to the heart of town, only about 130 feet northeast of the Minster, between it and an industrial district. Their prominence is suggested by a donation made in 1449 by the king for the rebuilding of their dormitory and library when these buildings burned down. And in 1524 the Dominicans made elaborate provision for anniversary masses and offices for Thomas Darcy, knight, and for Lady Edith his wife, who were to be recognized as "full and special partakers of all masses, prayers, fastings, donations, and of all other spiritual suffrages forevermore within our house," on account of their great generosity to the order.[77]

When the Dominicans first arrived at Beverley around 1240 they built a simple wooden church, but by the end of the century they had replaced it with a well-built stone church, still simple in plan, perhaps constructed by masons in town for work on the Minster, and then they proceeded to building the cloister and other parts of their friary complex in stone.[78] They could be expected to make an impact by their preaching, which early on they did not only for townspeople but also at nearby ports. But their links with the people of Beverley went further; by the late fifteenth century the local porters and creelers were holding their annual procession at the friary church, and at some point in the late Middle Ages a "Galilee" porch was added at the church's west end, which the laity used for processions or meetings.

The friars traditionally relied on alms for their sustenance, but in the late Middle Ages the Dominicans at Beverley and other friars elsewhere came to rely on other sources of funding: they could help make ends meet partly by accommodating lodgers in disused parts of the friary; they could do so even better, and raise money for further construction, by selling mortuary services such as chantries, "trentals" for the deceased, and burial rights within their churches. The summoner in Chaucer's *Canterbury Tales* tells of a friar who went to the region of Holderness, perhaps from nearby Beverley, and went about casting a spell with his preaching to persuade listeners to buy trentals, the funds from which enabled the friars to build their holy houses.[79] Thus, when the Beverley Dominicans added a south aisle to their nave, probably in the first half of the fourteenth century, they were not only adding considerably more space for congregations at services and sermons but also providing more places for lucrative burials. And when in the later fourteenth century they added a brick chantry chapel with at least one tomb in it, again this would have been a source of revenue. Individuals sometimes asked in their wills to be buried at particular places: one in 1428 wanted his body interred by the south door, and one in 1476 wished for a burial place in the middle of the nave before an image of the Virgin. For those who could not afford burial space inside the church, the Dominicans also provided interment in their churchyard. As Eamon Duffy has emphasized, laypeople had a strong businesslike sense of what they needed to secure a blessed state after death, and the religious houses patronized by these layfolk reciprocated with a businesslike approach to the provision of services, all of which presupposed that the services were genuine and worth securing.[80]

Further complicating the sacred topography of Beverley were the "hospitals" and almshouses, generally known at the time by the French name *Maison Dieu*, generally built along the town's north-south axis, and thus at or near the heart of town. Saint Nicholas Hospital housed indigent people who were known as brothers and sisters of Saint Nicholas; in 1226 the archbishop of York granted an indulgence to those who supported this institution. And the hospital of Saint Giles was placed under the authority of a religious house at Warter in 1277 because the archbishop had ascertained that it had fallen on hard times and was housing "nothing but persons deserving of censure," meaning the undeserving poor rather than pious paupers worthy of their alms. These institutions are relevant to the ecclesiastical geography of Beverley not only in themselves but because at least some of them would have had chapels attached.[81] A surviving parallel is at Browne's Hospital in Stamford, where the chapel is a room within the larger building; much more ambitious is the case of Saint Cross Hospital at Winchester, a complex comprising several buildings, extensive grounds, and a substantial work of ecclesiastical architecture for its chapel.[82]

The place of these various institutions in the life of Beverley is suggested with special clarity by documents relating to a wealthy draper named John de Ake and his wife Ellen. In 1398 John made his will, in which he gave his soul to almighty God, the Virgin Mary, and all saints, and his body for burial in Saint Mary's.[83] He then went on to bequeath specific amounts of money, and from the particulars we get a clear sense of a man endeavoring to cover a great many bases: 8 shillings 4 pence went to Saint Mary's and 6 shillings 8 pence to the Minster; specified sums to Saint Peter's church in York; donations to the Franciscans and Dominicans in Beverley, on condition that they pray for his soul; bequests to these houses and to others in Kingston-upon-Hull for daily mass over thirty days after his death; personal gifts for two specific friars and for the vicar of Saint Mary's; 40 shillings to his own rector "for tithes forgotten." But, most important, he gave lands and tenements for Trinity Hospital, in the center of Beverley, which housed twenty-four paupers under the supervision of the twelve governors of the town, with clergy hired to perform chapel services. By 1417 specific arrangements were being made at Saint Mary's for services on behalf of John and Ellen, with exact annual payments to the parish clerks for the tolling of four bells, to two thurifers, to four choristers, for the cloaking of the couple's sepulcher, for the provision of candles, and so forth. This hospital was rich in liturgical and artistic goods: an inventory of 1419 included a missal of the use of York, a processional banner, a silver chalice, various vestments and altar cloths, painted and gilt "tabernacles" (or hanging pyxes) to be suspended over the altar, iron candlesticks, a lead holy water stoup, an alabaster image of the Trinity with a tabernacle of painted wood, a gilt wooden image of Virgin and Child, a cheaper alabaster image of Virgin and Child, a wooden crucifix with Mary and John affixed to the wall above the altar, a portable image of the dead Christ ("very mean"), an image of Saint Anne and the Virgin, and much else, with a rather considerable total value of £30. And all this not for either of the major churches of Beverley but simply for a hospital chapel. Clearly even one of the more modest flowers in the ecclesiastical garden was exceedingly well gilded.

Beverley and the Ecclesiastical Landscape of Late Medieval England

What holds for Beverley holds also, at least broadly, for hundreds of other towns in late medieval Christendom. A town might routinely have within its walls churches of widely different types. Their concentration was not uniform: a large town such as Norwich might have forty-six churches (including various houses of religious orders) for a population of about ten thousand, but the nearby town of King's Lynn, which became a major urban center only after parish boundaries had become fixed around the twelfth century, had only one parish church and two major chapels for approximately six thousand people. Supporting a church and its clergy financially was a meritorious work, and one for which Christians could expect prayers that would ease their way out of purgatory. People could be particular about the churches they belonged to, but they also diversified their spiritual portfolios by investing in many religious institutions. By virtue of their size, their lavish design and ornamentation, and their proliferation, churches and chapels were a conspicuous feature of a late medieval townscape. And they had relevance to virtually every dimension of town life. In them the rich rubbed shoulders with the poor, the living encountered the dead, and sinners had saints held up to their view. Merchants had guilds that might be connected to churches, and their wealth was often memorialized along with them in death. (A wool merchant's brass memorial might depict him standing on a sack of wool, almost as though he were shown with his money bag.) Religion was so pervasive largely because it could take the form of a network of conventions, and for most people piety was no doubt conventional, but the conventions of religion were norms by which society regulated its life.[84]

One might expect the great diversity in types of religious architecture to result in corresponding diversity of form. In particular, one might suppose that if a town such as Beverley had a church that attracted pilgrims from far and wide to venerate the relics of a saint, a church with liturgy entrusted to a body of canons, it would differ not only in size and degree of splendor but in its basic plan from a more ordinary parish church. Remarkably, there was less variation in form than one might expect. Within a particular religious culture, broadly or narrowly defined—that of England, perhaps, or of Mediterranean France and Spain, or of Tuscany—forms of ecclesiastical design could spread beyond what liturgical necessity dictated. To some extent the major churches— cathedrals, monastic churches, and collegiate churches administered by canons—could establish norms that would be adopted and adapted by lesser churches. Thus, in its plan Saint Mary's at Beverley resembles Beverley Minster considerably more than it does, say, a parish church of comparable stature in an Italian town. The relative positions of sanctuary and choir and nave, the uses of transepts and aisles—in these respects Saint Mary's is not significantly different from the Minster. Church design is certainly in part a function of liturgical practice, but it is also determined by the shadows that the greater churches cast over the lesser ones in their vicinity. The influence of cathedrals and monastic churches on parish church design is sometimes conspicuous, as in the modeling of the church at Ottery Saint Mary on nearby Exeter Cathedral, but more pervasive is the subtler influence of design innovations highlighted by their use in major churches and then adopted elsewhere.[85]

The influence could work in the other direction as well: monastic churches adopted building habits from churches of their vicinity. One might expect the major religious orders with strong international connections and not only traditions but regulations that theoretically bounded their innovation to be relatively immune from such influence. But their internationalism was often tempered by local traditions in church-building. A Cistercian church might disregard Cistercian prohibition and build a typically Anglo-Norman crossing tower, and the Franciscans too might follow English custom by building the bell towers forbidden in their order's constitutions.[86] Best, then, to study churches in national and regional as well as global and theoretical perspective.

The people of late medieval Beverley clearly devoted a great deal of money to pious benefactions in the hope of release from the temporal punishment merited by their sins. At the same time, their generosity had a more public and more positive dimension. They were seeking not only to undo the spiritual effects of their misconduct but also to create works of public art and self-memorialization in a culture that had very little public art other than churches and their adornment. While the penitential motives for their bequests belong to a culture quite different from ours, the aesthetic and self-memorializing inspirations link these late medieval English men and women to us more directly. The chantries, the sanctuary privileges, and the pilgrimage of Beverley are historical facts that become as lively to us as we permit; for most people of our age, the devotional and penitential language is a foreign one requiring translation. But the aesthetic qualities of the surviving churches speak to us in a language we can grasp with some intuitive clarity. We can learn the other reasons a church was built, but we can see for ourselves why it was admired.

Conclusion

For those interested in the liturgical function of sacred space, the most obvious characteristic of the ecclesiological landscape in late medieval Beverley was perhaps its extraordinarily dense network of symbolic associations. Scarcely a single square inch in Beverley Minster was lacking in symbolic meaning, in historical reference, in relatedness to the social structure of the town and the county. The Minster was well known as a pilgrimage site and a place of refuge, and thus also as the beginning and ending place for the most important procession in town, but also as a center of musical activity, a mausoleum for local aristocracy and important townspeople, the liturgical center for several parishes, the home for several craft guilds, the location for several devotions other than to the patron saint, and of course the routine place for mass and sacraments. In varying ways and to different degrees, the other churches and chapels of Beverley would have shared many of these functions; they all had their patron saints, they all served as liturgical centers, and they all could be objects for pious munificence. If we want to take a holistic approach to the study of churches, all this must come prominently into view.[87]

A visitor to Beverley might take the Minster, like other buildings of its scale, as an expression of clerical dignity and in general "the Church's" domination of society. The most obvious complicating factor is that it was the archbishop of York, not the Minster, who was the lord of most of the town and its surrounding countryside, yet during the crisis of 1381 there were townsmen who distanced themselves from the Minster, allying themselves with the archbishop. Unqualified reference to "the Church" masks the reality of diverse institutions within the clergy and hierarchy, often working in tension or in conflict among themselves, and relating in various and shifting ways to different groups of laity. In any event, to the pilgrim arriving at Beverley from perhaps somewhere in East Anglia, the sight of the Minster from some miles away would have meant more than anything the termination of a long journey and the hope of favors perhaps both physical and spiritual. And for the fugitive, arrival at the Minster would have meant anything but domination: it would rather have been the opportunity for redemption from a judicial system ready to deprive him of his property, his limbs, or his life. As for the other churches, religious houses, and chapels of Beverley, they too would have held a great diversity of meanings, depending largely on where an individual had chosen to form affiliations by membership in a guild, by making bequests, by requesting burial, and the like. For many townspeople, probably for most, more than one institution would have some claim to personal significance. A layperson might belong to guilds at more than one place, might attend mass sometimes at one's parish altar in the Minster and sometimes at the Franciscan friary, and might bequeath property to several institutions.[88] This multiplicity of connectedness in itself made for a richness of association well beyond what we normally experience in our society. Those with financial resources to invest—and donations of all kinds were indeed forms of investment—could obviously cultivate special ties of patronage with the various institutions, but anyone in the society could become a beneficiary of ecclesiastical services, ranging from the purely spiritual to the straightforwardly material.

At least in the two major churches, the Minster and Saint Mary's, full and harmonious integration of the elements of the Gothic aesthetic provided a clear sense of dramatic power. The buildings were meant to be impressive; they were so, and are. But the impression one receives now can never be quite the same as that of a medieval visitor. This is partly because the buildings no longer have the dazzling color they would once have had in glass, wall paintings, and richly painted furnishings. More important, it is because we are sated with extravagant architecture, and churches such as these are less exceptional for us. We experience hotel atriums higher than these churches, and theater lobbies more opulently decorated. To have a fuller sense of the dramatic power such churches might have had, we need first to imagine ourselves into an era in which they would have been far more exceptional. Yet more important, we need to experience them as places for the drama of liturgy.

In both of the major churches at Beverley we find full development and use of processional space—these churches are typically English in their accentuation of long processional pathways—except that in rather different ways the longitudinal design is subject to segmentation and enclosure. As in many late medieval churches, the sense of dynamism would have come largely from the processions of clergy from one space into another. The special processions outside the church walls at Rogationtide and on the feast of Corpus Christi, in which laity as well as clergy participated, would have allowed for a different sense of ritual transition and dynamism. But the segmentation and enclosure of processional space, and the multiplication of nave altars, meant that most people's experience of the ordinary liturgy would have been in a relatively static setting: the congregation would be clustered about one or another altar, and the positions of both clergy and laity would have been rather sharply defined. For essentially the same reasons, there would have been a diffused sense of sacrificial action. No one would have doubted that the mass was a sacrifice, but Virginia Reinberg is surely right in saying that for the laity the greater emphasis was the dramatization of social realities in the bidding prayers, the kissing of the pax, the taking of blessed bread, and, at Easter time, the receiving of communion, while the sacrificial meaning of the mass might have been clearer to the clergy. The proliferation of altars and of screens meant that these churches did not have a single obvious focus, although during the mass there would have been sharp focus on one moment: the elevation of the host.[89]

If richness of symbolic association and aesthetic power seem the salient features of these churches, still it would be misleading to say that spatial dynamics and centering focus were sacrificed to these two factors. One might suppose late medieval Christians saw less need to cultivate dynamism and focused centers of meaning in their church design: their lives were on the whole perhaps less sedentary than ours, and the conflict between life and death too constantly present, for these matters to require architectural reminders. More important, the use of multiple altars and shrines, distributed through the church and its various chapels but all subordinated to the high altar, made for a distinctive kind of spatial dynamic, one in which townspeople and pilgrims might move through the interior as if through a spiritual landscape with multiple attractions and places of refuge and refreshment. The movement of devotees to chapels, altars, and shrines might be echoed by that of clergy in processions on liturgical feasts. And if there were several different focal points for different functions—the high altars, the subsidiary altars, the frith stool, the saint's shrine—a believer attending to any of the functions accommodated by the church would at that moment know which center was exerting the strongest attraction.

People's allegiance to the churches in late medieval Beverley, as in most late medieval towns, was clear enough by virtually every index, and that allegiance was largely a product of the intricate connectedness to people's lives. If personal investment in institutions is a criterion of their vitality, the most important fact to note is that a wide range of people in and around a town such as Beverley invested deeply and in multiple ways in their ecclesiastical institutions.[90]

In one respect Beverley Minster exemplifies a particular way a church may relate to society. Within the ecclesiastical landscape of any era, some churches maintain a more ambitious cultural profile, and in some respects they share the role of the medieval minster: a church of regional significance, between the rank of a cathedral and that of an ordinary parish or community church, bears the privilege and the responsibility of richer liturgical celebration and richer architecture, art, and music than other churches. Most large cities now have more or less centrally located churches that serve as cultural centers for the broader public. These are places that conceive their mission to include the integration of spiritual, ethical, and cultural expression. Their church buildings themselves, apart from the liturgical and cultural events they house, are meant as cultural statements, and whether the message received is one of generous aspiration or one of presumption will always depend on the posture the worshiping communities take toward the surrounding community. Here, as elsewhere, the meaning of church architecture can never be read in abstraction from local ethos.

6

Chicago

Traditional Churches in a Modern Culture

Widely known for its modern secular architecture, Chicago is among the best places to study church architecture as well.[1] Its claim to prominence in that field rests mainly on two foundations: the exceptional diversity of ethnic churches built in the later nineteenth and very early twentieth centuries, many of them still standing and functioning as churches, and the design of churches by some of the most prominent of modern architects working in the area.

Among the complicating factors in the history of American church architecture is the fact of high demographic transience, which can result in the quick destruction of churches or in their appropriation by new communities. Both certainly occurred in Chicago, but the city is fortunate in having both exceptional diversity of church design and a high rate of survival. Populations that have passed through a neighborhood have left traces of their presence, archeological layers of religious culture within the buildings that remain. In a highly mobile society with a plurality of religions and denominations, when one congregation moves out and a church is inherited by an entirely different population, the newcomers may or may not devote energy and revenue to reconfiguring the sacred space. As early as the 1860s, shifting population in Chicago resulted in transmission of church property, when Grace Episcopal moved to a new location and sold its building to a Jewish congregation. But the reverse phenomenon, sale of synagogues to churches, was more common, and in certain neighborhoods one can find Missionary Baptist churches profusely decorated with the Star of David. Douglas

Boulevard on the west side of Chicago was the center of an early Jewish district, and in the early decades of the twentieth century it was the address for several synagogues with the broadly round-topped facades that Jews had adopted in nineteenth-century Germany. But by the later twentieth century these buildings had generally become Baptist churches for the African Americans who now lived in the neighborhood. On a visit to one of these in the early 1980s, I inquired what remained from the days when the building was a synagogue; my guide escorted me out of the sanctuary, down the corridor, up a stairway, and down another corridor to a closet packed with vestiges of the old synagogue, including even the memorial plaques, all left behind when the Jews moved away from Douglas Boulevard. The building was transformed, but the stages of its transformation remained traceable.

The later nineteenth and early twentieth century was a time just before the rise of architectural modernism and liturgical reform. It was a time when traditional styles were still being used in a modern culture. If we want to examine the churches built in this period, Chicago presents itself as a particularly good place to begin.

Revival Styles in the History of Church Architecture

The Gothic revival arose out of nineteenth-century romanticism, and other revival styles flourished in a Victorian culture of eclecticism. One critic of architectural historicism spoke of the fascination with ruins as a development of the eighteenth century, then ascribed to the Gothic revival of the following century the "thoroughly insane idea" of living and even worshiping in ruins.[2] But the Neoclassical architecture of the seventeenth and eighteenth centuries was no less a succession of revival styles, and the history of building on tradition with greater and lesser degrees of liberty is virtually coextensive with the history of architecture. H. H. Richardson and other nineteenth-century architects designed Romanesque revival churches, but the Romanesque itself harked back to the architecture of ancient Rome. And Rome itself was famously retentive of classical styles: Santa Maria in Trastevere was built in the 1140s in faithful imitation of early basilicas, but for that matter even the basilicas of the fifth-century "Sixtine Renaissance" associated with Pope Sixtus III (432–40) were revivals of pre-Constantinian Roman design.[3] Indeed, most forms of church design are either revivals of earlier forms or borrowings from secular architecture, if not both. Historicism in church architecture has long been one aspect of the quest for symbolic resonance.

Daniel M. Bluestone has argued that the Gothic revival of the nineteenth century differed from earlier Neoclassicism: when American architects used Neoclassical idiom they did so in modern ways, without pretending that their buildings were ancient, but the Gothic revival indulged in just such fantasy.

"While neoclassicism pointed emphatically forward, the Gothic directed attention backward."[4] Perhaps so, but neither Neoclassical nor Gothic revival meant
the same thing to all its practitioners. Nineteenth-century classicism was in
large part vestigial and not inspired by a deep commitment to the culture of
antiquity, but in the fifteenth and sixteenth centuries, when Renaissance classicism was first inspiring revival of Roman and then Greek architectural forms,
this was part of a broader effort to revivify a noble ancient culture. The recreation of classical design in those early generations of Neoclassicism came far
closer to the Victorian sense that one could recreate and reenter a past age.

Newly built churches from the seventeenth to the early nineteenth century
were more often than not designed in one or another classical style, although
"Gothic survival" style (as distinct from the later "Gothic revival") remained an
option in both England and America.[5] The ascendency of classicism in architecture could be taken as a turning away from a Catholic and toward a Protestant aesthetic, but Catholic architects of Renaissance Italy were among the
chief pioneers of this classicism, and it would be truer to see this architecture
as bespeaking a broader catholicity that could embrace the architectural idiom
of ancient Rome, rather as the Pantheon and other temples were converted
into churches. Indeed, the Italian classicism of Andrea Palladio exerted long-
standing influence in the English-speaking world, and one of the leading English architects of the early eighteenth century, James Gibbs, not only took his
inspiration from Italy but was a Roman Catholic when he began his architectural career.[6] The development of English classicism in the later seventeenth
and early eighteenth centuries could be traced in the work of its best-known
practitioners: Christopher Wren, James Gibbs, and Nicholas Hawksmoor. Several eighteenth-century examples survive in America (Christ Church in Boston,
Saint Michael's in Charleston, Saint Paul's Chapel in New York, and First
Baptist in Providence); the "Colonial" style was not specifically colonial but a
phase in the broader movement of classical revival.[7]

Classicism was not just for churches: it was equally in vogue in secular
architecture, public and domestic. In fact, the only feature clearly distinguishing the exterior of a church from that of a secular edifice was one taken over
from medieval churches: the steeple, a vestige of the tower and spire of later
medieval design. The steeple of a classical church might be embellished with
classicizing details, but it might also be superficially Gothic; Wren, whose London churches are noteworthy on their exteriors mostly for the often elaborate
steeples that poked above the surrounding cityscape, worked in both modes.

The return to Gothic as a preferred style was inspired by various factors,
not always and everywhere the same. From one perspective it was a manifestation of the romantic medievalism widespread during the nineteenth century
in literature and the other arts. For many observers the Gothic looked more
specifically ecclesiastical and Christian, even though the style was also used
for secular buildings. In any event, the Gothic became well established—and

not just fashionable but justified on ideological grounds—in the 1840s, with the work of Augustus Pugin and others in England; in America it was Richard Upjohn's Holy Trinity Episcopal in New York (1839–46) that most clearly marked the arrival of the Gothic as the dominant style.[8] For an ideological purist such as Pugin it made an immense difference whether a church was designed in one architectural idiom or another. While the Neoclassical style Pugin reacted against had irredeemable pagan associations, the Gothic style he insisted on was densely vested with Christian associations, with symbolism of the Trinity, of the Resurrection, and much else.[9] Upjohn, too, was something of a purist, "the high priest of the Gothic in America," and he refused to design Gothic churches for low-church congregations that could not appreciate the Gothic and were thus unworthy of it.[10]

As with the Neoclassical, so too with Gothic, there were degrees of concern about historical accuracy, and degrees of success in attaining it. At least in some places, the mid-eighteenth century marked a turning-point: in colonial Virginia, builders had used generic classical idiom but then began to imitate particular churches, to take details from published manuals, and to take cognizance of distinct classical orders.[11] When Gothic came into prominence, some architects sought to replicate medieval forms as closely as possible, and the founders of the Ecclesiological Society strongly encouraged this striving for historical accuracy, while others designed more freely in what they took to be the spirit of the Gothic. Thus, the Gothic revival of George Gilbert Scott was grounded in a close study of surviving medieval churches.[12] His design at Halifax, in Yorkshire, was completed in 1859, and an amateur might on casual viewing take it for a medieval building that had just undergone restoration. Indeed, Scott was himself a major restoration architect as well as a designer of new buildings, and his patrons for church restoration generally shared his own confidence that he could replicate medieval forms—a confidence not uniformly shared by later architectural historians. His contemporary William Butterfield built All Saints, Margaret Street, in London, which was also completed in 1859, but the interpretation of the Gothic here was so free that even the putative amateur would not easily have taken it for a medieval design. For the exterior Butterfield used contrasting red and black brick, offset by decorative stonework, and he made the interior into a richly variegated showcase of decorative tile, terracotta, stone, and other work.[13]

In America, architects often relied heavily on books that gave them a keener sense of detail than of overall composition.[14] Thus, Trinity Church in New Haven, Connecticut, built between 1814 and 1816 as an early specimen of Gothic revival in America, was hailed at the time as perhaps the "only correct specimen" of Gothic architecture in the land.[15] But this judgment could only be passed on the details of the church, and particularly of the tower; the ordering of parts and the proportions of the building were far less close to any historical sources. When American architects aimed at historicity, they used

English sources more often than Continental, although James Renwick, Jr., drew on the French Gothic for inspiration,[16] and later in the nineteenth century Roman Catholic architects felt free to borrow from various national traditions. In varying degrees, the architects drew on a combination of published sources and personal experience of their prototypes, but without actually going abroad to see and perhaps sketch the historical models, they would always be liable to the limitations shown at Trinity Church in New Haven.

Most of the earliest surviving churches in Chicago are mid-nineteenth-century structures that display a relatively early phase of the Gothic revival: buildings such as Holy Family Roman Catholic and Saint James Episcopal.[17] Even these two early Gothic revival churches allow some insight into the different approaches to Gothic style and to the project of revival. Neither building could easily be mistaken for a medieval structure, but the architect of Saint James was clearly more interested in approximating what he took to be the forms of medieval church design, while Holy Family is a free and perhaps even to some degree fanciful reinterpretation of the Gothic.[18]

In surveying the history of the movement, Ralph Adams Cram distinguished a phase of amateurs and a phase of scientific investigators. In the first phase, Gothic art was studied in a purely empirical manner and admired for its superficial forms, with commentators producing "one silly theory after another." The scholars and archaeologists of the second phase examined the medieval cases more carefully and developed a coherent understanding of Gothic as a style in which ribbed groined vaulting with pointed arches controls all else in the structure. But this conception, Cram suggested, was overly narrow and excluded a great deal of architecture that on other grounds seemed clearly to qualify also as Gothic. Cram's own effort, then, was that of distilling the "substance" of the Gothic in a way that took into account its principles while allowing variation and flexibility in their implementation.[19]

One might speak of the difference between the spirit and the letter of the Gothic, but on a deeper level the contrast raises the question how far the appropriation of a tradition requires fidelity to its own standards of coherence and harmony. Arguably a church without any of the more superficial elements of the Gothic could be *more* in keeping with a Gothic aesthetic by reconceiving the Gothic sense of luminosity and harmonious articulation of design—but if an architect is going to use at all the Gothic vocabulary of pointed arches, window tracery, and so forth, then coherence and harmony may arguably demand consistent rather than fanciful use of this idiom.

For those who were not purists, greatly simplified versions of the Gothic could be provided, even for a congregation with limited resources. Richard Upjohn's *Rural Architecture* (1852) provided designs for wooden buildings in the Gothic idiom that could be erected by a local builder, as at Saint John Chrysostom in Delafield, Wisconsin (1856).[20] Strict fidelity to medieval precedent was not the goal with this "carpenter Gothic" style: little more than window frames with pointed arches marked them as Gothic at all, but this sufficed to give a church an ecclesiastical appearance, which was all congregations required. Already in 1849 the Gothic revival was interpreted very freely indeed when a wooden version, complete with pinnacles and spire, was built on canal boats to serve the seamen and dockworkers of Philadelphia, as the Floating Church of the Redeemer.[21]

In a much later period, the same rivalry between historical accuracy and freedom of adaptation can be seen in the revival of Eastern Orthodox architecture in America, and Serbian church design shows the distinction sharply. Many of the Serbian Orthodox churches built in North America after World War II, such as Saint Sava in Milwaukee or Saint Simeon Miroticivi in Chicago,[22] claim to be exact replicas of medieval Serbian monastic churches. But by the 1970s several Serbian churches were built with considerable freedom of design; the viewer would have to be closely sensitized to such details as the lantern dome to recognize an allusion to Serbian forms at Holy Trinity or Saint Nicholas in the suburbs of Pittsburgh or at Holy Resurrection in Chicago.[23]

Even when Gothic claimed hegemony, the romantic medievalism of the nineteenth century could also find room for a Romanesque revival. Henry Hobson Richardson, best known for his Trinity Episcopal in Boston, did much to popularize Romanesque architecture around the 1880s for American churches, courthouses, homes, and other structures.[24] His influence during this brief period can be seen throughout America; in Chicago, for example, the simple and elegant massiveness of Richardsonian Romanesque is unmistakable in the Episcopal Church of the Epiphany on the West Side of Chicago.[25]

In the later nineteenth and early twentieth centuries several architects specialized in designing Roman Catholic churches in a range of revival styles, and their eclecticism was meant to reflect the catholicity of the Church for which they built. Patrick Keely of New York was one of the earliest well-known representatives of that tradition.[26] For C. Grant LaFarge, who designed churches in a variety of revival styles on the East Coast, it was a matter of principle that "Catholics and catholicity go hand in hand."[27] Henry J. Schlacks in Chicago and John T. Comes in Pittsburgh were among the later practitioners of this ideologically grounded eclecticism in America, which found its counterpart in England in, for example, Westminster Cathedral and the Brompton Oratory.[28]

Early Chicago Churches (1833–71)

Chicago was incorporated as a city in 1837, with a population of approximately 4,200, and already in that decade churches were being constructed, purely vernacular wood frame structures designed by builders rather than by architects. In 1833 there were enough settlers in Chicago to justify the organization of a Roman Catholic parish, Saint Mary of the Assumption, with a French-speaking priest, and even during this decade the Roman Catholic population included French, Germans, Irish, and Native Americans, foreshadowing a time in midcentury when it could be said that "the nations are more mixed in Illinois than perhaps any State in the Union."[29] The first church building, thirty-six by twenty-four feet, conceived by Augustine Taylor, replaced the heavy beams and complex joints of traditional construction with a light and economical balloon frame.[30] An early spirit of harmony quickly eroded: in 1833 the Roman Catholic priest reported that many Protestants attended mass at his church regularly "and assist at it with much respect,"[31] but in 1834 the Presbyterian minister felt compelled "to kneel in prayer at dead of night outside the door" of the Catholic church, praying that it "might never know prosperity."[32] The frontier settlement had neither the resources nor the sense of permanent establishment required for ambitious construction, and one Methodist observer characterized the church architecture of early Chicago in unflattering terms:

> At this time the churches of the city were meager affairs. The St.
> James Episcopal society were worshiping on the North Side, in a
> dingey brick building, built in 1836. The Catholics had the only re-
> ally good church in town. The Unitarians had a passable frame. . . .
> The First and Second Presbyterian churches were low frame build-
> ings, and the Baptists were worshiping in a long, low, convent-like
> house. . . . The Clark Street Methodist church was a nondescript. It
> had first been twenty-six by thirty feet, and being twice doubled in
> size, it was a shaky affair, in whose ceiling and roof the joints were
> plainly visible. It was about forty-six by sixty-four feet, with twelve or
> fourteen foot walls. The outside, if ever painted, had lost all its
> whiteness, and presented a time-worn appearance.[33]

While the Presbyterians claimed the first church building in town, dedicated in January 1834, one newcomer's reaction was: "I have often heard of God's house, but I never saw his barn before."[34]

By 1845 there were thirteen churches serving the town's Methodist, Epis-copalian, Baptist, Presbyterian, Roman Catholic, Universalist, and Unitarian congregations. The simple wood frame buildings of the 1830s yielded in the 1840s to more permanent structures clustered along Washington Street, across from or at least nearby the public square at the center of town.[35] Like other contemporary public buildings, the churches along Washington Street were Neoclassical buildings of wood or brick, and they were distinguished from secular structures chiefly by their steeples. This arrangement replicated the pattern familiar in New England in the seventeenth and eighteenth centuries: churches were closely linked with their secular surroundings both by proximity to the heart of a town and by use of an architectural idiom shared with public and domestic buildings. But then in the 1850s and 1860s, one by one most churches were relocated away from the town center toward newly developed

and often affluent residential districts, first along Wabash Avenue, then further
out from the center. They moved partly because they felt increasingly constricted by the thriving business district, which left the church buildings
dwarfed and deprived them of open spaces and thus of visibility on all sides.
(It seemed unpleasant, said one observer, to "wind one's way to the sanctuary
through barricades of petroleum, molasses, salt, tea, and fish barrels, empty
soap boxes, stacks of heavy hardware and such worthy but worldly minded
institutions.") Furthermore, churches in Chicago were voluntary organizations
moving along with the wealthier and more prominent members, hoping to
retain their membership by relocating to the new residential districts.[36] But in
the process they severed the traditional link between religion and civic life and
moved instead toward a bond between religion and domestic life. And the
proceeds from the sale of their earlier property enabled them to build more
monumental churches in the newly fashionable Gothic style. Second Presbyterian was the first of the churches on Wabash, and when it was being planned
in 1849 the building committee rejected a plan for a Neoclassical building and
turned instead to James B. Renwick, an architect already known in New York
as an early advocate of the Gothic revival. Roman Catholics followed the trend:
although the version of Saint Mary's that was built in 1843 in Neoclassical
brick on Washington Street was adopted as the first cathedral, a new bishop
who arrived in 1859 took as his cathedral a Gothic structure, Holy Name
Church, north of the Chicago River, away from the center of the city.

The architects of the era were largely autodidacts, carpenters and builders
who learned the art of design from pattern books. John M. Van Osdel read
pattern books and builders' guides in New York before moving to Chicago and
becoming an architect in 1836. William W. Boyington worked in Massachusetts
as a joiner and carpenter before relocating to Chicago in 1853 and establishing
himself as a leading domestic and ecclesiastical architect in the fashionable
district along Wabash Avenue. Boyington and the Danish immigrant Theodore
V. Wadskier distinguished themselves for designs in the Gothic revival while
it was still in its early phases.[37] The flourishing of the untrained architect was
not a specifically American phenomenon; in England and elsewhere the transition to professional practice came over the course of the nineteenth century.
Sophia Gray was an enthusiast who around 1836 began to execute drawings
of historic English churches; it was largely on the strength of these drawings
that she served as an architect when her husband became the first bishop of
Cape Town in 1843.[38]

By 1868, when George S. Philips wrote *Chicago and Her Churches*, there
were clearly distinguishable phases that churches of almost all denominations
had passed through: from the wood frame buildings of the 1830s, to the Neoclassical designs along Washington Street of the 1840s, to the outlying
churches done usually in Gothic style in the 1850s and 1860s. The churches
built in the 1830s had generally cost $400 to $600. (The major exception,

Saint James Episcopal, spent $4,000 for the mahogany pulpit alone and $15,500 for brick construction.) By the 1840s the costs diverged widely: the building erected for First Baptist in 1848 cost around $4,500, while the new structure for First Presbyterian required $28,000. The combined effects of inflation and heightened ambition quickly mounted, and in 1870 First Baptist put up a new building that cost around $150,000.[39] Saint James Episcopal Church was rebuilt to a more imposing Gothic design in 1857, and when Trinity Episcopal replaced its structure of 1844 with a new one in 1860, a contemporary remarked that "it is built, like the ancient European churches, to stand for centuries."[40] It lasted in fact, until 1871, but while it stood it served as a monument to the idea of a church building as a sacrament of eternity.

The transition to churches designed by an increasingly professionalized group of architects paralleled the stylistic shift of the mid–nineteenth century: the chiefly Greek Neoclassicism that flourished in the early nineteenth century in ecclesiastical, civic, and even domestic architecture was succeeded by the Gothic revival. First Congregational Church at Lancaster, Massachusetts, was a classic of geometrical rationalism in the current Neoclassical idiom, and Baltimore Cathedral was built to a Neoclassical design rather than a Gothic alternative,[41] but "wherever reason travels in the realm of religion, mystery always follows close behind,"[42] and before long Gothic was the rage. The experience of Chicago, however, is surely not unique in suggesting that the dialectic of reason and mysticism, or of reason and romanticism, was linked to other factors, one of the most important being the quest for a culture of establishment. Those who knew the history of architecture knew that classical temples survived mainly as ruins, but Gothic churches (other than the picturesque remnants of dissolved monasteries) had endured, and it was Gothic more than Neoclassical that came to mark the status of a frontier town growing into a major commercial city.

Church-Building in Chicago after the Fire of 1871

The official seals of both the Roman Catholic archdiocese and the Episcopal diocese of Chicago include the phoenix among its devices, and no one familiar with the history of the city would miss the allusion to the fire of 1871, whose catastrophic effect was at the same time the occasion for ambitious new building, sacred as well as secular. Thirty-nine churches had been burned, including some of the most prominent: First and Second Presbyterian, Holy Name Roman Catholic, and Saint James Episcopal.[43] Of Roman Catholic churches, only Saint Patrick's and Holy Family survived, plus the shell of Saint Michael's. The story is told that a priest at Holy Family, on the west side of the city, made a vow during the fire that if his church was spared destruction seven lights would burn in perpetuity before an image of Our Lady of Perpetual Help, whereupon the winds shifted and the church was preserved.[44] But the historic churches remaining in Chicago were mostly built or rebuilt after 1871.

Churches were quickly rebuilt on a grand scale, and the monumentality characteristic of Chicago churches already in the 1850s drew criticism in later decades, perhaps most especially in the 1870s, after the fire. One observer lamented the reconstruction in grand style after the conflagration: the decision "to return to the flesh-pots of Egypt and gilded temples of the old time regime." A leading spokesman for liberal Christianity at the time protested what he called "limestone Christianity," preferring to invest limited resources in "great moral reform" rather than devoting them to "great architectural passion." One of the rebuilders, a Baptist leader, defended his plans for reconstruction by arguing that a cheap church building in an affluent town shows a "poverty of religious sentiment" and suggested that "parsimony and avarice in a people are far more to be dreaded than extravagance in church building."[45] Another, faced with the complaint that resources were needed for relief and mission labor rather than for costly churches, insisted that grand church buildings create "a great moral impression" and give evidence of dedication to a God for whom nothing is too good. In other words, as Daniel Bluestone notes, the proponents of monumental churches "turned on its head the critique of ostentation and materialism" by arguing that lavish churches indicate greed has been overcome by religious values.[46]

The Churches of Roman Catholic Immigrant Groups after the Fire

The period after the fire was also a time of rapid expansion for Chicago's immigrant population. In 1880, those living in Chicago who had come from Germany or Austria numbered 76,661; from Ireland, 44,411; from Poland, roughly 30,000; from Bohemia, 11,887. After 1880, larger numbers of Italians and Lithuanians, as well as Jews, entered the city.[47] Thus, In 1890, 68 percent of the city's population was foreign born. The nativist response was pronounced: the American Protective Association, founded to counteract "the Catholic menace" that was taken to be increasingly threatening, was centered in Chicago. Apart from resistance to the political power of immigrants, the nativist movement strove to ensure that children would be taught in English in schools responsible to public authorities. In this context, the cultural identity of the nativists was in some respects specifically American and in others— increasingly, in the religious sphere—Anglo-American. A sense of adherence to a venerable English tradition was, among other things, a way of asserting an alternative to the various ethnicities rising in prominence and power. The urge to assert Anglo-American identity and to glorify a heritage shared with England was a nationwide phenomenon; the surviving tower of the Old Church at Jamestown became the focus a romantic attachment to the Anglo-American heritage, a shrine of "that American Church which is the daughter of the Anglo-Saxon Church."[48] As for the immigrants themselves, Charles Shanabruch has pointed out that in the struggle to preserve their national identity they became more Americanized: they began by identifying themselves as ethnic Catholics, but they banded together in a common cause and entered into the thick of participatory democracy. Yet strong nationalist movements developed among the Irish, the Germans, and the Polish; many educated Poles, viewing America not as a permanent home but as a place from which to regain political independence in the old country, became disaffected with their assimilationist fellow Poles and by the turn of the century broke away and formed the Polish National Catholic Church.[49]

With the tide of immigrants from northern and then from eastern and southern Europe, the Roman Catholic population of Chicago significantly outnumbered the Protestant in the later nineteenth century: in 1890 there were over 260,000 Roman Catholics, while the seven leading Protestant denominations taken together had roughly 100,000.[50] The difference in membership of individual churches was even more pronounced: in 1889 the average Roman Catholic parish had 2,202 members, while the average Protestant congregation had only 315—a difference only partly explained by differing criteria of membership.[51]

Catholic church buildings differed in various ways from Protestant ones. First, they tended to be significantly larger; when Holy Name was rebuilt in 1853, it was 190 feet long, significantly longer than Saint James Episcopal and roughly twice the length of the largest Presbyterian or Methodist churches. Second, they were more often integrated into complexes with rectories, schools of various kinds, and convents, and frequently the buildings were architecturally coherent. Third, they tended to be less transient, not only because they represented considerably greater investment but also because they were under the control of a centralized diocesan administration that provided a force for stability even when populations shifted and one ethnic group was replaced by others.[52] And fourth, they were more clearly associated with territorial units or parishes.

The Roman Catholic Archdiocese of Chicago, like any diocese, was divided into parishes, and for many years members of one of these might identify themselves as much by the parishes they belonged to as by the neighborhoods they inhabited. But these "territorial" parishes served mainly the English-speaking population, which is to say in many cases primarily the Irish immigrants.[53] Overlapping the territorial parishes were "national" parishes for the various non-English-speaking immigrants, established with clergy fluent in the languages of the mother countries. Within a single territorial parish there might be more than one ethnic church, and relations among these churches could be complex and fluid.

The relevance of Roman Catholicism to the various immigrant groups was at least threefold. First, the Church provided an enclave in which the culture of the mother country could be preserved: priests could preach and hear confessions in the language of that country, while its patron saints and other emblems of ethnic identity could be honored. Second, the Church served as a means for easing immigrant groups into the mainstream of American culture; parochial schools produced pupils educated in the catechism but also assimilated into American social and political culture. Third, and for present purposes most important, the Latin mass guaranteed entry into a culture that transcended both the ethnic enclave and the American mainstream. A skeptic might suggest that the Latin mass provided everyone, native-born Americans and immigrants alike, equal opportunity for incomprehension, but there were always gradations of understanding and opportunities for deeper knowledge, and even a person with no grasp of the Latin formulas could still derive satisfaction from a sense of belonging to a worldwide community for which intercession was offered.

First-generation immigrants and especially those who saw their American presence as temporary had reason to maintain their ethnic distinctiveness, while others became in varying degrees assimilated into a broader culture of American Catholicism. Broadly speaking, the archdiocese accommodated the former impulse and encouraged the latter. In 1880, 42 percent of the thirty-eight parishes in the city were national; by 1902 the percentage had risen to 52.[54] Increasingly after World War I, the archdiocese sought to integrate the immigrants quickly into an American church without ethnic enclaves, turning national parishes into territorial ones; Cardinal George W. Mundelein (1916–39), in particular, adopted a policy of Americanization that meant calling an end to new national parishes and assimilating ethnic groups into the mainstream culture.[55] In church architecture and decoration, a corresponding tension arose between the impulse to preserve forms derived from the various homelands and the urge toward architectural assimilation—which could mean adopting other ethnic groups' traditions or building in what was taken for American tradition.

Among the earliest of the immigrant populations to settle in Chicago were the Irish, whose command of the English language gave them access to politics and other areas of public life that the Germans and Poles could not at first claim. Their first church was Old Saint Patrick's, still standing largely as it was built in 1852–56.[56] But this church exemplifies what can be seen in many other ethnic churches: the eventual cultivation of explicit ethnic identity well beyond what the immigrants would have known in their home country. The interior walls are decorated with Celtic interlace patterns, and the stained glass reflects an Irish identity both in its style and its depiction of Irish saints. These marks of ethnicity were not simply taken over from Ireland; the traditional churches in the mother country would rarely have featured such bold declarations of

Irishness. They were added to the church in the late nineteenth and early twentieth centuries, at the time when Celtic arts were experiencing an international revival, and they served the interests of a population that had long ago left or never seen the Old Sod and needed clear reminders of an Irishness that had been obvious to their parents and grandparents. The same development can be seen in other Irish churches, such as Saint Patrick's in Milwaukee, where a building with no visible marks of ethnicity was replaced by one lavishly decorated with interlace design on its interior walls.[57] Other ethnic groups as well would eventually follow suit, at least sometimes adopting for ecclesiastical use modes of decoration that declared an ethnic identity more explicitly than churches in the home countries. In the Italian Church of the Assumption, the ceiling was painted in 1939 with reproductions of recognized Italian masterpieces, while windows of 1966 displayed themes from Italian and Italian-American history.[58] That immigrant communities built churches in Chicago to remind them of churches in their home countries is at best a partial truth; when ethnicity was most explicit, it was generally least faithful to Old World prototypes.[59]

The most clearly defined and cohesive cluster of ethnic churches, as well as one of the earliest, is that built for Polish Roman Catholics in the old Polonia neighborhood along Milwaukee Avenue on the northwest side of the city.[60] The earliest of these churches, Saint Stanislas Kostka, was built between 1877 and 1881, inspired by a church in Krakow and designed by the prominent New York architect Patrick C. Keely (fig. 18). The pastor under whom it was constructed was Vincent Barzynski.[61] The church itself is designed in a Polish Renaissance style, with space for mass in both an upper and a lower church, both of which for some time had six masses every Sunday. With heavy Polish immigration into Chicago, five other Polish Catholic churches were built nearby between 1893 and 1921. All of these were in varying ways influenced by Polish Renaissance and Baroque architectural idiom, but only one (Holy Trinity) was designed by a Polish or Polish-American architect. Rather, these and other Polish churches of Chicago were designed by architects and architectural firms that deliberately worked in a diversity of revival styles, not always for Roman Catholics: the firm of Worthman and Steinbach worked for Polish Catholics, Italian Catholics, German Lutherans, and others.

Edward Kantowicz has surveyed the 165 Roman Catholic churches built in the vicinity of Chicago in the years 1891–1945 and found that seventy-nine of them were built by seven architects or firms: local Catholic architects, sometimes with specific ethnic connections. James J. Egan, who worked mostly for Irish parishes, built 12 of the 165 Chicago churches and cathedrals for three cities other than Chicago; in his later years he worked mostly in Romanesque. Herman J. Gaul designed six churches for Chicago's Germans, four of them in Gothic style. German parishes had a preference for Gothic style; Polish ones tended toward Polish Renaissance idiom, Italians opted for Romanesque or

FIGURE 18. Saint Stanislaus Kostka, Chicago, interior. Photograph by Richard Kieck-hefer.

Renaissance, and while the Irish were most eclectic in their taste, they used Gothic more than any other style. The Romanesque was a lowest common denominator, a modest and utilitarian idiom often preferred by less affluent parishes; it accounted altogether for 28 percent of the Roman Catholic churches in late nineteenth- and early twentieth-century Chicago, while 34 percent were Gothic, and 24 percent were Renaissance.[62]

The foremost of these eclectic architects, Henry J. Schlacks, had studied at the Massachusetts Institute of Technology, then he had worked in Chicago with Dankmar Adler and Louis Sullivan.[63] He traveled extensively in Europe, studying historical church architecture. His twelve churches in Chicago were designed for Germans, Poles, and Irish, in all the prevalent styles. His designs tended to be expensive, and he worked mainly for larger and more wealthy parishes. Among his early churches in Chicago were first Gothic and then Romanesque designs executed primarily for German parishes: his Gothic revival churches of Saint Peter in Skokie (1893–95), Saint Martin (1894–95), and Saint Paul (1897–99) are among the best specimens of his work, and were soon followed by Romanesque revival churches for the parish of Saint Boniface (1902–4) and for the now combined parish of All Saints and Saint Anthony (1913–15).

One might think of these churches as appealing to ethnic stylistic tastes: Saint Martin was done in a German style of Gothic, with glass and furnishings

largely imported from Germany, and the Romanesque revival was widely influential in Germany. But the models for Saint Paul were more French than
German, and the altar and mosaics were imported from Italy. After 1910
Schlacks drew heavily from Italian sources in building for various and often
mixed ethnic groups. Saint Adalbert, done for a Polish congregation, was modeled largely on San Paolo fuori le mura in Rome. Saint Mary of the Lake is
modeled partly on San Paolo fuori le mura and partly on Santa Maria Maggiore,
with a campanile modeled after that at Santa Pudenziana (fig. 19). Saint Ignatius, built for Jesuits near Loyola University, imitates the Renaissance church
of the Gesù, the mother church of the Jesuits in Rome. Somewhat later,
Schlacks returned to the Italian Renaissance style for Saint Clara, which was
originally a German parish. For Saint Ita, Schlacks turned to French Gothic
models at the suggestion of Cardinal Mundelein. In short, he used revival styles
both to cultivate a sense of ethnic particularity and to wean Roman Catholics
away from this particularism.

The complexity of relations between territorial and national parishes can
be seen in the far southern suburb of Chicago Heights, where the Inland Steel
Company built a factory in 1891 and immigrants from various countries
quickly began arriving as workers in that and other industries. The English-
speaking territorial parish of Saint Agnes, founded for a predominantly Irish
population, had a wood frame church by 1895, which was replaced in the 1920s
by a brick church-school complex of loosely classical design. But as other ethnic
groups grew in numbers they quickly established their own national parishes
where they might feel more at home. Polish Catholics formed Saint Joseph
parish in 1905 and by 1914 had built a Romanesque revival church. In 1906
the Italians formed a national parish of Our Lady of Pompeii, later dedicated
to Saint Rocco, and in the same year they built a Romanesque church. (By the
1970s the surrounding neighborhood had become largely Hispanic, but many
Italian families previously attached to Saint Rocco still returned there for worship even if they had moved elsewhere.) The parish of Saint Ann was founded
for the Germans in 1907, but by 1920 was only half the parishioners were
German, while the rest were French, Slovak, Austrian, Bohemian, and English-
speaking, and soon they were joined by Italians as well. (When a new church
was built in 1949–50, it was in Colonial style.) A church-school complex dedicated to Saint Casimir was built for Lithuanians in the years 1911–12, and the
parish remained Lithuanian until it saw an influx of Mexicans after World War
II. Slovak families who arrived at the turn of the century are said not to have
felt at home in other ethnic parishes, so in 1913 they obtained authorization
from the archdiocese to establish their own parish, but when they failed to
obtain sufficient membership and financial support the authorization was re-
scinded. Many of them continued to worship with the Germans at Saint Ann
Church while founding Slovak lodges in which they continued to raise funds
to buy property for their own church. In 1927 they organized a new parish of

FIGURE 19. Saint Mary of the Lake, Chicago, exterior. Photograph by Richard Kieck-hefer.

Saint Paul, for which a building complex in vaguely Romanesque style was constructed in 1928–29. All these developments occurred in a single suburb, and similar complexities could be found in other suburbs, as well as in neighborhoods through much of the city proper.[64]

Given these complications, one might suppose the link between ethnicity and church architecture had become minimal by the 1920s, but the link could easily be revived, particularly in a parish that remained officially national rather than territorial, as in the Lithuanian church of the Holy Cross (Joseph Molitor, 1913–15). The building is more eclectic than identifiably ethnic:

> The style of Holy Cross Church belongs to a time when architects were trying to harmoniously compose into one form all existing artistic styles or designs. Therefore in Holy Cross Church one can distinguish the architectural motif[s] of the Byzantine, Gothic, Renascence, Baroque, and pseudo-classic period; yet the Baroque theme is fundamental throughout.

But, as at Saint Patrick's, succeeding generations sought reminders of their ethnicity, and thus in 1951 the Lithuanian refugee Adolph Valesaka was invited to decorate the interior with paintings of specifically Lithuanian themes such as Our Lady of Valnius and the baptism of King Mindaugas, while a tile floor was installed that drew on traditional Lithuanian color patterns. The architecture itself might be highly eclectic, but those wishing to assert their ethnicity could still do so in a concerted way with decoration.[65]

Ethnic identity could be articulated in direct connection with religious observance through devotions focused on the early or prominent saints of the community's nationality. The choice of dedication was often the first and most obvious way of declaring national background, but the selection of saints for windows, wall paintings, and statues could also be crucial. Perhaps the most interesting devotional assertion of ethnicity was in the church of Saint Joseph and Saint Anne on the southwest side of Chicago, where a relic shrine (established in 1900) was modeled on that of Saint Anne at Beaupré in Quebec. Like the original site, if on a smaller scale, this church became the center of a pilgrimage, and cures ascribed to the relic were noted with crutches and other mementos affixed to the wall beside the shrine of the relic as *ex votos*.[66] In this striking case, not only was the devotion imported from a mother country, but even the very miracle-working relic serving as the center of devotion was traced (like the one at Beaupré) to a source in France. This is an exceptional case of carry-over by an ethnic group with keen awareness of its cultural identity, but in the realm of popular devotion, similar if less striking phenomena could be found throughout the archdiocese: images of Our Lady of Czestochowa, stained-glass windows featuring Irish saints, images of Christ with photographs pinned to them in Mexican fashion, and countless other devotional reminders of ethnic identity.

Ethnicity in Lutheran Church Architecture after the Fire

The immigration of the later nineteenth century brought Lutheran as well as Roman Catholic churches to Chicago, and Lutheran churches were built specifically for the various ethnic groups: thus, Roman Catholic churches for Polish and Irish immigrants might lie close to Lutheran churches built by German, Swedish, Norwegian, or Danish communities. There had been Swedish churches in the city since 1853, and by 1871 nearly a third of Chicago's Lutheran churches were Scandinavian.[67] But while these Lutheran buildings might contain markers of ethnic identity, such as the model ship suspended from the ceiling of a Danish church,[68] they were not on the whole so clearly and self-consciously indebted to national precedent for design or decoration, nor so prone to crossethnic borrowing, as were the Roman Catholic churches. The first circumstance can be explained in part by the relative simplicity of the buildings and their ornament and the second by the absence of a multiethnic institution that, like the Archdiocese of Chicago, could make assimilation its business.

One point along the spectrum from the most ambitious to the most modest of construction is represented by the work of Erick Gustaf Petterson, whose churches gained local recognition for the quality of their construction but made no claim to innovation or to influence outside the communities that built them.[69] Petterson was a Swede who migrated to America in 1868, worked as a carpenter and building contractor in Chicago after the fire of 1871, and studied architecture in the evenings, presumably from pattern books. By 1876 he was established as a builder-architect for the Swedish Lutherans in and around Chicago, and by 1906 he had designed some fifteen churches: seven in Chicago, six elsewhere in northern Illinois, and one each in Indiana and Kansas. His work combined Gothic with Romanesque features in varying proportions, and with Scandinavian elements in the detail; like other designers, he came under the influence of H. H. Richardson's Romanesque revival around the 1880s but then returned to designs that were more consistently Gothic. His early churches were all in wood; by 1888 he was using brick for a church in De Kalb.

Petterson's Swedish Evangelical Lutheran Bethany Church on the South Side of Chicago is representative of his work in its simplicity and in its piecemeal construction. Built in 1881, it was longitudinal in plan, with narrow, roundheaded windows, an altar set in an apse (clearly marked off from the nave by a round arch with strong molding) at the center of the west wall, a semicircular ballustrade rail defining a chancel that projected roughly nine feet in front of the altar, and a pulpit placed the the south of the chancel. In 1882 the tower was built after some hesitancy about whether to proceed with that part of the plan. A balcony at the back of the church (one element in the classic evangelical tradition of church-building) seems to have been included in the original plan but was not built until 1888. Deterioration of the building as early as the late 1890s led to the replacement of the wooden posts it rested on with a brick and stone foundation. Records from the early years of the church refer to "fresco painting" of the interior; the most notable art in early photographs is an altarpiece of the Ascension, installed in 1906. In short, this, like Petterson's other churches, was an exercise in the accommodation of architectural tradition to the resources of an immigrant community. His eclecticism of style and his emphasis on craft more than on what a broader community might recognize as art were perhaps characteristic of these Swedish communities but by no means distinctively Swedish. Many of the same traits can be found in the churches of other denominations and other ethnic groups. Thus is was not surprising, after the Swedish community gradually moved away from the neighborhood and left this church behind in 1949, that after some years as a National Guard armory the building served first a Baptist and then a Puerto Rican Pentecostal congregation.

Development of the Auditorium Sanctuary

The Roman Catholics and Lutherans who arrived in Chicago had clearly established forms of worship, and there was little experimentation in the basic forms of liturgical space. Among the Protestant churches that had come to America from England, however, the last quarter of the century was a time of significant innovation in design for worship.

The years 1832 and 1836 had been of vital importance in the history of American church architecture: in the former, Charles Grandison Finney was persuaded to move into the Chatham Garden Theater in Manhattan, which became the Chatham Street Chapel; in the latter, he and his congregation moved to the Broadway Tabernacle, which was designed in the form of a theater, with a fan-shaped arrangement of seats, a projecting stage, and a gallery on three sides. Jeanne Halgren Kilde suggests that this adaptation of theater design solved three critical problems facing preachers in traditional churches: the need to accommodate large congregations (Finney's two churches probably both had seating for two to three thousand), the need to improve acoustics so that large congregations could hear the preacher in an era without electronic amplification, and the need for unobstructed sight lines from the congregation to the preacher. Furthermore, the platform could allow the preacher far greater freedom to move about: the Chatham Street Chapel had a lectern placed on the platform, rather than an elevated and enclosed pulpit, and Finney could move freely across the expanse of the platform, punctuating his sermons with movement of more than just his upper body.[70]

And yet Finney's experiments were not widely adopted until the later

1860s. In 1859, Plymouth Church in Brooklyn held a competition for design of a church with an auditorium sanctuary to seat six thousand with the best possible sight lines and acoustics, but this ambitious plan was not carried to completion. It was in Chicago, during the years just before the great fire, that the new auditorium sanctuary was developed. Even as early as 1857, Edward Burling had designed an amphitheater sanctuary for First Methodist in Chicago to accommodate a congregation of a thousand.[71] But sustained development of the form came in the later 1860s, at First Baptist, First Congregational, and Union Park Congregational, which later became First Baptist Congregational (fig. 20).[72] In the following decade the new design was adopted at Third Presbyterian, Fourth Presbyterian, Plymouth, First Universalist, Unity, and Jefferson Park churches. Chicago architects of the later nineteenth century are best known for their use of metal frames in the development of skyscrapers, but they also brought new possibilities in structural engineering to bear on the construction of larger auditoriums, such as those at Unity Church and First Congregational of Oak Park.[73] One writer in 1873 noted approvingly that several Chicago churches had "abandoned the old long and narrow form for the broad semi-circular audience room. The audience is gathered about the speaker, as a crowd gathers itself in open air; not in the form of a brick, with the narrow ends toward the speaker, but in the form of a group that gathers about the old fireplace in mid-winter."[74]

FIGURE 20. First Baptist Congregational, Chicago, interior. Photograph by Richard Kieckhefer.

The most characteristic features of these churches—and the hundreds of other churches built in this style for several Protestant denominations across America over the ensuing decades—were the platform stage for the preacher, the fan-shaped arrangement of pews, and aisles that radiated outward from front to back. Typically their floors sloped downward from back to front in the manner of the amphitheater, galleries were wrapped around three or all four walls, risers behind the preacher provided space for a choir, and organ pipes soared dramatically upward on the wall behind the preacher and above the choir. These features could be accommodated in sanctuaries of varying shape, not only square or rectangular but also circular, oblong, octagonal, or otherwise.[75] The epitome of this development was Dwight L. Moody's Tabernacle, opened in 1876, with seating for nearly eight thousand in an auditorium 190 by 160 feet. The platform at the front of the sanctuary had room for the preacher, an organ, a substantial choir, and hundreds of "distinguished people." On the wall behind the preacher, scripture texts were inscribed, and on an illuminated cross the words "God is Love" ran in lights along the crossbeam.[76]

These buildings are sometimes thought to have borrowed their form from secular theaters of the day, but Kilde has shown that the relationship between sacred and secular design was more complex. It is true that American theaters in the mid–nineteenth century had begun to introduce the amphitheater design used earlier in Europe and in England. But architects such as Dankmar Adler were working simultaneously on secular and sacred auditoriums, experimenting with currently available technology to maximize the size of the interior while minimizing the use of internal supports that would obstruct the sight lines. Even the proscenium arch and use of gas jets and then electric fixtures for marquis lighting, which one might have thought distinctly theatrical, were developed at the same time in religious and secular buildings.[77]

These auditorium churches stand within the tradition of classic evangelical churches, as heirs perhaps to the Calvinist Temple du Paradis at Lyon. Arguably they represent the inevitable culmination toward which this classic design would tend when technology made broad, open spaces with good acoustics possible. But the auditorium church transformed the classic evangelical tradition. When the preacher had free access to the entire platform rather than being fixed to a pulpit, the preacher's role became more closely assimilated to that of an actor. When the auditorium was large enough to accommodate thousands, the congregation might still exert a determinative role in setting the basic expectations for worship,[78] but it was not in spontaneous interaction with the preacher to the same degree as in a more intimate space. From within the Reformed Church these auditorium churches have been criticized as succumbing to "choirolatry" by placing the choir on the platform behind the preacher. The choir members are members not of the clergy but of the congregation; their music is not a means of grace (according to this perspective)

but one of the expressions of gratitude for grace received, and confusion between music and the word of scripture is theologically unsound. Further, say
these critics, there are practical reasons against placing the choir on a platform:
the minister "competes with between four and forty faces behind him—some
intent in devout worship, others animated, some asleep, others beautiful in
their symmetry with well-placed noses, eyes, and mouths, topped with lustrous
hair, indeed a joy to behold."[79] Whatever one makes of this critique, the auditorium plan of the nineteenth century was not uniformly seen as the natural
and necessarily desirable culmination of development within the classic evangelical tradition of church-building.

Episcopal Churches and the Impact of "High Church" Worship

Another and very different influence in the later nineteenth century was the
spread of high church ceremonialism within the Episcopal Church and its
extension to other denominations as well. The Oxford Movement begun in the
1830s was primarily a revival of traditional theology, focused on a commitment
to the beliefs and practices of the Apostolic and Patristic eras, and emphasizing
apostolic succession as a sign of continuity with the early Church. But as it
developed, this movement also adopted a keen sense of social responsibility
on the one hand and a commitment to richly symbolic worship on the other.
The last of these tendencies was reinforced by the Cambridge Ecclesiologists,
who studied medieval church architecture, furnishings, vestments, and liturgies with an eagerness to restore to the Church of England the best of pre-
Reformation practice.

The ritualism of these movements took hold in the upper Midwest, in part
because of the efforts of James DeKoven in his work at Nashotah House seminary (in Wisconsin) and as bishop of Illinois. By 1856, some parishioners at
Saint James had split off to form a new parish at the Church of the Ascension,
Saint James having become too "high" or ritualist for them. But after a rapid
succession of rectors had passed through the parish, the canon Charles Palmer
Dorset arrived in 1869 and transformed the community, making it one of the
most staunchly ritualist or Anglo-Catholic churches in the region. Under Dorset and his successor Arthur Ritchie, weekly communion was established, then
reservation of the sacrament in a tabernacle, use of candles on the altar, and
(by 1884) benediction of the blessed sacrament. Critics charged that "the grand
old service of the Protestant Episcopal Church . . . is so distorted, patched, and
bedizened with old follies and new assumptions as to be repugnant to the
average Episcopalian." But the tradition was firmly established.[80]

The Episcopal Church did not at this time have a cathedral system, but
Bishop Henry John Whitehouse of Chicago was a leading proponent of the
idea, and he sought to establish a cathedral complex in the city that would

combine a chapter house, a library, a school, and other institutions along with the cathedral itself. In 1853 he was approached by an English architect of the Gothic revival, Jacob Wrey Mould, who offered to design this complex for no compensation other than the dignity of being its sole designer, but other Episcopal churches were reluctant to support the effort. Eventually Whitehouse gained his cathedral by moving to the Church of the Atonement, an English Gothic structure, redesigning its chancel in accordance with current liturgical norms, and rededicating it to Saints Peter and Paul.[81]

By no means all Episcopal churches, and not even all Anglo-Catholic ones, had the resources to build fully developed Gothic revival churches with full choirs in extended chancels. One place where the development was essentially complete was Saint Luke's Episcopal Church in the suburb of Evanston. The interior is clearly divided into nave, choir, and sanctuary, but with no structural distinction, the progression from one space to another being marked by modest rises in floor level, by low and partially open railings, by furnishings, and by differences in ornamentation (Fig. 21). Thus the congregation processing to the communion rail has a clear sense of unimpeded passage from one type of space to another. Indeed, the differentiation is all the clearer because the intended decoration of the nave was cut short by the Great Depression, leaving a sharp distinction between the ornate sanctuary and the relatively plain nave, where even the anticipated hammerbeam-style roof is merely hinted at by steel beams. At the same time, there is no screen or chancel arch to impede the sight lines, only a rood hanging from the ceiling at the crossing. While the transepts are shallow, there is a fully developed Lady Chapel on the north side of the church. This complex was built under the rector George Craig Stewart, one of the most prominent Anglo-Catholic churchmen of early twentieth-century America, who later became bishop of Chicago and continued to use Saint Luke's as his procathedral. Stewart was also an early leader in the World Council of Churches, and had dreams of establishing a cathedral of far greater proportions that would serve as such for the various denominations in the area.[82]

In the second half of the century other denominations as well began to adopt fixed liturgies at least as options for local use, and they adopted a more formal and liturgical style of worship partly because they feared defection of members to Episcopal churches. A Presbyterian minister writing in 1864 made the point explicit: in larger cities many Presbyterian youth were going over to the Episcopal Church simply because "a set form of worship is more in accordance with the etiquette of their social life, and therefore more consonant with their feelings."[83]

This flirtation with the Episcopal tradition made its mark on church architecture and furnishings as well. Very quickly the Gothic revival took hold outside the Anglican tradition. When Finney's Broadway Tabernacle moved to a new location in 1858, it was a Gothic revival church that it commissioned

FIGURE 21. Saint Luke's Episcopal, Evanston, Illinois, interior. Photograph by Richard Kieckhefer.

from Leopold Eidlitz, cofounder of the American Institute of Architects and a leading advocate of the Gothic revival. Evangelicals, as much as high church Anglicans, could recognize the Gothic as a specifically Christian architecture, neither Roman Catholic nor Protestant but the distinctively Christian form that might serve as a basis of unity among Christians. Jeanne Kilde quotes one straightforward formulation of the point: "Our religion has its style. We may hesitate, but there must be *unity; unity in religion, unity in architecture, and the union of both.*" The interiors of Evangelical churches might have auditorium seating focused on a centrally positioned pulpit within a shell whose stylistic idiom was indistinguishable from that of the Cambridge Ecclesiologists.[84] A further factor was the aesthetic attraction to the Gothic: one Presbyterian minister in Virginia in the mid-nineteenth century admitted a fondness for "a stone Gothic, rubble walls, crevices for moss and ivy: holes where old Time may stick in her memorials: cozy loopholes of retreat, where the sparrow may find a house."[85] But this sort of sentimental attraction could be indulged because Gothic could also be seen as a force for unity and an expression of Anglo-American cultural identification.

Thus, in denominations that had long since broken away from liturgical modes of worship, congregations adopted the Gothic style for their new buildings, even if internally the plan and furnishings followed some version of the auditorium style. In Chicago, Union Park Congregational Congregational Church (1869–71) and Second Presbyterian (1872–74) represent classic cases.[86] By 1895, the national trend evoked an aggrieved commentary:

> Whence the gross departures from Presbyterianism and primitive simplicity in our meeting-houses . . . ? Why have we gone back to the Middle Ages . . . ? Is there anything in the history of the old cathedrals, designed in sin, founded in iniquity, cemented with the tears and blood of the living temples of Christ, the monuments of idolatry and tyranny, dark and gloomy, chilly and fear-inspiring, to commend them to us who rejoice in the liberty and light of the gospel? . . . Why do we abuse the papists, and then imitate them?[87]

One answer to the last question, of course, is that churches of Calvinist background were imitating not Roman usage but Anglican, and by the second half of the nineteenth century Anglican churches were generally building in Gothic revival styles, whether they were higher or lower in their liturgy.

By around the turn of the twentieth century, churches built with platforms for a proclamatory worship were redesigned with some approximation on those platforms to the divided chancels of Anglican tradition, with facing choir stalls. On a single street corner in Evanston, just north of Chicago, First Baptist Church (now Lake Street Church) and First Presbyterian Church provide clear examples of this tendency. By 1933 it was possible to look back on the transformation and see it as a radical shift away from the Evangelical forms introduced earlier. A statement from that year is particularly interesting because it speaks not of Episcopal churches but of others influenced by Episcopal forms:

> A radical change has been noted in recent years for a more worship-
> ful church interior, and practically all new work is now designed
> providing a formal chancel instead of the old platform arrangement
> with its curved front rail, and overhead a great array of gilded organ
> pipes. This movement started as far back as 1912 when the Welling-
> ton Avenue Congregational Church was erected with a divided choir
> and a formal chancel. Since then other churches have been built
> along these lines, as far as the chancel is concerned, but the de-
> mand for this arrangement has reached great proportions in recent
> years until not only is this the accepted arrangement for new work,
> but we see many old churches undertaking remodelling programs of
> this character. It is a very encouraging sign, for with it will come an
> improvement in the order of worship, and today several of the de-
> nominations are studying the matter of worship with a zeal which
> promises much for the future church. One can readily see that no
> carelessly prepared service would be appropriate in the new chapel
> at the University of Chicago or in the First Unitarian Church, near
> the Midway, or in the Emerald Avenue Presbyterian Church.[88]

In most cases, to be sure, the borrowing from Anglican forms was partial. Churches that had had preaching platforms retained these but set choir stalls on them in a rough approximation of the divided chancel of the full Gothic revival. What these churches saw themselves as doing was taking an element of Anglican usage ("aping the Anglicans," as it was sometimes called) and integrating it with their own Presbyterian, Baptist, or other traditions.

A New Wave of Immigration and the Arrival of Eastern Orthodox Churches

While in the middle decades of the nineteenth century there was immigration to Chicago from the countries of northern Europe (especially Germans, Irish, Poles, and Scandinavians), the end of that century and beginning of the twen-tieth there was immigration from eastern and southern Europe as well, partic-ularly Jews from Russia and Ukraine; Eastern Orthodox from Greece; Eastern Rite Catholics from in and around Carpatho-Russia, many of whom soon con-verted to Orthodoxy; and Roman Catholics from Italy. While Italians were sub-ject to largely the same pressures toward assimilation earlier experienced by Poles and other Roman Catholics, the Eastern Orthodox maintained their national traditions of liturgy and quickly established distinct jurisdictions in America. While Irish and Polish Catholics belonged to a single diocese, Greeks and Serbs did not. Eventually Chicago became the see for bishops linked to the Greek Orthodox patriarch of Constantinople, the Russian Orthodox metropolitan or patriarch of Moscow, and the Serbian Orthodox patriarch of Belgrade, and in the course of the twentieth century the jurisdictions became further splintered. While in principle Eastern Orthodoxy represented a single Church, the jurisdictions were distinct. What this meant for architecture was a somewhat greater degree of adherence to traditional ethnic forms.

Holy Trinity Orthodox Cathedral (1901–3) was constructed with support by a grant from Czar Nicholas II. The local architect, Louis Sullivan, was familiar with Viollet-le-Duc's *L'Art russe* and with the liturgical function of Orthodox architectural forms, and the building is a close replica of a provincial Russian design. Some decorative touches, particularly on the porch, show Sullivan's hand. The use of stucco over brick for the walls and the overhanging roofs have been traced to the influence of the Prairie School. But the plan, the furnishing, and the aesthetic are Russian Orthodox: the bell tower at the west end, the dome on an octagonal drum over the square nave, the endonarthex that converts the nave from a square into a rectangle, the structurally distinct sanctuary (or "altar" in Eastern Orthodox parlance) that became closed to the nave by the insertion of an iconostasis with four ranks of icons set in a wooden frame.[89] In such a church the bishop or priest serving at liturgy would pass frequently out from the sanctuary, through the Royal Doors in the center of the iconostasis, and into the nave, in effect mediating between the inner and the outer space. The structure itself was also construed as having a mediating function: the interior of the dome was painted blue with stars, to reinforce the notion that the rounded inner dome represented heaven, the square beneath it was earth, and the liturgy itself mediated between celestial and terrestrial worship. And the profusion of images on the iconostasis, on walls and pillars, and on moveable stands grew out of the Eastern Orthodox conception of icons as mediating to Christ and the saints the veneration of those who kissed, incensed, or otherwise honored their icons.

Having no equivalent of archdiocesan support, and no linkage to religious orders, the Eastern Orthodox populations often began by purchasing buildings built for other communities; in 1927, for example, one Greek congregation moved into a former synagogue.[90] One of the most ambitious of the purpose-built Orthodox churches was Annunciation Cathedral, patterned after the cathedral in Athens and constructed after several years of worshiping in rented space.[91] While the colonnades marking aisles of the nave accentuate the longitudinal character of the nave more than at Holy Trinity Cathedral, and the stylistic idiom is in the tradition of Greek classicism, the plan of Annunciation is not fundamentally different from that of Holy Trinity.

Americanization and Establishment Gothic
in the Early Twentieth Century

Because revival styles and particularly the Gothic were so widely identified with the image of a church, architects working in more modern idioms were sometimes required to make compromises. When Marion Mahony Griffin was asked to design All Souls' Unitarian Church in Evanston (1902–3), her first plan was consonant with the early Prairie style she knew well from her association with Frank Lloyd Wright, combining strong geometrical forms with gestures toward historicism. But the building committee turned this plan down, preferring "something Gothic," and so Mahony gave them a simplified Gothic design with gestures toward Prairie School. As David Van Zanten has said, Mahony managed to imbue the church with "the exotic flavor of Wright's work through her handling of the skylights with their rich patterns casting a mottled light on the clean forms below." Behind the pulpit, in a shallow apse, she painted an angel with arms stretched outward to embrace the souls clustered before her.[92]

If the second half of the nineteenth century witnessed a diversity of styles among Roman Catholics, and some eclecticism also among Protestants, the early twentieth century was in some ways a period of greater conformity. After World War I, use of colonial classicism among Roman Catholics was a way of affirming that the Church was now emerging from ethnicity and on its way toward Americanization. The prime specimen is the chapel at the seminary in Mundelein (1925), which is designed in a Colonial style that might lead a casual observer to mistake it on the exterior for a Congregational church. In fact, it was modeled after just such a building, the Congregational Church in Old Lyme, Connecticut, because Cardinal Mundelein wanted it and the rest of the seminary campus to make a statement about Roman Catholic assimilation to American culture. The architect, Joseph W. McCarthy, was used by the archdiocese for several further churches, each them an exercise in assimilation to a perceived cultural mainstream. A concern to affirm American identity could be a factor again in the years just after World War II, when it was said of Our Lady of Perpetual Help in Glenview that a "combination of the Catholic and the genuinely American" prompted the pastor to use a Georgian Colonial style for a new church in this "typically American community," and while the church itself was being built a "Mount Vernon-style" rectory went up alongside it.[93]

The relative conformity of the early twentieth century came about also because some churches were more visibly acknowledging a connectedness to a social and economic elite. In the decades before the stock market crash of 1929, the Gothic style in America had become a symbol of status that was used well beyond the ecclesiastical sphere. While the Gothic had been used in England for the Houses of Parliament in the early nineteenth century, major public monuments in Gothic design had been mostly ecclesiastical. But in 1904 the firm of Ralph Adams Cram and Bertram Grosvenor Goodhue won a competition for design of the military academy at West Point in Gothic style, and the same firm went on to design university campuses and other nonecclesiastical buildings, as well as many churches for congregations that had attained or sought a high social profile.[94] Cram was passionately committed to the Gothic style and was the foremost American proponent and practitioner of that revival in his day, with Goodhue's assistance. The University of Chicago, well supported with funds donated by John D. Rockefeller, built a complex of highly accomplished Gothic revival buildings as part of its effort to attain national stature.[95] The business world itself adopted the Gothic, perhaps most prominently in the Tribune Tower of 1925, designed for a newspaper that used Gothic (or "Old English") lettering on its masthead.[96]

The popularity of this "Establishment Gothic," if one may call it that, is difficult to date with precision, because it is so much an extension and application of the Gothic revival begun in the second quarter of the nineteenth century. But something new had developed by 1912–14, when Fourth Presbyterian Church built a new church designed by Ralph Adams Cram.[97] What Cram produced was far more than simply a Gothic shell for a traditional Presbyterian auditorium: the interior is decidedly longitudinal (being 130 feet long and 50 feet wide), and the sanctuary is architecturally distinguished from the nave by the equivalent of a chancel arch. Furthermore, the ancillary buildings designed by Howard Van Doren Shaw include an arcaded walkway (or "cloister") and other facilities surrounding a "garth" in a fashion more to be expected in an Anglo-Catholic complex. Not far away is the Roman Catholic Quigley Seminary with its Saint James Chapel (1917–20), modeled after Sainte-Chapelle in Paris. It would be difficult to judge which of these two complexes is more self-consciously medievalizing, or which is more clearly designed to project a confident message of status to the developing community of Chicago's Near North Side.

Another of the most ambitious examples of the Gothic revival in this era is Goodhue's Rockefeller Memorial Chapel (1926–28) at the University of Chiago. This chapel sustained an already well-established tradition of ecclesiastical Gothic and at the same time contributed toward the Gothic style of its university surroundings. Like the Riverside Church near Columbia University in Manhattan, the chapel at Chicago was built with funding from John D. Rockefeller. It was built on an imposing scale, 265 feet long, with clerestory windows approximately 43 feet high, and a 207-foot tower. Done on a less ambitious scale but in the same tradition is the Bond Chapel, attached to the university's Divinity School, combining perpendicular window tracery of fifteenth-century inspiration with richly colored glass.[98] And the nearby First Unitarian Church also adopted the Gothic style, providing one of Chicago's best imitations of English design.[99] At First Unitarian, even the principles of construction approximate those of traditional Gothic architecture, with masonry unsupported by a steel frame. (At the pastor's insistence, and contrary to the architect's original plan, a spire was added above the tower, so for the tower steel support was needed.) But even more conspicuously marking the church's marriage with the business establishment was the building of the Chicago Temple. The First Methodist Church, which was bound to its early location on Washington Street by a clause in its deed, was the only one of the early churches along Washington to remain at the heart of the city. As soon as 1857 it occupied a building that combined ecclesiastical with commercial property, and in 1922–24 it replaced the current version of that hybrid with the Chicago Temple, a twenty-two-story French Gothic skyscraper in which the church itself occupies the first two floors, eighteen storeys of commercial office space soar above it, and a spire surrounded by Gothic ornament rises at the top above an upper sanctuary.[100]

For Cram, the Gothic was not only a pleasing style but an integral element in the medieval culture that he (rather like Pugin a century earlier) exalted as ideal. Gothic was the fruit of a spiritual and aesthetic golden age. Medieval Christianity might be often reviled, but "at least it was beautiful, one of the most beautiful things man has ever experienced, and I have never heard that the same attribute has ever been alleged of Calvinism, Puritanism, or any other of the substitutes that have taken its place."[101] English architecture had been "logical, consistent, [and] healthy" until the Reformation broke all continuity and led to artificial and valueless church designs. England itself had seen revitalization of its architecture in the nineteenth century; in America, Richard Upjohn and James Renwick had made some headway with reform, "but its vitality lapsed with their death," and Richardson with his eclectic Romanesque had "swept the very memory of it away." Only in Cram's own time was a renewed effort at reform underway that seemed to promise success.[102]

Cram also developed a theory of theological aesthetics in which his church designs were related to their liturgical purpose. The qualities required in a church, he suggested, were four. First, "a church is a house of God, a place of His earthly habitation, wrought in the fashion of heavenly things, a visible type of heaven itself." Second, it is "a place apart where may be solemnized the sublime mysteries of the Catholic faith," that is to say "a temple reared about the altar, and subordinate to it, leading up to it, as to the centre of honor, growing richer and more splendid as it approaches the sanctuary." Third, it is a place meant to create "spiritual emotion through the ministry of all possible beauty of environment," using art "to lift men's minds from secular things to spiritual, that their souls may be brought into harmony with God." Fourth, it is "a building where a congregation may conveniently listen to the instruction of its spiritual leaders." Cram listed these qualities in what he took to be descending order of importance. Properly designed, he went on, a church should be able to serve all four purposes well, but he reacted against what he saw as too narrow a focus on the fourth factor, for him the least important.[103]

It would hardly be surprising for a Episcopal parish with high liturgical leanings to grant a commission to a man with such views, but for a Presbyterian church such as Chicago's Fourth Presbyterian to engage such an architect is more unexpected. A generation earlier, even those Presbyterians who advocated a turn to Gothic style might have listed the fourth of Cram's characteristics of a church as the most important and might have had serious difficulty with the second. This marriage of Presbyterian worship with a "high church" conception of architecture must be seen in the context of the cultural éclat with which Gothic was vested at this time. If style of architecture could serve as a useful marker of ethnic identity for immigrant Roman Catholics, it could equally serve as a marker of cultural respectability for a social elite, even if this meant an apparent dissonance between the denomination's tradition and the theology associated with the architecture.

Church architecture in Chicago, as in most of the United States, came very largely to a standstill with the stock market crash of 1929. Between the fire of 1871 and the crash of 1929, church design had served in more than one way, and sometimes in a complex and nuanced variety of ways, as a cultural marker. Immigrants could build churches that either grew out of their Old World traditions or helped them move away from those traditions. Those who had long been established in America could embrace two trends both derived largely from England, the Gothic revival style and some measure of ritualism in liturgy, and could thereby assert a cultural identity distinct from that of the immigrants and closely tied to a sense of the continuities in Anglo-American culture. Even those who resisted the incursion of ritualism might still be attracted to the Gothic design, and use of the fully developed chancel could be a guarantor of dignified worship even in a congregation that would never think of using candles or incense. Not surprisingly, observers could become confused and wonder why anti-Romanists seemed to be borrowing traditions associated with Rome. But presumably each congregation—or at least each dedicated member of each congregation—had some way of conceiving and justifying each innovation.

Liturgical Disposition of Churches in Chicago: Intercession, Mediation, and Proclamation

Robert W. Jenson suggested that both Protestant and Catholic churches of the period I am discussing reflected traditional conceptions of church design "in vulgarized form," Catholics by building "holy theaters" with stages and auditoriums for viewing the sacred act, Protestants by designing "holy lecture halls" for the hearing of sacred discourse, but both contriving sacred space that was oriented toward a focal point.[104] The argument need not be expressed quite so bluntly, but it is true that Roman Catholic and Protestant churches of this era represented particular variants on—or deviations from—the classic sacramental and evangelical traditions.

In the Roman Catholic worship of modern centuries, the processional character of the longitudinal nave was diminished, and the church was divided sharply into two zones: the laity prayed in the nave, and the clergy rarely moved out from the sanctuary. Catholic reformers of the sixteenth century had insisted that the sanctuary should be fully visible—if not approachable—from nave. This was a change that Giorgio Vasari was called on to introduce at Santa Maria Novella and elsewhere in the sixteenth century;[105] it became the norm. Given the length of the nave, it might be difficult for the laity to hear what was being said at the altar, and in any case the priest would be speaking in Latin, facing away from the congregation and toward the high altar, not chiefly addressing the people, but rather God. Churches of this sort were built for *intercession*, with the priest interceding before God in Latin on behalf of those gathered. As J. J. Burke explained in 1892, "the prayers of the Mass are offered to God. Hence when the priest says Mass he is speaking not to the people, but to God, to whom all languages are equally intelligible."[106] The priest's space or sanctuary is separated from the congregation's space or nave by a low communion rail, and at the communion the clergy and laity met on opposite sides of that rail, which served as an effective barrier to movement if not to vision. The mass is a sacrifice to which immense dramatic power is ascribed, as is clear from a monologue that John Henry Newman puts into the mouth of a character in his novel *Loss and Gain*:

> to me nothing is so consoling, so piercing, so thrilling, so over-coming, as the Mass, said as it is among us. I could attend Masses forever, and not be tired. . . . It is, not the invocation merely, but, if I dare use the word, the evocation of the Eternal. He becomes present on the altar in flesh and blood, before whom angels bow and devils tremble.[107]

The mass may well have been spectacle, but it was not mere show: it was meant, at least, as drama that called attention beyond itself to realities far transcending ordinary experience.

The space within the church is differently segmented in Eastern Orthodox tradition.[108] If the Roman Catholic mass is fundamentally intercessory, one might perhaps say that the Orthodox liturgy is *mediatory*. Separating the sanctuary from the nave is a high iconostasis, or icon screen, which developed in Russia in the later Middle Ages out of a barrier that was less high and imposing. The visual focus is neither the altar nor the pulpit (an Eastern Orthodox church traditionally has no fixed pulpit), but rather the Royal Doors in the center of the iconostasis. The nave may or may not be elongated, but it is clearly distinguished from the sanctuary, and traditionally it has no fixed seating at all. The bishop, priest, and others serving at liturgy pass back and forth between the sanctuary and the nave, in effect mediating between the space occupied by the congregation and that from which laity are generally excluded. While the role of clergy is thus one of mediation between the inner and the outer sanctum, there are other forms of mediation at work as well. The entire church is conceived as mediating between heaven and earth. The dome represents the sphere of the heavens resting on the four-cornered earth, and those participating in earthly liturgy are joined with the saints and angels in celestial liturgy: the church and the liturgy thus mediate between earth and heaven. And the icons are seen as windows to the supernatural world, and means by which veneration is transmitted to the sacred personages: whether hung on the iconostasis, painted on the walls, or lying on stands, an icon mediates between the devotee and the object of devotion.

In one sense, then, an Orthodox church is more firmly segmented than a Roman Catholic church, and in another sense it is less so. The fully developed iconostasis poses a visual barrier between nave and sanctuary, but the clergy (not the laity) pass out into the nave and thus preserve a fuller sense of procession from one sacred space to another. While the Roman church of this period permits full visibility but very little mobility between sanctuary and nave, the Orthodox church allows considerable mobility (for the altar party) but little visibility.

From one perspective, church architecture in Chicago between the 1871 fire and the crash of 1929 represented a boisterous variety: the diversity of ethnic heritage was variously reflected in architectural design. But from the viewpoint of liturgical arrangement the diversity was considerably less. Roman Catholic churches, the most conspicuously diverse in style, were perhaps the most standardized in liturgical disposition. Longitudinal naves separated by communion rails from the sanctuaries were routine, as were altars to Mary and Joseph flanking the high altar, box confessionals along the sides or in back, stations of the cross, and other foci of devotional piety. Even Episcopal churches, which ranged from highly ceremonialist to relatively low in their churchmanship, did not range widely in their liturgical form. Chancels were almost always shallow, scarcely ever approximating the length found in many Anglo-Catholic chancel abroad, let alone that of a thirteenth-century English chancel; the Church of the Ascension, known for its high churchmanship, was built originally for a low church faction from Saint James and in its plan shows little of its later Anglo-Catholic leanings. Protestant churches underwent a significant shift in the last decades of the nineteenth century with the introduction of the fully developed auditorium design, which came to be imitated even in relatively small churches once it had been popularized in larger ones with high profile. Baptist or Presbyterian churches might rearrange their platforms to approximate the divided chancels of Episcopalians, but the extent of the rear-rangement was limited by the available place on the platforms. And among the Eastern Orthodox and Eastern Rite Catholics, the tradition of a sanctuary closed off by a high iconostatis was essentially unchallenged.

In effect, then, there were three basic approaches to liturgical space in these churches: the design of Roman Catholic churches was appropriate mainly for intercession, that of Protestant churches for proclamation, and that of Eastern Orthodox churches for mediation. The intercessory churches of Roman Catholics were built in the tradition of classic sacramental churches, but they used processional space in a particular way, limiting the sanctuary to the priest and servers, maintaining a clear distinction between sanctuary and nave, and bringing the congregation and priest together for communion at the boundary line formed by the communion rail. The proclamatory churches of Protestants were designed in the tradition of classic evangelical churches, but their size and their arrangement of the platform often tilted the balance in the direction of proclamation over response, giving preacher and choir a role more sharply defined than the congregation's. And the mediatory churches of the Eastern Orthodox represented another version of the classic sacramental church, with dramatic separation of sanctuary and nave and with those in the altar moving outward into the nave but not vice versa. Radical rethinking of the ways these liturgical spaces might be used was not widespread; in Prot-estant and Roman Catholic circles, if not in Orthodoxy, the next major step would be not the creative redeployment of traditional space but experiments with new types of space altogether.

7

Rudolf Schwarz

Modern Churches in a Modern Culture

Asked once about his personal religious convictions and their relevance to his work at Ronchamp, Le Corbusier responded: "I have
not experienced the miracle of faith, but I have often known the
miracle of ineffable space." His youthful Protestantism had been
transmuted into a vaguer "sense of higher things," a poetic sensibility and philosophical idealism, a program of moral and social better-
ment through change of the environment.[1] But what did he mean
by "the miracle of ineffable space"? Was he affirming the power of
signs without accepting the reality of what they signify? Or if it is
the immanent architectural space itself that is ineffable, does it lose
its quality as a sign pointing to some transcendent referent? Or was
the architect perhaps merely recognizing the meaningfulness of
church design without presuming to specify for his client what its
theological meaning should be?

In the twentieth century surely more than at any previous time,
clients for church architecture were willing to engage the services of
distinguished designers regardless of their beliefs, indeed regardless
of whether they had any faith at all. Seeking to show their openness
to the modern world, the Greek Orthodox might hire a Frank Lloyd
Wright and the French Dominicans a Le Corbusier. The Victorian
notion of the ecclesiastical architect as exercising a quasi-sacerdotal
calling was now remote.[2] In more than one case the client for a new
church has explicitly preferred an architect without previous experience in church design, and thus without the preconceptions of a
specialist in the field.[3] From the architects' perspective the alliance
could be a good one. God, it has been said, is "a demanding client

but one who could make your name if you got things right."[4] And so churches have always been "enviable opportunities for architects."[5] They are often highly visible, they provide good showplaces for striking exteriors and for large and potentially impressive interiors, and the clients are often less businesslike and more impressionable than secular clients. Churches give exceptional opportunities to meet challenges: the integration of the functional and the symbolic, the fraught relationship between tradition and modernity, the link between spatial dynamics and centering focus. In 1961 Oskar Söhngen went so far as to argue that "all knowledge requires distance from the object of knowledge," hence a Protestant who stands in "a dialectical position between distance' and lovingly careful sensitivity" can contribute something toward better knowledge and evaluation of a building such as the Ronchamp chapel.[6]

One of the leading American church designers of the twentieth century, Pietro Belluschi, was said to have remained deeply spiritual while casting off the Roman Catholic heritage of his youth. He was particularly fond of working on churches and became known largely as an ecclesiastical architect. An outsider to all denominations, he studied the liturgical demands of his clients, engaged them in sustained conversation, and on occasion instructed them with truisms, telling them perhaps that "a religious building must create an atmosphere conducive to prayer and meditation."[7] But an architect who is not a member of the religious community will not be in the same position to join with that community in articulating the relationship between architectural signs and the theological realities they are taken to signify. The architect who does belong to the tradition will have greater authority, not as an architect but as an interpreter of architecture.

One commentator in 1966 went so far as to question the "often stated dogma of religious design that architecture should be shaped by worship, not worship by the architect," expressing doubt that this principle was actually practiced in the past and insisting that it could not in the present.

> The unique conditions of our time, which combine a questioning theology and an experimenting architecture, accentuate the impossibility of church architecture as a preordained unity of religious dogma and architectural style. The modern architect is forced by a fragmented society to evolve a philosophy and explain the formal implications of his work, leading to the architect's personal evaluation of theology and ritual.

Even if not a member of the religious community, the architect collaborates in the creation of ritual space, serving "not the servant of theology but its interpreter" and "performing an act with theological implications."[8]

On virtually all these points, the German architect Rudolf Schwarz (1897–1961) was distinctive.[9] He was a lifelong Roman Catholic who studied theology and liturgy seriously in his youth and continued to travel in theologians' and

liturgists' company. He was well familiar with the earliest phases of the movement for liturgical renewal. One friend commented after his death, "Rudolf
Schwarz was a pious Christian. . . . I am convinced that only on this basis can
the man and his work be understood."[10] He thought and wrote a great deal
about all the crucial questions that concern us in this book: spatial dynamics
and centering focus, aesthetic impact and symbolic resonance, the relationship
between tradition and modernity. It is not only that he devoted himself intensely to working out the meaning of church architecture. More than that, he
never *stopped* telling people what his churches and other churches meant. He
was a theologically sophisticated theorist of church architecture and the author
of a book on the subject, *Vom Bau der Kirche* (1938), which appeared in English
as *The Church Incarnate* (1958). Among his other writings, his memoirs—
Kirchenbau: Welt vor der Schwelle (*Church Building: World before the Threshold*),
published in 1960, the year before his death—deserve particular attention for
their commentary on particular designs he executed.[11] His friend Mies van der
Rohe praised him as a great architect and in particular as a *thinking* architect,
as "the great German church builder" and "one of the most profound thinkers
of our time."[12] Along with his elder contemporary Dominikus Böhm and others, Schwarz was a leading figure in architectural modernism in the 1920s,
then in the years after World War II he reemerged as one of the leaders in the
reconstruction of Germany. There were other architects who had been pioneers
of modernism and now were its elder statesmen, but few of these were as
influential in the design of churches.

During his lifetime, his designs and his theories were intensely controversial. His Fronleichnamskirche (Corpus Christi Church) at Aachen was
hailed by some as the first fully modern church but condemned by others as
empty and barren. And while *Vom Bau der Kirche* was celebrated by some for
its depth of reflection, it was also branded as "one of the most dangerous books
ever written about church-building."[13] For some time after his death, his rep-
utation was eclipsed.[14] Liturgical reforms of the 1960s generated a sense of
novelty that made it harder to sustain interest in an earlier generation of reformers. Schwarz's churches attracted less attention than they had previously,
and his writings were cited relatively little. But in recent decades there has
been a revival of interest, with exhibitions of his architectural output and serious commentary on his writings: in the 1990s alone, three important books
on his architecture appeared. And with the advantage of historical perspective
it becomes possible again to perceive the stature of an architect who played so
central a role both in the 1920s and in the 1950s, both in theory and in practice.
Whatever one makes of his designs and his writings, it would be difficult to
find any other single figure whose work is more important for an understanding of twentieth-century church architecture. Yet in the English-speaking world
he remains little known, and when known he is sometimes badly misunder-
stood.[15]

Liturgical Background: Schwarz, Guardini, and Early Liturgical Renewal

To grasp Schwarz's place in liturgical architecture one must situate him vis-à-vis the movement of liturgical renewal that had begun in the early years of the twentieth century.[16] Central to this movement was the conviction that liturgy is an activity of the Christian community, the Church as a people, and neither a simply clerical exercise nor a form of private and individual prayer. This meant that the laity should be allowed and encouraged to participate fully in the liturgy rather than being observers of clerical action. It also meant that liturgy should be distinguished clearly from private devotional exercises, however much these were rooted in and derived from the liturgy. Sometimes the birth of this movement is dated to 1909, when the Belgian Benedictine monk Lambert Beauduin delivered an influential paper on "The True Prayer of the Church" at a conference in Malines. But what led to a movement in the sense of a sustained effort of reflection, publication, and regular meetings intended to stimulate renewal of liturgy was a Holy Week conference of 1914 organized by Ildefons Herwegen, abbot of Maria Laach, a Benedictine monastery in Germany. Herwegen himself produced relevant pamphlets in 1928 and many further works in succeeding years, and another monk of Maria Laach, Odo Casel, produced two influential books, *Die Liturgie als Mysterienfeier* (*Liturgy as Celebration of Mystery*) and *Das Christliche Kultmysterium* (*The Mystery of Christian Worship*), in 1922 and 1932, which emphasized the function of liturgy as the acting out of mystery and of mysteries of the faith.[17] Maria Laach became the focus for a circle of liturgists and architects who set out to study the problems of liturgy and liturgical space. It was under the impetus and auspices of these reformers at Maria Laach that Romano Guardini published his early book *Vom Geist der Liturgie* (*On the Spirit of the Liturgy*) in 1918.[18] And while Ildefons Herwegen was himself a close friend of Rudolf Schwarz's family during the architect's youth, it was Guardini with whom Schwarz was more closely associated during his formative years in the Catholic youth organization Quickborn and in his early professional life.

Guardini wrote on numerous aspects of theology, philosophy, and literature, but he never lost his early interest in liturgy, and he played a critical role in the history of twentieth-century liturgical renewal. If there is any one theme central to Guardini's conception of liturgy, apart from the shared convictions of the liturgical movement generally, it is the contemplative element. He notes in *Vom Geist der Liturgie* that in modern Western culture the practical will, a sense of active purpose, or Ethos, has taken priority over Logos, or the contemplative dimension of life. He urges a corrective view: "the basis of all genuine and healthy life is a contemplative one. No matter how great the energy of the volition and the action and striving may be, it must rest on the tranquil contemplation of eternal, unchangeable truth. This attitude is rooted in eternity."[19] Contemplation rather than action, Logos rather than Ethos, becomes the central focus of liturgy. Guardini speaks of a "playfulness" in liturgy, by which he means its orientation to meaning rather than to purpose. "When the liturgy is rightly regarded, it cannot be said to have a purpose, because it does not exist for the sake of humanity, but for the sake of God. In the liturgy man is no longer concerned with himself; his gaze is directed towards God. In it man is not so much intended to edify himself as to contemplate God's majesty."[20] This is by no means to deny the communal character of liturgy: when Guardini speaks of contemplation here he is speaking of the orientation of a community, not detached individuals, toward the divine, and the constitution of that community as sacred precisely through that orientation. Nor is it to deny that liturgy has ethical implications, even if these are indirect, as a source of moral strength more than of specific moral guidance.

Another early book of Guardini, *Von heiligen Zeichen* (*On Sacred Signs*), appeared originally in 1922 as a publication of the Quickborn movement, in which Schwarz was an active member.[21] This was a series of short meditations on the symbols, gestures, vessels, and other objects and acts associated with liturgy. The flavor of this work may be conveyed by an excerpt from Guardini's meditation on altars:

> In the still depths of man's being there is a region of calm light, and there he exercises the soul's deepest power, and sends up sacrifice to God.
>
> The external representation of this region of central calm and strength is the altar.
>
> The altar occupies the holiest spot in the church. The church has itself been set apart from the world of human work, and the altar is elevated above the rest of the church in a spot as remote and separate as the sanctuary of the soul. . . .
>
> The two altars, the one without and the one within, belong inseparably together. The visible altar at the heart of the church is but the external representation of the altar at the centre of the human breast.[22]

Schwarz was deeply affected not only by the general emphasis of the reformers on congregational participation and unity of laity with clergy but also by Guardini's emphasis on the assembly's contemplative presence before the divine, a theme developed in *Von Geist der Liturgie*, and the habit of meditative reflection on particular objects as signs, seen in *Von heiligen Zeichen*. He also shared Guardini's conception of the centrality of the altar. Of further importance is the collaboration of these two men in the design of Schwarz's earliest executed architecture for worship, the chapel in the Quickborn headquarters at Burg Rothenfels (1928).[23] Schwarz had already been associated with Guardini at Berlin in the early 1920s, but in 1927 Guardini was called to Burg Rothenfels as its director, and in the later years of the decade Schwarz worked at the Burg as architect for renovation of its facilities. When the chapel itself was redesigned, then, Guardini was the liturgist and Schwarz the architect for this project. There had earlier been a chapel with a Gothic revival altar, a pietà over the tabernacle, and traditionally ranked pews separated by a central aisle. All this was removed. What Schwarz and Guardini substituted was entirely different. The seating took the form of simple moveable stools, meant to be arranged in various configurations, including that of a horseshoe around three sides of the room, with the altar, also moveable, on the fourth side. The walls were pure white. The focus was entirely on the congregation and the priest, together forming a community gathered for worship, with no separation between them. The chapel was a place where liturgical reforms born in the monasteries could reach wider circles.[24]

Schwarz's Theory of Church Design: The Seven Plans

Even people who know little else about Schwarz have sometimes been exposed to his seven plans of church design, given in *Vom Bau der Kirche* (fig. 22). These plans vary in their visual complexity and in the complexity of interpretation given them. In the first, called "the sacred inwardness," the congregation is gathered in a ring about the altar. The second, "the open ring," is a variation on the first: the people are again gathered around the altar, but with a break in the ring. This second plan held a position of prominence in Schwarz's thought, in his architectural practice, and in his writings about the churches he executed: it is the one meant to be "valid for the average situation of every day and year."[25] The chapel at Burg Rothenfels was an early example. The third plan, "the chalice of light," adds a vertical dimension to the ring, with a complex dome above it as a source of illumination. The fourth, "the sacred journey," corresponds to the longitudinal church that would have been most familiar to most of Schwarz's readers. Deeply problematic for him, it was also intensely fascinating, and his chapter on it is significantly longer than any other. The fifth plan, "the dark chalice," is essentially a parabola with the altar placed near the apex. At first it appears to be a cheering and welcoming form of church, with the arms of the parabola taken to represent the outstretched arms of Christ, seated at the front, waiting to receive the people who come toward him, but what seems at first a cheering vision becomes complex and troubling. The Lord hesitates; rather than closing his arms in embrace he looks beyond the people's heads to the portal, where he sees the scene of judgment and with outstretched arms now implores the Father for mercy, asking that the cup of judgment may, if possible, pass by, "but it shall not pass by."[26] It is a relief,

"1. The sacred inwardness"

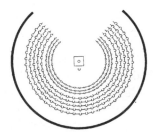

"2. The broken ring"

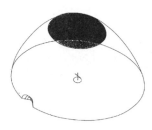

"3. The chalice of light"

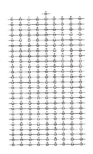

"4. The sacred journey"

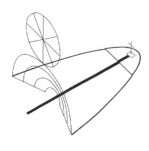

"5. The dark chalice"

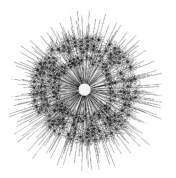

"6. The dome of light"

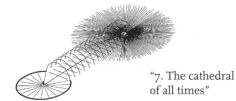

"7. The cathedral
of all times"

FIGURE 22. Plans from Rudolf Schwarz, *Vom Bau der Kirche* (Würzburg: Werkbund-verlag, 1938). Reproduced with permission of Maria Schwarz.

then, to turn to the sixth plan, "the dome of light," which Schwarz speaks of eloquently as a church bursting with luminosity.

> The building consists of light, light breaking in from all sides, light shining forth from all things, light fused with light, light turning to face light, light the answer to light. The earth is transformed into a star, her stuff afire, she is a monstrance of rays about the child in the center, her altar a flame, the people a sea of fire and each one of them a star. . . . The vault of the world is a pellucid infinitude, clear and transparent like an evening sky high in the mountains, ethereal and incorporeal, a golden effulgence where the heavenly beings are hovering motionless in bliss. Heaven is everywhere, earth every-where, the one melting into the other.[27]

What exactly this would look like remains uncertain, and indeed Schwarz says that this plan might be realized in various ways, all signifying that the world is bathed in eternal light. Similarly indeterminate is the seventh plan, "the cathedral of all times"; although Schwarz gives a diagram in which two rings are connected by a longitudinal pathway, he devotes very little attention in his text to the exact shape of either the church or the congregation, and he says rather obscurely that this is "a plan above all plans and no one man can build it."[28]

The plans are not meant as conventional architectural designs, with detailed specification of floor plan and elevation, but primarily (at least many of them) as images for the configuration of the assembly itself.[29] A conception of how the congregation forms itself underlies his design for a building to house the congregation. The spareness of the church is meant in part as empowerment for those who bring the space to life in worship. Alfred Döblin went so far as to suggest that Schwarz's focus on the congregation in his Fronleichnamskirche at Aachen brings an element of democracy to the old authoritarian hull of the church: it is the people themselves who define and create the sacred space.[30]

Toward the end of the book Schwarz maintains that his apparently accidental sequence of plans discloses "a profound inner order," and that they "are built upon each other and toward each other and they open up into each other." He then shows how each form can be transformed into the next in a topographic progression that one might now best represent with computer graphics. The inward-turned gathering around a center splits open, then the space "takes leave of the form and journey begins," an ascent "reaches the dead point in the apex," opposing forces lead to a standstill, "counteraction prevails," movement is thrown back, hesitates, and new space with a new center "unfolds out of the distended figure" and a "new world is gathered about it in a new sphere." All of this Schwarz compares to plant life, suggesting that the development of one form from another has a sort of organic character. Second, the progression is compared to the course of a human life, although this point is not developed. And third, the transmutation of forms is said to parallel the life of Christ, and indeed throughout the book one comes upon hints about this comparison—as the "dark chalice," for instance, becomes an allusion to the chalice of Gethsemane—but the parallel is never worked out systematically.[31]

Ultimately, however, it would perhaps be best to say that what Schwarz provides is not simply a series of plans for church design but a sequence of meditations showing how to *think* about church design, and then suggestions intimating how the plans themselves can be seen as linked. Each plan is the basis for a meditation; their connectedness is then subject matter for further meditation. While a system is implied, the series in fact serves mainly as a framework for other themes that prove more crucial for this book, for Schwarz's actual churches, and for his later thought. He turned back ever and again to some of the insights that might seem subordinate in their systematic context. But it was these apparently subsidiary themes rather than the system as such that were more significant for his practical work.

Theoretical Themes: Contemplative Space

Schwarz's discussion of the "open ring" requires closer examination. This is the plan in which one side of the ring has a gap, an opening, and this detail is significant on several levels. Schwarz speaks of the people as coming into the church and gathering in an open ring about the altar. Then the priest, the people's representative, steps forward to the altar, standing before it and facing the open space in the ring. The priest is "pushed to the boundary of the earth, the last man." He invokes God from across the altar, "that is to say across the holy earth with all her gifts." In this context, then, the opening represents the openness of the people and the world to that which lies beyond; the altar forms the center of the ring, and the ring itself allows the people to see each other, but the real orientation of people, priest, and altar is the open space beyond them all, and this point is essential for Schwarz's understanding of a church.

> In the priest, the congregation and Christ within it face across the earth into the openness. They go to the innermost brink of the world to the place where her shore curves in an open arc about the eternal. The congregation goes to the threshold of its house and calls out into God's eternity. The holy doctors have always compared this moment with the image in the Song of Songs where the bride steps into the doorway of her home to await the bridegroom. The people are borne forward through the priest as they step to the threshold and then "look out into the distance." They pour themselves out in the invocation of God and surrender themselves into the infinite direction.

The process is fourfold. First is the act of stepping forward to the opening, second that of looking out into that opening, and third an act of surrender— "then everything is still." Having invoked the Creator, the people stand in the breached and empty world, awaiting an answer. The fourth stage is that divine response, which "comes back as streaming light out of the direction into which the people have surrendered themselves."[32]

This passage is in some ways the most important for a grasp of Schwarz's theory. The first and perhaps most obvious observation to be made about this view of a church is that it is thoroughly contemplative, in the same way that Guardini's liturgical theology is contemplative: the focus is less on the liturgical process, scriptural reference, or ritual action than on consciousness of the divine presence. For Schwarz as for Guardini, a church is a place where "an intimation of God's presence can blossom forth."[33] The reference to mystical interpretation of the Song of Songs is one telltale sign of a contemplative conception of relationship to God. Most important, Schwarz's preference for the open ring over the simple or closed ring is a sign that his primary interest is not social but contemplative, or that the social dimension of such a church is subordinated to and dependent on its contemplative orientation. The people are gathered about the altar, but they are identified as a people open toward the divine. At one point Schwarz speaks of the divine answer to the human prayer as coming from afar: God answers "out of his remoteness." And yet the open ring is meant as a sign of the congregation's presence to God and (more to the point) of divine presence to the people thus assembled. If Schwarz had been asked whether his goal was to create space for kinetic or for verbal dynamism, he would presumably have replied that neither of these concepts was what he had in mind: contemplative rest, conceived as the terminus of process rather than in itself a process, was the main purpose of the spaces he designed.

While this contemplative thrust may be most explicit in the discussion of the second plan, in one form or other it pervades the book. Thus, the third plan is that "in which the church still gazes after the departing Lord," again emphasizing the contemplative tension between the presence and absence of the divine.[34] The architect in seeking to do God's work is akin to a mystic:

> the profound meaning of all church building is just this: to find, beyond all preliminary tasks, the absolute task and to introduce in incorrupted works the primal process itself, God's sacred maintaining of the world. Like the mystic who seeks the way to that innermost cell where God lives in the midst of the world, so the cathedral builder seeks to do God's true work, to render the process of all processes. Here in purity God's work should "be done."[35]

But the community too has a role in this approach to the divine, because the forms of architecture are not subjective inventions of the individual but are the work of a culture, a community, and to build "means to place great communal forms before God."[36]

This contemplative sense—this urge to bring people into a keener consciousness of the divine presence—is found in Schwarz's architectural practice as well as in his theoretical writings. It is nowhere clearer than in the Fronleichnamskirche (fig. 23), and one can hardly be surprised to find that when he designed that church Schwarz had been reading the sermons of Meister

FIGURE 23. Fronleichnamskirche, Aachen, Germany, interior. Early photograph, reproduced with permission of Maria Schwarz.

Eckhart, which were among his sources for the notion of an empty space for God to fill, a house prepared each night for "the Guest who may come."[37]

Theoretical Themes: Minimalism of Form

In describing the first of his plans, the ring, Schwarz says it has a table at its center, bread and wine on the table, perhaps candles for decoration.

> That is all. Table, space and walls make up the simplest church. . . . The little congregation sits or stands about the table. The Lord is in the center as he promised to be when he said that wherever a few should gather in his name he would be in the midst of them. There have been greater forms of church building than this one but this is not the right time for them. We cannot continue on from where the last cathedrals left off. Instead we must enter into the simple things at the source of the Christian life. We must begin anew and our new beginning must be genuine. The small congregation is given us to-day, the "coming together of two or three," the communion of the table, and certainly for us the Lord is in the midst of men.

But if the tone here seems uncompromising, even in the context of the second plan, the open ring, Schwarz speaks of the church in nuanced terms: a grand and appreciable edifice becomes an ideal eluding realization:

> The movement into the heights is something very great—the cathedrals of the mind are glorious. We should not be suspicious of them nor revile them. God did not wish men mildly modest and "moderate": he wished them bold. But these things remain a likeness, and even the fruitful earth is a likeness too. But in the end God is utterly different.
>
> And while the ascetic is scaling the lonely peaks perhaps God is in the valley, playing with the children and the flowers.[38]

The ambivalence seen in this passage is one easily detected in Schwarz's actual church designs: more often than not they are marked by an assertiveness, a monumentality, whether they are large or of moderate size, and yet his constant aim was to temper any sense of grandeur with a simplicity of design and undisguised use of utilitarian materials.

But the fullest and most thoroughly developed treatment of this theme comes in discussion of the seventh plan, the "cathedral of all times," and indeed it emerges as the central theme of that chapter. Schwarz here articulates two opposed conceptions of a church. In the first, it is an empty vessel, a tent, filled and activated only by the worshiping assembly.[39] Schwarz observed that many newer churches are almost wholly devoid of images, being "noble instruments for the act of worship" but nothing more, and intentionally so:

Only in the divine service should the plain form of the instrument
be raised to exalted reality. The space and its light should be created
from within, as sacred achievement; even the altar, which in the beginning is only a table, should itself be created; that which was
merely an earthly substance in the beginning should come into being as sacred body; and as the act of worship ends this creation
should die away again—it should be consumed just as the consecrated species themselves become food for the journey.[40]

This may seem to turn the church into a kind of Brigadoon, but perhaps the
closer analogy would be a nomadic encampment, created for the moment by
the worshiping community, rather than a lasting environment that helps to
create this community. Richness of imagery gives way to contemplative simplicity, and if the ritual has symbolic resonance it will come from the words,
the gestures, and the memories of those present.

But Schwarz immediately recognizes that for all its validity this approach
has its limits, and so he proceeds to an opposite understanding of a church.
Here he offers a sensitive appreciation of Eastern Orthodox architecture:

The eastern churches are even today filled with the sacred, steeped
in the palpable presence of God. Usually they are dark and almost
without windows. As an area set apart the holy of holies lies behind
the golden iconostasis whose images show the Saints in their final
form, bathed in the golden ground and with the wide-open eyes of
the beatific vision. Hanging lamps and candles illumine these pictures so that they become holy lights in holy darkness. Where, in
the same neighborhood, a church of the western cult stands with
her "emptiness," devoid of mystery in her sober obviousness, she
cannot stand the comparison, even though she and her cult are also
permeated by the faith in a sacred presence, by the faith in consecration and benediction, in sacred imagery and in sacred building and
above all by the faith in the Lord's presence; nor is she conceived
without a storing up of the sacred [ohne heilige Aufbewahrung], and
to her, too, the sacral act interweaves with the present.[41]

The two goals, then, are "process" and "lastingness" (Vorgang und Dauer), and
churches must be built of both. But in the first instance these are concepts not
of liturgy but of history: that which is deposited in architecture and becomes
lasting form or image has arisen in the course of historical process and become
deposited at a favorable moment. One might go further and say that this is
true of the liturgy itself, which may be experienced as coming from an im-
memorial past but which in each of its moments is the product of historical
creation and enactment, received and transmitted by a community that honors
the lasting vestiges of historical process.

Theoretical Themes: Multivalent Symbolism

Although Schwarz may not have been a poet, he was familiar with Goethe and Rilke, and with Guardini's study of the *Duino Elegies*, and his own mentality was deeply symbolist. More important, his symbolism was always multivalent.[42] The opening of the ring in the second plan is also a wound, representing "the open, injured, bleeding form of this earth, her wounded heart." While Christ is present in the church, he is in a different sense absent, "and thus the empty side is also Christ's empty seat at the table of this world." The plan is a reminder "that when emptiness breaks into a thing, God is near, for this invasion of emptiness is not meaningless annihilation: it is the beginning of growth into the light." If the configuration of the assembly around the altar takes on the form of an open ring, the pattern is also like an eye, "God's own sacred eye, which, dark and opened wide, is looking into God's own sacred light," and the meaning of the plan is that the people are "taken up into the dark eye of providence and up into the resplendent response." But equally the form can be that of a great bird with outstretched wings, or of a tree, and each of these images can be the bearer of spiritual meaning. This approach to symbolism may seem to have much in common with early Christian exegesis of scripture, in which each text has not one but many meanings, potentially an indefinite number, not necessarily known to the human author of the scriptural book yet implanted by the divine source of inspiration.

Schwarz showed very much the same mentality when writing about his various designs for actual churches. Along with Dominikus Böhm he won an architectural competition for the Frauenfriedenskirche (Women's Peace Church) at Frankfurt am Main (1927) with a design entitled *Opfergang*, or "Sacrificial Passage," a long and dark passageway leading to the brightly lighted sanctuary with its crucifixion group.[43] The title made reference to Christ's way of the cross, and thus to Christ's sacrifice renewed in the sacrifice of the mass, but also to the life of the Christian as a way of sacrifice, the world itself as a processional space, and most particularly the passage of soldiers into death, the church being conceived as a memorial to the fallen in World War I. Sankt Michael, also at Frankfurt (1954) (fig. 24), was for Schwarz an embodiment of the open ring; that was the governing factor in the liturgical design. Yet in addition Schwarz saw in Sankt Michael the form of a star, of a castle protecting against inimical forces, and even of a gorge; he had recently been hiking in the Aare Gorge and had come upon a place hemmed in by rocks, with a small opening to the sky high above: "a menacing world towering all around with but a glimpse of the open sky whose silver light shimmers down from the highest region," and Sankt Michael gave expression to this common human experience.

Ultimately, then, the multivalent symbolism of *Vom Bau der Kirche* and Schwarz's other writings must be taken less as a fixed code of meanings and

FIGURE 24. Sankt Michael, Frankfurt, Germany, interior. Early photograph, reproduced with permission of Maria Schwarz.

more as a method for finding meaning, as a guide to symbolist meditation on architectural design. Taken as a code, the meanings Schwarz ascribes to his designs may seem arbitrary and artificial; understood as examples of a method, they open further possibilities for the reader, as they did for Schwarz himself in his later reflections.

While in his early book *Vom Bau der Kirche* Schwarz lays out a more or less systematic sequence of ways churches accommodate congregations, his later book *Kirchenbau* dispenses with any attempt at system and acknowledges that in reflection on particular church buildings designed over his career numerous further images had come to mind: some taken from the realm of creation, such as the star, the mountain, the firmament, the valley or ravine, the flower or tree or forest; others from mathematics, such as the cube or parabola; some from the sphere of human labor, including the harbor, the castle, or the tower, or from history, such as the throne, the crown, or the city; yet others suggested by the human body, as the eye or the hand; and finally images from salvation history such as the crown of thorns. All of creation is formed of such images, and the task of the architect is to replicate this creation: the architect "constructs the world once again." What Schwarz's conception of imagery leads to, then, is an understanding of any church as a building with deep resonance, alluding to multiple dimensions of experience, and to a conception of the architect's creative activity—and presumably any other creative undertaking—as a mimesis of divine creation. The multivalence of a church building replicates that of the world of creation from which the architect draws inspiration.[44]

But along with the withdrawal from systematization, this renewed flexibility in the later work brings a further shift in Schwarz's focus. While the primary symbolic forms in the earlier work are configurations of people assembled in particular patterns, in the later work it is the buildings themselves that become the primary bearers of symbolic weight. The focus shifts to the building, not the people, as the gorge, or the mystical rose, or the outstretched arms of Christ. And the symbols in the later work are more objectifying, in a way that would seem inappropriate if they were symbols for the congregation: they do not illuminate the active role of the assembly, but they do give further depth and richness of meaning to the objective environment surrounding the assembly in worship.

Frédéric Debuyst, who had no patience for the lyrical and symbolist dimensions of Schwarz's work, looked askance at the more obviously symbolic elements such as the "mystical rose" design for Maria Königin at Saarbrücken, and preferred a simpler design such as Schwarz's late commission at Sankt Christophorus—evidently not recognizing that for Schwarz even this simple rectangular structure could bear symbolic meaning. Indeed, one key to understanding Schwarz's work both as architect and as theorist is that he combined minimalism of form with plenitude of meaning. Anyone seeking symbolic resonance in Schwarz's churches, and expecting to find it in the manner of an Eastern Orthodox or a Baroque church replete with symbolic imagery, would be disappointed by the minimalism of both structural form and ornamentation, even in the later churches where this minimalism is tempered. Schwarz's designs are implicitly rather than overtly associative. But perhaps the most crucial point in Schwarz's writings is that even a visually minimalist church can be vested with a richness of symbolic associations if every detail not only of its decoration but of its structure, and even the configuration of people assembled within it, is taken into account. Even the simplest of geometrical forms could to his mind and to his eye be charged with a range of symbolism. We are now aware, he said, how deeply creation is infused with geometric structures: how the form of a spiral, for example, grows in every tree. Even simple geometrical forms, then, can serve as signs of the Creator who implants these forms, although they are not the only possible signs for God, and in themselves they are not divine.[45]

Some of the symbolic meanings Schwarz assigned to church design were particular to specific churches, but not all. Underlying any church, for Schwarz, was a fundamental Trinitarian structure. The architect devises a landscape of worship consisting of three regions: first the world of pure creatureliness, open toward God; second the threshold, where Christ dwells as mediator; third the region of Openness itself, or Heaven. The first is the space of the Spirit, the comforter; the second that of Christ, the mediator (who as such dwelt with humankind in history); the third that of the Father—but also, perhaps unexpectedly, of Christ seen as sent forth from eternity. Schwarz mentions that it was fashionable to speak of churches as Christocentric because in them the congregation is gathered around Christ's altar, but he insists that properly speaking a church is, rather, Trinitarian. The ordering of space is an ordering of people toward the triune God. The architect's task is to lay the threshold that separates the people standing on one side from the inaccessible region of God on the other, but at the same time this threshold opens each side to the other, as the people enter upon the threshold and God responds from the other side. The church as a threshold marks "the edge of earthly things, the shoreline of eternity," beyond which every assertion contains its own denial, and what the architect undertakes must acknowledge its own limitation. Beyond and behind the altar, then, what Schwarz preferred was a bare wall.

Throughout his work, the symbolist vocabulary that goes most directly to the core of his perceptions is that which touches on his contemplative understanding of sacred space. In *Vom Bau der Kirche*, the images underlying the seven plans may not seem contemplative at first but lend themselves to contemplative interpretation, as when the open ring becomes a ring of worshipers standing in the divine presence. In *Kirchenbau*, the symbolist vocabulary may serve a meditative function, inviting meditation on the church building itself as a symbol for multiple realities in various worlds of experience. But the notion of the church as providing a threshold at which the assembly stands facing eternity is perhaps the most fully and explicitly contemplative of all Schwarz's images; its entire point is that a church is a place for contemplative awareness of the uncontainable divine presence not within but from the vantage point of a sacred enclosure.

It might seem odd to think of symbols of any sort as contemplative; contemplation is traditionally seen as rising above the discursive vocabulary of images and symbols. But, as Evelyn Underhill remarks, "the cloud of unknowing," and indeed even the apophatic images "emptiness," "darkness," and "the nothing," however much they are meant to lead beyond the world of sensory experience, are drawn from that world.[46] Similarly, Schwarz intends to construct clearly material structures as links between the created world and eternity.

Theoretical Themes: "Ringkirche" and "Wegkirche"

From another perspective, the key to understanding the link between Schwarz's theory and his practice is the relationship between the *Ringkirche* ("ring-church") and the *Wegkirche* ("way-church"), which is to say the relationship between two ways the assembly can be configured, in a ring turned inward or as a collectivity moving forward. The first plan is most obviously that of a ring, but in Schwarz's usage the term *Ringkirche* sometimes becomes shorthand for the second plan, the open ring. The Wegkirche is most straightforwardly represented by the fourth plan, the sacred journey, which gathers the people together in rank order as if they were marching forward with the priest in the lead.

> In this marching army the men stand shoulder to shoulder, each
> man a link in a chain, each chain a rank. The next ranks stand a
> step ahead and a step behind, and many weave together into the or-
> der of the marching column. At the very front stands the leader. He,
> too, is facing in the same direction, and like all the others, he, too, is
> a man on the way.[47]

While the second plan is meant for the ordinary situation of the worshiping community, this fourth one is of the greatest significance not only for its historical prominence but for its prevalence in the traditional architecture Schwarz's readers would have known, and, most important, it is important as a counterfoil to the "open ring." It is hardly surprising, then, that Schwarz devoted more sustained attention to it than to any other plan.

Schwarz's account of the sacred journey is forbidding:

> Here no eye looks into another, here no man looks to his fellow—all
> look ahead. The warm exchange from hand to hand, the surrender
> from human being to human being, the circuit of heart-felt com-
> munion—all are lacking. Here, each human being stands alone
> within the network of the whole. . . . The bond which binds each one
> to the others is cool and precisely measured—actually it is only a
> bond of the pattern and not a bond of the heart . . . The people can-
> not feel heartfelt warmth for one another since this pattern has no
> heart at all.[48]

The people on this journey have "a hard lot," homeless fugitives on the earth, and the plan of their church has no charm, its special virtue being "rigorous austerity."[49] They have no altar, no sacred spot where God enters the world and their journey ends; God is remote, going ahead of them as they process toward him.[50] Each step, it seems, must reach him, "yet he too advances one step further."[51] Their being and their power are "consumed in sacred journey," yet they cannot arrive at God's dwelling, "for the horizon flees ever before them."[52]

The biblical image behind this theme is clearly that of the Israelites wandering in the desert. And yet from another perspective a promised land is held out, the altar is found as a place of final sacrifice, and the distant light that the people's eyes cling to is itself "a form of communion" that "binds the human beings together." The ring-form had turned out to be more foreboding than it seemed at first, because the eyes of each person were blocked to those standing behind in the next ring out, and the ultimate bond among individuals was their common link to the center. So too, the way-form proves "richer in love than we at first suppose."[53]

Schwarz realizes (perhaps far better than most writers on the theory of church architecture) that the longitudinal church was meant for processional movement. "In earlier times the liturgy was richer in movement, but much of this has since died out." The one remaining movement is the communion procession, with its pattern of "way forward, union and way back." Characteristically, Schwarz places special emphasis on the moment of union. As for the return, he acknowledges that this is properly understood as a sending back out into the world, "to our work"—but again the meditation becomes dark, as he suggests that a "profounder and more valid" meaning is that of proceeding toward the portal, and thus toward the final judgment which the portal represents, with the eucharistic supper as food for the journey.[54]

Elsewhere in the chapter Schwarz speaks with remarkably deep respect for the medieval and Eastern forms of processional church, in which "a small consecrated group" go off to a separated space (the chancel or sanctuary), sent there as representatives from the people, "that there, like a lowest order of angels, they may celebrate a heavenly liturgy." They are at first remote, but later the people are permitted to draw near to their area. "All this provides a completely correct and wonderfully beautiful representation of the Christian way-form," although its use of a representative group may risk polarization and cleavage, and it is a difficult form of church to design.[55] But lest we mistake this for an enthusiastic endorsement, it must be noted that Schwarz commends such churches specifically as fine manifestations of a plan that is the most austere and forbidding of all the seven.

All seven plans, ultimately, can be seen as versions of the ring, the sacred journey, or some interplay of the two. Four of the plans—sacred inwardness (plan 1), the open ring (plan 2), the chalice of light (plan 3), and the dome of light (plan 6)—can be taken as variations on the theme of the Ringkirche. The dark chalice (plan 5) and the cathedral of all times (plan 7) can be seen as compromises, composites, or syntheses of the Ringkirche and the Wegkirche. Thus, the dark chalice, with a parabola for its plan, combines the clear sense of direction of the Wegkirche with the gathering of the assembly around a focal point characteristic of the Ringkirche, and the cathedral of all times in its complexity links two rings with a mediating processional way.

The interplay of the forms extends even to a hint of processional movement within the "open ring": the priest proceeds to the altar from one particular direction, stands on one particular side, and looks across the altar, and his movement is part of a longer path, that of his own life story, with an origin and destiny, and because this path leads from God and to God it is a "sacred way."[56] Here as elsewhere, then, Schwarz begins with bold claims and ends with nuance.

In his designs for actual construction, Schwarz can be seen as constantly negotiating the relationship between the Ringkirche and the Wegkirche. His chapel at Burg Rothenfels and some of his churches of the 1950s were designed to allow seating on three sides of the altar, in a variation on the open ring. Heilig Kreuz at Bottrop, with its parabolic plan, combines the directionality of the Wegkirche and the gathering around a common focus of the Ringkirche, in the manner of the dark chalice. But, as I will show, Schwarz designed other churches—in particular the Fronleichnamskirche at Aachen and Sankt Michael at Frankfurt—that in interesting ways test and extend his thinking about Ringkirche and Wegkirche.

From the Radical Modernism of the 1920s to the Modern Mainstream of the 1950s

That Schwarz's career began in the 1920s and flourished in the 1950s makes him a useful reference point for a transition within architectural modernism and in modernism generally. The contrast between these periods is worth noting. In the early years of the twentieth century, from World War I into the early 1930s, various phases of modernist aesthetic had a radical edge and a power to galvanize both supporters and opponents. T. S. Eliot's *Love Song of J. Alfred Prufrock* (1917) and *The Waste Land* (1922) marked him as the *enfant terrible* of modernist poetry.[57] Dada had emerged as a movement of cultural protest during World War I and retained its vitality into the early 1920s, while Surrealism in literature and painting arose to public acclaim and notoriety precisely in the twenties. It was an age of artistic creeds and manifestos, most notably André Breton's *Manifeste du Surréalisme* (1924). Modernism often had the power to evoke strong reaction, not simply because artists meant to shock but because their convictions placed them at odds with a still well-established traditionalist mainstream, and in architecture the stakes were especially high because buildings require funding well beyond the artist's own resources, because they are inescapably public, and because they remain on display and in use well beyond the moment of their production. The rise of "Establishment Gothic" around the 1920s represented more than simply a reaction against early modernist architecture, but along with all else it was also that.

By the period of reconstruction after World War II, the cultural landscape was transformed. Modern artists no longer needed to define and assert themselves with their earlier insistence, having become widely enough established to have achieved a measure of familiarity, even at times domestication. T. S. Eliot, no longer an *enfant terrible*, had become a dominant figure in a new cultural establishment, and if some forms of modernism were suspect because they had been exploited by the Nazis, others could take pride in having been disdained under the Third Reich for their supposed degeneracy. Modernism had entered the mainstream. To the extent that it lost the vigor of its convictions and its ideological grounding, modernist architecture became simply modern architecture. The danger now was not so much that of shocking the public and being ostracized but rather of succumbing on the one hand to formulaic patterns or on the other to mere idiosyncrasy in the name of innovation.

In church architecture, the clearest manifestations of early modernism are in France and especially Germany, where churches built in the 1920s—or more precisely between 1922 and 1932—demonstrated the potential of modernist architecture for ecclesiastical design.[58] The best known of these churches are marked by boldness of conception, by vigorous use of sharply defined forms, and by a strong commitment to an aesthetic that is strikingly different from that of traditional churches. Auguste Perret's Notre Dame du Raincy (1922–25), in the northeast suburbs of Paris, was innovative most obviously in exploiting the potential of reinforced concrete for church design, but this technical innovation made it possible for Perret to cultivate an aesthetic vision with only approximate parallels in earlier church building.[59] The dominant impression is one of openness. The columns placed between the nave and the aisles are reduced to slender shafts that barely impinge on the sight lines and afford a sense of uninterrupted length and breadth. While the floor of the nave follows the inclination of the site, sloping downward from west to east, and the sanctuary is built up to what appears a dramatic height, there is no architectural articulation of the sanctuary as a distinct space. The walls are reduced to a honeycomb of concrete matrices for colored glass. The effect has sometimes been compared to that of a Gothic church, and the building at Le Raincy does have something of the character of those "glass houses" built at Aachen and Cologne, or Sainte-Chapelle in Paris. But in all these cases the glass has a density of color that emphasizes the role of the windows as boundaries for defining space and containing the objects within. At Le Raincy, the glass has that kind of density only at the far east end, while toward the west it is more muted, lighter, and more suggestive of permeability through the concrete honeycomb. The openness within the interior is thus complemented by a suggestion of openness to the surrounding environment.

Equally striking but following an entirely different aesthetic is Dominikus Böhm's Sankt Engelbert (1931–32) in Riehl, on the north side of Cologne, a classic Expressionist building with boldly defined forms and dramatic interplay of light and shadow. In plan it is round, with the sanctuary and altar on one side. Around the edges are eight concrete ribs that rise to the top, forming parabolic arches and making up a kind of vaulted dome. The sanctuary is bathed in light from an adjacent window, and the contrast with the dark rotunda makes clear that the altar is meant as the visual focus of the building. Dramatic form and variably dramatic lighting combine to create a cavernous interior of dramatically mysterious intensity.[60]

The architectural minimalism of these years served to endow furnishings and vessels with a greater prominence. One priest who had frequent experience of these churches reported that they allowed the meaning of the liturgy to emerge more effectively than in any other setting but the catacombs:

> On the whole this architecture shows a strong and manly tendency toward sobriety and honesty. The "sacred things," the altar, the candles, the crucifix, the light, the steps, the walls, the ground—in short, the *Urdinge*, the first, the original things, stand before us and delight us as if we had discovered them again. . . . These white walls, the local stone or brick floors, these plain altar blocks, these plain *things* serving the holy mysteries, are liturgical in a unique sense. The "emptiness" . . . conveys to us a feeling of true grandeur, although the material of the church building and its sacred furniture is very plain and strictly local. . . . The emptiness and sobriety emphasize God's wealth and majesty in an overwhelming and impressive way.[61]

Later critics would point out, correctly enough, that these churches of the 1920s are more traditional in their liturgical than in their aesthetic design, all having either a longitudinal plan or a clear distinction between nave and sanctuary, if not both. One might see these experiments as a necessary stage in the evolution of modern church design, pointing sometimes more clearly and sometimes less so toward the bolder liturgical innovations of the future, prophetic even in raising the relationship between sanctuary and nave as a matter for reconsideration. Or one could argue that the aesthetic transformation of church design is never merely that, because it inevitably affects the way the church as a whole and thus the liturgy within it is experienced—that the openness of the church at Le Raincy gives a sense of solidarity between priest and congregation even when mass is celebrated at the altar in a dramatically elevated sanctuary, or that the use of architectural form and lighting at Riehl binds the congregation with the clergy more closely than a more conventional interior.

In varying degree, the modernist initiative in ecclesiastical architecture was sustained into the 1930s, as in the English churches of N. F. Cachemaille-Day.[62] But the economic depression brought a temporary lull in church-building in some countries, or at least a lessening of its pace. Among the exceptional cases of noteworthy modernist church-building in North America during the depression were Madonna della Strada in Chicago and Saint Mark's Episcopal in St. Louis, the latter noteworthy in part for its windows depicting striking workers and other motifs of contemporary relevance.[63] In Germany the effects were uneven: Bavaria generally and Munich in particular did have significant church-building under the Nazis, but there was less in Cologne.[64] In any case, what was built was no longer in the radical avant-garde mode of the twenties. If the 1930s represented on the whole a slow decade for church-building, even less ecclesiastical construction was carried out during World War II.

In the postwar architectural boom, innovation was more widely accepted than in the 1920s, and before long it was the expectation. Church design more often broke away from traditional ideas about the basic form of a church, sometimes embracing circular, parabolic, or irregular forms.[65] Frequently, however, it was not community churches with lay congregations but special institutions that took the lead, as they had earlier amid the youth group gathered at Burg Rothenfels. Some of the most innovative designs were done for communities of religious orders that had little if any need to justify themselves in the eyes of lay congregations or to be apprehensive about their openness to innovation: among the most famous cases are Notre Dame de Toute Grâce at Assy, the Chapelle du Rosaire at Vence, the Benedictine monastery at Las Condes in Chile, and the Abbey Church of Saint John the Baptist in Collegeville.[66] (Particularly the first two of these serve also as showcases for religious arts other than architecture.) Widely noted minimalist designs were made for university chapels, notably at the Massachusetts Institute of Technology, at the Illinois Institute of Technology, and at Otaniemi in Finland. Notre Dame du Haut at Ronchamp was rebuilt as a pilgrimage chapel with a single primary patron who was willing to endorse the architect's intensely personal conception of sacred space. Many other churches, sometimes equally innovative, were done for congregations that for one reason or other were eager to embrace modern design: Christ Church Lutheran in Minneapolis, Sankt Albert at Saarbrücken, the parish church at Salzburg-Parsch, Sankt Maria in den Benden at Düsseldorf-Wersten, and Annunciation Greek Orthodox Church at Wauwatosa, Wisconsin. But winning the approval of ecclesiastical authorities and a broader public could still be a perilous undertaking in midcentury, as Oscar Niemeyer and his patrons at Pampulha in Brazil discovered in 1943, when the bishop refused to consecrate the modern structure, one mayor proposed its demolition, and in the end the building went under the protection of the National Department of Historical and Artistic Patrimony without ever being used as a church.[67]

Far more than in earlier decades, architectural tendencies had become international.[68] In the United States, for example, the most widely noted modern churches of the 1950s were designed by architects born and for the most part trained in Europe: Eliel and Eero Saarinen, Ludwig Mies van der Rohe, Marcel Breuer. Francis Barry Byrne, who had worked in Frank Lloyd Wright's studio early in the twentieth century and designed Saint Thomas the Apostle in Chicago during the 1920s, and who built his famous fish-shaped churches in Kansas City and Saint Paul in the late 1940s, maintained a lively interest in Continental church architecture.[69] Other American architects as well drew on European inspiration, and at Resurrection Church in St. Louis the parabolic design suggested by Schwarz in the late 1930s was implemented before Schwarz himself actually built such a church.[70] The most distinctly American designer was Frank Lloyd Wright, who had designed Unity Temple in Oak Park in the early years of the century. He was hardly a specialist in ecclesiastical architecture, but he did return to this field in the 1950s with the First Unitarian Society Meeting House at Madison and Annunciation Greek Orthodox Church at Wauwatosa in Wisconsin.[71]

If any one church is generally recognized as a model of mid-twentieth-century ecclesiastical innovation, it is surely Le Corbusier's Notre Dame du Haut at Ronchamp (1955). The design drew attention largely because of its unconventionality, which some took as inspiring and others saw as idiosyncratic or grotesque. (Rudolf Schwarz referred to it as "trash.")[72] The architect demonstrated here that neither roof nor walls nor even floor were bound to consistent rectilinear planes. The roof is sometimes compared to a nun's coif and sometimes to an airplane, although the architect claims it was inspired by a crab shell. Rather than resting directly on the walls, it sits on impost blocks that allow a slit of light along the top of the walls. The visitor proceeding around the exterior finds that the white walls do not turn corners but curve about from one side to another. They are punctuated with a silo-type tower. The south wall, which appears massively thick but is in fact a hollow shell, displays a series of irregularly distributed, deeply recessed windows. The viewer is meant to be drawn by the mystique of these openings and is expected to move from one to another, gazing at the colors, the drawings, or the inscriptions found on the glass.

One early commentator on Ronchamp, John Ely Burchard, judged its vaunted spontaneity both a strength and a weakness, finding it "confusing, too exciting, too theatrical," seeing it as filled with "too much personal caprice, interesting or not," and judging the architect too careless about details. Not without reason, Burchard takes issue with Ronchamp's "billing as the hall of light": praised for the mysterious subtlety of its light, the chapel in fact has lighting "neither so brilliant nor, paradoxically, so serene as the light of Le Raincy."[73] Frédéric Debuyst also gave Ronchamp a nuanced review.[74] He found it "amazingly clever and complex," "at once lyrical and controlled, primitive and sophisticated, defying any description," but he insisted it should have been left to stand alone, a *hapax legomenon*, unique of its kind, to be admired rather than imitated.[75] Instead, it had been harmful through its imitations, having inspired excesses of all sorts, in particular a showy monumentality. And indeed, one may well suppose that Ronchamp brings into convergence the Scylla of idiosyncrasy and the Charybdis of formulaic imitation that threatened church design in midcentury, precisely because some of its most distinctive features quickly became formulas. The proliferation of irregularly arranged windows on the south wall, for example, was soon imitated elsewhere—at times perhaps with improvement over Le Corbusier's original design, as in the new Sankt Alban im Stadtgarten at Cologne.[76]

But more than any particular motifs of design, it was the exuberant fondness for innovation in form detached from liturgical purpose that aroused the liturgists' critique during this period: George Pace sneered in 1962 at architects who "like to be given churches as it gives them opportunities to evolve strange shapes," and a later commentator noted that in the early 1950s lightweight building materials made it easier to bridge wide spans, which tempted architects "to treat a church simply as a sculptural space."[77]

There had been fewer examples of modern church-buildings in the 1920s, but those built were often fairly pure expressions of clearly defined concepts; there were numerous buildings in the 1950s, but more often they were products of a complex interaction of inspiration and expectation, including the expectation aroused by earlier inspiration. The bold, pure, radical, and profoundly impressive churches of the 1920s were succeeded in the 1950s by work that was often formulaic or idiosyncratic, because in architecture, as in other media, the high modernism cultivated after World War I was marked by a greater intensity of conviction and energy in execution than the later, more domesticated, and more commercialized modernism popular after World War II. Schwarz himself had some sense of this contrast. Looking back at the Fronleichnamskirche late in his life, he commented: "Thirty years ago, the ideas that inspired our construction plans were very simple," and "it seems to me that we understood the great ideas of church architecture in those days." At that time the bold ideas that inspired new church design were shared by a relatively narrow circle. Since then "much has happened since then to dilute and weaken [these] ideas and concepts."[78]

Schwarz's Churches Designed in the 1920s

Rudolf Schwarz's work of the 1920s and early 1930s is in this respect very much a product of its time: it shares with other churches of the time a clarity and vigor of conception, a boldness of design, a willingness to disregard the cultural mainstream and carry a principle to its extreme. The centerpiece of Schwarz's early work, and indeed one of the classic monuments of twentieth-century church architecture, is the Fronleichnamskirche at Aachen (1930), better known within the congregation as Sankt Fronleichnam.[79] He went on in subsequent years to design the Werktagskapelle Liebfrauen in Leipzig (1930) and the Albert-Kapelle in Leversbach (1932), but the church at Aachen in particular calls for attention. Schwarz himself singled this church out as uniquely uncompromising;[80] it surely was that. Frédéric Debuyst hailed it as "the first clearly and totally *modern* church." Peter F. Smith proclaimed that it "must rank as one of the most revolutionary churches of all time" and that "no building better expresses the modern revolution."[81] Fronleichnam stands alongside the churches of Le Raincy and Riehl as a classic instance of early modernist architecture, striking in its clear articulation of a sharply defined aesthetic. But while the dominant impression at Le Raincy is one of openness, and at Riehl one of cavernous enclosure, the aesthetic at Aachen is one of pure luminosity. If Notre Dame du Raincy impresses with its wash of color, and Sankt Engelbert with its atmospheric play of shadows, the Fronleichnamskirche is so uncompromising in its use of white for the walls and ceiling, black for the floor and furnishings, and the windows placed high on the walls provide such even lighting, that one is forcefully struck with a sense of all-encompassing brightness. A church made entirely of glass conveys a sense of openness to the world beyond itself rather than of pure light. It is Fronleichnam, rather, that gives a clear embodiment of luminosity. What people sometimes say of other churches is particularly appropriate to the Fronleichnamskirche: its effect cannot be captured in photographs, not for the usual reason, that photographs fail to convey a sense of the three-dimensional whole, but because the white of the paper is merely a blankness, an absence of ink, and can only faintly suggest a realm of luminosity.[82] The church is longitudinal in form, like the design for the Frauenfriedenskirche, but while that was at heart a study in darkness this is a study in light.[83]

The main block of the church—69 feet high, a 159 feet long, and 68 feet wide—is precisely that, a rectangular block, entirely white on the exterior as on the interior. A plain white shaft stands as a bell tower. Beside the main block, which encompasses nave and sanctuary, is a much lower aisle, in which the Marian altar and the stations of the cross (in the form of a long tapestry) are placed, reflecting Guardini's emphasis on the liturgy itself as public and devotion as distinct from liturgy. Just beneath the roof are windows with colorless glass; lower windows at the front of the church allow a greater flow of light onto the altar. The floor has veined black marble. The sanctuary floor is also of black marble, as is the high altar that stands monumentally against a towering white wall. The wooden benches are simple and dark. On either side of the interior, string lighting hangs from the ceiling. Schwarz noted that anything brought into this space has exceptional strength and density of presence: a small cross, less than a foot tall, suffices for a space over sixty feet high. At the same time he acknowledged that such a space has dangers, and that anything of inferior design can easily distort and undermine the effect of the room. Even the church's most devoted admirers are generally more cool toward the exterior than the interior. (When Alfred Döblin was taken to Fronleichnam, he emerged from the car, looked around, and asked: "So where is it?") Schwarz himself referred to the exterior as a "melody of rectangular bodies," but the stronger impact is made by the interior space.

The distinction between liturgical and devotional emphasis is signaled already by differing interpretations of the church's dedication. The priest who commissioned Schwarz saw the dedication as referring to eucharistic devotion, but Schwarz conceived it more in ecclesial terms: if the Church is the Body of Christ, then the church building should not only be called Fronleichnam (Corpus Christi, or Body of Christ) but *be* that for the assembly there gathered.

One of the church's harshest critics, Edward Maufe, decried it as "an extreme example of sans-serif architecture" and as "something of a functionalist's dream—a functionalist who has swung so far on the pendulum of revolt against over-statement that he denies us the graces of life, and becomes stingy and rather negative."[84] Maufe reacted against this sort of modernism because it seemed a glorification of the utilitarian, of the machine.[85] This notion was nearly as remote from Schwarz's intention as it could be; Schwarz had indeed written on the aesthetics of technology, but he expressed disdain for the notion of the church as "a machine for performing the liturgy."[86] Others made a similar observation in a more positive spirit, seeing the building as a kind of sacred factory, a consecration of the factory as a workplace of God, and Schwarz himself repudiated this perception too. First of all, he argued, there is nothing special about a factory building, which is a building like any other, and has occupied a position of special dignity only for incidental historical reasons, in particular when well-known architects such as Walter Gropius designed such works as the Fagus Factory (1910–11). There might be some appeal in the notion of a church as a workplace of God, declaring labor itself as holy. But while labor is after all honorable, it is not the same as prayer, and indeed on the Lord's Day labor ceases and a day of rest is celebrated. As Guardini had said, "the church has itself been set apart from the world of human work." The church is related to the factory, then, as a place where the labor of the factory is set aside.[87]

When Fronleichnam encountered criticism in its early years, Guardini published an article in its defense, emphasizing the sense of a "holy presence" that he found in this church.[88] To be sure, one might experience such a space as empty, as some had called it. But what people refer to as emptiness is in fact stillness, "And in the stillness is God. Out of the stillness of these broad walls an intimation of God's presence can blossom forth." Perhaps people have forgotten what silence is, Guardini continues, and no longer realize that silence belongs together with speech, as inhaling goes with exhaling. Devout silence is the deepest prayer; when silence is no more, the prayer of words is no longer possible. Yet people often perceive silence as a pause, and when a pause occurs in speech others will immediately fill it, perhaps with a cough, to close the gap. So too with the great stillness found in the Fronleichnamskirche, the broad surfaces unbroken by any articulation, images, or ornaments. The powerful impression of a holy presence is there all along, and when evening comes and the church grows dark, suddenly the lights will be turned on and the entire space will shimmer with light.

That Guardini needed to leap to his friend's defense in this way is one index to the controversial nature of the Fronleichnamskirche, but it tells only a small part of the controversy. That the church was ever built was something of an accident: the plans had been rejected more than once by the ecclesiastical authorities, until a moment came in the administrative history of the diocese when more sympathetic personnel could give the required authorization. The church very nearly suffered the same fate as the Frauenfriedenskirche that was never built at Frankfurt.

While the Fronleichnamskirche appears to be a Wegkirche, and some have so identified it, Schwarz maintained it was not. In his memoirs he insisted that this church had nothing in common with the processional space of an Egyptian temple, with its progression through gateway, through courtyard, through pillared hall, and on into the narrow cell deep in the interior; nor with the longitudinal monastic church, where a screen separates the consecrated community from the assembly of people in the nave; nor even with the interior of a cathedral, with its space for grand festal processions. None of this, Schwarz said, is to be found in the Fronleichnamskirche.

> Here there is nothing but the still presence [stille Gegenwart] of the congregation and of Christ. The goal is attained, and every way is brought to rest [gestillt] in pure presence, in a common, bright, high, and entirely simple space. The people and the Lord are to-gether, having become one body in a celebratory architectural form, in the higher body of their sacred presence.[89]

Which is to say that the distinction between Wegkirche and Ringkirche is here expressed only imperfectly in concrete architectural forms, and that even a form that might suggest processional dynamism may be understood not as an invitation to movement but rather as space for contemplative experience of the divine presence. The key term *Stille* and its cognates can refer to an absence of sound, a state of quietness, but also to a restraint from motion, a state of rest or repose, an Augustinian sense of the rest desired by the *cor inquietum*, and in either case to that state of contemplative consciousness so fundamental to Schwarz's conception of this or any other church.

Schwarz hardly meant to deny that the plan of the Fronleichnamskirche is longitudinal; it manifestly is so. Nor could he convincingly have denied the church's potential as processional space, since its longitudinal form and clear orientation toward the altar would fit it well for that purpose, whatever the architect's intent. Rather, the point is that even in a clearly longitudinal church the emphasis can be on the numinous presence perceived as filling the space, present simultaneously to the entire assembly and not simply the terminus of a liturgical process. This contemplative view of sacred space may seem rarefied, and one may well ask how far it corresponds to the experience of any worshiper or congregation, but that question can be posed with reference to any conception of liturgy and its environment.

Schwarz's Churches Designed in the 1950s

At the end of World War II, the widespread need to rebuild destroyed churches and to construct new ones made Germany again an important center in ecclesiastical architecture, as it had been in the 1920s. The archdiocese of Cologne, where the losses in the war had been severe, took a position of prominence in this rebuilding.[90] Approximately eight thousand churches needed to be built or restored in Germany between 1945 and 1960. In several dioceses a church was dedicated almost every Sunday. According to one survey there were 323 churches built in the archdiocese of Cologne by 1955, and 240 further ones planned. In the nearby diocese of Aachen, 29 percent of the Roman Catholic churches had been totally destroyed and a further 63 percent were damaged.[91] New churches were needed not only because thousands of old ones were destroyed or damaged but because millions of refugees were resettled in West Germany, and population shifted from inner cities to outlying areas.[92] Many other architects played a role in designing churches as well as secular buildings, but Schwarz was in some ways the most important church-builder of the era, much sought after as a designer of churches and widely recognized as an authority on church design. Over the course of his career he designed, reconstructed, or renovated fully thirty-nine churches.

Within the context of postwar Germany, when Schwarz was recognized as a leading architect and served as director of reconstruction in Cologne, his modernism was no longer avant-garde and no longer required the same sort of pleading.[93] On the whole, he steered a course between idiosyncrasy and formula. Only on occasion did his work manifest an element of idiosyncrasy, as at Sankt Joseph in Cologne-Braunsfeld (1954), where the windows are ranged as a series of hexagons that inspired wags to dub the church "Saint Zigzag."[94] He might be accused of having created a series of formulas for his own imitation, but both in his theory and in his execution there is enough subtlety, flexibility, and variety that on closer examination what appears formulaic often reveals elements of nuance and freshness. Still, none of his postwar churches have the bold and uncompromising character, the single-minded working out of principle, that mark the Fronleichnamskirche.

Three of Schwarz's postwar churches are cruciform, with curved rather than square terminations. All three are large, but only moderately so, seating some five hundred people. If they appear more monumental than their seating capacity would suggest, this is partly because they call attention to themselves with their bold and unaccustomed forms, partly because they rise abruptly to full height on all sides. More than Schwarz's other postwar churches, these convey the impression of a fortress or "mighty refuge" against the perils of the surrounding world, a theme sometimes taken as central to his work in the 1950s but manifested more in some buildings than in others. The effect is intensified in early photographs, in which the churches stand by themselves without the contextualization of later buildings or the softening of landscape.

Sankt Michael at Frankfurt am Main (1954),[95] the earliest and most famous of the three churches, is the one that Schwarz himself interpreted variously as an open ring, a gorge through which one passes, a star, and a castle. The concrete supports were built first, and when the walls were added the supports remained exposed, providing a rhythmic sequence of vertical shafts punctuating the flow of the darker brick walls on the exterior, the lighter surface on the interior. An even flow of natural light comes from a clerestory of glass blocks placed just below roof level. The main axis is approximately elliptical; conches on the sides form the arms of the cross. The altar is placed at the crossing. The congregation occupies the long end, one of the arms accommodates the choir, the other serves as a weekday mass chapel, and the third forms an apse reserved for the clergy. Schwarz was among thirty architects who entered the competition for design of this church; with it, the man who had been a radical innovator in the Weimar years clearly and effectively reasserted himself as a leading church designer in postwar Germany.

The fusing of Wegkirche and Ringkirche at Sankt Michael is particularly subtle. The main body of the church might seem at first a Wegkirche because of its elongation. Indeed, as one moves from the back to the front of Sankt Michael one can experience a clear dynamic pull toward the altar, reinforced by the curving transepts that open on either side of the altar. But the curvature of the nave walls, punctuated by the vertical concrete shafts, creates something like an optical illusion, so that even at the far end one can have a sense of being not in a longitudinal space but in the Ringkirche that Schwarz intended. When Dominikus Böhm designed Sankt Engelbert at Cologne-Riehl with a circular nave and a niche to the north for a sanctuary, he suggested that the circular plan would appear broader than it is deep and convey a sense of proximity to the altar;[96] a similar effect is achieved at Sankt Michael, giving an approximately elliptical form something of the feel of a ring. If one views Sankt Michael as a Ringkirche, the effect of the transepts is to support not so much a sense of linear direction but rather a sense of the building as a whole formed around the altar.

Sankt Andreas at Essen (1954–57),[97] and the better known Maria Königin, built on the slope of a hill overlooking Saarbrücken (1959) (fig. 25),[98] have essentially the same shape as Sankt Michael, but with one important difference: instead of providing natural light only through a high clerestory, Schwarz has windows extending nearly from floor to ceiling at each of the four corners of the crossing. At Maria Königin the windows are sweeping half-parabolas of colored glass. Whether these windows call attention more effectively to the altar or to themselves may be an open question. One commentator speaks of a "dazzling architectural spotlight at the crossing" in Maria Königin, while another refers to the space as a "mighty parable for the breaking in of the

FIGURE 25. Maria Königin, Saarbrücken, Germany interior. Early photograph, reproduced with permission of Maria Schwarz.

divine."[99] In any case, this church like others by Schwarz lends itself to more than one level of interpretation: it can be taken as a crown for Mary the Queen to whom the church is dedicated, or as a chalice or a mystical rose, as Schwarz himself suggested. It has perhaps the most interesting approach of all Schwarz's churches. Normally one would come toward it from below, but one can ascend further up the hill on which it is built and see it from a vantage point overlooking the city and across the valley into France. On entering the church one first passes a stairway leading down to the crypt, then a small chapel or "upper crypt"; then a broader stairway to the right leads to the baptismal font and then turns back and divides, leading on either side into the church proper. In short, the building takes ample advantage of its hillside site for a complex and symbolically charged passage through lower and subsidiary spaces and into the common liturgical space above. It has been said that if this church were in France rather than across the river in Saarbrücken it would be visited by throngs of Germans.[100]

Heilig Kreuz at Bottrop (1957) is again one of Schwarz's better known churches.[101] Apart from a side chapel and a detached but prominent tower, it is utterly simple, parabolic in plan, with the altar near the apex, and exposed brick on both exterior and interior. The open end of the parabola forms a single massive window, with glass by Georg Meistermann in a swirling design entitled "Infinity"; the back-lighting that floods in through this window is balanced by a clerestory over the altar, with the "Eye of God" depicted in a manner that has been called "painfully realistic."[102] While the overall form is thus far simpler than at Sankt Michael, Maria Königin, and Sankt Andreas, and the lighting is based on entirely different principles, the curvilinear walls rise similarly to an imposing height, and the single exterior apex at Bottrop is closely reminiscent of the corresponding projections in these three other churches. What most clearly distinguishes Heiliz Kreuz is that it was the only one of Schwarz's churches directly derived from the fifth plan of Von Bau der Kirche, the initially cheering but then foreboding "dark chalice." Schwarz was himself reluctant to use the parabolic form, having discussed it more as a theoretical than as a practical option, but the pastor at Bottrop, having read Schwarz's book and seen the diagrams in it, insisted on this plan, and its more disturbing implications were played down.[103]

These churches, reflecting the lyricism of Vom Bau der Kirche in their curvilinear shapes and richness of symbolism, might seem to represent an altogether new phase in Schwarz's career, distinct from the prewar designs with their severe rectilinearity. But other postwar churches, on the whole less well known and less widely celebrated, seem more clearly grounded in prewar precedent, with clearer allusions to the Fronleichnamskirche and Schwarz's other earlier designs. Heilige Familie in Oberhausen (1955–58) is a simple rectangular space with seating on three sides of a broad altar platform toward the east and a weekday mass chapel to the west.[104] Sankt Christophorus in Cologne-Niehl is also a plain rectangle, with the altar platform toward the west.[105] (This church was singled out for special praise by Frédéric Debuyst and Edward Sövik for its "air of simplicity, of economy, tranquil harmony and plain, radiant humanity" and its "humble earthiness" and clarity.)[106] Elsewhere, as at Sankt Mechtern in Cologne-Ehrenfeld, Schwarz adds a low side aisle to a high rectilinear nave, as he had done in the Fronleichnamskirche.[107]

In a category largely by itself is Sankt Anna at Düren (1956).[108] Elsewhere Schwarz handled renovation of a church badly damaged in the war, but this church at Düren, both a parish church and the center of a pilgrimage to Saint Anna, was completely demolished, along with most of this small town. The new church was made of tawny stone recovered from the rubble of the Gothic revival church that had been destroyed. Schwarz made use of differential height here perhaps more effectively than anywhere else except at Aachen: the main entrance is through a broad, low, and relatively dark narthex along the south side of the nave, which has the stations of the cross on its walls and a shrine of Saint Anna at its eastern (and broader) end. After passing through this narthex, one emerges into the far higher nave, which is illuminated by a window that stretches all along its south wall, above the narthex. The transition from the darkened enclosure of the narthex to the bright and open space of the nave is more dramatic than at Aachen, in part because the narthex is wider and the contrast between the two units is more pronounced. But the most noteworthy feature of this church is its integration of a larger nave with a smaller one that serves as a weekday chapel, converging in an L-shape on a single altar.[109] Each nave is visible from the other through the narthex-corridor, and the entire church thus has unity of form without confusion of its parts. The altar is designed as a square, the same in form whether viewed from the main nave or from the chapel.

The postwar designs, then, are less bold and uncompromising than the work of the 1920s, less severe, less insistently rectilinear and monochrome. Among the elements of continuity, these later churches are still clearly grounded in geometrical forms, and like the earlier work they make creative use of natural light, often through windows placed high on the walls but brought lower beside the sanctuary. If Schwarz's churches attain a high degree of dramatic power, it is neither by use of lighting alone nor by handling of space, but through the combination: by the creative and evocative interaction of light in space. They often juxtapose high central space with low aisles, and devotional foci such as stations of the cross are placed in the latter; at Düren, the shrine of Saint Anna is at the end of the long and low narthex. And in his later work, as at Fronleichnam, Schwarz typically added free-standing towers that lent a touch of asymmetry to the exterior.

Perhaps the clearest difference in the postwar buildings is Schwarz's willingness to add color and figurative art. Commenting on Sankt Michael in Frankfurt, Schwarz noted that it already contained certain representative art—a mosaic of Saint Michael, another of the Resurrection, a band of glass in the crypt by Georg Meistermann depicting the theme of creation in abstract shapes—and he trusted that gifted artists would provide more such images for the church, which he said was never intended (like Fronleichnam) to be devoid of them. At Sankt Anna in Düren there was even a stylized Tree of Life built into the masonry behind the altar and visible on both interior and exterior. All such images, Schwarz said, are well and good, even if they are not necessary for the building or for the liturgy, but brought forth out of "a holy excess." They should not be inserted into a church at random but should be organized in accordance with the structure of the building: themes of separation should be used at the portal, where earlier artists depicted the Judgment, or perhaps Mary the Gate of Heaven; stations within the church might be appropriate for depiction of saints. But in any case the all-holy space behind the altar is fit only for "the stillness of eternity, the pure being of the holy" and should thus be free of such images.

The Later Reordering of Schwarz's Churches

Although Schwarz was in close contact with the liturgical reforms inaugurated in the early twentieth century and resumed after the war, he died in 1961, just before the Second Vatican Council (1962–65). In later decades many of the liturgical changes undertaken before and after the Council have been ascribed to the Council itself, whose main contribution was to ratify and make official what had previously been more tentative or provisional. It was in the years after the council, under Pope Paul VI, that the mass was translated into the various vernacular languages and a new missal and liturgical calendar were produced. Among the other reforms instituted after the council was the reordering of the sanctuary, with relatively simple and low free-standing altars brought nearer to the congregation, for celebration of the mass *versus populum*, or facing the people. Churches with larger high altars against the far end of the church now had free-standing altars added, closer to the congregation, and new churches were built with free-standing altars. At the same time, three other major changes in liturgical furnishing were introduced: ambos were designed as places for scriptural reading in the vernacular, the tabernacle for the reserved sacrament was displaced from the high altar to a position either on the side of the sanctuary or in a separate chapel, and the communion rail was done away with. All these reforms were introduced first in the interest of engaging the congregation in fuller participation, and second to distinguish more clearly between liturgy and devotion, including paraliturgical devotion to the reserved sacrament. In other words, the fundamental principles were those that Guardini and Schwarz had advocated in the early decades of the century, even if implementation of those principles had now been reconceived. But Schwarz's own churches, and other modern churches from before the 1960s, were subjected to much of the same reordering that was done in older, revival-style churches that predated even the early stages of liturgical renewal. While Schwarz could see his earlier judgments mostly confirmed by liturgical renewal after the war—as expressed, for example, in a diocesan synod at Cologne in 1954—new developments in liturgical thinking called into question features of his early churches such as the elevated altar platforms.[110]

The churches Schwarz had designed in the 1950s did not have the status of architectural classics whose original integrity needed to be preserved. Sankt Mechtern at Cologne-Ehrenfeld (1954) was reordered in 1966; the altar platform had originally been elevated far higher than the level of congregational seating, and its height was now much reduced, while a new altar and ambo were provided.[111] At Sankt Joseph in Cologne-Braunsfeld (1954), the tabernacle stood originally on the altar designed by Schwarz but was transferred in 1968 to a stele or pillar designed by Heribert Calleen, who also designed a new ambo and altar cross.[112] Schwarz's wife, the architect Maria Schwarz, was often consulted in the reordering in a gesture of fidelity to her husband's intent, but the prevailing voices were not always in consonance with the architect's original vision.

A great deal more controversial was the reordering of the Fronleichnamskirche. Even during the architect's life there were relatively minor changes, but he noted in his memoirs that when restoration was needed the pastor, the bishop, and the preservationists had been unanimously in favor of preserving it as a monument in its original form. Already in 1966, five years after Schwarz's death, a new ordering of the church was tentatively proposed, and in 1975 and 1980 the sanctuary was adapted to new liturgical standards. The marble platform in front of the altar was extended to allow for the furnishings now required, and in front of the black marble high altar a much smaller altar was placed on a lower level. The tabernacle remained on the high altar, which thus became a platform for sacramental reservation, while celebration of the mass was moved forward to the new free-standing altar, as had already been done in countless other Roman Catholic churches. In this case the reordering aroused an outcry from those who viewed the church as a monument of early modernist architecture and who resented the alterations introduced by the parish and the diocese. One architectural group insisted (in vigorous italic type) that this church did not belong to its congregation alone, or to Aachen alone, but was a monument of modern church architecture and required preservation as such.[113] In any case, the design of the new altar was sufficiently different from that of the original furnishings to make clear that it was not part of Schwarz's design, and those responsible for the new arrangement took pains to represent it as provisional, as a solution adequate for their time, not necessarily for all time.[114]

It is no doubt futile to speculate how far Schwarz would have modified his views if he had lived into the later 1960s. The conception of the sanctuary underlying his own designs represents anything but an unconsidered traditionalism, or indeed even vestigial traditionalism, and one cannot say that in the 1950s he was simply adhering to an unreconstructed reformist vision of his own earlier years. He continued to think, often in new ways, about the meaning and purpose of liturgical design. But between his interiors and those of the later 1960s there are important differences. The removal of the communion rail, the addition of an ambo, and even the displacement of the tabernacle might have seemed the least problematic of the novelties. More clearly central to his vision was the conception of a church as an open ring that is not closed by the altar or by the priest but rather remains open to the eternal and transcendent, and the reordering of churches with the priest facing the congregation across a low free-standing altar would have been problematic because it brought closure in the form of a turning inward rather than outward by the liturgical community.[115]

And yet, while it is sometimes pointed out that in his later years Schwarz was not enthusiastic about celebration *versus populum*,[116] and in his discussion of the "open ring" he represents the priest as standing *with* the people and facing outward to the opening, at a later point in *Vom Bau der Kirche* he had assumed that the priest is indeed across the altar from the people. Even so, he does not take the priest to be speaking *to* the people, apart from relatively brief moments of dialogue. For the most part the priest speaks, rather, to God. And if in doing so the priest stands on the other side of the altar from the people, the point is to speak the words of prayer "into it [the altar] as if into a center which opens into the infinite."[117] Which is to say that Schwarz was not opposed to this arrangement of a church, even though his conception of it differed from that of most of its later advocates and arose once again from a profoundly contemplative understanding of liturgy and liturgical space, and even the social dimension of worship was for him a function of a contemplative sense of priest and people standing together in the presence of God.

For my purposes, Schwarz's place in the evolving process of liturgical reform is important mainly as one part of a broader discussion about the various factors in church design. His was one of the formative voices in discussion of the spatial dynamics of a church. Unlike most writers who have addressed the issue, he knew well the range of processional capacities found in longitudinal space; his contemplative view of liturgy led him to set this option aside, even when his spaces were in fact longitudinal. On the question of centering focus he sided with the early generation of liturgical reformers: the altar was paramount, and giving the altar prominence and clarity was the prime concern, not bringing it down into proximity with the congregation. The aesthetic he cultivated was meant to convey a sense of divine presence through effective diffusion of light within dramatically conceived space. And if the symbolic message of his work was rarely explicit in the design and decoration, both the shape of the building and his multifaceted reflection on its meaning gave a depth of symbolic resonance that was exceptional in twentieth-century church design.

Schwarz's buildings, like much of the writing of Romano Guardini, are marked by a strong simplicity—but (to adapt the language of Paul Ricoeur) it is a *second* simplicity, that of a person grounded in the richness of tradition and seeking to bring its main symbols and insights into clear focus, not the first simplicity of a person coming to the tradition as a beginner.[118] What happens, then, if the next generation has never known the richness from which simplicity is distilled? The challenge for those who cherish the second simplicity is to raise a new generation with more than an attenuated tradition, with more than only the first simplicity. Fidelity to the principles of Schwarz, Guardini, and other early reformers means not only accepting their way of appropriating tradition but being grounded with them in the tradition they appropriated.

8

Issues in Church Architecture

In the decades after World War II a shift in thinking about churches emerged that some might call a revolution. Already in the late 1940s a document on church architecture endorsed by the Roman Catholic hierarchy of Germany was an early harbinger of this shift, and in America it was soon echoed in an influential statement from the diocese of Superior, Wisconsin.[1] In England issues were brought into sharp focus by the writings of Peter Hammond and his collaborators, who called for fundamental reconception of church design in and beyond the Anglican Communion.[2] Revisionist thinking about liturgical architecture went hand in hand with new currents of thought regarding liturgy itself, and this conjunction was clear even in the title of Theodor Filthaut's book *Church Architecture and Liturgical Reform* (1965).[3] Fundamental to thinking about both liturgy and its environment was an enthusiasm for bringing congregations into fuller participation, but the reformers went further, condemning traditional church architecture as extravagant, anachronistic, isolationist, inappropriately ornamental, and monumental. The Second Vatican Council and its supporting statements did not have a great deal to say about church architecture, and what it did have to say was on the whole moderate and not highly specific.[4] Still, conciliar statements about liturgy entered into and reinforced a movement in thinking about church design that was already well underway. The practical result of the rethinking in these decades was the emergence and development of what I am calling the modern communal church. And while formulations have changed since the 1960s, the basic agenda for discussion has remained largely the same.

Beginning in the late twentieth century, however, there has been a vigorous reaction against the reformers' conceptions of church architecture. Steven J. Schloeder's *Architecture in Communion* begins by noting the "banality" and lack of inspiration that Schloeder finds in recent Roman Catholic churches. He touches on more fundamental theological issues with the argument that churches exist not primarily for gathering of the people but for worship of God.[5] Duncan Stroik, on the architecture faculty at the University of Notre Dame, publishes the journal *Sacred Architecture* as a forum for architects and liturgists who lament what they regard as widespread banality and defection from specifically Roman Catholic norms in church architecture. In the Roman Catholic tradition, recent trends in church design are said to be mandated by documents of the Second Vatican Council; the traditionalists insist that these documents have been misread and that the changes in church architecture in fact run counter to the Council's teaching. In making this argument Schloeder and Stroik are joined by others, such as Michael Davies and Michael S. Rose.[6]

Rose's most recent book, *Ugly as Sin*, is one of the more aggressive salvos in this campaign.[7] For him, the difficulty with the emphasis on congregational participation is that it goes hand in hand with the banality and iconoclasm of the reformers' churches by leading to the removal of art and furnishings that are deemed distracting. Beautiful churches have been destroyed, and uninspiring ones built, in the name of congregational participation. For the same purpose, altars have been moved forward and sanctuaries thus disfigured, statues and communion rails have been removed, and murals and mosaics covered over as distractions from active participation.[8] He links his aesthetic critique of modern churches to a theological perception: the word "ugly" refers here "not just to that which is aesthetically offensive, but also to that which is theologically inappropriate." Modern churches lead worshipers "away from the goodness, beauty, and truth of the Faith to a false notion of God and of themselves in the face of God," and thus they are literally "ugly as sin."[9] The traditionalist movement is not limited to the United States; in 1999 an International Exhibit on Liturgical Architecture was held at Rome that produced a volume of essays and photographs meant to demonstrate the possibilities for renewal of traditional forms in church architecture.[10]

On both sides of the debate, dogmatism is routine. Indeed, people who might think it distasteful to stake out dogmatic positions on other matters (the Trinity, say, or the divinity of Christ) often know just where they must stand on matters of church design. Preferences are justified by polemic against alternatives. Members of a congregation are educated, which is to say they are told which tradition of church-building is right-minded and which is wrong-minded; those who resist such education are themselves deemed wrong-minded, a spiritual if not a moral offense. To be sure, even more pragmatic forms of architecture can arouse controversy, because buildings are so public, so costly, and so lasting. But church architecture arouses principled passion, harnessing aesthetic taste to theological conviction. Churches *must* be built and liturgical space *must* be arranged in particular ways because tradition requires it, or because current liturgical thinking demands it. For one current architect the full array of Gothic effects, from cruciform plan to hammer beams and from rood beam to gargoyles, is indispensable to church design: "the absence of these forms and linguistic elements, as well as many others, is the absence of the very essence of Christian space."[11] No gargoyles, no churches.

Problems are compounded by four factors. First is the tendency of reformers and traditionalists to talk past each other, perhaps in part because the reformers tend to be professional liturgists mainly interested in the worship accommodated by architecture, while the most vocal traditionalists are often practicing architects with greater interest in the aesthetic and symbolic qualities of buildings themselves. Second is the more general tendency to see more clearly what we have experienced as valuable than to grasp what others have so experienced. Imagination and learning alike are applied to disparagement rather than to understanding. Caricature is frequent, almost routine, from Edward Sövik's prosopopoeia of good- and bad-talking churches to Michael Rose's protest that modern churches are "ugly as sin." Drama is reduced to mere show, and the biblically mandated eucharistic sacrifice is taken for a bizarre ritual. Third, voices on both sides of the debate are informed by only limited experience of church architecture. Those who condemn longitudinal churches are likely to be thinking about certain types of longitudinal space that do in fact distance altar and clergy from people. Those who disparage modern churches as banal may know little beyond neighborhood churches that may indeed be uninspired. Fourth, and perhaps most important, architecture is blamed for deficiencies in liturgical use or in ethos.

The Reaction Against Traditional Church Design

Six main themes in the movement of reform can be seen as reactions against perceived abuses of traditional church design: extravagance, revival styles, distinctively ecclesiastical forms, a spirit of withdrawal, ornamentalism, and monumentalism.

(1) *The reaction against extravagance.* Many Christians as well as outsiders have always been uncomfortable with the artistic elaboration of churches, and this discomfort can be articulated in several ways. A church built on a grand scale and lavishly decorated is perceived not only as a sacrament of the divine presence but as a monument to clericalism and triumphalism, a glorification of its builders. As Ludwig Feuerbach suggested, "temples in honour of religion are in truth temples in honour of architecture."[12] Already in late antiquity Saint Jerome asked how one could justify the adornment of churches when Christ was starving to death in the person of the poor.[13] Amid the boom in church-

building after World War II the question recurred, as in the characteristically pointed formulation of J. G. Davies: "If the choice is between erecting a church and meeting human need, the Christian community has no grounds for hesitation."[14] Extravagance in church-building became an embarrassment. One writer proposed in 1973 that if there could be "one simple method of saving the Church's mission" it might be "the decision to abandon church buildings," which after all are "basically unnatural places" having little connection with people's normal everyday lives.[15] The purpose of soup kitchens was obvious; that of sanctuaries was less so. As Giovanni Catti pointed out, the lesson of evangelical poverty always becomes more difficult to communicate when ever greater sums are expended for the space in which the lesson is preached.[16]

In many places sensitivity to these issues has resulted in churches that are more modest in scale and in decoration. Already in the early 1950s, architects were devising relatively economical forms of church, such as the A-frame design in which "the walls are also the roof, the roof is also the walls and the nave is also the steeple," producing "a lot of tall church for very little money."[17] In some places what this has meant is that indigent communities have inherited highly ornate churches of the nineteenth and early twentieth centuries, while more affluent ones have built churches for themselves designed in homage to an ideal of modesty. (Edward Sövik noted ironically that those who request "the very humblest of materials and the least expensive construction possible" may not apply the same standards to their own homes.)[18] A church built of simple and economical materials, like Our Lady of Hungarians Roman Catholic Chapel at Cegléd in Hungary, will be celebrated as a "people's church."[19]

But an ethically grounded striving for simplicity may run afoul of other ethical goals. Horst Schwebel notes that the reformers' idea was to build a "church for others" that would eschew all "self-assertive display" but that in the concrete situation the moral ideal of the "church for others" might mean instead relieving a drab environment with a more colorful and distinctive building.[20] In some cultures the artistic embellishment of churches provides virtually the only setting in which professionally conceived and executed art is publicly accessible. Indeed, churches are still often the only places in which public art is fully and regularly integrated with public activity: people may eat their lunches at the foot of a monumental sculpture, but public rituals involving such art are rare, and they are not usually occasions for marking critical passages in the lives of individuals and in the experience of communities. Does an ethic of service also mean no art museums, no theaters, and no music halls? If large sums are spent on those forms of culture, why not also on buildings where culture is integrated with community-building, inspiration, consolation, and worship?

For the Uruguayan architect Eladio Dieste, church architecture has an inherently populist mission: it articulates a conception of the people for whom it exists. Gothic cathedrals and Mayan or Peruvian temples might achieve this purpose, but such expression of a people's culture seemed to Dieste now lacking. He spoke of conversing with a group of affluent women who had asked him to give a series of talks about religious architecture—women who spoke about art as a luxury commodity, "as they would talk, let's say, about a French perfume, about a fine horse." He and his audience had little in common. For Dieste, art in general and religious architecture in particular is not a luxury but a basic commodity, like potatoes. While there may be refined art for those souls who have a special need for it, as there will be a need, say, for Saint John of the Cross's *Spiritual Canticle*, what concerned Dieste was the "great art shared by the community."[21] His perspective has much in common with that of some Anglo-Catholic priests of the late nineteenth and early twentieth centuries who took their ceremonialism into the British slums in an effort to give the working classes a taste of the splendor they experienced so little of in their environment,[22] although he seems to have envisaged a stronger correlation between a particular people and a particular idiom for church-building.

(2) *The reaction against revival styles.* As late as the 1950s it was possible to find large numbers of churches still being designed in Gothic and other revival styles.[23] Further, congregations making a transition from sect to denomination sometimes sought to adopt a more recognizably churchly style to gain recognition for their new self-conception, as when Seventh Day Adventists in Nashville built a new "cathedral-type chapel" with Gothic arches as late as 1967.[24] But the assumption that a church should look like some historical model could no longer be taken for granted, and one of the main themes in discussion of church architecture from the mid–twentieth century onward was a reaction against revival styles. The Modernist movement at the turn of the twentieth century had turned away from historicism in secular architecture, and church builders followed this lead. No one supposed that Gothic and Baroque had been traditional when they were first built, and Edward Maufe distilled this observation into the principle that "it is traditional to be modern."[25] Being anything other than modern could seem pretentious or simply odd. In Peter Hammond's memorable formulation, "It is better to come before God naked than in period costume."[26]

Revival architecture seemed a nostalgic throwback to the past, irrelevant to the needs of the present. A church built in contemporary architectural idiom was taken to declare: "We want to worship today."[27] If a church was to serve contemporary members, it need not and must not be archaic in its design: it need not, precisely because the aesthetic idiom of any age can be accepted as valid, and modern architecture was as appropriate as any other; and it must not, because use of archaic style confirms the unbeliever's argument that Christianity is "merely the by-product of a vanished culture."[28] Revival styles, it was argued, are used only to arouse the emotional impact of conventional church design, to titillate the religious emotions by evoking association with what a church is assumed to look like. People fall back on them because they make a church "look like a church." But function, not form, should in this respect be decisive: once people have moved beyond that concern with what a church should look like, and concern themselves instead with what a church *is*, what purpose it serves, they will realize that to fulfill that purpose a church must be designed in "a living language."[29] Edward Sövik phrased the matter somewhat differently, suggesting that the appearance of a church is indeed important, but that if one wishes a church to look like a church this cannot mean that it should look like *familiar* churches, rather "a church ought to look like *the* church," serving as a visual symbol of the congregation it shelters.[30] Besides which, different members and committees within the congregation might want a building that "looks like a church," but each would propose a different notion of what a church in fact looks like.[31]

Rudolf Schwarz argued that architects could indeed imitate the deeply recessed doorways and the "mighty pillars" of Romanesque style, or Gothic pointed arches, but "it would not be true." In an age of steel frames and strengthened materials, walls are no longer thick and heavy masonry but taut membranes, and replication of structural forms where they are not needed makes of them "theatrical trappings," an "empty wrapping."[32] Sharing this concern about honesty, Paul Tillich also proposed that imitation stifles creativity: study of past models circumvents the "unconscious, symbol-creating side of the artistic process."[33]

Even those who advocate modern idiom sometimes allude to revival styles, as Maufe did when he used simplified Gothic forms at Guildford Cathedral. But by midcentury, compromise was scorned as a kind of "vestigial historicism," meaning the use of allusion to historic styles within modern buildings, which one critic disdained as simply unserious: "the broad effect is that of a kind of architectural baby talk, analogous to the Gothic script in which *Ye olde Tea-Shoppe* used to be written."[34] A prominent architect might still profess a need for grounding in architectural tradition, might declare that "the joy and stimulus in architecture is the discovery of fresh combinations of old ingredients appropriate to present problems," and might even conclude: "Faced with the choice, I would rather be right than contemporary." But the prominence of this architect would rest on his capacity to reinterpret any historical impulses so radically that an untrained eye might see only the modern and not the traditional in his work.[35]

Rudolf Arnheim's assessment is more discriminating. He notes an "almost desperate attempt" to eschew revival styles and "to proclaim that religion has kept up with the times." In seeking "to attract a dwindling clientele," churches take their cues from "their leading competitors, the entertainment and catering industries," the nature of religion itself being now uncertain. Yet churches that succeed both in their modernity and in their identity as churches, "translating dignity and spiritual devotion into twentieth-century idioms," represent the highest ideal.[36]

(3) *The reaction against distinctively ecclesiastical forms*. Why in any case should ecclesiastical architecture be distinct from secular design? Lance Wright suggested in 1962 that it is better for churches to follow the stylistic norms of the broader culture. The Church is meant to mold and inspire people, which "is best done by her being within rather than without," and the distinctive architectural dress tends to place the church without and impede its work in the world.[37] Churches should thus be indistinguishable from secular buildings. When the Church uses distinctive architectural dress it separates it from the world it is meant to mold and inspire, thus making its work more difficult: architects must use "the pure vernacular" in building churches, avoiding forms they would avoid in any other buildings.[38] In keeping with this counsel, churches soon sprang up that looked little different from secular buildings, sometimes serving as multipurpose space.[39]

(4) *The reaction against withdrawal*. The reaction against the notion of specifically sacred architecture is linked to a conviction that churches should not be places of withdrawal. A working party of the World Council of Churches once suggested that there can be "heretical" church buildings: those that foster a sense of security in isolation, a flight from the world, a quest for the delights of heaven, or a diversion from work in the world and from the realization of heaven on earth through sanctification of human relations.[40] In a similar vein, Edward Sövik has suggested that traditional church structures are "otherworldly by inference, detaching themselves from the architecture of the world around them," insulated from the world's realities by "their saccharine charm" or providing a "sentimental and esoteric escape" with their "dim religious light."[41]

Some churches are therefore consciously opened to a social and specifically urban setting. Sometimes integration with the outer world receives token obeisance: an American clergyman saw a church in Scotland where the window behind the altar opened onto the workaday world, reminding people of their social responsibilities, and he wanted something of the sort for his church back at home, but what he got was a window along the side of the nave, with a view of a garden, and beyond it trees and rooftops.[42] Elsewhere the integration is more fully developed. Saint Peter's Lutheran Church in Manhattan sold its land to Citicorp in the 1970s, but on the condition that the bank would construct a new church with a distinctive architectural presence.[43] One way to accomplish this goal would have been to place the church on the top of the skyscraper.[44] Instead, the Citicorp Center skyscraper was propped on massive columns, and the new Saint Peter's was nestled under one corner, at street level. One critic mused that "there is a bit of disturbing symbolism to the church's position at the base of the tower—the granite church seems from some angles to cower beneath the huge skyscraper, a rather awkward reminder that the bank is big and rich and the church less so."[45] But of course a church placed at the top of a skyscraper is considerably less accessible to the public than one at street level, and for a church such as Saint Peter's, with its vigorous cultural programs, accessibility is of paramount importance. Another observer commented that the large window behind the altar, looking down from the sidewalk level into the recessed main sanctuary, "distracts the eye and unfocuses the concentration."[46] In any case, the church is manifestly integrated into its urban setting and open to that environment, while at the same time providing a fully enclosed chapel (with sculpture by Louise Nevelson in the form of white-painted wooden *objets trouvés*) for prayer and meditation.

The usual criticism of all such forms of openness to the environment is that it can make for distraction. What if the view outside is of a mall or a parking lot?[47] The deeper critique is that an insistence on this kind of openness rests on a questionable assumption about the way liturgy relates to life in the world. In its intercessory moments, liturgy brings to mind hospital rooms, battlefields, decaying neighborhoods in inner cities, and other settings that are not likely to lie conveniently outside a window, and one point of intercession is to be in relationship with broad networks of people in need, to cultivate responsiveness not only to those in one's immediate sphere but to those well beyond it.[48] A view of the immediate environment need not inhibit this broader consciousness, but an insistence on its necessity does easily suggest that the focus of liturgical attention is constricted to the world at hand, the environment that can be seen. Relevance to the world may be better achieved by bringing the world at large into it in prayer, symbol, and at times practical action than by opening windows onto the patch of turf immediately outside. Rafael Moneo's cathedral at Los Angeles, set alongside an expressway, is meant as "a space where people feel more able to isolate themselves from daily life."[49]

Still, the church building is often linked to ancillary structures, and, viewed as part of a broader architectural context, a church may also be in dialogue with its environment through service. One of the most important aspects of the recent renovation at Saint John the Evangelist Cathedral in Milwaukee is its integration of liturgical space with facilities for the homeless: the complex is designed so that liturgical processions can begin in an atrium directly attached to an outreach center. The cathedral can be distinguished from the outreach center, but they are meant to support each other in the related acts of worship and community service.

(5) *The reaction against ornamentalism.* Liturgical reform has shared with modernist aesthetic an emphasis on minimalism, a paring away of superficialities and distractions, a seeking out of the essential. For some, the avoidance of ornament is a way of restoring an emphasis on the craft, the workmanship of the structure itself. W. R. Lethaby thought ornament on churches was like tattoos on the body, something belonging to a primitive stage in civilization.[50]

Ninian Comper admired the simpler medieval churches as little more than whitewashed barns that "became glorious by beautiful workmanship within."[51] More extreme is the minimalism of Ludwig Mies van der Rohe, worked out in his secular architecture but applied also to his chapel at the Illinois Institute of Technology. Reversing Louis Sullivan's dictum that form follows function, Mies argued that the functionality of a building is much enhanced if it is made in "a practical and satisfying shape" that can serve multiple and changing functions. In its stark simplicity the chapel exemplifies the modular and functional conception of architecture that Mies championed. He used uniform rectilinear units of steel, glass, and in this case brick, in modules that could just as well be assembled differently to serve various functions. But at the same time he demanded that the units and their assembly be crafted with precision and balance that would endow each structure with a simple elegance and beauty—God being, after all, "in the details."[52]

Minimalism can be a form of iconoclasm.[53] For Karl Barth, "images and symbols have *no place at all* in a building designed for Protestant worship" because they "dissipate attention and create confusion."[54] More often economy of images and symbols is recommended for greater effect, a single image being more arresting and compelling than a multiplicity. The tradition more relevant than Puritan iconoclasm as precedent for modernist minimalism is the monastic and especially Cistercian tradition, which hardly disdains symbolism but does insist on an economy and clarity in the use of symbols. Not surprisingly, one of the most notable examples of minimalist remodeling of a church was William Schickel's work for the Trappists at Gethsemani Abbey, where the Gothic revival vaulting and tracery were removed and a purely Cistercian white brick box was left in place.[55]

The minimalism of modern church architecture can be meant as "holy emptiness," a term behind which two distinct but related ideas lie. First is the notion (articulated by Rudolf Schwarz) that a church should be a place chiefly for liturgical action, and that the spareness of design and of ornament forces awareness that everything important happening in the church comes not from objects but from actions. It is perhaps no coincidence that many of the most successful modern churches are those of monastic and other nonparochial religious communities: not only are the planners free of pressure from parish members but, more important, they can cultivate a symbolic minimalism with assurance that those in the community will bring a richness of associations to the liturgy independent of the liturgical environment.

The second, related reason for "holy emptiness" is that of Paul Tillich, whose main theological concern here was the relationship between the sacred and the holy, and the importance of preserving the primacy of the holy and the provisional character of every sacred symbol. Tillich granted that in some cultures a grand profusion of sacred symbols might be fitting; he had experienced the "vegetative abundance" of Indian temples and the "wild-growing abundance of holy forms and figures" in Mexican churches. For his own culture he preferred holy emptiness, in large part because the symbols of a more exuberant culture seemed to him to have lost their power but also because the very emptiness of a church seemed a fitting sign of God's absence: religious symbols now appear hollow and dishonest, and while we await God's return we must acknowledge that divine absence with holy emptiness. "Therefore the expression of church building should be 'waiting' for the return of the hidden God who has withdrawn and for whom we must wait again."[56]

(6) *The reaction against monumentalism.* Akin to the minimalism of modern church architecture is an aversion to monumentality. This tendency gained force in midcentury in reaction against the monumentality of state-sponsored architecture under totalitarian regimes. Monumental architecture continued to be used for public and commercial architecture as well as some ecclesiastical designs,[57] but it could no longer be taken for granted in secular design, and for churches it seemed even less appropriate. "What kind of being is this God for whom churches are to be erected? Is he one who delights in monuments to his honour rather than in loving care for men?"[58]

Bishop Robert J. Dwyer spoke of the need to dispense with the cathedral, by which he meant any church built with the mass and height associated with the cathedral.[59] The massiveness of the cathedral was never a function of its actual use; it was a symbol of wealth and power. Such churches may have been necessary at one time, when religion needed to dominate society, but this is not the function of religion now, when it has set aside claims to political power but deepened and widened its social mission. Rather than conceiving the church as a cathedral, Dwyer said, one should think of it in biblical terms as the house of God and the gate of heaven. Dwyer's theme was quickly taken up by other writers.[60] The *complexe du monument* seemed less fitting to some than a domestic model: the ideal church was essentially "a kind of great livingroom, a place where the faithful come together to meet the Lord, and one another in the Lord." The church building designed for celebration should resemble domestic architecture, should be "free of monumental overtones," serving the assembled community *"in the simplest possible form."* The vision inspiring it should be one of peace rather than of glory: *Non gloriae, sed pacis visio.*[61]

Perhaps the fullest and most nuanced articulation of this antimonumentalism came in an essay of 1962 by Lance Wright, for whom the sense of the provisional, of economy, and of the continuing nature of space are the three basic marks of modern architectural expression.[62] It may once have made sense to build churches for eternity, but our awareness of the geological time scale makes clear that whatever we build is destined to pass, and we should build accordingly, diagramatically and informally, without monumentality and the accentuation of sculpted forms superimposed on architectural surfaces. In the past, even when funds were limited, the ideal was to built on a magnificent scale, but a sense of social responsibility now requires economy in church building; this does not require cheapness but does involve "simplicity and asceticism." Earlier architecture was meant to enclose space, but modern technology makes a more open form of building possible, and the Church's openness to the world makes it desirable.

The Traditionalist Counterreaction

Reformers' notions about church architecture were not uniformly well received when first implemented, and expensive modernization sometimes evoked resentment and return to traditional form. At Telfs in the Austrian Tyrol, a church built in 1859–63 in Romanesque style was modernized with drastic starkness and reordered for current liturgy in 1962, then restored to something of its ornate condition under a new pastor who arrived in 1970.[63] One study in Germany traced the histories of seventeen "parish centers" originally designed as multipurpose buildings. Each one of them eventually was reconfigured and made to resemble more closely a traditional church. Typically the first step was increasing separation of the worship space from other parts of the complex, then the flexible arrangement of furnishings became fixed, then the area around the altar was given some marker of special dignity such as a carpet, a cross was set up by the altar, walls were adorned, and simple liturgical furnishings were replaced by more expensive alternatives. At Baunatal, an utterly simple parish center built in 1973 for both Roman Catholics and Protestants was eventually replaced by separate churches of more clearly confessional and "churchly" design.[64]

The multipurpose church was always intensely controversial. Willem Gerard Overbosch was not the only opponent to find such churches marked by an unhappy compromise: neither quite a place to feel at home nor a place for concentration and worship, with acoustics that may be appropriate for discussion but not for congregational singing.[65]

Mark Allen Torgerson has traced the evolution in use of Edward Sövik's churches, where congregations sometimes lived with the original arrangements for some years but then reverted to a more traditional pattern. Sövik deliberately positioned the altar table, the pulpit, and the lectern asymmetrically; in later adaptation the altar table might be centrally placed on the platform, with pulpit and lectern flanking it. The architect preferred three blocks of seating on three sides of the platform; after some time, as little as two years, the seats might be rearranged in a semicircle facing the platform, or in parallel rows in front of the platform.[66] These congregations did tend to continue using their worship spaces for multiple purposes, but when using them specifically for worship they opted for more traditional disposition of the interior.

If grassroots resistance to reform emerged almost immediately, another factor became operative only in the later decades of the century: the shift from modernist to postmodern architecture in a secular context. The postmodern attempt to reconceive and recover an architectural heritage has brought rethinking of the modernist reaction against revival styles in architecture generally.[67] And if postmodern architecture harks to historical models in secular design, it becomes harder to argue that the exclusion of historicizing architecture is important for contemporaneity: historicism is no longer a turning back from contemporary culture, but an essential part of that culture.[68] Christ Church at Lake Forest, Illinois, with its adaptation of colonial classicism, demonstrates how a church can be at the same time thoroughly modern and thoroughly historicist.[69] Saint Jerome in Waco, with its postmodern homage to Santa Maria Novella in Florence, demonstrates historical allusion as appliqué on a church that has little in common structurally with its supposed Renaissance prototype.[70] Perhaps even more daring, churches of the 1990s could again be Gothic in style: one could be described as "a contemporary interpretation of a neo-Gothic form," and another could be said to evoke Victorian Carpenter Gothic while remaining entirely modern.[71] In the context of this ecclesiastical equivalent of secular Postmodernism, it is only surprising that no one yet has published a book entitled *From Bauhaus to God's House*.[72]

It was against this background of grassroots resistance and shifting architectural tastes that Stroik, Schroeder, Rose, and others launched a sustained attack on ecclesiastical modernism in the late twentieth century. As a consciously articulated position, this recovery of tradition has involved at least three forms of reaction against modern church design: against banality, against loss of tradition, and against a one-sided emphasis on church as place of assembly.

The charge of banality in modern church design was made already during the 1940s in Protestant circles,[73] and more recently critics have lambasted many, indeed most recent Roman Catholic churches as banal and uninspiring.[74] Duncan Stroik notes that despite a perhaps unprecedented boom in church construction in the second half of the twentieth century, remarkably few churches of the period are recognized as major works of architecture.[75] What may seem a question of taste also has a social dimension. Critics of traditional ornamentation tend to associate it with chilly formality, but its defenders reply that on the contrary it can appear more inviting and "friendly" than a minimalist architecture. A South African architect converted from strict modernism, Jack Barnett, made this point when he was struck by a revival-style church in Cape Town and compared it with the minimalist buildings around it: traditional and ornamented church architecture has a stronger sense of personality than those in modern idiom, a more generous share of friendliness and approachability.[76]

But a deeper issue, particularly for Roman Catholic critics, is what they take to be a diminished rootedness in tradition. Traditional reaction can arise from a simple and practical urge to establish identity—or, in the words of one observer, to find "some architectural way to say, loud and clear, 'Church Here!'"[77] But it arises also from a sense that a church is meant to be symbolic and that it should be that already in its form: a church should look like a church, and as Schloeder insists, "a Catholic church ought to look like a Catholic church." One architect thus proposes a revival of traditional forms and symbols in church architecture:

> I believe we should see the law and the gospel conveyed through works of art in the Church, and on our church buildings. We should have murals depicting the history of God's people through the ages; we should have stained glass honoring the heroes of the faith; we should make use of symbols, provided they are understood.[78]

Another protests that modern art often prefers geometric abstraction to symbolism; that "we live in an age of religious iconoclasm"; that what the building looks like inside and out is important for individuals and communities; and that architects would do well to tap the supply of "symbol-laden building forms" available in Western civilization, modifying them to accommodate modern needs.[79]

Loss of tradition is in part a loss of meaning in traditional symbolism. Camilian Demetrescu wishes to revive appreciation for such traditional symbols as solar orientation of churches, churches perceived as arks, portals and processional paths as symbolic elements in church design. But he realizes the odds he faces and the difficulty of his challenge: "To speak of sacred architecture today, to a Church which is crushed, humiliated and degraded by the ignorance of its symbols, by the painful alienation of the remaining iconography, drowned in the schemes of disembodied abstraction, is equivalent to turning a knife in the wound."[80] But more deeply the loss of tradition is seen as reflecting a loss even of faith. Thus, Giampaolo Rossi argues that faith must be restored to church design in opposition to the nihilism and despair of modern culture.[81]

In Roman Catholic circles the argument takes specific form: whatever other denominations may choose to do with their church buildings, a Roman Catholic church should uphold the specific values of that tradition. Thus, Schloeder is willing to concede that certain twentieth-century churches may be great as architecture while still insisting that they are not appropriate specifically as Catholic churches.[82] One particular reform that evokes frequent protest is the displacement of the tabernacle from the high altar to a side chapel, a shift that is blamed for diminished eucharistic devotion, weakened consciousness of the real presence of Christ, and an impoverished sense of the sacred. One archbishop asked the faithful how they responded when a church was rededicated with its tabernacle restored to "its proper place," and the congregation broke into applause.[83]

The critics protest further against a one-sided emphasis on church as place of assembly. Among the themes prevalent in recent literature is that of the church as *domus Dei* (house of God) or *domus ecclesiae* (house of the assembly). Duncan Stroik's response to those who accentuate the latter conception is that Catholicism is a religion of "both/and" rather than "either/or," and that these two notions of a church express complementary emphases on the divine presence and on the community assembled by God. Steven Schloeder insisted that the Second Vatican Council "did not change the *purpose* of the church building. That building still exists primarily for the worship of the Lord."[84] In this theocentric emphasis the critics stand in a tradition most vigorously articulated in the earlier twentieth century by Evelyn Underhill in her general study of worship.[85]

The Movement for Congregational Participation

When an influential document of 1978 emphasized that people at worship should be "involved as participants and *not* as spectators,"[86] this was hardly a new or controversial stance. Thirty years earlier, the Second Vatican Council's *Constitution on the Sacred Liturgy* urged that the entire assembly should be engaged in "full, conscious and active participation" in liturgy.[87] This emphasis had already been a key theme in liturgical reform throughout the twentieth century, in Anglican and other churches as well as in the Roman communion.[88] Decades before the Council, publication and distribution of bilingual missals was itself a way of enabling the laity in Roman churches to pray the mass along with the priest rather than saying the rosary or engaging in other devotions, and this too was a way of cultivating conscious and active (if perhaps not full) participation.[89] Through the second half of the twentieth century one main concern of liturgists was to define various ways of involving the laity in liturgical responses, in music, in roles such as lector and minister of communion. In the Roman Church, even translating the mass into the vernacular in the 1960s was a basic way of engaging the laity more fully. This emphasis on participation was not an isolated phenomenon: as E. Brooks Holifield points out, it was "part of a broader impulse in the society" that was manifested in participatory democratic practices in politics, management, labor, and higher education.[90]

Architects' main concern in this regard has been twofold: first to devise unified space that does not distinguish or at least does not emphasize a sharp distinction between clerical and congregational spaces, and second to rearrange seating in such a way that worshipers have closer contact both with the clergy and with each other. Both these developments can be seen already at Rudolf Schwarz's chapel in Burg Rothenfels as early as 1928. But in general it was the sense of unified space that came first and the reordering of the congregation—in denominations where this had not already been done generations ago—that came later.

Unification of space required transformation of the church design in both plan and elevation: it meant a movement away from the apsidal or otherwise architecturally distinct sanctuary, creating an interior readily perceived as a single space.[91] Advocates of this unification in the mid–twentieth century often emphasized the importance of a balance: the unification should not be complete but should retain some distinction between clerical and lay space. Because the Church is a hierarchical society whose members have distinct functions, the space for clergy should be distinct from those of laity; yet they form a single worshiping community in which all should be participants and none mere spectators, so there should be no visual or architectural separation, no long and narrow spaces that "remove the laity from close contact with the altar."[92]

Reordering of seating vis-à-vis the altar might mean a fully centralized arrangement, with seating in the round. Frederick Gibberd chose this option for the Metropolitan Cathedral of Christ the King in Liverpool, as Gyo Obata did for the Priory Church of Saint Mary and Saint Louis, but both architects disclaimed any intent that this design should be generally adopted.[93] Critics emphasized that the arrangement puts one large block of worshipers (often the choir) behind the back of the clergy, can undercut clear recognition of a processional axis, and emphasizes the organic but not the hierarchical nature of the assembly.[94] Most common were compromises, versions of the centralized arrangement that placed the altar in the midst of the assembly but without literally surrounding it.[95] Largely under the influence of German precedent, such arrangements were exported to other countries soon after World War II.[96] It then became one of the most popular arrangements, although it is sometimes criticized as encouraging attention to the central focal point rather than promoting a sense of close contact among worshipers in the congregation. Not all liturgical reformers of the later twentieth century advocated the use of centralized space; one early reformer, who preferred to have clergy and people facing each other in a transversal arrangement, argued that a centralized disposition disrupts the unity of the assembly and distracts from "an undisturbed, recollected attitude," exposing worshipers to "the curious gaze of others."[97] In the 1960s and 1970s, however, some version of centralized space with seating on three sides of the liturgical center came to prevail in architecture for liturgical reform. The seating might wrap around the center in a fan pattern. Alternatively it might be arranged in three blocks, one in front of the altar and one to each side, as for example at Nuestra Señora de Fátima at Moreno in Argentina.[98] In all these arrangements the fundamental goal is the "gathering around" that Edward Sövik speaks of as fundamental to establishing the unity of a congregation. "If you ask a group of people, young or old, to sing together to an empty space without an audience, they will almost inevitably gather in a circle." The experience of gathering around in a circle or some other cluster gives a sense of being "a single body whose parts belong together."[99]

It is harder to plan for participation when the size of the assembly varies greatly, from a small cluster on weekday mornings to a multitude on Christmas or Easter. The usual solution is to set aside a weekday chapel for smaller groups. Robert Maguire and Keith Murray's church of Saint Paul's, Bow Common, in London, is above all else a solution to the problem of providing space for either larger or smaller congregations without relegating the latter to a chapel. The building is designed to accommodate as many as two hundred and as few as about ten. The chief means for achieving this flexibility are two. First, the central space has a high clerestory wall above it, something like a square dome, which illuminates this space enough that it is visually distinct and can serve by itself for a smaller congregation, while at the same time those on the periphery of a larger assembly have their attention drawn toward the center by its relative brightness. Second, slender columns go around all four sides of the central area, again defining the inner space for a smaller group but allowing a larger congregation to extend outward without being cut off from the rest of the assembly.[100]

Much of the history of modern church architecture, then, has been a series of experiments designed to enhance congregational participation. But not all observers have been persuaded that these experiments have been successful, and some have argued that they have been counterproductive: in the words of Steven Schloeder, "despite the millions of dollars spent in reordering churches and redirecting the liturgy, the laity have been brought into neither a more profound sense of active participation nor a deeper sense of community."[101] On several points critics have suggested, in effect, that participation and community bonding are something like joy, which, as C. S. Lewis famously proposed, must be a by-product: "Its very existence presupposes that you desire not it but something other and outer."[102] If people are shy about singing generally, they may be more so if the seating is semicircular and others can see and more easily identify them singing. If the church has a domestic appearance, this may foster a habit of thinking of worship as a private affair, an activity of the family, in which outsiders are made to feel not more welcomed but more like outsiders.[103] An environment comfortable for one activity may be distinctly uncomfortable for another.[104] Churches may limit their own success precisely by conveying a sense of domestic and intimate space that makes visitors feel like intruders.[105]

A perhaps deeper problem is that none of the configurations of seating quite solves the problem of how the congregation relates to the presider, and in attempting to overcome detachment of clergy from laity most of these experiments run the risk of giving the clergy an even more prominent role. Giles Dimock complains that in one renovation a carved reredos served as backdrop no longer to the altar but rather to the celebrant's chair, making it appear like

a throne.[106] But the traditionalists' chief complaint is about seating arrangements that may be meant to foster participation but in fact bring the preacher
into greater prominence.[107] Any arrangement of sacred space can give rise to
clericalism. Any form of church design can lead to a sense that it is the clergy
who act and the laity who merely react, or that the clergy are active and the
laity passive. Processional space can create this effect if it is the clergy alone
or chiefly who are perceived as processing. Auditorium space can do so by
calling clear attention to the preacher who proclaims the gospel to the congregation and by making that one person the center of attention. In a church
segmented for intercessory worship, it is the clergy who do the work of interceding on behalf of the congregation. In a church segmented for mediatory
liturgy, it is the clergy and their attendants who mediate between one sacred
space and another. One might distinguish a clericalism of distance and a clericalism of proximity: one in which the clergy are detached in isolation from
the laity and one in which they are exalted in a special role immediately before
the congregation.

Louis Bouyer expressed concerns about clericalism in *Liturgy and Architecture*.[108] When this book appeared in 1967, Bouyer was seeking many of the
same goals as other reformers. He was as insistent as anyone on overcoming
the clericalist approach to liturgy, with its assumption that liturgy is something
done by clergy on behalf of the laity. But while for many people the chief ways
to attain these goals were use of the vernacular and celebration of mass *versus
populum*, or with the priest facing the congregation, Bouyer envisioned more
venturesome ways to attain the reformers' goals. He had been an early advocate
of celebration *versus populum*, at a time when the priest stood at a distance
from the congregation and did even the scripture readings from a missal placed
on the altar. Turning the priest to face the congregation seemed an improvement. But by 1967 a far better solution for Bouyer was having the priest stand
with the people, in their midst, facing the same direction. Facing toward the
congregation seemed to him a step in the wrong direction, a step toward greater
rather than lesser clericalism: "far from uniting the community focused on the
altar," he warned, just as this change was becoming normative, "it will emphasize the separation and opposition between clergy and laity; the altar will
just become itself the most formidable barrier between two castes among
Christians." Instead, he urged, the priest should stand *with* the people, and the
people should be clustered closely around the priest, first at the ambo and then
at the altar.

Michael Rose suggests that what the Second Vatican Council had in mind
when it called for participation was not specifically outward action but a broader
type of participation that includes a contemplative dimension. The crucial term
in conciliar documents is not *activa participatio*, which Rose says might imply
external acts of participation only, but *actuosa participatio*, which allows more
fully for a contemplative form of engagement.[109] But this is wishful thinking;

actuosa simply does not differ from *activa* in that way.[110] It is true that the Council clearly and explicitly wished to encourage participation on both levels, inward and outward, and was particularly interested in congregational participation in music.[111] And yet participation as usually conceived may indeed be too timid, both demanding and offering too little. For the congregation to sing five or six hymns and to join in a series of scripted responses—and for these to be conceived as the participatory moments—makes of liturgy a bumpy ride in which those carried along go through long periods of passivity only to be jolted into participatory moments. One might suggest that the congregation should participate not some of the time but all the time, and that every moment people are *not* participating represents a squandered opportunity. But this is to suggest an expanded range of participatory modes. If one person is singing every hymn and reciting every prayer but in a merely mechanical way, while another is silent but attentive to every nuance, which is more fully participating? Watching and listening with one's attention fully engaged, with what the Buddhists call mindfulness, alert to the patterns and surprises, the references and the relevance of what is said and done—this is not a passive or inactive state; it is one mode of deeply active participation. The congregation may at certain junctures be engaged in singing and in speaking, but to define these as the moments of participation is to betray a restricted notion of what participation can be.

Sacrality Debated and Defined

In the early twentieth century, the architect Otto Bartning participated already in a reaction against revival styles, which he saw as "hiding the profane visage of the preaching hall behind an untrue, symbolically sacred mask." He preferred a utilitarian space that would allow for practical gathering of hearers around a pulpit, and also for lectures, concerts, and meetings. A few years after building such a church Bartning had occasion to revisit it, but when he saw it now he was crushed. He suddenly perceived that the conceptions he had upheld in his youth stood before him more clearly and inexorably in this structure than he had grasped them when they were stated in words. He had meant to create a spacial form that would embody his faith, his conviction, but it was an empty shell. "This knowledge seemed to me like a second expulsion from Paradise. Unseen and unrecognized, I slipped out of my church and went away on the next train. But I could not slip so easily away from the problem."[112] For him and for others, the problem was the proper sense in which a church should be seen as sacred.

When a panel from the archdiocese of Paderborn declared that the Ronchamp chapel was "an unsurpassable example of arbitrariness, disorder, and the craving for novelty," altogether lacking in the sacral character requisite to religious architecture, the Protestant Oskar Söhngen replied that the very strangeness of the building gives it a numinous quality, making it a symbol of the wholly other, and that even the elements which seem capricious turn out to spring from deep primordial levels of sacrality. "I have seldom come to know a liturgical space that breathes the sacral more strongly and convincingly than Ronchamp."[113] But soon the question under discussion was whether and in what ways a church should after all be sacred.

One of the most influential books of the 1960s on the conception and use of churches was John Gordon Davies's *Secular Use of Church Buildings*. The book was in some ways typical of the theological rapprochement with secularization that was characteristic of the 1960s, appearing as it did three years after Harvey Cox's book *The Secular City*.[114] While some of its polemics may now appear dated, in other respects it articulated assumptions that still linger in discussion of church architecture.[115] Davies traced a fundamental shift in thinking about church buildings: already in the early years of the basilicas, but more fully in the Middle Ages, and then definitively in the writings of Cardinal Bellarmine in the sixteenth century, the church was interpreted as a Christian analogue to the Temple in Jerusalem and was vested with corresponding sacrality.[116] The veneration of saints' relics inside churches did much to reinforce the notion that a church is a holy place.[117] Nonetheless, churches (particularly naves) were used for a range of functions: incubation at saints' shrines, sanctuary, sheltering of travelers, feasting on various occasions, dancing, sale of even purely secular goods, meetings, legal proceedings, publishing notices of general interest to the community, storage of goods for the church and for individual parishioners, teaching, library facilities, distribution of poor relief, games, drama, and military defense.[118] The list is motley, and includes both routine and exceptional functions, some of which might have interfered with liturgy while others would not. Holding markets in church naves was a widespread practice but would not normally have been done while the nave was needed liturgically. Using the church as a fortress would have been more disruptive but more exceptional. In any case, Davies's conclusion is both cogent and important:

> There can be no question that in the Middle Ages the church was an all-purpose building. It is difficult to think of any secular activity that had no connection with it. . . . In all, there was no conscious irreverence. The church was a home [away] from home, where people could sleep, live, eat, drink, play, act and meet. It was part and parcel of everyday life; it was there to be used and used it was. . . . Sacred and secular were united and while excesses were perpetrated, what made them condemnable was not the place but the excesses themselves.[119]

In the Reformation period, then, voices arose in almost all denominations calling for the reservation of churches for purely sacred functions, so that gradually the multiuse church came to serve more strictly liturgical purposes. Joseph Mede, in *Several Discourses concerning the Holiness of Churches*, distinguished between the essential holiness proper to God, the holiness of integrity or righteousness that comes of freedom from sin, and that "relative" holiness, "a state of Relation of peculiarity to Godward, either in respect of presence or propriety and dominion," that characterizes churches.[120] J. B. Thiers held that within a church the altar is holier than the rest of the sanctuary, the sanctuary than the choir, the choir than the nave, the nave than the porch.[121] And for Augustus Pugin, as for many writers on the subject, the sanctity of a church implied separation: "from the earliest ages there has been a separation between priest and people, between a sacrifice and the worshippers, in every church," but the chancel in particular is "the place of sacrifice, the most sacred part of the edifice," reserved for that clerical act.[122] Even where sacralization was not theologically grounded, Calvinists and other Christians soon adopted a practical equivalent and treated their churches as sacred space. The Puritans might criticize the Anglican Church on its lapse into Judaism in this regard,[123] but their own descendants were not immune to the lure of sacralization.

Crucial for Davies's argument is his view of scriptural theology. Those who conceived churches as distinctly holy places, analogous to the Temple in Jerusalem, were "seemingly ignorant of the fact that in so doing they were behaving contrary to the New Testament outlook."[124] Sacrality implies that God resides in a distinct world, transcendent and remote from the secular world of ordinary experience; that the sacred and the secular must be kept separate; and that God acts mainly within the sacred sphere.[125] What Davies finds as a general outlook of New Testament writers is, rather, a conception of the sacred and secular as unified, as two aspects of an integral whole. The old dichotomy between the sacred and the profane had been ended with Christ. No longer was there any particular place where alone God could be encountered. And if there was now a Christian "temple" in any sense, it was the living community of Christians.[126]

Davies's voice was not alone. Harold W. Turner's book *From Temple to Meeting House* (1979) sustains Davies's line of critique, giving a polemic for "the normative Christian position" on church-building. He distinguishes a "temple" tradition from a "meeting-house" tradition and concludes that "even at the phenomenological and historical level the meeting-house type presents the authentic norm for the Christian tradition."[127] Only "Jesus within the Church" community can be recognized as a true Christian temple; the building for meeting should not take the form of a temple or aspire to the splendor of a temple but should be simply a meeting house. This book resembles Davies's in its synthesis of phenomenology and history, both conceived as providing material for theological reflection.[128]

Giovanni Michelucci went yet further, mischievously reversing usual assumptions and turning the secular into the sacred:

I have my idea of the sacred. They say: the church is sacred. But it is
not the church that is sacred, it is the city that is sacred, and the
church should fundamentally represent the spiritual values of the
city. But the strange thing is that the church refuses to allow a presence of the "sacred" (that is, the city) in its temples. It closes its
doors; it keeps the city from coming in.[129]

In Germany, Christof Martin Werner argued that the very concept of sacrality is a modern invention, arising out of eighteenth-century efforts to cor-
relate types of buildings with particular effects they should have. Werner traces
the history of the concept in nineteenth- and twentieth-century discussion,
showing, for example, how sacrality takes on sensual dimensions in the work
of some writers.[130] The argument does not, of course, prove that architecture
before the modern era was not considered sacred, but rather that sacrality as
an abstract philosophical or theological category is a modern arrival. What
Werner's work relativizes is not the way people relate to buildings as sacred
but the way they articulate and theorize that reaction.

Patrick J. Quinn argued in 1967 for a kind of multipurpose church that
"offers a meeting place for the sacred and the profane, or rather a renewed
appreciation of the sacredness of all life" in a "desacralized" age; the church is
a place where secular activities can be brought into close association with the
sacred, restoring a sense of their own sacrality.[131] Whether this approach supports or undermines the case of Davies and others depends mainly on how
the sacredness of the church is defined, and in what ways it is meant to affect
the world outside.

What does it mean to speak of a church as sacred space? What is the sacred? What Davies rejects, and what theorists like Rudolf Otto assume, is
chiefly a quality of distinction or separation. The sacred is sacred by virtue of
its separation from the profane. A particular time or place is set apart not because it is already sacred but rather so that it may become sacred. In other cases
the sacred may be conceived as so powerful that it must be kept away from profane individuals for their own protection, like a live electrical line.[132] In yet others the sacred may be seen as marked by a purity it might lose if touched by
profane hands: a place or an object may be held sacred of itself, not by human
designation, and that sacrality may be compromised by defilement. In all these
cases a sharp distinction between the sacred and the profane or secular is either
the source of sacrality or its clear and vitally important consequence. But in
chapters 3 and 4 I have considered alternative notions: suggestions that a place
might be sacred not by separation, or by a power or purity that requires separation, but from consciousness of holiness as a living presence, or from richness of symbolic reference. Presence and association may be compatible with
secular activities, so long as these enrich rather than diminishing what the
church is meant to provide. Davies and his followers forcefully challenge a con-

ception of sacrality grounded in separation—but sacrality of presence and of symbolic association may remain vital to the conception of a church.

Steven Schloeder's response to the movement Davies inspired is in a way common-sensical: "to make all things 'sacred' is to allow nothing to be truly sacred."[133] Only the saint or mystic can genuinely perceive all things as sacred; for the rest, sacred things and sacred places remain necessary.

Davies's critique gives rise to a further concern. More than once he mentions the Puritans' fear that sacred forms meant relapse into Judaism, and Davies himself shares something of that apprehension. Without noting it, Davies raises one of the oldest issues in Christianity. Among the most pressing questions among early Christians was how far and in what ways their belief and practice could build on that of ancient Israel. Marcion in the second century represented the extreme form of anti-Judaism, repudiating the Hebrew scriptures and distinguishing the God of those scriptures from the Father of Christ. In opposition to such anti-Judaism, other Christians took a step we should not take for granted as simply inevitable: they accepted the Hebrew Bible as their Old Testament and saw in it not only a source of prophecies (now fulfilled) but also a repository of prayers and valid moral teaching. Ancient Israel had developed a tradition rich in narratives, rituals, festivals, sacred geography, and sacred architecture for the sacralization of communal and domestic life. Both rabbinic Judaism and early Christianity borrowed and adapted the cultural goods of that tradition. The anti-Judaism of Marcion and others represented not only a spiritual impoverishment but a discontinuity with the past that few found attractive or useful. It is true that the earliest generations of Christians were unable to build churches, and that even when they could do so they sometimes insisted it was the assembly rather than the buildings themselves that were sacred. Yet the struggle for identity and expression seen in the early Christian churches must be seen in the broader context of an effort to define how far and in what ways—not whether—the sacral culture of ancient Israel could and should serve as a model. When they began building basilicas and interpreting them as having something of the sacrality of the Temple, they were not "behaving contrary to the New Testament outlook" but finding ways they could remain faithful to the gospel while preserving that richness of symbolic expression that Christ and his disciples would have taken for granted even while they sought to reform it. They could claim to be following the disciples, who after the Ascension "were continually in the Temple blessing God" (Luke 24:53) and who afterward "spent much time together in the Temple" (Acts 2:46).[134]

It is possible to say, of course, that the Temple-worship of early Christians was the result of syncretism and "initial uncertainties" and that greater clarity led to independence from both Temple and synagogue.[135] This emphasis would be in keeping with the recognition that Christ himself, while honoring and in various ways participating in the system of worship focused on the Temple, viewed that worship as provisional.[136] After the destruction of the Temple in the year 70, Jews and Christians alike had to find alternatives to Temple worship. But as it became increasingly clear that the Second Coming was not imminent and that Christians, like Jews, would have to find ways of celebrating the sacred within the ongoing course of history, Christian communities faced the question whether to develop festivals and seasons, codes for behavior, organizational structures, canons of authoritative texts, and (when circumstances permitted) places of worship with symbolic resonance. They did so. When they did not look to the traditions of ancient Israel for inspiration, they looked to Greece and Rome. One may sneer that they were "relapsing" into Judaism, or one may see them as using in worship, as in belief and in moral norms, the resources of the tradition to which they claimed inheritance.[137]

Conclusion: Orthodoxy versus Dogmatism in Church Architecture

Paul Tillich, who in his youth considered a career as architect but instead devoted himself to the architectonics of theology, reflected late in his life on the opportunities and the hazards of modern church design:

> One can say that every new church in a new style is an experiment. Without the risk of experiments that fail, there is no creation. Perhaps people in the future will point to many failed experiments; but they will also point to the wondrous success: the triumph over the dishonest, the unquestioned, the anxiously conservative. New church building is a victory of spirit, of the creative human spirit and of the spirit of God that breaks into our weakness.[138]

In short, faced with the challenge of developing new forms in their work, architects should be sinners and sin boldly. But tolerance for inevitable failures is easier when there is agreement about the need for change and about its general direction. That sort of consensus is precisely what is now lacking. There is disagreement on the most basic questions. Reformers ask how to promote bonding within the local church gathered here and now, traditionalists ask how to regain a sense of bonding to a Church extending over millennia. But the differences extend much further, into conceptions of authority and of fidelity as well as community.

Dogmatic positions make too hasty a leap from consensus to consequence. They begin with widely accepted but vaguely formulated premises: that congregational participation is to be encouraged, that a sense of tradition is valuable, that people should feel welcome in church. They proceed then too quickly to concrete implementation, which may or may not serve the purpose on which there is consensus but which is probably not the *only* way to serve it. Those who question the consequence are then taken to be challenging the consensus.

One might speak of conflict as raging between adherents of the classic sacramental church and proponents of the modern communal church, to which the classic evangelical church is tacitly but misleadingly assimilated. But too often the debate is between partisans who generally have shallow grounding in the range of possibilities, superficial understanding of the traditions they reject, and often a weak hold even on the traditions they prefer.

One form of dogmatism prevalent in our culture rejects churches in the classic sacramental tradition because it supposes they must be imperial in their inspiration and clericalist in their effect, it misconceives the theology of eucharistic sacrifice, it perceives these churches as declaring the transcendence of God, and it sees their richness of symbolism as arcane or superstitious. It is grounded in a reaction against specific types of traditional architecture, such as those built in Chicago in the late nineteenth and early twentieth centuries. It knows nothing of the way processional space can be used to enhance community and to clarify the shape of the liturgy. It is ignorant of writers such as Louis Bouyer and of churches such as Saint Gregory of Nyssa in San Francisco, or it judges them hastily. It sees modern communal churches alone as hospitable and adequate for forming community.

The classic sacramental church is the easiest to misrepresent, precisely because it represents a fusion of diverse historical influences. They may readily be grasped at an intuitive level, without need of learning. But they are difficult to articulate individually, and more difficult to present as a conceptually coherent whole.

For those who find classic sacramental churches confusing, one response to dogmatic repudiation might be to begin with any one feature of this design and trace its implications. One could take the rhythm of *procession and return* as the basic feature that gives meaning and context to everything else: the altar becomes the terminus of the progression and point of departure for return, the interplay of transcendence and immanence becomes a vertical counterpart to the horizontal movement of procession and return, and the symbolic density highlights the dignity of the sanctuary and the altar. Alternatively, one could construe the liturgy as at heart an act faithful to Christ's command to reenact the eucharistic sacrifice, so that the *sacrificial altar* would become the foundation for all else: for the processional path as the route to the altar, the dramatic setting as appropriate for the drama of sacrifice, and for the high symbolic resonance as a reminder of the multiple ways the sacrifice of the cross is relevant in Christian doctrine and history. Just as well, the dramatic emphasis on aspiration, mystery, and timelessness—all elements in the *interplay of transcendence and immanence*—could be taken as the heart of the liturgy and the liturgical space: procession toward the altar, sacramental participation in

Christ's sacrifice, and high symbolic resonance could all be seen as ways of entering into and participating in realities that transcend ordinary experience. From this perspective, the church would be fundamentally a place for sharing in something deeper and more momentous than ordinary life: participation in divine life, in the sacrifice and resurrection of Christ, and in the sacramental life of the Church extended in space and time. Finally, the *high symbolic resonance* could serve as the foundation on which all else rests: processional movement, the sharing in sacrifice, and all the aesthetic features of the church could be taken as elements in or dimensions of the symbolic world that one enters on stepping through the church's doors. But while these links are all possible, none of them is necessary. Sacramental participation in Christ's sacrifice, for example, could take place in an entirely different space, and the other factors interwoven in the tradition of the classic sacramental church could also in principle be detached from that tradition. It may be helpful to begin with one or another of these perspectives, and to entertain them one at a time, while still recognizing that they remain independent and irreducible one to another.

The opposite dogmatism sees modern communal churches as banal in their design, bland in their worship, and impoverished in their symbolic reference. It knows nothing of the way a minimalist aesthetic can build on long-standing traditions of simplicity in design and be infused with a richness of meaning. It is ignorant of architects and writers such as Rudolf Schwarz, or it misjudges them. While easier to understand than the classic sacramental church, the modern communal church also lends itself to misconception and caricature for the opposite reason: precisely its relative simplicity. If the worship space is considered in isolation, it may seem bland in its conception, and it may seem to encourage sedentary habits among worshipers, who may move about in a limited way within a single space, but not from one space to another, and who for the most part are expected merely to sit. This perception is corrected only by looking toward the complex as a whole, meant to accomplish what in a more traditional society might not have been necessary: the gathering of people from disparate places in the workaday world and the formation of a social group that then can become a worshiping assembly. If neither the form of the building nor its decoration suggests obvious richness of symbolic meaning, it may be that the observer has not reflected (or been invited to reflect) deeply on its possible meanings. Here the writings and designs of Rudolf Schwarz are particularly instructive; some of his churches anticipate the development of the modern communal church, and his writings point to multiple levels on which minimalism of form allows for plenitude of meaning. As with any church, the liturgical use of a modern communal space can transform it entirely: a space that seems uninspired when sparsely populated by a sluggish congregation may allow a fuller and more lively assembly to gain a strong sense of its own presence, and one that seems impersonal when filled with an anonymous crowd may serve well in its simplicity when a small contemplative circle is gathered at daybreak or by candlelight.

It does not help, of course, that people who value these traditions often have limited notions of how their own buildings can be conceived and used, that longitudinal space as it is actually employed often *does* distance the altar from the congregation, or that modern communal churches often *are* banal in their design and bland in their liturgical use. Dogmatism arises not in the perception of a problem but in too narrow a view of the solution.

The classic evangelical church is perhaps less often caricatured or mis-understood, not only because the purpose it serves is relatively easy to grasp but also because the burden of fulfilling that purpose is largely shifted from the building to the preaching that occurs within it. One may criticize a partic-ular church because of its awkward design or its imperfections as a space for preaching, but the idea of a preaching-hall is easy enough to grasp, and once the building has fulfilled its role of providing adequate accommodation, proper acoustics, and decent sight lines it has done its job of enabling the preacher to do the real work. The building's role is clearly and straightforwardly a sup-portive one. And yet this simplicity is misleading, because within the broader tradition of evangelical architecture there are variations in which the building is given fuller significance. Jeanne Kilde demonstrates how the auditorium church of the later nineteenth century, grounded as it may be in earlier evan-gelical conceptions, shares characteristics with the newly developing theaters of the era, and shares in a sacrality derived from an unexpected source, from the features it shares with the home, sacralized as a kind of domestic shrine. Here as elsewhere, there is more in church architecture than is dreamed of in the standard accounts.

Another widespread dogmatism holds that buildings conceived and de-signed as sacred must thereby be cut off from the profane world outside—that sacrality means detachment. This misconception underlies the insistence (by those who want sacred space) that churches must have traditional sacred form, distinct from secular architecture. The same misconception lies also behind the demand (from those who do not want sacred space) that churches should be *like* secular buildings of their time. With or without traditionally distinctive idiom, churches can be sacred through recollection of sacred narrative and sacred community widely extended in space and time. They can arouse a lively perception of the holy as a living presence and provide a context for the assem-bly's response to that presence.

The sacred is easily confused with the holy. In their understanding of church architecture, as in their conception of religion generally, people easily succumb to the temptation of taking as absolute what begins in service to the absolute. They do this not necessarily by simple transference, or even out of fondness for the familiar or the novel, but primarily out of sheer clarity of perception and strength of devotion for what they experience as sacred. This perception and this devotion are in themselves positive and valuable. It is for lack of careful consideration of alternatives ("I experience this as sacred—but I might experience that too as sacred") that the perception and the devotion become limiting.

The opposite of dogmatism is orthodoxy: an orthodoxy that looks askance at one-sided formulations, preferring paradox over simple resolution and open-endedness over closure. An orthodox Christology resists the dogmatic assertion that Christ is fully human but in only an extended sense divine. It might see this Christology as sacrificing the conviction of divine compassion and solidarity with humankind, as undermining the Christian claim that God has become flesh and shared its capacity for both grief and pleasure. It would equally distrust the privileging of Christ's divinity, if it encountered that position. So too, an orthodox conception of church architecture is critical of all dogmatic simplicities. While dogmatism claims to have correct positions on every manner of issue, orthodoxy as here understood knows nothing of a single answer to any theological question, or a fixed meaning for any symbol, but rather demands constant pursuit of fuller and richer meanings. It disdains easy or simple answers. Far from requiring cessation of thinking, orthodoxy *forbids* closure of thought. It unmasks supposed truths as partial truths and never ceases to urge further reflection.

History can serve the interests of dogmatism, but it is a better ally of what I am here calling orthodoxy. History relativizes formulations taken as absolute by showing that they are not necessary, but rather grounded in and conditioned by historical circumstances: thus the tabernacle, an invention of the later Middle Ages, may be convenient but cannot be a necessary feature of Roman Catholic (or Anglican) church furnishing. History reveals possibilities that may inspire creative appropriation: Syriac church design may be revived in San Francisco, at Saint Gregory of Nyssa Church, demonstrating that the classic sacramental church can take forms strikingly different from the familiar ones. Less obvious but just as important, history demonstrates that judgments are not stable. What we today call progressive innovation will soon become traditional. What we think of as retrograde may have new purpose and new life breathed into it by some later generation of reformers. Quick judgments will pass quickly into oblivion. History, like life, should breed modesty of claims; like life, it seldom does.

Sövik tells a story about a meeting between the architectural historian Sigfried Giedion and Frank Lloyd Wright. The illustrious architect extended his hand to Giedion, asking: "And who are you?" Giedion replied: "My name is Sigfried Giedion. I am an historian." To which Wright rejoined: "Oh, you write history, you don't make history."[139] Historians identifying with Giedion might find themselves pondering how they might have responded to Wright's withering jibe. "But it is historians who judge whether other people have made history," he might have said. Or, more simply, "Yes, that is why I can sleep well at night." But perhaps the best answer would be that history is what keeps options open and possibilities alive for architecture and for theology.

Apart from any specific formulation or recommendation, Louis Bouyer in the 1960s meant to recommend a renewed focus on the most basic principles of church design in the context of both theology and history. He wrote as a historically informed scholar whose grasp of history was liberating and enabling, calling attention to the broad range of possibilities from the past, and recognizing that the very diversity of options undercuts the claim of any particular norm to be binding for the present and the future. He had a broader and livelier sense of the possibilities for church architecture than most writers on the subject. He could have taken as his motto what any good historian might claim: you shall know the past and the past shall make you free.

Notes

INTRODUCTION

1. Robertson Davies, *The Rebel Angels* (New York: Viking, 1982), 178.

2. Otto Clemen, *Die Volksfrömmigkeit des ausgehenden Mittelalters* (Dresden: C. Ludwig Ungelenk, 1937), 6, referring to an unspecified work of Paul Drews.

3. Augustus J. C. Hare, *The Story of My Life* (New York: Dodd, Mead, 1896), 1:422–23, s.a. 1853. For a *reductio ad absurdum*, see Roz Chast, "Tour of Cathedral #4,019," *New Yorker*, Sept. 10, 2001, p. 112. But then on seeing Matisse's chapel at Vence, Picasso is supposed to have said, "Very pretty, very pretty. But where is the bathroom?" See Rudolf Stegers, *Räume der Wandlung, Wände und Wege: Studien zum Werk von Rudolf Schwarz* (Wiesbaden: Vieweg, 2000), 122, and Oskar Söhngen, "Der Begriff des Sakralen im Kirchenbau," in *Kirchenbau und Ökumene: Evangelische Kirchenbautagung in Hamburg 1961* (Hamburg: Friedrich Wittig Verlag, 1962), 185–86.

4. "Reinterpreting an Ancient Liturgy," *Progressive Architecture* 47, no. 3 (Mar. 1966), 145.

5. For literature on the Romanesque one might begin with Norbert Nußbaum, *St. Aposteln in Köln*, 2nd ed. (Cologne: Rheinischer Verein für Denkmalpflege und Landschaftsschutz, 1985); Werner Schäfke, *Kölns romanische Kirchen: Architektur, Ausstattung, Geschichte* (Cologne: DuMont, 1984); Clemens Kosch, *Kölns Romanische Kirchen: Architektur und Liturgie im Hochmittelalter* (Regensburg: Schnell & Steiner, 2000); and Godehard Hoffmann, *Rheinische Romanik im 19. Jahrhundert* (Cologne: Bachem, 1995). For the cathedral and its context, see Herbert Rode, et al., *Der Kölner Dom: Bau- und Geistesgeschichte* (Cologne: Historisches Museum, 1956); Arnold Wolff, *Cologne Cathedral: Its History—Its Works of Art*, trans. Margret Maranuk-Rohmeder (Cologne: Greven, 1995); Norbert Nussbaum, *German Gothic Church Architecture*, trans. Scott Kleager (New Haven, Conn.: Yale University Press, 2000); and Chris Brooks, *The Gothic Revival* (London: Phaidon, 1999), 261–68.

6. Harold Cave, "Mission Churches in a New Nation," *Churchbuilding* 18 (Apr. 1966), 8.

7. On this church and on Guardini's interpretation see chapter 7.

8. Sally A. Kitt Chappell, "On First Seeing Hagia Sophia," *Chicago Architectural Journal* 8 (1989), 26–27.

9. Paul Tillich, *On Art and Architecture*, ed. John and Jane Dillenberger, trans. Robert P. Scharlemann (New York: Crossroad, 1989), 221–28.

10. J. N. Comper, *Of the Atmosphere of a Church* (London: Sheldon, 1947), 7: "The Doyen of Fécamp Abbey, in Normandy, years ago said to me of his church that it 'prays of itself.' It was a beautiful way of expressing what we mean when we say that a church has an atmosphere."

11. James F. White, "Liturgical Space Forms Faith," *Reformed Liturgy and Music* 22 (1988), 59–60.

12. John Ely Burchard, "A Pilgrimage: Ronchamp, Raincy, Vézelay," *Architectural Record* 123, no. 3 (Mar. 1958), 171–78.

13. See the examples in Laura Chester, *Holy Personal: Looking for Small Private Places of Worship* (Bloomington: Indiana University Press, 2000).

14. The image may be fitting on more than one level. Oskar Söhngen, "Die Wallfahrtskirche von Ronchamp: Zum Problem des Sakralen im modernen Kirchenbau," in *Reich Gottes und Wirklichkeit: Festgabe für Alfred Dedo Müller zum 70. Geburtstag* (Berlin: Evangelische Verlagsanstalt, 1961), 184, comments that the chapel presents itself as a cave on the height, *eine Höhle auf der Höhe*. See also Söhngen, "Der Begriff des Sakralen im Kirchenbau," 6. Söhngen finds Ronchamp a model of sacrality more effective for Catholic use than many churches built by Catholic architects, which of course presupposes a particular understanding of Catholicity.

15. Karl Rörlich, "Gemeinde und Kirche im Wandel," in Peter Müllenborn, et al., *St. Fronleichnam, Aachen, 1930–1980* ([Aachen: The Church, 1980]), 40–43.

16. Lindsay Jones, *The Hermeneutics of Sacred Architecture: Experience, Interpretation, Comparison* (Cambridge, Mass.: Harvard University Press, 2000), 2:213. For a popular account of San Francisco Acatepec, see Judith Dupré, *Churches* (New York: HarperCollins, 2001), 72–73.

17. E. F. Jansson, "Church Building in Chicago since 1833," in *The Place of the Church in a Century of Progress, 1833 to 1933* (Chicago: Chicago Church Federation, 1933), 28.

18. Eric Gill, "Mass for the Masses," in *Sacred & Secular &c* (London: Dent, 1940), 153–54.

19. "Meeting House of the First Unitarian Society of Madison, Wis.," *Architectural Forum* 97, no. 6 (Dec. 1952), 86.

20. Edward A. Sövik, "A Portfolio of Reflections on the Design of Northfield Methodist Church," *Your Church* 13, no. 5 (Sept./Oct. 1967), 57.

21. Rainer Volp, "Space as Text: The Problem of Hermeneutics in Church Architecture," *Studia liturgica* 24 (1994), 175. Volp cites Bernhard Schneider, "Der Raum als Text," *Kunst und Kirche* 39 (1976), 175–78.

22. Patrick J. Quinn, "The Symbolic Function of Church-Building," *Churchbuilding* 10 (Oct. 1963), 4.

23. Friedrich Wilhelm Deichmann, "Entstehung der christlichen Basilika und Entstehung des Kirchengebäudes: Zum Verhältnis von Zweck und Form in der

frühchristlichen Architektur," in *Rom, Ravenna, Konstantinopel, Naher Osten: Gesammelte Studien zur spätantiken Architektur, Kunst und Geschichte* (Wiesbaden: Steiner, 1982), 35–46. See Sible de Blaauw, "Architecture and Liturgy in Late Antiquity and the Middle Ages," *Archiv für Liturgiewissenschaft* 33 (1991), 28.

24. Jones, *Hermeneutics of Sacred Architecture*. Jones shows a strong preference for monastic churches and for certain churches of Renaissance Italy but generally neglects ordinary parish and community churches—even though he argues the importance of lay experience.

25. Dupré, *Churches*, 144–45. Alexander Liberman, *Prayers in Stone* (New York: Random House, 1997), is another book mainly of photographs, with personal commentary on the buildings seen mostly apart from their liturgical use.

26. Margaret Visser, *The Geometry of Love: Space, Time, Mystery and Meaning in an Ordinary Church* (New York: North Point, 2001). Visser sees a church as "laid out with a certain trajectory of the soul in mind" (p. 4), as "a recognition, in stone and wood and brick, of spiritual awakenings" (p. 11), but more "mystical" than liturgical.

27. For example, Alec Clifton-Taylor, *The Cathedrals of England* (London: Thames and Hudson, 1976), 99–106. Thomas Cocke and Peter Kidson, *Salisbury Cathedral: Perspectives on the Architectural History* (London: HMSO, 1993), touches glancingly on the use of Sarum.

28. Thomas F. Mathews, *The Early Churches of Constantinople: Architecture and Liturgy* (University Park: Pennsylvania State University Press, 1971); Rowland J. Mainstone, *Hagia Sophia: Architecture, Structure and Liturgy of Justinian's Great Church* (London: Thames and Hudson, 1988), and Robert Ousterhout, "The Holy Space: architecture and the Liturgy," in Linda Safran, ed., *Heaven on Earth: Art and the Church in Byzantium* (University Park: Pennsylvania State University Press, 1998), 81–120. De Blaauw, "Architecture and Liturgy, 9–10, notes that for Constantinople we have exceptional wealth of both archeological and documentary evidence, making it possible to study in some detail the relations between architecture and liturgy. (At the beginning of this excellent review, de Blaauw gives further examples of inattention to the liturgical use of churches.)

29. Daniel Lee, "Architecture's role in Christianity," *Sacred Architecture* 2 (fall 1998), 15.

30. See the comments of Donald Schell, "Rending the Temple Veil: Holy Space in Holy Community," in John Runkle, ed., *Searching for Sacred Space: Essays on Architecture and Liturgical Design in the Episcopal Church* (New York: Church Publishing, 2002), 156–61, on Christopher Alexander's conception of sacred space, in Christopher Alexander, Sara Ishikawa, and Murray Silverstein, *A Pattern Language: Towns, Buildings, Construction* (New York: Oxford University Press, 1977), 131–34 (chap. 24, "Sacred Sites"), and 331–34 (chap. 66, "Holy Ground"); the chief goal here is not that access should be limited to special individuals (priests) but that sacred space should require the effort of passage through a succession of spaces. For recent advocacy of restricted visibility see Michael R. Carey, "Veiling the Mysteries," *Sacred Architecture* (winter/spring 2000), pp. 23–27.

31. For an important critique of this approach to interpretation see Paul Crossley, "Medieval Architecture and Meaning: The Limits of Iconography," *Burlington Magazine* 130 (1988), 116–21.

32. Françoise Fromonot and Renaud Ego, "Shigeru Ban: L'élegance et l'urgence,"

Architecture d'aujourd'hui, 306 (Sept. 1996), 40–47, refers to Shigeru Ban's cardboard churches at Kobe and Takatori. Less to the point, perhaps, is the "inflatable church" marketed in 2003 by Michael Gill.

33. Martin Foreman, *Beverley Friary: The History and Archaeology of an Urban Monastery* (Beverley: Hutton Press, 1998), 38. Ronald Tallon, "Knockanure Church,"in John Donat, ed., *World Architecture 2* (London: Studio Vista, 1965), 75, complains that in Ireland churches "cannot be built without copying past styles," barely recognizable in their modern form yet generally acceptable if made of stone. But see John Ely Burchard, "Architecture for the Good Life," *Architectural Record* 120, no. 1 (Jul. 1956); 198: "The first temple of Apollo at Delphi was of wood and legend follows it with one of feathers and beeswax and one of brass but it ended in stone. It did not end in stone because the Greeks who built it cared only about what their successors would think; but because they expected both to gain current enjoyment and profit from its use and to leave it to a posterity which would enjoy it and for the same reasons."

34. Rudolf Arnheim, *The Dynamics of Architectural Form* (Berkeley: University of California Press, 1977), 146.

35. Michael Hall, "What Do Victorian Churches Mean? Symbolism and Sacramentalism in Anglican Church Architecture, 1850–1870," *Journal of the Society of Architectural Historians* 59 (2000), 83.

36. Edwin Heathcote, "On the Fast Track to the Middle of Nowhere: Architect Renzo Piano Talks to Edwin Heathcote about How and Why He Is Building the Largest Modern Church in Europe," *Financial Times*, Jun. 16/17, 2001, weekend sec., p. viii. See also Rahel Hartmann, "Muschel, griechisches Theater, gotische Kathedrale: Kirche für Padre Pio in San Giovanni in Rotondo, Foggia, von Renzo Piano," *Kunst und Kirche* 2001, no. 3, 154–56, and Cesare de Seta, *Architetture della fede in Italia* (Milan: Bruno Mondadori, 2003), 207–9, for placement of this church in a broader Italian context.

37. L. F. Salzman, *Building in England down to 1540: A Documentary History*, new ed. (Oxford: Oxford University Press, 1997), 119.

38. R. R. Langham-Carter, "South Africa's First Woman Architect," *Architect and Builder* 17 (Mar. 1967), 17.

39. *Built of Living Stones: Art, Architecture, and Worship: Guidelines of the National Conference of Catholic Bishops* (Washington, D.C.: United States Catholic Conference, 2000).

40. *The Oxford English Dictionary*, s.v. "church," discusses the controverted technicalities of the etymology and inclines to take the word as derived from the Greek *kuriakon*, meaning "house of the Lord." See also Bruno Bürki, *La case des chrétiens: Essai de théologie pratique sur le lieu de culte en Afrique* (Yaounde, Cameroon: CLE, 1973), 23.

CHAPTER I

1. Douglas R. Hoffman, "Seeking the Sacred: A Response to Edward Sövik's 'Remembrance and hope,'" *Faith and Form* 30 2 (1997), 12–13.

2. Thomas Barrie, *Spiritual Path, Sacred Place: Myth, Ritual, and Meaning in Sacred Architecture* (Boston: Shambhala, 1996).

3. Ibid., chap. 5, pp. 79–148.

4. Ibid., 28.

5. Ibid., 213–32; the discussion of liturgy is on pp. 230-31. He seems to confuse daily mass with Sunday mass, interprets the kiss of peace as priest's kissing of the gospel book (which he places after the offertory), takes no notice of the canon of the mass, and conflates the dismissal at the end of mass with the early Church's dismissal of the catechumens. And he appears not to grasp the difference or relationship between a monastic church and a cathedral.

6. Particularly important for the architecture and its liturgical use is Sible L. de Blaauw, *Cultus et decor: Liturgie en architectuur in laatantiek en middeleeuws Rome: Basilica Salvatoris, Santae Mariae, Sancti Petri* (Delft: Eburon, 1987), 163–218, also available in Italian. See also Roberto Luciani and Francesco Maria Amato, *Santa Maria Maggiore e Roma* (Rome: Palombi, 1996).

7. Richard Krautheimer, "The Architecture of Sixtus III: A Fifth-Century Renascence?" in *Essays in Honor of Erwin Panofsky*, ed. Millard Meiss, (New York, 1961), 291–302; Richard Krautheimer and Slobodan Curcic, *Early Christian and Byzantine Architecture*, 4th ed. (Harmondsworth: Penguin, 1992), 89–92. See now also Gabriele Bartolozzi Casti, "Battisteri presbiteriale in Roma: Un nuovo intervento di Sisto III?" *Studi romani* 47 (1999), 270–88.

8. Giovanni Battista Piranesi, "Veduta interna della Basilica di S. Maria Maggiore," in *Piranesi: Rome Recorded: A Complete Edition of Giovanni Battista Piranesi's "Vedute di Roma" from the Collection of the Arthur Ross Foundation* (New York: Arthur Ross Foundation, 1989), p. 175, no. 86, with text by Robin B. Williams, 102.

9. Thomas F. Mathews, *The Clash of Gods: A Reinterpretation of Early Christian Art*, rev. ed. (Princeton, N.J.: Princeton University Press, 1999), 92–94.

10. Susan Twyman, *Papal Ceremonial at Rome in the Twelfth Century* (Woodbridge, Suffolk: Boydell and Brewer, 2002).

11. Peter Hammond, *Liturgy and Architecture* (London: Barrie and Rockliff, 1960), 47; Christopher V. Stroik, *Path, Portal, Path: Architecture for the Rites* (Chicago: Liturgy Training, 1999), 60; Robert Maguire and Keith Murray, "Anglican Church in Stepney," *Churchbuilding* 7 (Oct. 1962), 15.

12. Notice on Richard J. Neutra and Robert E. Alexander's interdenominational chapel at Miramar, California, in *Architectural Record*, 119, no. 6 (Jun. 1956), 212–14, referring to Neutra's notions about the physiological basis for processions, in *Survival through Design* (New York: Oxford University Press, 1954).

13. Reinhard Gieselmann, *Contemporary Church Architecture* (London: Thames and Hudson, 1972), 70; Egon Tempel, *New Japanese Architecture*, trans. E. Rockwell (London: Thames and Hudson, 1969), 136–39. The cathedral was built in 1967–69.

14. Frédéric Debuyst, *Modern Architecture and Christian Celebration* (London: Lutterworth, 1968), 45, represents traditional seating as fixing the congregation in "a kind of static procession."

15. Giuseppe Bovini, *The Churches of Ravenna* (n.p.: Instituto geografico de Agostini, 1960), *Sant'Apollinare Nuovo in Ravenna*, trans. J. Templeton (Milan: Silvana, 1961), and *San Vitale Ravenna*, trans. Basil Taylor (Milan: Silvana, 1956). On Desider-

ius Lenz and his attempt to accomplish a similar processional effect with murals in the early twentieth century, see Rudolf Schwarz, *Vom Bau der Kirche*, new ed. (Salzburg: Pustet, 1998), 119–21, in English as *The Church Incarnate: The Sacred Function of Christian Architecture*, trans. Cynthia Harris (Chicago: Regnery, 1958), 145–47.

16. Albert Christ-Janer and Mary Mix Foley, *Modern Church Architecture: A Guide to the Form and Spirit of Twentieth-Century Religious Buildings* (New York: McGraw-Hill, 1962), 103–17.

17. Gieselmann, *Contemporary Church Architecture*, 64–66. The church was built in 1959–62.

18. Maguire and Murray, "Anglican Church in Stepney," 15–16. Maguire and Murray point out that the aisles of a Gothic church building, particularly when they are vaulted, have a longitudinal direction distinct from that of the nave; each aisle becomes "a compartment with its own directional 'pull' unrelated to the place of the altar." See also Robert Maguire, "Church Design since 1950," *Ecclesiology Today* 27 (Jan. 2002), 2–14; Edwin Heathcote and Iona Spens, *Church Builders* (Chichester, England: Academy, 1997), 68–73.

19. Rudolf Arnheim, *The Dynamics of Architectural Form* (Berkeley: University of California Press, 1977), 158–61; the comment on Alberti's church follows a suggestion by Nikolaus Pevsner.

20. Robert W. Jenson, "God, Space, and Architecture," *Response* 8 (1967), 157–62; reprinted in Jenson, *Essays in Theology of Culture* (Grand Rapids, Mich.: Eerdmans, 1995), 9–15.

21. John A. T. Robinson, *Honest to God* (Philadelphia: Westminster, 1963), and Gregory Baum, *Man Becoming: God in Secular Language* (New York: Herder and Herder, 1970), popularized a debate regarding divine transcendence.

22. Perhaps most obviously in Matthew 6:9–10. Jenson's sharp distinction between "the God of religion" and "the God of the gospel" also assumes, with Marcion, that the New Testament is not contextualized by traditions of Israel rooted in what the earliest Christian communities had accepted as the Old Testament.

23. Terence Bailey, *The Processions of Sarum and the Western Church* (Toronto: Pontifical Institute of Mediaeval Studies, 1971).

24. Ibid., 1–26.

25. George J. Booth, *The Offertory Rite in the Ordo Romanus Primus: A Study of Its Bearing on the So-Called "Offertory Procession"* (Washington, D.C.: Catholic University of America Press, 1948).

26. Claudio Zaccaria, Gino Bandelli, and Mario Mirabella Roberti, *Aquileia romana e cristiana fra II e V secolo* (Trieste: Editreg, 2000).

27. Joseph A. Jungmann, *The Mass of the Roman Rite: Its Origins and Development (Missarum Sollemnia)*, trans. Francis A. Bruner, vol. 2 (New York: Benziger, 1955), 374–75.

28. By Benjamin D. Sommer, March 1, 2001, at the corner of Chicago Avenue and Church Street in Evanston, Illinois.

29. Sible de Blaauw, "Architecture and Liturgy in Late Antiquity and the Middle Ages," *Archiv für Liturgiewissenschaft* 33 (1991), 26–27; Paul Binski, "The English Parish Church and Its Art in the Later Middle Ages: A Review of the Problem," *Studies in Iconography* 20 (1999), 10–14.

30. Nancy Edwards, *The Archaeology of Early Medieval Ireland* (Philadelphia: University of Pennsylvania Press, 1990), 122.

31. Eamon Duffy, *The Stripping of the Altars: Traditional Religion in England, c. 1400–c. 1580* (New Haven: Yale University Press, 1992); Jacqueline Jung, "Beyond the Barrier: The Unifying Role of the Choir Screen in Gothic Churches," *Art Bulletin* 82 (2000), 622–57.

32. Charles James Stranks, *Dean Hook* (London: Mowbray, 1954); John Jebb, *The Choral Service of the United Church of England and Ireland: Being an Enquiry into the Liturgical System of the Cathedral and Collegiate Foundations of the Anglican Communion* (London: Parker, 1843), especially 17–20.

33. Elain Harwood, "Liturgy and Architecture: The Development of the Centralised Eucharistic Space," in *Twentieth Century Architecture: The Journal of the Twentieth Century Society*, 3 (1998), 56; Basil F.L. Clarke, *Church Builders of the Nineteenth Century* (London: SPCK, 1938, 209–15.

34. H. Benedict Green, "A Liturgical Brief," in Peter Hammond, ed., *Towards a Church Architecture* (London: Architectural Press, 1962), 102–3; see Hammond, *Liturgy and Architecture*, 44.

35. Wolfgang Pehnt, *Gottfried Böhm* (Basel: Birkhäuser, 1999), 74–79.

36. John Harvey, *English Cathedrals*, rev. ed. (London: Batsford, 1961), 17–18, 31–32; Alec Clifton-Taylor, *The Cathedrals of England* (London: Thames and Hudson, 1976), 19–21.

37. Bernard Bevan, *History of Spanish Architecture* (London: Batsford, 1938), is dated but still worth consulting on Spanish churches. At Morella, space constraints on the site led the builders of the collegiate church to devise a choir erected on stilt-like pillars over the nave.

38. Margaret Haines, ed., *Santa Maria del Fiore: The Cathedral and Its Sculpture: Acts of the International Symposium for the VII Centenary of the Cathedral of Florence, Florence, Villa I Tatti, 5–6 June 1997* (Fiesole: Cadmo, 2001); Timothy Verdon and Annalisa Innocenti, eds., *Atti del VII centenario del Duomo di Firenze* (Florence: Edifir, 2001).

39. Royal Commission on Historical Monuments, *St. Albans Cathedral* (London: HMSO, 1952); Eileen Roberts, *The Hill of the Martyr: An Architectural History of St. Albans Abbey* (Dunstable: Book Castle, 1993); Martin Henig and Phillip Lindley, eds., *Alban and St Albans: Roman and Medieval Architecture, Art and Archaeology* (Leeds: British Archaeological Association, 2001).

40. Ernest Woolley, "The Wooden Watching Loft in St. Albans Abbey Church," *Transactions of the St. Albans and Hertfordshire Architectural and Archaeological Society* (1929), pp. 246–54.

41. Robert Ridgway Lloyd, *An Architectural and Historical Account of the Shrines of Saint Alban and Saint Amphibalus in Saint Alban's Abbey* (St. Albans, Hertfordshire: Langley, 1873). On "Saint Overcoat," see John Morris, "Celtic Saints: A Note," *Past and Present* 11 (Apr. 1957), 9.

42. G. H. Cook, *The English Mediaeval Parish Church* (London: Phoenix House, 1954), 61–70.

43. Paul Binski, "The Murals in the Nave of St Alban's Abbey," in D. Abulafia, M. Franklin, and M. Rubin, eds., *Church and City, 1000–1500: Essays in Honour of*

Christopher Brooke (1992), 249–78; Eileen Roberts, *The Wall Paintings of Saint Albans Abbey*, rev. ed. (St Albans, Hertfordshire: Fraternity of Friends of St Albans Abbey, 1993).

44. C.N.L. Brooke, "Religious Sentiment and Church Design in the Later Middle Ages," *Bulletin of the John Rylands Library* 50 (1967), 13–33; reprinted in *Medieval Church and Society: Collected Essays* (London, 1971), 162–82.

45. See now H. M. Taylor, "The Anglo-Saxon Cathedral Church at Canterbury," in *The Archaeology of Anglo-Saxon England: Basic Readings* (New York: Garland, 1999), 155–94.

46. Frederick Hancock, *Dunster Church and Priory: Their History and Architectural Features* (Taunton: Barnicott and Pearce, 1905); Katherine L. French, "Competing for Space: The Monastic-Parochial Church at Dunster," *Journal of Medieval and Early Modern Studies* 27 (1997), 215–44.

47. Dell Upton, *Holy Things and Profane: Anglican Parish Churches in Colonial Virginia* (Cambridge, Mass.: MIT Press, 1986), 222.

48. Designed by John Goldman (1995); see Richard Fabian, *Worship at St Gregory's: Millennium Edition* ([San Francisco]: All Saints', 2001), 11–17; Richard Giles, "St Gregory of Nyssa, San Francisco," *Church Building* (March–April 1999), 47–48; Michael J. Crosbie, "Urban Religious Spaces: Designing for Liturgy," *Faith and Form: Journal of the Interfaith Forum on Religion, Art and Architecture* 31 2 (1998), 16–17; Michael J. Crosbie, *Architecture for the Gods* (New York: Watson-Guptill, 2000), 128–34. See also Donald Schell, "Rending the Temple Veil: Holy Space in Holy Community," in John Runkle, ed., *Searching for Sacred Space: Essays on Architecture and Liturgical Design in the Episcopal Church* (New York: Church Publishing, 2002), 149–81.

49. This solution obviously breaks from the tradition of orientation, a matter on which Bouyer was willing to make accommodation, although for Joseph Cardinal Ratzinger, *The Spirit of the Liturgy*, trans. John Saward (San Francisco: Ignatius, 2000), 74–84, this is a crucial feature in Bouyer's interpretation.

50. Louis Bouyer, *Liturgy and Architecture* (Notre Dame, Ind.: University of Notre Dame Press, 1967).

51. Bouyer gives a generic account of each type of church he deals with, distilling what he finds useful; he thus draws from history but does not pretend to be making a contribution specifically to historical scholarship. For the Syriac churches see G.W.O. Addleshaw, *The Ecclesiology of the Churches of the Dead Cities of Northern Syria* (London: Ecclesiological Society, 1973); Howard Crosby Butler, *Early Churches in Syria: Fourth to Seventh Centuries*, ed. E. Baldwin Smith (Princeton: Department of Art and Archaeology of Princeton Universtity, 1929; Lizette Larson-Miller, "A Return to the Liturgical Architecture of Northern Syria," *Studia liturgica* 24 (1994), 71–83; and de Blaauw, "Architecture and Liturgy," 6–7.

52. Krautheimer and Curcic, *Early Christian and Byzantine Architecture*, 75–78. For an Alsatian church in this tradition, see Judith and Hans Jakob Wörner, *Abteikirche Ottmarsheim* (Lindenberg: Kunstverlag Josef Fink, 1998).

53. Krautheimer and Curcic, *Early Christian and Byzantine Architecture*, 144–51.

54. Josef Fink, *Das Petrusgrab im Rom* (Vienna: Tyrolia, 1988); Graf Franz Woff Metternich and Hildegard Giess, *Die Erbauung der Peterskirche zu Rom im 16. Jahrhundert* (Vienna: Schroll, 1972–); Thea and Richard Bergere, *The Story of St. Peter's* (New York: Dodd, Mead, 1966).

55. Nnamdi Elleh, *African Architecture: Evolution and Transformation* (New York: McGraw-Hill, 1997), 168.

56. On the influence of the Jerusalem church see Richard Krautheimer, "Introduction to an 'Iconography of Mediaeval Architecture,'" *Journal of the Warburg and Courtauld Institutes* 5 (1942), 3–20.

57. Dorothée Hugot, *Aachen Cathedral: A Guide*, trans. Peter Marsden (Aachen: Einhard, 2000), 27–29; Ernst Günter Grimme, *Der goldene Dom der Ottonen* (Aachen: Einhard, 2001). The original position of the throne has been established only recently; see Sven Schütte, "Der Aachener Thron," in Mario Kramp, ed., *Krönungen: Könige in Aachen, Geschichte und Mythos* (Mainz: Von Zabern, 2000), 213–22, and "Überlegungen zu den architektonischen Vorbildern der Pfalzen Ingelheim und Aachen," 203–11.

58. Steven J. Schloeder, *Architecture in Communion: Implementing the Second Vatican Council through Liturgy and Architecture* (San Francisco: Ignatius, 1998), 182; Robert Ousterhout, "The Holy Space: Architecture and the Liturgy," in Linda Safran, ed., *Heaven on Earth: Art and the Church in Byzantium* (University Park: Pennsylvania State University Press, 1998), 87; Sharon E. J. Gerstel, *Beholding the Sacred Mysteries: Programs of the Byzantine Sanctuary* (Seattle: College Art Association and University of Washington Press, 1999), 5–14.

59. Sally A. Kitt Chappell, "On First Seeing Hagia Sophia," *Chicago Architectural Journal* 8 (1989), 26.

60. Thomas F. Mathews, *The Early Churches of Constantinople: Architecture and Liturgy* (University Park: Pennsylvania State University Press, 1980); de Blaauw, "Architecture and Liturgy," 9–10.

61. Thomas F. Mathews, "Religious Organization and Church Architecture," in Helen C. Evans and William D. Wixom, eds., *The Glory of Byzantium: Art and Culture of the Middle Byzantine Era, A.D. 843–1261* (New York: Metropolitan Museum of Art, 1997), 20–35.

62. Martin S. Briggs, *Puritan Architecture and Its Future* (London: Lutterworth, 1946), 15–18; Stephen C. Humphrey, ed., *Churches and Chapels of Southern England (Blue Guide)* (New York: Norton, 1991), 519; Christopher Stell, "Puritan and Nonconformist Meetinghouses in England," in Paul Corby Finney, ed., *Seeing beyond the Word: Visual Arts and the Calvinist Tradition* (Grand Rapids, Mich.: Eerdmans, 1999), 51.

63. John von Rohr, *The Shaping of American Congregationalism, 1620–1957* (Cleveland: Pilgrim, 1992), 44–45 (on "Old World antecedents"), and Jeanne Halgren Kilde, *When Church Became Theatre: The Transformation of Evangelical Architecture and Worship in Nineteenth-Century America* (New York: Oxford University Press, 2002), 77.

64. Joseph Siry, *Unity Temple: Frank Lloyd Wright and Architecture for Liberal Religion* (New York: Cambridge University Press, 1996); Robert McCarter, *Unity Temple: Frank Lloyd Wright* (London: Phaidon, 1997).

65. The same is true of Willow Creek Church, on which see Jeanne Halgren Kilde, "Architecture and Urban Revivalism in Nineteenth-Century America," in Peter W. Williams, ed., *Perspective on American Religion and Culture* (Malden, Mass.: Blackwell, 1999), 185.

66. Robert G. Calkins, *Medieval Architecture in Western Europe: From A.D. 300 to 1500* (New York: Oxford University Press, 1998), 133–34, 271, 275–76.

67. To cite merely one concrete example, the efforts of the town council and of Jakob Fugger to provide for preaching in Augsburg are traced in some detail in Rolf Kießling, *Bürgerliche Gesellschaft und Kirche in Augsburg im Spätmittelalter: Ein Beitrag zur Strukturanalyse der oberdeutschen Reichsstadt* (Augsburg: Mühlberger, 1971), 147–50, 301–5. Bernd Moeller, "Religious Life in Germany on the Eve of the Reformation," in Gerald Strauss, ed., *Pre-Reformation Germany* (London: Macmillan, 1972), 28–29, speaks briefly about the role of preaching.

68. Quoted in Margaret Whinney, *Wren* (London: Thames and Hudson, 1971), 48 (capitalization modernized).

69. Upton, *Holy Things and Profane*, 199; Upton goes on to analyze the church as the terminus of movement from the surrounding community.

70. Karen B. Westerfield Tucker, "'Plain and Decent': Octagonal Space and Methodist Worship," *Studia liturgica* 24 (1994), 129–44. Tucker points out that the German architect Leonhard Christoph Sturm had used the octagonal plan earlier in the eighteenth century and that it was known among the Dutch Reformed in Holland itself and in North America.

71. On Protestant church architecture generally, see James F. White, *Protestant Worship and Church Architecture: Theological and Historical Considerations* (New York: Oxford University Press, 1964), and Klaus Raschzok and Reiner Sörries, eds., *Geschichte des protestantischen Kirchenbaues* (Erlangen: Junge and Sohn, 1994). On the Anglican tradition, see Nigel Yates, *Buildings, Faith and Worship: The Liturgical Arrangement of Anglican Churches, 1600–1900*, rev. ed. (Oxford: Oxford University Press, 2000).

72. Built 1563, destroyed 1567; attributed to Jean Perrissin. See André Steyert, *Nouvelle Histoire de Lyon*, 3 (Lyon: Bernoux and Cumin, 1899), 143–44 (fig. 185–86); Natalis Rondot, *Les Protestants à Lyon au dix-septième siècle* (Lyon, 1891), 16–17 and 172–73.

73. On Finney and his career, see Charles E. Hambrick-Stowe, *Charles G. Finney and the Spirit of American Evangelicalism* (Grand Rapids, Mich.: Eerdmans, 1996).

74. James Brand and John M. Ellis, *Memorial Addresses on the Occasion of the One Hundredth Anniversary of the Birth of President Charles G. Finney* (Oberlin: Goodrich, 1893).

75. Kilde, "Architecture and Urban Revivalism in Nineteenth-Century America," 183–84.

76. Sara Holmes Boutelle, *Julia Morgan, Architect* (New York: Abbeville Press, 1988), 69. The building dates from 1906–7.

77. Michael Burden, *Lost Adelaide: A Photographic Record* (Melbourne: Oxford University Press, 1983), 81. The architect was Edmund Wright.

78. Walter A. Taylor, "A Survey: Protestant Church Design in America," *Architectural Record* 86, no. 1 (Jul. 1939), 67.

79. Hélène Guicharnaud, "An Introduction to the Architecture of Protestant Temples Constructed in France before the Revocation of the Edict of Nantes," trans. Raymond Mentzer, in Finney, *Seeing Beyond the Word*, 133–55; Andrew Spicer, "Architecture," in Andrew Pettegree, ed., *The Reformation World* (London: Routledge), 514–15.

80. Among older works, Murk Daniël Ozinga, *Protestantsche kerken hier te land gesticht, 1596–1793: onderzoek naar hun bouw- en ontwikkelingsgeschiedenis* (Amsterdam: H. J. Paris, 1929), and F. A. J. Vermeulen, *Handboek tot de geschiedenis der Nederland-*

sche bouwkunst ('S-Gravenhage: Nijhoff, 1928–41), vol. 2, pt. 1, pp. 354–404. More recently, W. Kuyper, *Dutch Classicist Architecture: A Survey of Dutch Architecture, Gardens and Anglo-Dutch Architectural Relations from 1625 to 1700* (Delft: Delft University Press, 1980), 1–56; Jakob Rosenberg, Seymour Slive, and E.H. ter Kuile, *Dutch Art and Architecture, 1600 to 1800* (Harmondsworth: Penguin, 1966). For background, see Jeremy Dupertuis Bangs, *Church Art and Architecture in the Low Countries before 1566* (Kirksville, Mo.: Sixteenth Century Journal, 1997).

81. Arie van Deursen, "Church and City Government in Amsterdam," in Peteer van Kessel and Elisja Schulte, eds., *Rome, Amsterdam: Two Growing Cities in Seventeenth-Century Europe* (Amsterdam: Amsterdam University Press, 1997), 175–79.

82. Frederik F. Barends, *Geloven in de schaduw: Schuilkerken in Amsterdam* (Gent: Snoeck-Ducaju and Zoon, 1996). Two particularly important examples survive: Ons' Lieve Heer op Solder was originally created as an attic chapel in 1663; and the Begijnhof Chapel was created in 1680 by remodeling interiors at the lower levels of adjacent houses.

83. While synagogues are beyond the scope of this book, it is worth noting that the classical period of church-building was also the prime era of synagogue construction. Particularly noteworthy—and recognized as such immediately—was the Portuguese Synagogue, built in 1671–75, designed by Elias Bouman in a classical idiom, with broad windows affording a sense of spaciousness and openness comparable to that of the Westerkerk. The synagogues of Amsterdam are treated in the general histories of Dutch architecture; see also Helen Rosenau, "The Synagogue and Protestant Church Architecture," *Journal of the Warburg and Courtault Institutes* 4 (1940), 80–84.

84. Ernest Kurpershoek, *The Nieuwe Kerk, Amsterdam*, trans. Sammy Herman (Amsterdam: Nationale Stifting De Nieuwe Kerk, 1999); Marijke Beek and Ernest Kurpershoek, *Amsterdams Nieuwe Kerk* (Amsterdam: Tiebosch/Scala, 1983).

85. *Grote of St.-Bavokerk, Haarlem, Holland* (Haarlem: Kerkvoogdij Hervormde Gemeente Haarlem, n.d.).

86. Walter Kramer, *De Noorderkerk in Amsterdam* (Zwolle, The Netherlands: Waanders, 1998); J. Kramps-van Drunen, *Ontmoeting met de Westerkerk* ([Amsterdam: The Church], n.d.).

87. Kuyper, *Dutch Classicist Architecture*, 10.

88. Jebb, *The Choral Service*, 202–3, complained about the use in England of conspicuous organs, a custom that he blamed on Holland, which in the seventeenth century was "seized with the mania of building gigantic and noisy organs," "enormous music-mills" whose "barbarous crash is more fit for Nebuchadnezzar's festival, than for that sweet and grave accompaniment for which our best Cathedral organs were fully sufficient."

89. Kramps-van Drunen, *Ontmoeting*, 7.

90. Jeroen Giltaij and Guido Jansen, eds., *Perspectives: Saenredam and the Architectural Painters of the Seventeenth Century: 15/9–24/11/91, Museum Boymans–Van Beuningen Rotterdam* (Rotterdam: Museum, 1991); *Dutch Church Painters: Saenredam's Great Church at Haarlem in Context: National Gallery of Scotland 6 July–9 September 1984* (Edinburgh: National Gallery of Scotland, 1984).

91. Gary Schwartz and Marten Jan Bok, *Pieter Saenredam: The Painter and His Time* (New York: Abbeville, 1989), 15, 21, 33–34, 74–75, 83–84, 97, 138, 204–6, 228–32.

92. Mark Allen Torgerson, "Edward Anders Sövik and His Return to the 'Non-Church,'" (Ph.D. diss., University of Notre Dame, 1995); Mark A. Torgerson, "An Architect's Response to Liturgical Reform: Edward A. Sövik and His 'Non-Church' Design," *Worship* 71 (1997), 19–41 (response from Sövik, "Forum: Notes on Mark Torgerson's Quire," 244–47, drawing back from the term "non-church"). Michael S. Rose, *Ugly as Sin: Why They Changed Our Churches from Sacred Places to Meeting Spaces and How We Can Change Them Back Again* (Manchester, N.H.: Sophia Institute Press, 2001), 154–66, gives a critique.

93. Donald J. Bruggink and Carl H. Droppers, *When Faith Takes Form: Contemporary Churches of Architectural Integrity in America* (Grand Rapids, Mich.: Eerdmans, 1971), 62–67.

94. Debuyst, *Modern Architecture and Christian Celebration*, especially 9–10 and 13. The idea of a church as a livingroom is in a quotation from Bishop Wilhelmus Bekkers, to which Debuyst assents with the specified condition.

95. Ralph Edward Peterson, "Social Values and Religious Architecture," *Faith and Form* 9 (fall 1976), 7; see Gretchen T. Buggeln, "Architecture as Community Service: West Presbyterian Church in Wilmington, Delaware," in David Morgan and Sally M. Promey, eds., *The Visual Culture of American Religion* (Berkeley: University of California Press, 2001), 95–96. An item in a church newsletter, reproduced as an ironic newsbreak in *The New Yorker*, Dec. 20, 1976, p. 114, tells of a filmstrip on "how to make church buildings more functional," with arrangements for "intimacy, hospitality, futility and flexibility."

96. James F. White, "From Protestant to Catholic Plain Style," in Finney, *Seeing beyond the Word*, 473–76: "Reformed principles in the design of church architecture live on but now in a different community—Presbyterians seem to have forgotten these principles while Roman Catholics have appropriated them!"

97. Gieselmann, *Contemporary Church Architecture*, 28–29 (*Langräume*), 74–75 (*Querräume*), and 122–23 (*Zentralräume*).

98. Appendix to Liturgy Constitution, art. 128 (Declarations of Preparatory Commission for a clearer explanation of certain articles), in *Church Architecture: The Shape of Reform* (Washington, D.C.: Liturgical Conference, 1965), 98–102: "The fitting place for the main altar is midway between the presbytery and the people, i.e., in the middle of the assembly (ideally, not mathematically computed). It is praiseworthy, in as much as the edifice permits, to have this altar covered with a canopy or baldachin in order to show its holiness."

99. E.A. Sovik, *Architecture for Worship* (Minneapolis: Augsburg, 1973), 33.

100. E.A. Sovik, "The Place of Worship: Environment for Action," in Mandus A. Egge, ed., *Worship: Good News in Action* (Minneapolis: Augsburg, 1973), 94–110; also Sövik, "Remembrance and Hope," *Faith and Form* 30 no. 2 (1997), 9–11.

101. Edward A. Sövik, "A Portfolio of Reflections on the Design of Northfield Methodist Church," *Your Church* 13, no. 5 (Sept./Oct. 1967), 59.

102. James F. White and Susan J. White, *Church Architecture: Building and Renovating for Christian Worship*, new ed. (Akron, Ohio: OSL Publications, 1998), 2–3. For the ideal of hospitality in the rather different context of colonial Virginia, see Upton, *Holy Things and Profane*, 164–66.

103. Maurizio Abeti, *Un'architettura cristiana: per una nuova assemblea celebrante* (Naples: Luciano, 1998), 61–82.

104. White and White, *Church Architecture*, 38–39.

105. At another point the Whites do note the traditional role of the long aisle in weddings, while suggesting alternative possibilities: ibid., 14.

106. Ibid., 8, 12.

107. The principle might be applied also in a Greek Orthodox church. On Edward Dart's Holy Apostles Greek Orthodox Church in Westchester, Illinois, see "Reinterpreting an Ancient Liturgy," *Progressive Architecture* 47, no. 3 (Mar. 1966), 141.

108. M.W. Newman, "Sacred Space," *Architectural Forum* 137, no. 5 (Dec. 1972), 40–45; Kevin Seaholtz, "Contemporary Monastic Architecture and Life in America," in Timothy Gregory Verdon, ed., *Monasticism and the Arts* (Syracuse, N.Y.: Syracuse University Press, 1984), 332–35.

109. Theodor Filthaut, *Church Architecture and Liturgical Reform*, trans. Gregory Roettger (Baltimore: Helicon, 1968), 97–99.

110. Gieselmann, *Contemporary Church Architecture*, 119–21; Ignazio M. Calabuig, "The Rite of Dedication of a Church," trans. Matthew J. O'Connell, in Anscar J. Chupungco, ed., *Liturgical Time and Space* (Collegeville, Minn.: Liturgical Press, 2000), 376.

111. Roberto de Alba and Alan W. Organschi, "A Conversation with Giovanni Michelucci," *Perspecta* 27 (1992), 122. See also Cesare de Seta, *Architetture della fede in Italia* (Milan: Bruno Mondadori, 2003), 185–89, and Sandro Benedetti, *L'architettura delle chiese contemporanee: Il caso italiano* (Milan: Jaca, 2000), for further discussion of Michelucci and of other modern ecclesiastical architecture in Italy.

112. Giacomo Grasso, *Tra teologia e architettura: analisi dei problemi soggiacenti all'edilizia per il culto* (Rome: Borla, 1988), 68.

113. Designed by Friedrich Zwingmann (1976–78); see J. Rinderspacher, Friedrich Zwingmann, and Emil Wachter, *Autobahnkirche St. Christophorus, Baden-Baden*, with preface by Katharina Sandweier, 4th ed. (Munich: Schnell and Steiner, 1992). Justus Dahinden's work also displays a recurrent tent motif; see Edwin Heathcote and Iona Spens, *Church Builders* (Chichester, England: Academy, 1997), 87–89. Jules Gregory's Luther Memorial Evangelical Lutheran Church at New Shrewsbury, N.J., has also been called "a tent along the highway" for "born-again" people; see "Church Design: The Architecture of Collaboration," *Progressive Architecture* 47, no. 3 (Mar. 1966), 163. Perhaps the best use of the tent image in church architecture is Gottfied Böhm's pilgrimage church at Opfenbach-Wigratzbad (1972–76), made of "an accumulation of prefabricated tent-shaped units" which could be taken apart and set up elsewhere, suggesting "the image of a flexible tented city, which is anyway associated with pilgrimage"; see Wolfgang Pehnt, *Gottfried Böhm* (Basel: Birkhäuser, 1999), 90.

114. Walter M. Abbott and Mauro Paolo Wolfler, "Church of the Encounter," *Liturgical Arts* 37, no. 2 (Feb. 1969), 42–49.

115. Donald J. Bruggink and Carl H. Droppers, *Christ and Architecture: Building Presbyterian/Reformed Churches* (Grand Rapids, Mich.: Eerdmans, 1965), 264.

116. J.G. Davies, *Temples, Churches and Mosques: A Guide to the Appreciation of Religious Architecture* (Oxford: Blackwell, 1982), 35–37; W.R. Lethaby, *Architecture, Mysticism and Myth* (London: Percival, 1892), chap. 7; Craig M. Wright, *The Maze and the Warrior: Symbols in Architecture, Theology, and Music* (Cambridge, Mass.: Harvard University Press, 2001); Judith Dupré, *Churches* (New York: HarperCollins, 2001), 144–

45. On the recent interest in labyrinths, see especially Lauren Artress, *Walking a Sacred Path: Rediscovering the Labyrinth as a Spiritual Tool* (New York: Riverhead, 1995). The best-known historical example is in the nave at Chartres Cathedral, on which see Malcolm Miller, *Chartres Cathedral*, 2nd ed. (Andover, Hampshire: Pitkin, 1996), 18.

CHAPTER 2

1. Donald J. Bruggink and Carl H. Droppers, *When Faith Takes Form: Contemporary Churches of Architectural Integrity in America* (Grand Rapids, Mich.: Eerdmans, 1971), 24, on John Knox Presbyterian Church, Marietta, Georgia (the firm of Henry Toombs, Joseph Amisano, and Edwin Wells).

2. Ibid., 24; see p. 40 (St. Jude, Grand Rapids, Michigan (Progressive Design Associates, George E. Rafferty).

3. Eric Gill, "Mass for the Masses," in *Sacred & Secular &c* (London: Dent, 1940), 146; *Letters of Eric Gill*, ed. Walter Shewring (London: Jonathan Cape, 1947), 414–15; Malcolm Yorke, *Eric Gill: Man of Flesh and Spirit* (New York: Universe, 1982), 234–35. See Ralph Adams Cram, *Church Building: A Study of the Principles of Architecture in Their Relation to the Church*, 3rd ed. (Boston: Marshall Jones, 1924), 7.

4. "Diocesan Building Directives: Diocesan Liturgical Commission, Superior, Wisconsin," *Liturgical Arts* 26, no. 2 (Feb. 1957), 7–9. See also Frédéric Debuyst, *Modern Architecture and Christian Celebration* (Richmond, Va.: John Knox Press, 1968), 66–67. See also Peter Hammond, *Liturgy and Architecture* (New York: Columbia University Press, 1960), 28; Virgil Michel, "Architecture and the Liturgy," *Liturgical Arts* 5 (1936), 15–17; DeSanctis, *Renewing the City of God The Reform of Catholic Architecture in the United States* (Chicago: Liturgy Training, 1993), 18.

5. *Directives for the Building of a Church* (Collegeville, Minn.: Liturgical Press, 1957), 6–7; see Robert J. Dwyer, "Art and Architecture for the Church in Our Age," 2–6.

6. Frederick Gibberd, *Metropolitan Cathedral of Christ the King, Liverpool* (London: Architectural Press, 1968), 10.

7. Louis Dupré, *Symbols of the Sacred* (Grand Rapids, Mich.: Erdmans, 2000), 28–41, surveys the usual range of theories of sacrifice in relation to Christian understandings; Kent S. Knutson, "Contemporary Lutheran Theology and the Eucharistic Sacrifice," *Lutherans and Catholics in Dialogue* (New York: U.S.A. National Committee for Lutheran World Federation, 1967), 3:167–80, points to agreement in Lutheran-Reformed dialogue that Christ's atoning sacrifice "becomes contemporary" in the sacrament. René Girard, *Things Hidden since the Foundation of the World*, trans. Stephen Bann and Michael Metteer (Stanford, Calif.: Stanford University Press, 1987), 180–223, argues for a "nonsacrificial" reading of the Gospels but does not take into account the eucharistic institution narratives, which (alongside the identification of Christ with the Passover lamb) constitute the most relevant evidence. Girard draws a sharp contrast between the allegedly nonsacrificial interpretation of the Gospels with the later sacrificial theology of Hebrews, but well before the Gospels were written 1 Corinthians explicitly identified Christ's death as sacrifice.

8. New Age books such as Peg Streep *Altars Made Easy: A Complete Guide to Creating Your Own Sacred Space* (San Francisco: Harper San Francisco, 1997), and D.J.

Conway, *A Little Book of Altar Magic* (Freedom, Calif.: Crossing Press, 2001), tend not belabor instructions for sacrificing rams and bullocks; the former does mention animal sacrifice in passing (p. 13) but emphasizes images of animals as sources of spiritual power.

9. Thomas Aquinas, *Summa theologiae*, 3, qu. 83, art. 1 ad 2.

10. Christine Smith, Lude LeBlanc, and George Liaropoulos-Legendre, *Retrospection: Baccio Bandinelli and the Choir of Florence Cathedral* (Cambridge, Mass.: Harvard Graduate School of Design, 1997).

11. Sacrifices might be distinguished minutely in terms of *purpose*, but in *form* this distinction was fundamental. The concept of *olah* ("that which goes up" because it ascends to God) was related to *minkha* ("gift"). The term *zébakh* is short for *zébakh ha shelamim*, "slaughter of well-being," often rendered as "peace-offering." See W. Robertson Smith, *Lectures in the Religion of the Semites: The Fundamental Institutions* (Edinburgh: Black, 1889; reprint New York: Schocken, 1972), 213–43 (dated yet useful); Roland de Vaux, *Studies in Old Testament Sacrifice* (Cardiff: University of Wales Press, 1964), 27–51 (especially helpful); Gary A. Anderson, *Sacrifices and Offerings in Ancient Israel: Studies in Their Social and Political Importance* (Atlanta: Scholars Press, 1987), 27–34 (on *minhâ*). De Vaux emphasizes that the communion sacrifice in Hebrew tradition was not alimentary (God did not *eat* the offering), although there may be some reminiscence of archaic notions of this sort. Still, the communion sacrifice did involve a sharing with God, whatever God did with the offering. (For help with the terminology and for the correlation with divine transcendence and immanence I am indebted to Benjamin D. Sommer.)

12. Jack Miles, *Christ: A Crisis in the Life of God* (New York: Knopf, 2001), 219.

13. Josef A. Jungmann, *The Early Liturgy: To the Time of Gregory the Great*, trans. Francis A. Brunner (Notre Dame, Ind.: University of Notre Dame Press, 1959), 29–38, 45–49. Steven J. Schloeder, *Architecture in Communion: Implementing the Second Vatican Council through Liturgy and Architecture* (San Francisco: Ignatius, 1998), 51, citing Jungmann, insists that the early Church persisted in seeing eucharist as sacrifice. But Jungmann acknowledges that sacrificial notions soon became subordinated to others. See also *La Maison-Dieu*, 123 (1975); Robert J. Daly, *Christian Sacrifice: The Judaeo-Christian Background Before Origen* (Washington, D.C.: Catholic University of America Press, 1978), and *The Origins of the Christian Doctrine of Sacrifice* (Philadelphia: Fortress Press, 1978); Rowan Williams, *Eucharistic Sacrifice: The Roots of a Metaphor* (Bramcote, Nottinghamshire: Grove, 1982); and Colin Buchanan, ed., *Essays on Eucharistic Sacrifice in the Early Church* (Bramcote, Nottinghamshire: Grove, 1984). J. Delorme et al., *The Eucharist in the New Testament: A Symposium*, trans. E. M. Stewart (Baltimore: Helicon, 1964), includes an important article by P. Benoit.

14. Much of the theological literature on eucharistic sacrifice simply presupposes that the notion to be accounted for is that of the people's sacrificial act; see Gordon W. Lathrop, *Holy Things: A Liturgical Theology* (Minneapolis: Fortress, 1993), 139–58.

15. Kenneth Leech, *The Sky Is Red: Discerning the Signs of the Times* (London: Darton, Longman and Todd, 1997), 164.

16. C.S. Lewis, *Reflections on the Psalms* (London: Bles, 1958), 52.

17. *The Book of Alternative Services of the Anglican Church of Canada* (Toronto: Anglican Book Centre, 1985), 213.

18. F.L. Cross and E.A. Livingston, eds., *The Oxford Dictionary of the Christian*

Church, 2nd ed. (Oxford: Oxford University Press, 1974), 25–26; Marion J. Hatchett, *Commentary on the American Prayer Book* (San Francisco: Harper, 1995), 380–81.

19. Edward King introduced into the Church of England the use of the Agnus Dei, along with other elements of high-church ceremonialism; complaints were raised against him, but in 1890 the archbishop of Canterbury found in his favor.

20. Another text sometimes used at the fraction, "Christ our Passover is sacrificed for us, therefore let us keep the feast" (from 1 Corinthians 5:7–8), appears in a more embellished form in the *Book of Common Prayer* of 1549.

21. Charles Davis, "Church Architecture and the Liturgy," in Peter Hammond, ed., *Towards a Church Architecture* (London: Architectural Press, 1962), 120.

22. E.A. Sövik, *Architecture for Worship* (Minneapolis: Augsburg, 1973), 31–33.

23. Edward A. Sövik, "A Portfolio of Reflections on the Design of Northfield Methodist Church," *Your Church* 13, no. 5 (Sept./Oct. 1967), 54–55.

24. Robert Maguire and Keith Murray, "Anglican Church in Stepney," *Church-building* 7 (Oct. 1962), 15–16. The church was built in 1956–60.

25. M. Minucius Felix, *Octavius*, 10.2 and 32.1, ed. Bernhard Kytzler (Leipzig: Teubner, 1982), p. 8 (asking why Christians have "no altars, no temples, no publicly-known images") and p. 30 (responding, in essence, that Christians conceal nothing and that God transcends temples and all creation); see *The Octavius of Marcus Minucius Felix*, trans. G.W. Clarke (New York: Newman, 1974), 66 and 111. Interpretation of Minucius has assumed a crucial role in our understanding of early Christian worship and its environment. J. G. Davies begins the first chapter of *The Secular Use of Church Buildings* (New York: Seabury, 1968) quoting him. But the question and the answer in Minucius refer to the absence of *public* facilities for worship, and of the sort of altars (*arae*, not *altaria*) found in such temples. And for apologetic purposes Minucius generally gives a minimalist version of Christian belief and practice; see Harry James Baylis, *Minucius Felix and His Place among the Early Fathers of the Latin Church* (London: SPCK, 1928), 145 and 152.

26. Maurice M. Hassett, "History of the Christian Altar," in *The Catholic Encyclopedia: An International Work of Reference on the Constitution, Doctrine, Discipline, and History of the Catholic Church* (New York: Encyclopedia Press, 1913), 1:362.

27. L. Michael White, *The Social Origins of Christian Architecture* (Valley Forge, Pa.: Trinity Press, 1996–97), reviewed (with usefully sharp distinction of phases, followed here) by Steven J. Friesen, Edgar Krentz, Ulrike Outschar, and Carolyn Osiek, in *Religious Studies Review* 27 (2001), 223–31. For a summary of the historiography prior to White's work and of an early version of White's study, see Paul Corby Finney, "Early Christian Architecture: The Beginnings (a Review Article)," *Harvard Theological Review* 81 (1988), 319–39. White discusses Dura especially on pp. 1:21–22, 40–44, 50–55, 120–22, 2:123–34, 261–93.

28. Carl Hermann Kraeling, *The Synagogue*, new ed. (New York: Ktav, 1979); Joseph Gutmann, ed., *The Dura-Europos Synagogue: A Re-Evaluation (1932–1992)* (Atlanta: Scholars Press, 1992).

29. A. R. Bellinger, "The plan of the temples," in P. V. C. Baur, M. I. Rostovtzeff, and Alfred R. Bellinger, eds., *The Excavations at Dura-Europos: Preliminary Report of Third Season of Work* (New Haven: Yale University Press, 1932), 18–24; "Discoveries in the temple of Artemis-Nanaia, I. History and architecture," in M. I. Rostovtzeff, A. R. Bellinger, C. Hopkins, and C. B. Welles, eds., *The Excavations at Dura-Europos: Prelimi-*

nary Report of Sixth Season of Work (New Haven: Yale University Press, 1936), 397–411.

30. H. Seyrig, "Altar Dedicated to Zeus Betylos," in *Preliminary Report*, 4:68–71.

31. "The Temple of Adonis," in *Preliminary Report*, 7/8:135-57; "The temple of Zeus Theos, I. Architecture," pp. 180–96.

32. Clark Hopkins and P.V.C. Baur, *Christian Church at Dura-Europos* (New Haven: Yale University Press, 1934), is reprinted from the preliminary reports of the excavation; Carl H. Kraeling, *The Christian Building* (New Haven: Dura-Europos, 1967), is the pertinent section of the final report.

33. Michael D. Swartz, *Place and Person in Ancient Judaism: Describing the Yom Kippur Sacrifice*, International Rennert Guest Lecture Series 9 (Ramat Gan, Israel: Ingeborg Rennert Center for Jerusalem Studies, Bar-Ilan University 2001), 1–2.

34. Gregory Dix, *The Shape of the Liturgy*, 2nd ed. (London: Dacre, 1945), 50–54.

35. To be sure, a permanent altar may simply not survive, but no other evidence suggests the earliest churches would have had anything more than modest and portable tables.

36. Arnold Wolff, *Cologne Cathedral: Its History—Its Works of Art*, trans. Margret Maranuk-Rohmeder (Cologne: Greven, 1995); more fully in Sebastian Ristow, Lothar Bakker, and Dorothea Hochkirchen, *Die frühen Kirchen unter dem Kölner Dom: Befunde und Funde vom 4. Jahrhundert bis zur Bauzeit des Alten Domes* (Cologne: Kölner Dom, 2002). The parallel does not extend to the precise forms of the two buildings but to their origins in domestic architecture along the Roman *limes*. There is also an early chapel (not easily visited, but worth the effort) beneath St. Severinus, while the early fabric at St. Gereon is integrated at ground level into the later construction.

37. Schloeder, *Architecture in Communion*, 44.

38. The periods suggested here are from Edmund Bishop, "On the History of the Christian altar," in *Liturgica Historica: Papers on the Liturgy and Religious Life of the Western Church* (Oxford: Clarendon, 1918), 20–38, but the descriptions for those periods are not quite those given by Bishop. See also C. E. Pocknee, *The Christian Altar in History and Today* (London: Mowbrays, 1963); Joseph Braun, *Der christliche Altar in seiner geschichtlichen Entwicklung* (Munich: Alte Meister Guenther Koch, 1924); Karl Heimann, *Der christliche Altar: Übersicht über seinen Werdegang im Laufe der Zeiten*, new ed. (Abensberg: Aventinus–Verlag J. Kral, 1954); Andreas Schmid, *Der christliche Altar: Sein Schmuck und seine Ausstattung*, rev. Oscar Doering (Paderborn, Germany: Schöningh, 1928).

39. *The Book of Pontiffs (Liber Pontificalis): The Ancient Biographies of the First Ninety Roman Bishops to AD 715*, trans. Raymond Davis (Liverpool: Liverpool University Press, 1989), 16–26. The structure now in place at the Lateran basilica dates from 1367.

40. A document attributed to Pope Sylvester, and thus to the time of Constantine, requires stone for an altar, but the ascription is quite surely false.

41. Hassett, "History of the Christian Altar," 362–67.

42. Peter Brown, *The Cult of the Saints: Its Rise and Function in Latin Christianity* (Chicago: University of Chicago Press, 1981), 36–37.

43. The Catharijneconvent museum in Utrecht has interesting examples of the containers in which relics were placed before being sealed in the altar.

44. Gary Macy, *The Theologies of the Eucharist in the Early Scholastic Period: A*

Study of the Salvific Function of the Sacrament According to the Theologians, c. 1080–c. 1220 (Oxford: Oxford University Press, 1984), and "The Dogma of Transubstantiation in the Middle Ages, *Journal of Ecclesiastical History* 45 (1994), 11–43.

45. Pocknee says the earliest known color sequence is from the Latin Church of the Holy Sepulchre at Jerusalem, where a sequence used from the twelfth century included black for Christmas and Marian feasts, blue for Epiphany and Ascension.

46. Hassett, "History of the Christian Altar," 366.

47. Donald J. Bruggink and Carl H. Droppers, *Christ and Architecture: Building Presbyterian/Reformed Churches* (Grand Rapids, Mich.: Eerdmans, 1965), 253–63. The architects are F.A. Eschauzier and Frits Eschauzier.

48. Christopher Stell, "Puritan and Nonconformist Meetinghouses in England," in Paul Corby Finney, ed., *Seeing beyond the Word: Visual Arts and the Calvinist Tradition* (Grand Rapids, Mich.: Eerdmans, 1999), 53 n. 14.

49. George Hay, *The Architecture of Scottish Post-Reformation Churches, 1560–1843* (Oxford: Clarendon, 1957), and Andrew Spicer, "Architecture," in Andrew Pettegree, ed., *The Reformation World* (London: Routledge), 513–14, 517–20.

50. G.W.O. Addleshaw and F. Etchells, *The Architectural Setting of Anglican Worship* (London: Faber and Faber, 1948); Nigel Yates, *Buildings, Faith and Worship: The Liturgical Arrangement of Anglican Churches, 1600–1900*, rev ed. (Oxford: Oxford University Press, 2000); Horton Davies, *Worship and Theology in England* (Princeton, N.J.: Princeton University Press, 1961–75), esp. 1:365.

51. John Crook, *The Architectural Setting of the Cults of Saints in the Early Christian West, c. 300–1200* (Oxford: Clarendon, 2000).

52. Walter Horn and Ernest Born, *The Plan of St. Gall: A Study of the Architecture and Economy of, and Life in a Paradigmatic Carolingian Monastery* (Berkeley: University of California Press, 1979), 1:127–43.

53. Sible L. de Blaauw, *Cultus et decor: Liturgie en architectuur in laatantiek en middeleeuws Rome: Basilica Salvatoris, Santae Mariae, Sancti Petri* (Delft: Eburon, 1987), 196–98 and 200–201.

54. Sible de Blaauw, "Architecture and Liturgy in late Antiquity and the Middle Ages," *Archiv für Liturgiewissenschaft* 33 (1991), 21–22.

55. G.H. Cook, *Mediaeval Chantries and Chantry Chapels*, rev. and enl. ed. (London: Dent, 1963; reprint, J. Baker, 1968); Peter Draper, " 'Seeing That It Was Done in All the Noble Churches in England,' " in Eric Fernie and Paul Crossley, eds., *Medieval Architecture and Its Intellectual Context* (London: Hambledon, 1990), 137–42, discusses Lady chapels of the twelfth and thirteenth centuries.

56. Richard Kieckhefer, "Major Currents in Late Medieval Devotion," in Jill Raitt, ed., *Christian Spirituality*, vol. 2 (New York: Crossroad, 1987), 75–108.

57. Bishop, "On the History of the Christian Altar," 36, and Pocknee, *The Christian Altar*, 51–54.

58. Joseph Armstrong Baird, Jr., *The Churches of Mexico, 1530–1810* (Berkeley: University of California Press, 1962), 28.

59. Rui de Pina, "Relazione del Regno di Congo," in *O chronista Rui de Pina e a "Relação do Congo": Manuscrito inédito do "Códice Riccardiano 1910,"* ed. Carmen M. Radulet (Lisbon: Commisão Nacional para es Comemorações dos Descobrimentos Portugueses, Imprensa Nacional—Casa da Moeda, 1992), as cited by Albert J. Raboteau in a lecture at Northwestern University, November 13, 2000. See Lindsay Jones,

The Hermeneutics of Sacred Architecture: Experience, Interpretation, Comparison (Cambridge, Mass.: Harvard University Press for Harvard University Center for the Study of World Religions, 2000), 2:106 and n. 87, on the Church of the Trinity at Stadl-Paura (1714–25), which "has not only three identical facades, each framed by three towers, but also three main portals and three altars, each of which is explicitly dedicated to a member of the Trinity."

60. Marcel Durliat, *L'Église Saint-Jacques, Perpignan* (n.p., 1997). The vicinity of Perpignan provides good evidence for the earlier history of the altar: the main altar at Saint-Michael de Cuxa, consecrated in 974 (rediscovered in 1969), was a slab of white marble, about seven feet long and four and a half feet wide, taken from Roman ruins at Narbonne; see *Cuxa* (Saint Michael de Cuxa's Abbey, n.d.), 8 and 11–14.

61. [Theodor Klauser,] *Directives for the Building of a Church, by the Liturgical Commission of the German Hierarchy*, English trans. (Collegeville, Minn.: Liturgical Press, 1949), 8–9, echoed in the United States by the highly influential "Diocesan Building Directives: Diocesan Liturgical Commission, Superior, Wisconsin," *Liturgical Arts* 26, no. 2 (Feb. 1957), 7–9.

62. Both a supplementary document prepared for the Second Vatican Council and the instructions issued for implementation of the Council's constitution specified that side altars should not distract from the main altar and as much as possible should be in special chapels; see appendix to Liturgy Constitution art. 128 (Declarations of Preparatory Commission for a clearer explanation of certain articles), in *Church Architecture: The Shape of Reform* (Washington, D.C.: Liturgical Conference, 1965), 98–102, and Kevin Seasoltz, "Devotions and Other Uses of the Church," in the same volume, 63.

63. Gervase Rosser, "Communities of Parish and guild in the later Middle Ages," in S. J. Wright, ed., *Parish, Church and People: Local Studies in Lay Religion, 1350–1750* (London: Hutchinson, 1988), 29–55, and "Parochial Conformity and Voluntary Religion in Late-Medieval England," *Transactions of the Royal Historical Society*, ser. 6, 1 (1991), 173–89.

64. Caryl Coleman, "Ambo," and Gerald Gietmann, "Pulpit," 12: 563–65, in Herberman, *Catholic Encyclopedia*, 1:381–82. G. P. P. Vrins, "De ambon: Oorsprong en verspreiding tot 600," in *Feestbundel F. van der Meer* (Amsterdam: Elsevier, 1966), 11–55.

65. Crispino Valenziano, "Liturgical Architecture," trans. Matthew J. O'Connell, in Anscar J. Chupungco, ed., *Liturgical Time and Space* (Collegeville, Minn.: Liturgical Press, 2000), 385–86.

66. Otto Lehmann-Brockhaus, "Die Kanzeln der Abruzzen im 12. und 13. Jahrhundert," *Römisches Jahrbuch für Kunstgeschiche* 6 (1942–44), 259–428 (reprint, Vienna: Schroll, [1945?]).

67. Michael Ayrton, *Giovanni Pisano: Sculptor* (London: Thames and Hudson, 1969), 157–64 (plates 155–79).

68. J. Charles Cox, *Pulpits, Lecterns, and Organs in English Churches* (London: Oxford University Press, 1915), 18–26.

69. Stephen Friar, *A Companion to the English Parish Church* (Stroud, Gloucestershire: Alan Sutton, 1996), 367; F. E. Howard and F. H. Crossley, *English Church Woodwork: A Study in Craftsmanship during the Medieval Period, A.D. 1250–1550* (London: Batsford, 1917), 275–96.

70. Spicer, "Architecture," 511.

71. Jakub Pokora, "Word and Picture as Keys for Solving the Ideological Programme of Protestant Pulpits in Silesia, 1550–1650," *Polish Art Studies* 8 (1987), 48.

72. Friar, *A Companion to the English Parish Church*, 367–69 and 425.

73. Spicer, "Architecture," 511–20.

74. Bruggink and Droppers, *Christ and Architecture*, 229–31; George Hay, *The Architecture of Scottish Post-Reformation Churches, 1560–1843* (Oxford: Clarendon, 1957), especially 18–35 and 178–90.

75. J. Kramps-van Drunen, *Ontmoeting met de Westerkerk* ([Amsterdam: The Church], n.d.), 14–18.

76. Bruggink and Droppers, *When Faith Takes Form*, 18, and "A Baptist church by Weese," *Architectural Record* 138, no. 12 (Dec. 1965), 113–17; the architect is Harry Weese.

77. Gietmann, "Pulpit," 565.

78. Andreas Rothe, "Theologie in Stein und Bild," in *Die Schloßkirche zu Torgau: Beiträge zum 450 jährigen Jubiläum der Einweihung durch Martin Luther am 5. Oktober 1544* (Torgau, Germany: Torgauer Geschichtsverein and Evangelische Kirchengemeinde Torgau, 1994), 7–26. Rothe speaks of the building as a church but acknowledges a longstanding controversy about whether it should more propertly be called a chapel. See also Spicer, "Architecture," 509.

79. Spicer, "Architecture," 509–11.

80. Oskar Thulin, "Der Altar in reformatorischer Sicht," in *Reich Gottes und Wirklichkeit: Festgabe für Alfred Dedo Müller zum 70. Geburtstag* (Berlin: Evangelische Verlagsanstalt, 1961), 193–204. Luther's liturgical writings are gathered in *Works of Martin Luther*, vol. 6 (Philadelphia: A.J. Holman and Castle Press, 1932), trans. P.Z. Strodach, L.D. Reed, A. Steimle, and C.M. Jacobs; the pertinent passage from "The German Mass and Order of Service" of 1526 is on 178–79; see also the 1523 "Formula of Mass and Communion for the Church at Wittenberg," 95.

81. Albrecht Steinwachs and Jürgen M. Pietsch, *Der Reformationsaltar von Lucas Cranach d.Ä. in der Stadtkirche St. Marien, Lutherstadt Wittenberg* (Spröda: Akanthus, 1998).

82. Martin Luther, "Sermon at the Dedication of the Castle Church in Torgau: Luke 14:1–11, October 5, 1544," in *Luther's Works*, ed. Jaroslav Pelikan and Helmut T. Lehmann, vol. 51 (Sermons, 1), ed. and trans. John W. Doberstein (Philadelphia: Muhlenberg, 1959), 333–54. For classics of the genre see Sermons 336–38, in *The Works of Saint Augustine: A Translation for the twenty-first Century*, part 3, vol. 9 (Sermons on the Saints), trans. Edmund Hill, ed. John E. Rotelle (Hyde Park, N.Y.: New City Press, 1994), 266–78.

83. Valenziano, "Liturgical Architecture," 389.

84. Richard Krautheimer, "Introduction to an 'Iconography of Mediaeval Architecture,'" *Journal of the Warburg and Courtauld Institutes* 5 (1942), 20–33; J.G. Davies, *The Architectural Setting of Baptism* (London: Barrie and Rockliff, 1962).

85. Bruggink and Droppers, *When Faith Takes Form*, 56.

86. Aelred Tegels, "Resurrection: The Reformed Liturgy and the Other Sacraments," in *Church Architecture: The Shape of Reform* (Washington, D.C.: Liturgical Conference, 1965), 52–60

87. This is the report of Leigh Waggoner, who visited the church in February 2002. See Judith Dupré, *Churches* (New York: HarperCollins, 2001), 57.

88. Otto Bartning, "Der evangelische Kultbau," in Curt Horn, ed., *Kultus und Kunst: Beiträge zur Kläring des evangelischen Kultusproblems* (Berlin: Furche-Kunstverlag, 1925), 47–54, esp. 51.

89. Martin Elsässer, "Evangelische Kultbaufragen," in Horn, *Kultus und Kunst*, 55–64, esp. 59–60.

90. Rupert Spade, *Eero Saarinen* (New York: Simon and Schuster, 1971), plates 97–100 and p. 124; Bruggink and Droppers, *When Faith Takes Form*, 94–107.

91. Bruggink and Droppers, *Christ and Architecture*, give illustrations of thirty-one churches, historical and modern, illustrating the possibilities. W.J.G. van Mourik te Velp, *Hervormde Kerkbouw na 1945* ('s-Gravenhage: Boekencentrum N.V., 1957), also gives a rich assortment of modern examples. Willem Gerard Overbosch, "Kirchenbau in Holland," in *Kirchenbau und Ökumene: Evangelische Kirchenbautagung in Hamburg 1961* (Hamburg: Friedrich Wittig Verlag, 1962), 53, notes that this reform may leave too little room for the old Dutch custom of sitting at the Lord's Supper, which is them administered in the pews.

92. Davis, "Church Architecture and the Liturgy," 117–24.

93. Debuyst, *Modern Architecture and Christian Celebration*, 62. For a Roman Catholic church Debuyst inclined to add the tabernacle as a fourth element.

94. Klemens Richter, "Verschiedene Wegen nach Rom: Prozessionskirche versus Communio-Raum," *Kunst und Kirche* 3 (2001), 148–50.

95. Designed by the firm of Guy Prisco, Marty Serena, and William Sturm (1995).

96. From a pamphlet of spring 1996, with an opening letter signed by Father Rich Homa.

97. Sövik, *Architecture for Worship*, 76–77.

98. Sövik, "A Portfolio of Reflections," 48–49; see Bruggink and Droppers, *When Faith Takes Form*, 64. Christopher V. Stroik, *Path, Portal, Path: Architecture for the Rites* (Chicago: Liturgy Training, 1999), 59, argues against the "objective isolationism" of foci within a church.

99. Stephen Wilson, "Cults of Saints in the Churches of Central Paris," in Stephen Wilson, ed., *Saints and Their Cults: Studies in Religious Sociology, Folklore and History* (Cambridge: Cambridge University Press, 1983), 233–60, gives an interesting case study.

100. Jones, *The Hermeneutics of Sacred Architecture*, 1:77–78 and n. 15.

CHAPTER 3

1. E.A. Sövik, "The Place of Worship: Environment for Action," in Mandus A. Egge, ed., *Worship: Good News in Action* (Minneapolis: Augsburg, 1973), 108; see Sövik, "Living on the High Wire," *Faith and Form* 26 (fall 1993), 10, and "Remembrance and Hope," *Faith and Form* 30 (1997), p. 10.

2. *Environment & Art in Catholic Worship*, issued by the Bishops' Committee on the Liturgy, National Conference of Catholic Bishops (Chicago: Liturgy Training Publications, 1993), 21. For a straightforward statement, see Victor A. Lundy, quoted

in "Churches—1961," *Architectural Forum* 115, no. 6 (Dec. 1961), 92: "I think the important question in a church building, after all the intellectualizing, is *does it move you?* I think a church has to. That's the important thing."

3. Paul Tillich, *On Art and Architecture*, ed. John and Jane Dillenberger, trans. Robert P. Scharlemann (New York: Crossroad, 1989), 207. Scarcely anyone would agree with Angelique Arnauld's statement, quoted by Anselme Dimier, *Stones Laid Before the Lord*, trans. Gilchrist Lavigne (Kalamazoo: Cistercian Publications, 1999), 122, "I love all that is ugly. Art is only a lie and a vanity. Everything that feeds the senses takes away from God."

4. Leon Battista Alberti, *On the Art of Building in Ten Books*, bk. 7, trans. Joseph Rykwert, Neil Leach, and Robert Tavernor (Cambridge, Mass.: MIT Press, 1988), 194.

5. Peter Hammond, *Liturgy and Architecture* (London: Barrie & Rockliff; New York: Columbia University Press, 1960), 29.

6. J.N. Comper, *Of the Atmosphere of a Church* (London: Sheldon, 1947), 31.

7. Horst Wenzel, *Hören und Sehen, Schrift und Bild: Kultur und Gedächtnis im Mittelalter* (Munich: Beck, 1995), 95–127.

8. Ralph Adams Cram, *Church Building: A Study of the Principles of Architecture in Their Relation to the Church*, 3rd ed. (Boston: Marshall Jones, 1924), 8; see John Jebb, *The Choral Service of the United Church of England and Ireland: Being an Enquiry into the Liturgical System of the Cathedral and Collegiate Foundations of the Anglican Communion* (London: Parker, 1843), 23–24.

9. "Proposed Episcopal Church, Riverside, California: Ralph C. Flewelling and Associates, Architects," *Progressive Architecture* 28, no. 7 (Jul. 1947), 57.

10. Asher Ovadiah, "Early Churches," in Ephraim Stern, ed., *The New Encyclopedia of Archaeological Excavations in the Holy Land* (New York: Simon & Schuster, 1993), 1:305–9.

11. Crispino Valenziano, "Liturgical Architecture," trans. Matthew J. O'Connell, in Anscar J. Chupungco, ed., *Liturgical Time and Space* (Collegeville, Minn.: Liturgical Press, 2000), 394.

12. For example, Marco Mulazzani, "Mauro Galantino: chiesa di S. Ireneo = Church of S. Ireneo, Cesano Boscone 2000," *Casabella* 65, no. 687 (Mar. 2001), 74 (on the role of the *sagrato*); "Richard Meier: The Church of the Year 2000, Rome, Italy, 1996," *A + U: Architecture and Urbanism* 4 (319) (Apr. 1997), 40–51, esp. 40 (the competition brief).

13. Tillich, *On Art and Architecture*, 221–28.

14. Saint Caesarius of Arles, *Sermons*, vol. 3, trans. Sister Mary Magdeleine Mueller (Washington, D.C.: Catholic University of America Press, 1973), p. 175. Caesarius has three relevant sermons: nos. 227–29 (pp. 164–79).

15. Another way to make the point: nothing in a church is meant to suggest that God is *not* present; everything is meant to suggest that God *is* present, although the mode of divine presence may be mysterious and the presence itself indirectly perceived.

16. William P. Hund, "The Emotion of Reverence in Church Architecture," *Liturgical Arts* 34 (Feb. 1966), 50–51, 56, defends this view of church design.

17. Robert Campbell, "A Church Struggles to Look Like One," *Faith and Form* 26 (spring 1993), 35 (reprinted from *The Boston Globe*, Sept. 8, 1992): "if you banished all tall impractical spaces, there'd be few good churches left in the Western world."

18. Terry Eagleton, *Literary Theory: An Introduction* (Minneapolis: University of Minnesota Press, 1983), 2–6, with specific reference to the Russian Formalists.

19. Albert Christ-Janer and Mary Mix Foley, *Modern Church Architecture: A Guide to the Form and Spirit of Twentieth-Century Religious Buildings* (New York: McGraw-Hill, 1962), 293–300.

20. Leopold Eidlitz, "Christian Architecture," *Crayon* 5 (Feb. 1858), 53, quoted in Jeanne Halgren Kilde, *When Church Became Theatre: The Transformation of Evangelical Architecture and Worship in Nineteenth-Century America* (New York: Oxford University Press, 2002), 70.

21. Oskar Söhngen, "Der Begriff des Sakralen im Kirchenbau," in *Kirchenbau und Ökumene: Evangelische Kirchenbautagung in Hamburg 1961* (Hamburg: Friedrich Wittig Verlag, 1962), 200.

22. Romano Guardini, *Sacred Signs*, trans. Grace Branham, rev. ed. (Wilmington, Del.: Michael Glazer, 1979), 39.

23. This occurred at Winchester, Worcester, Ely, Beverley, and elsewhere.

24. Old Saint Paul's in London (1561); Lincoln Cathedral (Sixteenth century), Chichester (Nineteenth century). West towers, built on their own foundations, were never as vulnerable to collapse as central towers, but at times they too gave way; at Saint John the Baptist in Chester, the west tower collapsed in 1881. Even if it remained standing, a tower whose foundations settled after construction might develop a nervous-making list. The most famous case is the campanile at Pisa, but the examples are numerous; Ravenna has more than one leaning tower. During World War II, an engineer wanted to pull down the leaning tower of the Temple Church in Bristol, not knowing that it had been tilting since it was built in 1460. According to local legend it had been built on sacks of wool—a story that no doubt rested on figurative truth. See *Bristol Heritage: A Walking Guide to Bristol's Churches* (Bristol: Redcliffe, 1991), 50–51. Hund, "The Emotion of Reverence," 51, construes the awesomeness of a church as "a feeling of wonderment mixed with slight fear about whether or not such great masses of masonry will stay up there."

25. "The Horizontal Cathedral: A Discussion with Mario Salvadori on Today's Structural Potentials," *Architectural Record* 119, no. 6 (Jun. 1956), 183.

26. Edward A. Sövik, "A Portfolio of Reflections on the Design of Northfield Methodist Church," *Your Church* 13, no. 5 (Sept./Oct. 1967), 49.

27. Athanasius, *De incarnatione Verbi* 54.3, in *Patrologia Graeca*, vol. 25, col. 192; see Irenaeus, *Adversus haereses* 3.19.1, in *Patrologia Graeca*, vol. 7, pt. 1, col. 939. Aspiration is a central value in, for example, 2 Peter 1:4, Matthew 5:48, Colossians 3:2, and Hebrews 11:1. One might say much about the range of forms aspiration takes, and the differences between one writer and another, but simply to say that Christianity is not a religion of aspiration is to make a stunningly implausible claim.

28. The phrase is quoted from Henry Drummond, *Natural Law in the Spiritual World*, 8th ed. (London: Hodder and Stoughton, 1883), 117.

29. Jacob Needleman, *Lost Christianity: A Journey of Rediscovery to the Center of Christian Experience* (Garden City, N.Y.: Doubleday, 1980), 33. The bishop is Metropolitan Anthony of Sourozh, who published in earlier years as Anthony Bloom.

30. Ronald Goetz, "Protestant Houses of God: A Contradiction in Terms?" *Faith and Form* 19 (fall 1986), 20; reprinted from *Christian Century*, Mar. 20–27, 1985. Goetz takes Anselm of Canterbury as corresponding to the Romanesque with his em-

phas on human fallenness and dependence on divine restoration, but Augustine, Calvin, Barth, and many others were at least as insistent on the matter. Goetz wishes thirteenth-century Scholastic confidence in the capacity of the human mind to be reflected in the Gothic style, but his Romanesque theologian Anselm was yet more confident in the mind's ability to provide necessary reasons for the existence of God and many other doctrines on which Thomas Aquinas and his contemporaries were far more cautious. Erwin Panofsky, *Gothic Architecture and Scholasticism* (Cleveland: World, 1967), a classic of this genre, is far more nuanced but has still been subject to much criticism. More dubious still in characterization and chronology is Judith Dupré, *Churches* (New York: HarperCollins, 2001), 6.

31. Otto von Simson, *The Gothic Cathedral: Origins of Gothic Architecture and the Medieval Concept of Order*, 3rd ed. (Princeton, N.J.: Princeton University Press, 1988), 3.

32. "Kaleva Church, Tampere, Architect Reima Pietila," in section on Finland, ed. Esko Lehesmaa, in John Donat, ed., *World Architecture Today* (New York: Viking, 1964), 206. Judith Dupré, *Churches*, (New York: HarperCollins, 2001), 140: "Light, the generator of architecture, is conspicuous everywhere in [Tadao] Ando's buildings, either by its presence or absence. Capturing light is Ando's most fundamental and poetic tool for communicating with the human spirit."

33. Comper, *Of the Atmosphere*, 26–27; see Richard Hurley Mriai, "Modern Church Design in Ireland," *Liturgical Arts* 35, no. 1 (Nov. 1966), 7 ("Well designed and sympathetic abstract stained glass . . . helps to create an atmosphere conducive to devotion").

34. Richared Lacayo, "To the Lighthouse: What Should a Church Look Like Today? One Bold Answer: Rafael Moneo's L.A. cathedral," *Time*, Sept. 2, 2002, p. 65.

35. The first words of Solomon at the dedication of his temple (1 Kings 8:12).

36. William A. Christian, Jr., *Apparitions in Late Medieval and Renaissance Spain* (Princeton: Princeton University Press, 1981).

37. Leroy A. Campbell, *Mithraic Iconography and Ideology* (Leiden: Brill, 1968), 6–11 (especially the quotation from Euboulos on p. 6), and David Ulansey, *The Origins of the Mithraic Mysteries: Cosmology and Salvation in the Ancient World* (New York: Oxford University Press, 1989), 35–36 (on parallels to the myth and cult of Perseus, born in a cave, as Christ was, according to one Christian tradition).

38. Designed by Joseph H. Saunders, Jr. (1948).

39. Laura Burns Carroll, "Revisiting a Church of Radical Design—and Its Visionary Priest," *Faith and Form* 28 (fall 1994), 14; see Harold W. Turner, *From Temple to Meeting House: The Phenomenology and Theology of Places of Worship* (The Hague: Mouton, 1979), 334.

40. Dennis McNally, *Sacred Space: An Aesthetic for the Liturgical Environment* (Bristol, Ind.: Wyndham Hall, 1985), 80.

41. Erwin Panofsky, ed. and trans., *Abbot Suger, on the Abbey-Church of St.-Denis and Its Art Treasures*, 2nd ed. by Gerda Panofsky-Soergel (Princeton, N.J.: Princeton University Press, 1979); see Peter Kidson, "Panofsky, Suger, and St. Denis," *Journal of the Warburg and Courtauld Institutes* 50 (1987), 1–17; Bernard McGinn, "From Admirable Tabernacle to the House of God: Some Theological Reflections on Medieval Architectural Integration," in Virginia Chieffo Raguin, Kathryn L. Brush, and Peter Draper, eds., *Artistic Integration in Gothic Buildings* (Toronto: University of Toronto Press,

1995), esp. 46–51; and Lex Bosman, "'De uitvinding van de gotiek: abt Suger sinds Erwin Panofsky," *Madoc* 12 (1998), 251–56.

42. Jean-Michel Leniaud and Françoise Perrot, *La Sainte Chapelle* (Paris: Nathan, 1991).

43. Dorothée Hugot, *Aachen Cathedral: A Guide*, trans. Peter Marsden (Aachen: Einhard, 2000), 37–39.

44. John Harvey, *English Cathedrals*, rev. ed. (London: Batsford, 1961), 44.

45. Bernard Bevan, *History of Spanish Architecture* (New York: Scribner, 1939). Tobias Smollett, in his jaundiced reflections on churches, admits that the hot climate of Spain is suitable for churches that are "vast, narrow, dark, and lofty, impervious to the sun-beams, and having little communication with the scorched external atmosphere" and thus provide "a refreshing coolness, like subterranean cellars in the heats of summer": Tobias Smollett, *The Expedition of Humphry Clinker*, ed. Angus Ross (Harmondsworth: Penguin, 1967), 214–5. For an equally strong but opposite reaction, see Ralph Adams Cram, *The Substance of Gothic: Six Lectures on the Development of Architecture from Charlemagne to Henry VIII*, 2nd ed. (Boston: Marshall Jones, 1925), xi–xii.

46. See the entire issue of *Kunst und Kirche* 38, no. 4 (1975), on the quality of light in architecture.

47. *Acoustics for Liturgy: A Collection of Articles of The Hymn Society in the U.S. and Canada* (Chicago: Liturgy Training, 1991), 7–16; Scott R. Reidel, *Acoustics in the Worship Space* (St. Louis, Mo.: Concordia, 1986); Jürgen Meyer, *Kirchenakustik* (Frankfurt: Verlag Erwin Bochinsky, 2003), supplements thorough technical discussion with historical and modern case studies.

48. Jebb, *The Choral Service*, 231–32, recognized the value of "advancing up the long-drawn Aisle" as "a holy preparation to the service" but frowned on singing in the process.

49. Terry K. Boggs, "A Pastor's View: Acoustics and Meaningful Places for Worship," in *Acoustics for Liturgy*, 51–59.

50. The chief distinguishing feature of classical chant is not that it is monophonic but that it is nonmetrical. Most of the music heard in contemporary culture is metrical but handles its meter with varying degrees of subtlety. At one extreme is strictly and even mechanically metrical music in which an insistent, inexorable drive sweeps everything else along with it, and if there are words they are clearly subordinated to the beat. Church music accompanied by guitar and bass can sometimes have this character. A poem read in unrelievedly metrical fashion is a poem read badly, and strict metrical drive rarely enhances musical performance. But meter is by no means necessarily mechanical; in music as in poetry, meter can provide a framework of expected accentuation that becomes nuanced with metrical variations, and melody too can cut across metrical expectations and lend a sense of freedom and personality. Musicianship is largely a matter of lending nuance and grace to what could otherwise be mechanical performance. It holds the metrical framework and the variations from this framework in creative tension. Some of the most striking examples of sacred music juxtapose a floating, sustained melody line against a strictly metrical background (one famous example being Handel's "Holy Art Thou"), which again establishes a tension between the potentially mechanical tendencies of meter and the freedom of melody that is not strongly punctuated or accentuated. But classical chant represents

the other end of the spectrum, dispensing with meter altogether and thus with the tension. To speak of chant as relaxing, as some listeners do, comes near the mark but not quite on it: it has neither the drive of strictly metrical music nor the tension that comes from a subtle play with meter, and its release from these formal qualities may be experienced as relaxing, but if sung with grace what it substitutes for a mechanical drive is a sense of intense personal engagement, with the fluid, spontaneous, unpredictable rhythms of speech. (I would not want to take the further step of identifying chant as "spiritual" and metrical music as "carnal," unless "spiritual" were redefined to mean *free* in this sense, which might still be more misleading than helpful.)

51. Comper, *Of the Atmosphere*, 10. On the architect's work, see John Betjeman, "A Note on J. N. Comper: Heir to Butterfield and Bodley," *Architectural Review* 85 (Feb. 1939), 79–82; Anthony Symondson, "Unity by Inclusion: Sir Ninian Comper and the Planning of a Modern Church," in *Twentieth Century Architecture: The Journal of the Twentieth Century Society* vol. 3 (1998), 17–42; Michael Hope, "Sir John Ninian Comper, 1864–1960," *Transactions of the Royal Institute of British Architects* 3 (1984), 90–99. On timelessness in liturgical arts see Josef Kreitmaier, *Beuroner Kunst: Eine Ausdrucksform der christlichen Mystik*, 2nd ed. (Freiburg: Herder, 1914), 64; Steven J. Schloeder, *Architecture in Communion: Implementing the Second Vatican Council through Liturgy and Architecture* (San Francisco: Ignatius, 1998), 46.

52. The argument here is thus not fundamentally at odds with the emphasis on "God's good time" in Jeremy Begbie, *Theology, Music, and Time* (Cambridge: Cambridge University Press, 2000).

53. Many people will report that a church built of concrete has a cold atmosphere, because its color and texture are less warm and subtle than those of most stone and brick, and because it is associated with utilitarian structures. Worshipers may report that they do not perceive concrete as cold—to which a critic would probably reply that they were insensitive (or had been desensitized) to the building's qualities. See Donald J. Bruggink and Carl H. Droppers, *When Faith Takes Form: Contemporary Churches of Architectural Integrity in America* (Grand Rapids, Mich.: Eerdmans, 1971), 60.

54. David Beevers, *All Saints, Margaret Street* (Andover, Hampshire: Pitkin, 1990).

55. McNally, *Sacred Space*, 80–81.

56. Kjell Lund, "The Spirituality of Space: Scandinavian Culture," *Faith and Form* 26 (spring 1993), 15.

57. Rudolf Otto, *The Idea of the Holy*, trans. John W. Harvey, 2nd ed. (London: Oxford University Press, 1950), 68.

58. Douglas R. Hoffman, "Seeking the Sacred: A Response to Edward Sövik's 'Remembrance and Hope,'" *Faith and Form* 30 (1997), no. 2, p. 13.

59. Söhngen, "Der Begriff des Sakralen," 194.

60. Built in 1984–87; Clare Lorenz, *Women in Architecture: A Contemporary Perspective* (London: Trefoil, 1990), 72 and 75.

61. Susan Dart, *Edwart Dart, Architect* (Evanston, Ill.: Evanston, 1993); "Reinterpreting an Ancient Liturgy," *Progressive Architecture* 47, no. 3 (Mar. 1966), 140–45; Linda Legner, "A City Church in the Village: Sandburg Village, That Is," *Inland Architect* 16, no. 10 (Dec. 1972), 20–21; Michael E. Komechak, "Ed Dart's Last Church, Completed after His Death," *Inland Architect* 21, no. 10 (Oct. 1977), 17–20.

62. Sövik, "A Portfolio of Reflections," 50–51.

63. Sergius Bulgakov, "Hagia Sophia," in *A Bulgakov Anthology*, ed. Nicolas Zernov and James Pain (Philadelphia: Westminster, 1976), 13–14; Catherine Evtuhov, *The Cross and the Sickle: Sergei Bulgakov and the Fate of Russian Religious Philosophy* (Ithaca, N.Y.: Cornell University Press, 1997), 230–33.

64. Ruth Webb, "The Aesthetics of Sacred Space: Narrative, Metaphor, and Motion in *Ekphraseis* of Church Buildings," *Dumbarton Oaks Papers* 53 (1999), 59–74. The term *ekphrasis* means simply "description" but came to be used as a kind of technical term for a particular kind of description of art or architecture.

65. Ibid., 68.

66. R. Macrides and P. Magdalino, "The Architecture of *Ekphrasis*: Construction and Context of Paul the Silentiary's Poem on Hagia Sophia," *Byzantine and Modern Greek Studies* 12 (1988), 47–82.

67. Procopius's description in *De aedificiis*, trans. Aubrey Stewart (in the Palestine Pilgrims' Text Society), is reprinted with consultation of the original in W.R. Lethaby and Harold Swainson, *The Church of Sancta Sophia, Constantinople: A Study of Byzantine Building* (London: Macmillan, 1894), 24–29, and parts are reprinted in Deno John Geanakoplos, ed., *Byzantium: Church, Society, and Civilization Seen through Contemporary Eyes* (Chicago: University of Chicago Press, 1984), 195–96. Paul the Silentiary's *Descriptio S. Sophiae* is translated by Lethaby and Swainson in *The Church of St. Sophia Constantinople*, 35–52 and 54–60, and parts are reprinted in Geanakoplos, *Byzantium*, 196–97; also W. Salzenberg, *Alt-christliche Baudenkmale von Constantinopel vom V. bis XII. Jahrhundert* (Berlin: Ernst and Korn, 1854; reprint, Leipzig: Hirsemann, 2001). The report of the Russian envoys from *The Russian Primary Chronicle* is in Serge A. Zenkovsky, ed., *Medieval Russia's Epics, Chronicles, and Tales* (New York: Dutton, 1963), 67–68, and in Geanakoplos, *Byzantium*, 189–90. On Hagia Sophia generally, see Rowland J. Mainstone, *Hagia Sophia: Architecture, Structure and Liturgy of Justinian's Great Church* (London: Thames and Hudson, 1988); Thomas F. Mathews, *The Early Churches of Constantinople: Architecture and Liturgy* (University Park: Pennsylvania State University Press, 1980); Robert Ousterhout, "The Holy Space: Architecture and the Liturgy," in Linda Safran, ed., *Heaven on Earth: Art and the Church in Byzantium* (University Park: Pennsylvania State University Press, 1998), 81–120; and Robert Ousterhout, *Master Builders of Byzantium* (Princeton, N.J.: Princeton University Press, 1999).

68. Cyril Mango and John Parker, "A Twelfth-Century Description of St. Sophia," *Dumbarton Oaks Papers* 14 (1960), 233–45.

69. Evliyá Efendí, *Narrative of Travels in Europe, Asia, and Africa, in the Seventeenth Century*, trans. Ritter Joseph von Hammer (London: Oriental Translation Fund of Great Britain and Ireland, 1846–1950), 55–65 (here p. 58). This account is replete with wonders.

70. Goetz, "Protestant Houses of God", 19–20; Ousterhout, "The Holy Space: Architecture and the Liturgy," 90.

71. This aspect of the building would have been brought to the foreground when Sultan Murád IV had cages with songbirds introduced to complement the singing of the muezzins and fill the space "with a harmony approaching to that of Paradise"; see Efendí, *Narrative of Travels*, 58.

72. Söhngen, "Der Begriff des Sakralen," 193; for the French text, *La Confession*

helvétique postérieure (texte française de 1566), with an introduction by Jacques Courvo-isier (Paris: Delachaux and Niestlé, 1944), 127.

73. James F. White, "From Protestant to Catholic Plain Style," in Paul Corby Fin-ney, ed., *Seeing beyond the Word: Visual Arts and the Calvinist Tradition* (Grand Rapids, Mich.: Eerdmans, 1999), 462.

74. Dell Upton, *Architecture in the United States* (New York: Oxford University Press, 1998), 111.

75. Tillich, *On Art and Architecture*, 214–20.

76. K.L. Sijmons, *Protestantsche kerkbouw* ('s-Gravenhage: D.A. Daamen, 1946), especially 16–21 and 34–38. G.J. van der Harst, *Monumentale kerkgebouwen: Een lust voor de kerk!* (Zoetermeer, The Netherlands: Boekencentrum, 2000), 26–29 ("Een typ-isch protestantse sfeer"), builds on Sijmons' observations. See Trevor Wyatt Moore, "Of God and Place and the Future: A Conversation with Karel L. Sijmons," *Faith and Form* 2 (1969), 15–16. On Sijmons's work, see the notices in *Bouwkundig weekblad ar-chitectura* 71 (Jan. 20, 1953), 22–26, and 74 (Mar. 27, 1956), 141–47; in *Forum* (Am-sterdam) 12, nos. 1–2 (Mar. 1957), 5–9; and 13, no. 12 (1958–59), 372–75 and 378–81; Roger Ortmayer, "Critique: Thomas Kerk Reformed Church Center, Amsterdam, The Netherlands," *Faith and Form* 1 (Apr. 1968), 6–11; Willem Gerard Overbosch, "Kir-chenbau in Holland," in *Kirchenbau und Ökumene: Evangelische Kirchenbautagung in Hamburg 1961* (Hamburg: Friedrich Wittig Verlag, 1962), 55. Sijmons has comments on Ronchamp in *Forum* 10, no. 9 (Nov. 1955), 302–9. I have not been able to locate Wim J. Van Heuvel, *Karel Sijmons Architect* (Voorburg: Heuvel, 1998).

77. Oswald Spengler, *The Decline of the West*, trans. Charles Francis Atkinson (New York: Knopf, 1926), 1:250. Sijmons's phrasing simplifies the conception slightly.

78. Louis P. Nelson, "Building Confessions: Architecture and Meaning in Nineteenth-Century Places of Worship," in Virginia Chieffo Raguin and Mary Ann Powers, eds., *Sacred Spaces: Building and Remembering Sites of Worship in the Nine-teenth Century* (Worcester, Mass.: Iris and B. Gerald Cantor Art Gallery, College of the Holy Cross, 2002), 11.

79. James F. White, *Protestant Worship and Church Architecture: Theological and Historical Considerations* (New York: Oxford University Press, 1964), 29.

80. *Architectural Record* 119, no. 6 (Jun. 1956), 214, on Richard J. Neutra and Robert E. Alexander's interdenominational chapel at Miramar, California. A Congre-gational minister prayed in 1835, "may the time never come, when the sons of Con-necticut, into whatever part of the world wandering, on returning home, shall not be greeted from the distant hills and smiling valleys of their native state, by the church-spire . . . pointing their soul to heaven"; see Louis P. Nelson, "Building Confessions: Architecture and Meaning in Nineteenth-Century Places of Worship," in Raguin and Powers, ed., *Sacred Spaces*, 12.

81. Tillich, *On Art and Architecture*, 193.

82. "Crystal Chapel: Bruce Goff, Architect," *Architectural Forum* 93, no. 1 (Jul. 1950), 87 (praised for its "crystalline purity of emotion based on other-worldly won-der"); Robert E. Fischer, "The Crystal Cathedral: Embodiment of Light and Nature," *Architectural Record* 168, no. 7 (Nov. 1980), 77–85; Barbara Goldstein, "New Crystal Palace: Crystal Cathedral, Garden Grove, CA," *Progressive Architecture* 61, no. 12 (Dec. 1980), 76–85; Manfredo Tafuri, "Subaqueous Cathedral: Crystal Cathedral, Garden Grove, California, 1980; Architects: Johnson Burgee Architects," *Domus* 608 (Jul.–

Aug. 1980), 8–15; John Pastier, "Soaring Space Wrapped in Metal and Glass: Crystal Cathedral, Garden Grove, Calif., Johnson/Burgee," in *American Architecture of the 1980s* (Washington, D.C.: American Institute of Architects Press, 1990), 30–39.

83. Peter W. Williams, "Metamorphoses of the Meetinghouse: Three Case Studies," in Paul Corby Finney, ed., *Seeing beyond the Word: Visual Arts and the Calvinist Tradition* (Grand Rapids, Mich.: Eerdmans, 1999), 485.

84. Söhngen, "Der Begriff des Sakralen," 200–201.

85. White, "From Protestant to Catholic Plain Style," 457–76.

86. Ernest Kurpershoek, *The Nieuwe Kerk, Amsterdam*, trans. Sammy Herman (Amsterdam: Nationale Stifting De Nieuwe Kerk, 1999).

87. "Christ Church (Minneapolis, Minn.)," *Architectural Forum* 93, no. 1 (Jul. 1950), 80–85; "Église à Minneapolis," *Architecture d'aujourd'hui* 21, no. 33 (Dec. 1950–Jan. 1951), 79–83; Albert Christ-Janer and Mary Mix Foley, *Modern Church Architecture: A Guide to the Form and Spirit of twentieth-Century Religious Buildings* (New York: McGraw-Hill, 1962), 146–53; and Albert Christ-Janer, *Eliel Saarinen: Finnish-American Architect and Educator*, rev. ed. (Chicago: University of Chicago Press, 1979), 117–21; Rolf T. Anderson, *Architectural History of Christ Church Lutheran* (United States Department of the Interior, National Park Service, National Register of Historic Places Continuation Sheet, sec. number 8, 2001).

88. Christ-Janer, *Eliel Saarinen*, 118.

89. Ibid., 121.

90. Christ-Janer and Foley, *Modern Church Architecture*, 147.

91. Basil F.L. Clarke, *Church Builders of the Nineteenth Century* (New York: Macmillan, 1938), 204, quoted in Elizabeth and Wayland Young, *London's Churches* (Topsfield, Mass.: Salem House, 1986), 71.

92. Frédéric Debuyst, *Modern Architecture and Christian Celebration* (Richmond, Va.: John Knox Press, 1968), especially p. 70.

93. "First Presbyterian Church, Cottage Grove, Oregon, Pietro Belluschi," *Progressive Architecture* 33, no. 3 (Mar. 1952), 64; "Meeting House of the First Unitarian Society of Madison, Wis.," *Architectural Forum* 97, no. 6 (Dec. 1952), 86 and 89.

94. Debuyst, *Modern Architecture and Christian Celebration*, 70.

95. *Environment and Art in Catholic Worship.*

96. Ken Sidey, "So Long to Sacred Space: Consumer-Minded, User-Friendly Buildings—Not Glorified Monuments—Are Driving Church Designs," *Christianity Today* 37, no. 13 (Nov. 8, 1993), 46.

97. Debuyst, *Modern Architecture and Christian Celebration*, 43, 47, 50.

98. Edward Anders Sövik, "Tea and Sincerity," *Liturgical Arts* 37, no. 1 (Nov. 1968), 4–7; see Mark Allen Torgerson, "Edward Anders Sövik and His Return to the 'Non-Church'" (Ph.D. diss., University of Notre Dame, 1995), 216–25.

99. Austin C. Lovelace, "A Musician's View: Good Acoustics for Music and Word," in *Acoustics for Liturgy*, 25–32.

100. Dennis Fleisher, "An Acoustician's View: Acoustics for Congregational Singing," in *Acoustics for Liturgy*, 7–16.

101. Christian Norberg-Schulz, *Intentions in Architecture* (Cambridge, Mass.: MIT Press, 1965), 139 and 151; in Norberg-Schulz's *Meaning in Western Architecture*, trans. Anna Maria Norberg-Schulz (New York: Praeger, 1975), articulation is one of the basic organizing categories.

102. Sara Holmes Boutelle, *Julia Morgan, Architect* (New York: Abbeville Press, 1988), 70–72.

103. Mary E. Osman, "Julia Morgan of California: A Passion for Quality and Anonymity," *AIA Journal*, Jun. 1976, 44–48; and Dell Upton, *Architecture in the United States* (New York: Oxford University Press, 1998), 276–77. Diane Favro, "Sincere and Good: The Architectural Practice of Julia Morgan," *Journal of Architectural and Planning Research* 9, no. 2 (summer 1992), 112–28, provides a useful analysis of Morgan's career (noting on p. 116 that she "demonstrated commitment by becoming a workaholic, devoting almost every waking hour to architecture while subsisting on a few hours of sleep and a diet of chocolate bars and coffee"), and especially her status as a woman in the male-dominated field of architecture, but does not discuss her churches. For another woman architect, see John Edward Powell, "Edith Mortensen Northman: Tower District Architect," *Fresno Bee*, May 11, 1990, p. F4 ("She was proud of her Danish Lutheran Church in Los Angeles, built in 1937 in the Danish country-church style, which she described in total understatement as 'not too bad' ").

104. Sally B. Woodbridge, "Preservation: St. John's," *Architectural Forum* 139, no. 2 (Sept. 1973), p. 18.

105. Joseph Armstrong Baird, Jr., *The Churches of Mexico, 1530–1810* (Berkeley: University of California Press, 1962), 28–29.

106. Built in 1871–98; see Clarke, *Church Builders of the Nineteenth Century*, 196–209; Roger Dixon and Stefan Muthesius, *Victorian Architecture* (London: Thames and Hudson, 1978), 218–21; Young, *London's Churches*, 69–72 ("Is there anywhere a Victorian church which is entirely harmonious, which is pleasing without and within, which lacks neither prettiness nor grandeur, which invites the eye both to dwell and to proceed, which is in short quite beautiful? There is, and this is it").

107. The most important precedent was Albi Cathedral, on the influence of which see John Thomas, *Albi Cathedral and British Church Architecture: The Influence of Thirteenth-Century Church Building in Southern France and Northern Spain upon Ecclesiastical Design in Modern Britain* ([London]: Ecclesiological Society, 2002).

108. Elisabeth Beazley, "Watts Chapel," in J. M. Richards and Nikolaus Pevsner, eds., *The Anti-Rationalists* (London: Architectural Press, 1973), 170–80, Edwin Heathcote and Iona Spens, *Church Builders* (Chichester, Sussex: Academy, 1997), 16; Mary S. Watts, *The Word in the Pattern: A Key to the Symbols on the Walls of the Chapel at Compton* (London: W. H. Ward, n.d.).

109. Stanley Abercrombie, " 'A Building of Great Integrity': Fay Jones' Thorncrown Chapel, Eureka Springs, Ark.," in *American Architecture of the 1980s* (Washington, D.C.: American Institute of Architects Press, 1990), 22–29; Robert Adams Ivy, Jr., *Fay Jones: The Architecture of E. Fay Jones, FAIA* (Washington, D.C.: AIA, 1992; New York: McGraw-Hill, 2001), 32–45 (reference to the AIA survey on p. 13), reviewed in *Faith and Form*, 26 (winter 1992–93), 40; Euine Fay Jones, *"Outside the Pale": The Architecture of Fay Jones* (Fayetteville: University of Arkansas Press, 1999); Heathcote and Spens, *Church Builders*, 176–85, includes reference to more recent work.

110. Ivy, *Fay Jones*, 32.

111. Upton, *Architecture in the United States*, 127.

112. Boutelle, *Julia Morgan*, 89–91.

113. Designed by R. S. D. Harman (1935); see John Stacpoole and Peter Beaven,

New Zealand Art: Architecture, 1820–1970 (Wellington, New Zealand: Reed, 1972), p. 84, no. 62.

114. By Josias Joesler (1936). See the similar use of site at Faith Lutheran Church in Tucson (designed by Arthur T. Brown): there is a short account in "Religion," *Progressive Architecture* 32, no. 1 (Jan. 1951), 76.

115. See the listing of IFRAA International Architectural Design Awards in *Faith and Form* 25 (winter 1991–92), 20. Yet another good example is First Unitarian Church in Westport, Connecticut (Victor A. Lundy), on which see "Churches—1961," *Architectural Forum* 115, no. 6 (Dec. 1961), 90-93; the church is built on eight acres of dense woodland, left largely intact, and the architect is quoted as saying, "The real sanctuary is the nature left there on the land."

116. Built in 1966–78; see Roberto de Alba and Alan W. Organschi, "A Conversation with Giovanni Michelucci," *Perspecta* 27 (1992), 123.

117. Stephen A. Kliment, "Labor of Love: Metropolitan Community Church, Washington, D.C.; Suzanne Reitag, Architect," *Architectural Record* 181, no. 10 (Oct. 1993), 79.

118. Built 1949–51; see "Wayfarer's Chapel (Palos Verdes, Calif.)," *Architectural Forum* 95 (Aug. 1951), 153–55; "Swedenborg Memorial Chapel (Wayfarer's Chapel), Rancho Palos Verdes, California, 1946–1971; Architect: Lloyd Wright," *Space Design* 11 (182) (Nov. 1979), 9–15; Allison J. Colborne, *Prints and Drawings: Guide and Inventory to the Papers of Lloyd Wright's Wayfarers' (Swedenborg Memorial) Chapel* (Montreal: Canadian Centre for Architecture, 1990); Alan Weintraub, Thomas S. Hines, Eric Lloyd Wright, and Dana Hutt, *Lloyd Wright: The Architecture of Frank Lloyd Wright Jr.* (New York: Abrams, 1998); and Patrick Joseph Meehan, *Lloyd Wright, a Prairie School Architect* (Monticello, Ill.: Vance Bibliographies, 1978).

119. Ivy, *Fay Jones*, 52–75.

120. Upton, *Architecture in the United States*, 127.

121. Ivy, *Fay Jones*, 35.

CHAPTER 4

1. Rudolf Arnheim, *The Dynamics of Architectural Form* (Berkeley: University of California Press, 1977), 208–9.

2. J. Rinderspacher, Friedrich Zwingmann, and Emil Wachter, *Autobahnkirche St. Christophorus, Baden-Baden*, with preface by Katharina Sandweier, 4th ed. (Munich: Schnell and Steiner, 1992), and Emil Wachter, *Die Bilderwelt der Autobahnkirche Baden-Baden* (Freiburg: Herder, 1980).

3. "Crystal Chapel: Bruce Goff, Architect," *Architectural Forum* 93, no. 1 (Jul. 1950), 87.

4. Paul Tillich, *On Art and Architecture*, ed. John and Jane Dillenberger, trans. Robert P. Scharlemann (New York: Crossroad, 1989), 204–13.

5. Built in 1943; see Stamo Papadaki, *The Work of Oscar Niemeyer* (New York: Reinhold, 1950), 92–103; Henry-Russell Hitchcock, *Latin American Architecture since 1945* (New York: Museum of Modern Art, 1955), 66–67.

6. First Unitarian Church of Fairfield County, Westport, Connecticut (Victory A. Lundy, 1961–65); see "Churches—1961," *Architectural Forum* 115, no. 6 (Dec. 1961),

91, and Patricia M. Snibbe and Richard W. Snibbe, *The New Modernist in World Architecture* (New York: McGraw-Hill, 1999), 78–79.

7. Peter Hammond, "A Radical Approach to Church Architecture," in Peter Hammond, ed., *Towards a Church Architecture* (London: Architectural Press, 1962), 24–25.

8. Edwin Heathcote and Iona Spens, *Church Builders* (Chichester, Sussex: Academy, 1997), 15.

9. Ibid., 160.

10. Douglas R. Hoffman, "Seeking the Sacred: A Response to Edward Sövik's 'Remembrance and hope,'" *Faith and Form* 30 no. 2, (1997), p. 13, distinguishes three types of archetypal factor in sacred architecture: universal themes (earth, air, water, fire), religious or mythic motifs (axial pillars, trees, stones, mountains), and pure geometric forms. See also Dennis McNally, *Sacred Space: An Aesthetic for the Liturgical Environment* (Bristol, Ind.: Wyndham Hall, 1985), 4 and 81–82.

11. "Meeting House of the First Unitarian Society of Madison, Wis.," *Architectural Forum* 97, no. 6 (Dec. 1952), 86.

12. Michael J. Crosbie, *Architecture for the Gods* (New York: Watson-Guptill, 2000 [reprint]), 86, referring to Light of the World Catholic Church in Littleton, Colorado (Hoover Berg Desmond, 1984).

13. Translation from Asher Ovadiah, "Early Churches," in Ephraim Stern, ed., *The New Encyclopedia of Archaeological Excavations in the Holy Land* (New York: Simon & Schuster, 1993), 1:305–9; see Kathleen McVey, "The Domed Church as Microcosm: Literary Roots of an Architectural Symbol," *Dumbarton Oaks Papers* 37 (1983), 95.

14. Guillelmus Durandus, *The Symbolism of Churches and Church Ornaments*, trans. J.M. Neale and B. Webb, 3rd ed. (London: Gibbings, 1906).

15. Anthony Sparrow, *A Rationale upon the Book of Common Prayer of the Church of England* (Oxford: Parker, 1843), 299–302; Charles James Stranks, *Anglican Devotion: Studies in the Spiritual Life of the Church of England between the Reformation and the Oxford Movement* (London: SCM, 1961), 150–54.

16. The parish church of Holy Trinity at Stratford-on-Avon, where Shakespeare is buried, provides one good example of this phenomenon. Often there were constraints on the site, or the builders miscalculated; see Warwick Rodwell, *The Archaeology of the English Church: The Study of Historic Churches and Churchyards* (London: Batsford, 1981), 60–61.

17. Durandus, *The Symbolism of Churches*, xix–cxxvii.

18. Steven J. Schloeder, *Architecture in Communion: Implementing the Second Vatican Council through Liturgy and Architecture* (San Francisco: Ignatius, 1998), 195–208; L.H. Stookey, "The Gothic Cathedral as the Heavenly Jerusalem: Liturgical and Theological Sources," *Gesta* 8 (1969), 35–41.

19. A. Welby Pugin, *Contrasts: Or, a Parallel Between the Noble Edifices of the Fourteenth and Fifteenth Centuries, and Similar Buildings of the Present Day, Showing the Present Decay of Taste, Accompanied by Appropriate Text* (London: Pugin, 1836), 5.

20. Michael Hall, "What Do Victorian Churches Mean? Symbolism and Sacramentalism in Anglican Church Architecture, 1850–1870," *Journal of the Society of Architectural Historians* 59 (2000), 78–95.

21. Robert W. Jenson, "God, Space, and Architecture," in *Essays in Theology of Culture* (Grand Rapids, Mich.: Eerdmans, 1995), 15.

22. Frédéric Debuyst, *Modern Architecture and Christian Celebration* (London: Lutterworth; Richmond, Va.: John Knox Press, 1968), 70.

23. Stephen A. Kliment, "Labor of Love: Metropolitan Community Church, Washington, D.C.; Suzanne Reitag, Architect," *Architectural Record* 181, no. 10 (Oct. 1993), 79.

24. Joanne Deane Sieger, "Visual Metaphor as Theology: Leo the Great's Sermons on the Incarnation and the Arch Mosaics at Santa Maria Maggiore," *Gesta* 26 (1987), 83–91; Sible L. de Blaauw, *Cultus et decor: Liturgie en architectuur in laatantiek en middeleeuws Rome: Basilica Salvatoris, Santae Mariae, Sancti Petri* (Delft: Eburon, 1987), 176–77.

25. Sixten Ringbom, *Icon to Narrative: The Rise of the Dramatic Close-up in Fifteenth-Century Devotional Painting*, 2nd ed. (Doornspijk: Davaco, 1984).

26. Richard Kieckhefer, *Unquiet Souls: Fourteenth-Century Saints and Their Religious Milieu* (Chicago: University of Chicago Press, 1984), 76–77.

27. Jole Vichi Imberciadori, Piero Torriti, and Marco Torriti *The Collegiate Church of San Gimignano and its Museum of Sacred Art* (San Gimignano, Italy: Nencini, 2001), and Gianna Coppini, *San Gimignano: A Medieval Dream* (San Gimignano: Il Furetto, 2000). On Pickering in Yorkshire, where the elements of coherence are far from total, see Christopher Ellis, *St. Peter and St. Paul Parish Church, Pickering* (Derby: English Life, 1996), and Kate Giles, "Pickering: Parish Church of SS Peter and Paul," *Archaeological Journal* 154 for 1997 (1998), 250–55.

28. Lucien Bégule, *La peinture décorative en Savoie: Les peintures murales des chapelles Saint-Sébastien et Saint-Antoine a Lanslevillard et Bessans (Maurienne)*, Étude présentée à *l'Académie des sciences, belles-lettres et arts de Lyon, en la Séance du 25 Juin 1918*, vol. 16, 397–434) (Lyon: A. Rey, 1918); Bégule does not fully resolve the question of dating, but I incline toward an earlier date than the early sixteenth century.

29. Marcia B. Hall, *Renovation and Counter-Reformation: Vasari and Duke Cosimo in Sta Maria Novella and Sta Croce, 1565–1577* (Oxford: Clarendon, 1979), 1–15.

30. Antoine Gardner, "Le couvent des Dominicains de Guebwiller," *Congrès archéologique de France* 136 (1978), 249–63.

31. Joseph Polzer, "Andrea di Bonaiuto's *Via Veritatis* and Dominican Thought in Late Medieval Italy," *Art Bulletin* 77 (1995), 262–89.

32. On the use of frescoes within the orders, see generally Dieter Blume, *Wandmalerei als Ordenspropaganda: Bildprogramme im Chorbereich franziskanischer Konvente Italiens bis zur Mitte des 14. Jahrhunderts* (Worms, Germany: Werner, 1983).

33. Phyllis Williams Lehmann, "Alberti and Antiquity: Additional Observations," *Art Bulletin* 70 (1988), 388–400

34. J. Wood Brown, *The Dominican Church of Santa Maria Novella at Florence: A Historical, Architectural, and Artistic Survey* (Edinburgh: Otto Schulze, 1902), 69–70.

35. Kathleen Giles Arthur, "The Strozzi Chapel: Notes on the Building History of Sta. Maria Novella," *Art Bulletin* 65 (1983), 367–86; Joanne Snow-Smith, "Masaccio's Fresco in Santa Maria Novella: A Symbolic Representation of the Eucharistic Sacrifice," *Arte lombarda* 84–85, nos. 1–2 (1988), 47–60; Jack Miles, *Christ: A Crisis in the Life of God* (New York: Knopf, 2001), 295.

36. *Benediktinerinnen-Abtei St. Hildegard, Rüdesheim-Eibingen*, 5th ed. (Regensburg: Schnell and Steiner, 1999), 14–15.

37. Ann Lumley, *Sydney's Architecture* (Melbourne: Longman Cheshire, 1992), 50–51. The architect was William Wardell; the cathedral was built in stages 1868–1928.

38. Charlene Rooke, *Edmonton: Secrets of the City* (Vancouver: Arsenal Pulp Press, 2001), 34.

39. Theodor Maas-Ewerd, "Liturgie der Kirche—Liturgie des Himmels," in Jürgen Lenssen, ed., *Liturgie und Kirchenraum: Anstösse zu einer Neubesinnung* (Würzburg: Echter, 1986), 71.

40. *The Divine Liturgy according to St. John Chrysostom, with Appendices* (New York: Russian Orthodox Greek Catholic Church of America, 1967), 52–55; see Bishop Chrysostomos of Oreoi, "Heaven Meets Earth: Eastern Orthodox Church Art and Architecture," *Faith and Form* 19 (fall 1986), 25–27.

41. Liviu Streza, "The Mystagogy of Sacred Space according to Orthodox Theology," *Studia liturgica* 24 (1994), 90.

42. Romano Guardini, *The Spirit of the Liturgy*, trans. Ada Lane (New York: Herder and Herder, 1998), 67. See also Dennis McNamara, "So, You're on the Parish Building Committee?" *Adoremus Bulletin* 4, no. 9 (Feb. 1999): "The primary consideration in building a new church is the recognition that a church building is a domus Dei, or House of God, in which we 'sing a hymn to the Lord's glory with all the warriors of the heavenly army' in an earthly liturgy which provides a 'foretaste of the heavenly liturgy.' [SC 8]"

43. Caesarius of Arles, *Sermons* 227, trans. Mary Magdelein Mueller (New York: Fathers of the Church, 1956–73), 3:168; *Sancti Caesarii Arelatensis Sermones*, ed. Germanus Morin, 2nd ed. (Turnhout: Brepols, 1953), 900 ("ut cum dies iudicii venerit, in illa aeterna ac beata ecclesia . . . audire mereamur: 'Venite, benedicti patris mei.'"). Jean Fouquet's Enthronement of the Virgin, "Hours of Étienne Chevalier," ca. 1445, Musée Condé, ms. fr. 71, fol. 14, is reproduced in Barbara Newman, "Intimate Pieties: Holy Trinity and Holy Family in the Late Middle Ages," *Literature and Religion* 31, no. 1 (1999), 77–101, fig. 1 (and on the cover of that issue of the journal).

44. George Craig Stewart, *Six Altars: Studies in Sacrifice* (Milwaukee: Morehouse, 1930), 47–48. See also A.G. Hebert, *Liturgy and Society: The Function of the Church in the Modern World* (London: Faber and Faber, 1935; reprint, 1961), 246–49; Cettina Militello, "A Theology of Liturgical Space," trans. Matthew J. O'Connell, in Anscar J. Chupungco, ed., *Liturgical Time and Space* (Collegeville, Minn.: Liturgical Press, 2000), 402–03.

45. Augustine, *Concerning the City of God against the Pagans* 22.11–30, trans. Henry Bettenson (Harmondsworth: Penguin, 1972), 1049–91, is a sustained reflection on the community in heaven (but here I give my own translation, to convey more of the rhetorical effect of the original). Even the digressions in the text are the result of Augustine's clear insistence that contemplative prayer and liturgical prayer, the act of the individual and that of the worshiping community, are ultimately and ideally fused (22.29). Why, en route to his finale, must Augustine ponder in what sense the angels are ours and in what sense God's? And why must we know whether the saints will see God with their bodily eyes, and whether their vision will be interrupted if they blink? The angels are ours in the sense that we and they are fellow citizens of the heavenly city. And Augustine's interest in the role of bodily vision leads to a suggestion with stunning implications: perhaps, he says, our vision of God in eternity will be a refracted one, perhaps individuals will perceive God in each other

and throughout the new heaven and the new earth, and when the thoughts of one saint lie open to the mind of another this too may be a means for perceiving God, and if the blessed see each other's bodies with their bodily eyes this too may be a form of what later theologians would call beatific vision. What Augustine entertains here is the possibility that beatitude will not mean turning from the many to the One but even in eternity partaking of the One through the many, in an ideal life that is radically and necessarily social.

46. T.S. Eliot, *Four Quartets* (New York: Harcourt, Brace, 1943), 32 ("Little Gidding," lines 52–3).

47. Kliment, "Labor of love," 81.

48. Ernest R. Suffling, *English Church Brasses* (London: Gill, 1910), 170.

49. H. B. McCall, *Richmondshire Churches* (London: Stock, 1910), 187–209.

50. On funerals and their significance, see C.R. Burgess, "A Service for the Dead: The Form and Function of the Anniversary in Late Medieval Bristol," *Transactions of the Bristol and Gloucestershire Archaeological Society* 105 (1987), 183–211, and "Late Medieval Wills and Pious Convention: Testamentary Evidence Reconsidered, in Michael Hicks, ed., *Profit, Piety and the Professions in Later Medieval England* (Gloucester, England: Sutton, 1990), 14–33.

51. In the village church at Alne there is a "virgin's crant," a garland made of paper, meant to be carried in front of a maiden's body at her funeral procession.

52. Giles Knox, "The Colleoni Chapel in Bergamo and the Politics of Urban Space," *Journal of the Society of Architectural Historians* 60, no. 3 (2001), 379; see Giles Robert Morgan Knox, "Church Decoration and the Politics of Reform in Late-Sixteenth and Early-Seventeenth-Century Bergamo" (Ph. D. diss., University of Toronto, 1999).

53. Similarly, despite the dedication, few today are aware how far Saint Patrick's Cathedral once served as a tribute to the Irish, who could behold such monuments and "laugh to scorn" their English oppressors; see Thomas Keneally, "Cold Sanctuary: How the Church Lost Its Mission," *New Yorker*, Jun. 17 and 24, 2002, p. 62.

54. Andrew Martindale, "Patrons and Minders: The Intrusion of the Secular into Sacred Spaces in the Late Middle Ages," in Diana Wood, ed., *The Church and the Arts* (Oxford: Blackwell, 1995), 175.

55. Mircea Eliade, *Images and Symbols*, trans. Phillip Mairet (New York: Sheed and Ward, 1961), 120–21; Guilford Dudley III, *Religion on Trial: Mircea Eliade and His Critics* (Philadelphia: Temple University Press, 1977), 56.

56. William A. Christian, Jr., *Apparitions in Late Medieval and Renaissance Spain* (Princeton, N.J.: Princeton University Press, 1981).

57. William A. Scott, *Historical Protestantism: An Historical Introduction to Protestant Theology* (Englewood Cliffs, N.J.: Prentice Hall, 1971), 90–91.

58. C.E. Pocknee, *The Christian Altar in History and Today* (London: Mowbrays, 1963), chap. 5.

59. Josef Andreas Jungmann, "The New Altar," trans. John J. Galvani, *Liturgical Arts* 37, no. 2 (Feb. 1969), 36–40.

60. Steven J. Schloeder, *Architecture in Communion: Implementing the Second Vatican Council through Liturgy and Architecture* (San Francisco: Ignatius, 1998), 173–75. Otto Scriba, "Zur Orientierung mittelalterlicher Kirchen," *Kunst und Kirche* 41 (1978), 101–2, finds evidence at Bad Wimpfen on the Neckar for the positioning of churches

not strictly toward the east but rather toward the direction of sunrise on the feast of the church's patron. Whether this practice was widespread in England has been debated. See Hugh Benson, "Church Orientations and Patronal, Festivals," *Antiquaries Journal* 36 (1956), 205–13; Sidney Searle, "The Church Points the Way," *New Scientist*, 61, no. 879 (Jan. 3, 1974), 10–13, followed by correspondence in nos. 881 (Jan. 17), 155–56; 882 (Jan. 24), 219–20; 883 (Jan. 31), 284; and 884 (Feb. 7), 365; Davies, "Church Orientation in Rutland," *Rutland Record* 4 (1984), 142–43; W. C. B. Smith, *St Mary's Church, Beverley: An Account of its Building over Four Hundred Years from 1120 to 1524* (Beverley: The Friends of St Mary's Church, 1978 [i.e., 2001]), 140–42; and, for a useful survey of the literature, Bob Trubshaw, "Church orientation," *Mercian Mysteries* 5 (Dec. 1990), 4–6, available on-line at www.indigogroup.co.uk/edge/chorien.htm.

61. In Rome, which was less in need of such assurance, orientation was for complex reasons much less the norm; early Roman churches were more often directed westward, with the priest facing east, but this arrangement was not consistent or rigorous.

62. Herbert Thurston and Donald Attwater, eds., *Butler's Lives of the Saints*, rev. ed. (New York: Kenedy, 1956), 4:68.

63. Philippe Guigon, *Les églises du haut Moyen Age en Bretagne* (Saint-Malo, France: Centre régional d'archéologie d'Alet, 1997–98); the relevant volumes of Marcel Aubert, ed., *Les églises de France* (Paris: Letouzay and Ane, 1932–); Heinz Vestner, ed., *Brittany*, trans. Michael Cunningham and Simon Knight (Munich: Nelles Verlag, 1993).

64. For English parallels, see P. E. H. Hair, "The Chapel in the English Landscape," *Local Historian* 21 (1991), 4–10.

65. Georg Gerster, *Churches in Rock: Early Christian Art in Ethiopia*, trans. Richard Hosking (London: Phaidon, 1970), 85–92; Irmgard Bidder, *Lalibela: The Monolithic Churches of Ethiopia*, trans. Rita Grabham-Hortmann (New York: Praeger, 1960); Caroline Orwin, "Lalibela (Amara, Ethiopia)," in *International Dictionary of Historic Places* (Chicago: Fitzroy Dearborn, 1996), 4:444–47; Marilyn Eiseman Heldman, "Legends of Lalibala: The Development of an Ethiopian Pilgrimage Site," *RES: Anthropology and Aesthetics* 27 (Spring 1995), 25–38; Nnamdi Elleh, *African Architecture: Evolution and Transformation* (New York: McGraw-Hill, 1997), 134–37.

66. Augustus Joseph Schulte, "Consecration," in *The Catholic Encyclopedia: An International Work of Reference on the Constitution, Doctrine, Discipline, and History of the Catholic Church* (New York: Encyclopedia Press, 1913), 4:276–83; J. G. Davies, *The Secular Use of Church Buildings* (New York: Seabury, 1968), 249–64; Brian V. Repsher, *The Rite of Church Dedication in the Early Medieval Era* (Lewiston, N.Y.: Edwin Mellen, 1998); Ignazio M. Calabuig, "The Rite of Dedication of a Church," trans. Matthew J. O'Connell, in Chupungco, *Liturgical Time and Space*, 333–79; Ignazio M. Calabuig, *The Dedication of a Church and an Altar: A Theological Commentary* (Washington, D.C.: United States Catholic Conference, 1980); Thomas G. Simons, *Holy People, Holy Places: Rites for the Church's House* (Chicago: Liturgy Training, 1998); Schloeder, *Architecture in Communion*, 170–73. For a concise statement on consecration in Eastern Orthodoxy, see Streza, "The Mystagogy of Sacred Space According to Orthodox Theology," 86–87.

67. Calabuig, "The Rite of Dedication of a Church," 337, relates 1 Kings 8 with

Ezra 6:13–18 (Zerubbabel's dedication) and 1 Maccabees 4:36–61 (the dedication in the time of Judas Maccabeus).

68. There is an alternative tradition, of course, that ascribes the construction of the Temple to a very different sort of collaboration; see F.C. Conybeare, "The Testament of Solomon," *Jewish Quarterly Review* 11 (1899), 1–45.

69. Davies, *Secular Use of Church Buildings*, 252; Calabuig, "The Rite of Dedication of a Church," 344, doubts that this meaning was originally intended.

70. Davies, *Secular Use of Church Buildings*, 38 (referring to the author of this liturgical source as "Dodo" of Metz). Elsewhere, p. 256, Davies asks, "Can anyone indeed point to a virgin patch of ground on which a church is to be built and seriously declare that it is demon infested?" But on this point see Calabuig, "The Rite of Dedication of a Church," 369: the new dedication rite prescribed in 1977 for the Roman Church did not think it appropriate "to eliminate every reference to the ancient *lustratio*, which reminds the faithful of the mysterious influence of the Evil One even on material structures, which are subject to transiency and corruption (see Rom 8:20–21)."

71. On these changes see Simons, *Holy People, Holy Places*, especially 1–14.

72. Davies, *Secular Use of Church Buildings*, 262.

73. "Chapel of the Snows destroyed," *Antarctic Journal of the United States*, 13, no. 4 (Dec. 1978), p. 6, and "New Chapel of the Snows dedicated at McMurdo Station," *Antarctic Journal of the United States*, 24, no. 4 (Mar. 1989), 13–4. The original chapel was destroyed, with irony that some might find fitting, by fire. Andrei Zolotov, Jr., "Orthodox Church on Its Way to Antarctica," *St. Petersburg Times (Russia)*, Feb. 27, 2002 (posted on the internet site of the Orthodox Peace Fellowship), discusses a wooden church designed for King George Island (with special provisions enabling it survive the Antarctic climate) and mentions a makeshift Chilean chapel in Antarctica as well.

74. Theoharis David, curator, *Contemporary Third World Architecture: Search for Identity: Amer-Indian, Africa, India, Cyprus, Egypt, Mexico: A Traveling Exhibition Organized by the Department of Exhibitions, Pratt Institute, and first shown at the Pratt Manhattan Center Gallery, 160 Lexington Avenue at 30th Street, September 13–October 8, 1983*, 65, with diagrams and photo of model on 65–67. On the architect, see *Amancio Guedes* (London: Architectural Association, 1980), and Elleh, *African Architecture*, 60–61. For his later work, including a mosque (designed, he says, one Friday night when he had dinner with an old friend, who wished it built quickly to make peace with Allah before undergoing heart surgery) and a cricket pavilion converted into a chapel, see Pancho Guedes, "Recent Work," *AA Files* 1, no. 1 (winter 1981–82), 129–32.

75. Monastery of San Luis Potosí, Mexico (Antonio Attolini Lack, 1980), shown in David, *Contemporary Third World Architecture*, 21; and "Church of Saint Paul: a Catholic Church of Concrete at Karuizawa, Japan," *Architectural Record* 79, no. 1 (Jan. 1936), 29.

76. Bruno Bürki, *La case des chrétiens: Essai de théologie pratique sur le lieu de culte en Afrique* (Yaounde, Cameroon: CLE, 1973), 106–8.

77. Manfred Ludes, *Sakralbauten: Projekte, 1964–1998* (Wuppertal, Germany: Müller und Busmann, 2001), 52.

78. Terrence M. Curry, "Designing a Building for a Nigerian Church," *Faith and Form* 24 (winter 1990–91), 36–39.

79. "Prototype Mission Churches," *Churchbuilding* 18 (Apr. 1966), 3–6.

80. Elleh, *African Architecture*, 168–69, 175; Udo Kultermann, *New Architecture in Africa*, trans. E. Flesch (London: Thames and Hudson, 1963), 18; Heathcote and Spens, *Church Builders*, 91–94. See also Justus Dahinden, *New Trends in Church Architecture*, trans. Cajetan J.B. Baumann (New York: Universe, 1967).

81. Designed by William P. Wenzler (1971); see Mary Ellen Young and Wayne Attoe, *Places of Worship—Milwaukee*, 2nd ed. (Milwaukee: [Dept. of Architecture, University of Wisconsin–Milwaukee], 1977), 12–13.

82. Designed by Stanley-Love-Stanley (completed 1999); see Rose Marie Berger, "Unless the Lord Builds the House: Ebenezer Baptist Church, Atlanta," *Sojourner* 30, no. 2 (Mar.–Apr. 2001), 34–35.

83. Horst Bürkle, "Kirchenbau in Übersee: Eine Ausstellung als Diskussionsbeitrag," in *Kirchenbau und Ökumene: Evangelische Kirchenbautagung in Hamburg 1961* (Hamburg: Friedrich Wittig Verlag, 1962), 99.

84. Terence J. Mangan, "The Doman Moon Chapel," *Liturgical Arts* 36, no. 1 (Nov. 1967), 2–7. See also the letter on "Moon people's liturgy," in the same issue, 11–12.

85. Julian Beinart, "Amancio Guedes, Architect of Laurenço Marques," *Architectural Review* 129, no. 770 (Apr. 1961), 247.

86. Amancio d'Alpoim Guedes, "Architects as Magicians, Conjurors, Dealers in Magic Goods, Promises, Potions, Spells—Myself as a Witchdoctor," in John Donat, ed., *World Architecture 2* (London: Studio Vista, 1965), 171, largely reprinted in the Architectural Association's *Amancio Guedes*, 5. On the "habitable woman," see *World Architecture 2*, 176–77; the description of this project is meant to be read aloud "in the manner of a circus barker." Compare Michelucci, in Alba and Organschi, "A Conversation with Giovanni Michelucci," *Perspecta* 27 (1992), 120, on the consequences of pursuing *order* by attending to a single precise concept: "We don't allow the element of the fantastic to come into play, and it's precisely this element that's so extremely important in architecture. . . . It's from fantasy that architecture comes."

CHAPTER 5

1. Virginia Reinburg, "Liturgy and the laity in late medieval and Reformation France," *Sixteenth Century Journal* 23 (1992), 526–47; see Eamon Duffy, *The Stripping of the Altars: Traditional Religion in England, c. 1400– c. 1580* (New Haven: Yale University Press, 1992), and my review article "A Church Reformed though Not Deformed?" *Journal of Religion* 74 (1994), 240–49; also John Bossy, *Christianity in the West, 1400–1700* (Oxford: Oxford University Press, 1985).

2. The best general source is R.E. Horrox, "Medieval Beverley," in K.J. Allison, ed., *A History of the County of York, East Riding*, vol. 6 (London: Oxford University Press, 1990), 2–62. Much material is found in the classic work of George Poulson, *Beverlac, of the Antiquities and History of the Town of Beverley in the County of York, and of the Provostry and Collegiate Establishment of St. John's, with a Minute Description of the Present Minster and Church of St. Mary, and Other Ancient and Modern Edifices*, vol. 2 (London: Longman, 1829), although Poulson's transcriptions are not beyond chal-

lenge. Keith Miller, John Robinson, Barbara English, and Ivan Hall, *Beverley: An Archaeological and Architectural Study* (London: Royal Commission on Historical Monuments, 1982), is particularly important.

3. See, most recently, Rosemary Horrox, ed., *Beverley Minster* (Beverley: Friends of Beverley Minster, 2000), and Allison, *History of the County*, 2–11 and 231–38; also Richard Morris and Eric Cambridge, "Beverley Minster before the Early Thirteenth Century," in Christopher Wilson, ed., *Medieval Art and Architecture in the East Riding of Yorkshire* (London: British Archaeological Association, 1989), 9–32. Apart from the further literature cited hereafter, see also Christopher Wilson, "The Early Thirteenth-Century Architecture of Beverley Minster: Cathedral Splendours and Cistercian austerities," in P.R. Coss and S.D. Lloyd, eds., *Thirteenth Century England*, vol. 3 (Woodbridge: Boydell and Brewer, 1991), 181–95; and Charles Hiatt, *Beverley Minster: An Illustrated Account of Its History and Fabric* (London: Bell, 1911).

4. Venerable Bede, *The Ecclesiastical History of the English People*, 5.2–6, ed. Judith McClure and Roger Collins (Oxford: Oxford University Press, 1994), 237–44.

5. D.M. Palliser, "The Early Medieval Minster," in Horrox, *Beverley Minster*, 23. For legendary material on Saint John, see Alan Deighton, "The Sins of Saint John of Beverley: The Case of the Dutch 'Volksboek' *Jan van Beverley*," *Leuvense Bijdragen* 82 (1993), 227–46; and Alan Deighton, "Julian of Norwich's Knowledge of the Life of St John of Beverley," *Notes and Queries* 238 (1993), 440–43.

6. Paul Barnwell and Rosemary Horrox, introduction to Horrox, *Beverley Minster*, 3.

7. Palliser, "The Early Medieval Minster," 24–25. On the king, see Michael Wood, "The Making of King Aethelstan's Empire: An English Charlemagne?" Donald A. Bullough, and Roger Collins, in Patrick Wormald, eds., *Ideal and Reality in Frankish and Anglo-Saxon Society* (Oxford: Blackwell, 1983), 250–72, and Michael Lapidge, "Some Latin Poems as Evidence for the Reign of Athelstan," *Anglo-Saxon England* 8 (1979), 61–98.

8. Barnwell and Horrox, introduction, 3.

9. Arthur Francis Leach, ed., *Memorials of Beverley Minster: The Chapter Act Book of the Collegiate Church of S. John of Beverley, A.D. 1286–1347* (Durham, England: Andrews, 1898), 1:xxii–xxiii, gives a translation of one version of the legend, then assesses its (meager) historical value (pp. xxiii–xxiv) and surveys further versions (pp. xxiv–xxviii).

10. Palliser, "The Early Medieval Minster," 32.

11. Rosemary Horrox, "The Later Medieval Minster," in Horrox, *Beverley Minster*, 39–40; Barnwell and Horrox, introduction, 4. On the general phenomenon of saints' shrines, see Christina Hole, *English Shrines and Sanctuaries* (London: Batsford, 1954), where Beverley is mentioned on pp. 85–87, and Ben Nilson, *Cathedral Shrines of Medieval England* (Woodbridge, Suffolk,: Boydell and Brewer, 1998)

12. Horrox, "The Later Medieval Minster," 40–41.

13. Barnwell and Horrox, introduction, 3.

14. Horrox, "The Later Medieval Minster," 48. While John is said to have died on May 7, the translation of his relics occurred on October 25, and he shared the latter feast (observed in northern English dioceses) with Saint Crispin and Crispinian; Shakespeare, in *Henry V*, 4.3, associates Agincourt with the latter saint, but it was to John's tomb that Henry went on pilgrimage.

15. Horrox, "The Later Medieval Minster," 47.

16. Palliser, "The Early Medieval Minster," 27; James Raine, ed., *The Priory of Hexham* (Durham, England: Andrews, 1865), 2:lxv–lxvii.

17. Jacobus de Voragine, *The Golden Legend: Readings on the Saints*, trans. William Granger Ryan (Princeton, N.J.: Princeton University Press, 1993), 2:387.

18. J.G. Davies, *The Secular Use of Church Buildings* (New York: Seabury, 1968), 19–21, 41–44, and 157–58. At Durham in the years 1464–1524 there were 302 fugitives. The privilege was restricted by Henry VIII in 1540 and abolished for criminal offenses in 1603 and for civil offenders in 1723. See also Hole, *English Shrines and Sanctuaries*, 20–37.

19. Leach, *Memorials of Beverley Minster* 1:303–4 (*jurans asseruit*). The victim's willingness not to pursue the case might be taken as reinforcing or undercutting this conjecture about the identity of the assailant.

20. Richard Morris, *Churches in the Landscape* (London: Dent, 1989), 131.

21. Palliser, "The Early Medieval Minster," 25–27. The organization of the Minster and its staff is usefully compared with that of York Minster, for which see Barrie Dobson, "The Later Middle Ages, 1215–1500," in G.E. Aylmer and Reginald Cant, eds., *A History of York Minster* (Oxford: Clarendon, 1977), 44–109.

22. Horrox, "Medieval Beverley," 16–19; R.B. Dobson, "Beverley in Conflict: Archbishop Alexander Neville and the Minster Clergy, 1381–8," in Wilson, *Medieval Art and Architecture*, 156–57.

23. Palliser, "The Early Medieval Minster," 27–28, with interesting speculation about Celtic influence.

24. Ibid., 28.

25. Ibid., 28.

26. Horrox, "The Later Medieval Minster," 43; Leach, *Memorials of Beverley Minster*, 1:lxx.

27. Horrox, "The Later Medieval Minster," 44.

28. Leach, *Memorials of Beverley Minster*, 1:ix–x, and Horrox, "The Later Medieval Minster," 45.

29. Leach, *Memorials of Beverley Minster*, 1:liii–liv, lix, lix–lx, lxvi–lxvii, lxx, and lxxv.

30. Dobson, "Beverley in Conflict," 149–64; Horrox, "The Later Medieval Minster," 43–44.

31. Palliser, "The Early Medieval Minster," 30; Horrox, "Medieval Beverley," 11–16.

32. Martin Foreman, *Beverley Friary: The History and Archaeology of an Urban Monastery* (Beverley: Hutton Press, 1998), 10–11.

33. Horrox, "The later medieval Minster," 47.

34. Ibid., 37.

35. See the interesting estimates in R. Willis, "The Architectural History of York Cathedral," in *Memoirs Illustrative of the History and Antiquities of the County and City of York, communicated to the annual meeting of the Archæological Institute of Great Britain and Ireland, held at York, July, 1846* (London: Murray, 1847–48), pt. 2, [sect. 2], Note A, pp. 54–57, "On the Time Required for the Erection of the Different Parts of York Minster," including comparisons with Canterbury, Salisbury, Ely, Westminster, and Exeter.

36. Palliser, "The Early Medieval Minster," 30–31.

37. Francis Bond, *An Introduction to English Church Architecture: From the Eleventh to the Sixteenth Century* (Oxford: Oxford University Press, 1913), 1:177–80.

38. Ivan Hall, "Beverley Minster observed," in Horrox, *Beverley Minster*, 92–93.

39. Palliser, "The Early Medieval Minster," 33. One famous case is the church at Patrington; see John Maddison, "The Architectural Development of Patrington Church and Its Place in the Evolution of the Decorated Style in Yorkshire," in Wilson, *Medieval Art and Architecture*, 13–15.

40. Leach, *Memorials of Beverley Minster*, 1:ix–x.

41. Hall, "Beverley Minster Observed," 93–94.

42. *The Itinerary of John Leland in or about the Years 1535–1543*, ed. Lucy Toulmin Smith (London: Bell, 1907), 1:46, quoted in Horrox, "The Later Medieval Minster," 37.

43. Hall, "Beverley Minster Observed," 93.

44. *Nicholson's Guide to English Churches* (London: Robert Nicholson, 1984), 199.

45. Foreword from the vicar and churchwardens in Peter Rogerson, *Beverley Minster: Visitors' Guide* (Andover, Hampshire: Pitkin, 1990), 3.

46. Horrox, "The Later Medieval Minster," 41–42.

47. Barnwell and Horrox, introduction, 4. On nave altars generally, see Duffy, *Stripping of the Altars*, 112–16.

48. Horrox, "The Later Medieval Minster," 42–43.

49. Ibid., 45–46. In the reports submitted by guilds to chancery in 1389, 70 percent spoke of the provision of candles to altar as among their functions; see Ben R. McRee, "Religious Gilds and Civic Order: The Case of Norwich in the Late Middle Ages," *Speculum* 67 (1992), 69–97. This does not necessarily mean, of course, that all these guilds had altars specifically their own.

50. Leach, *Memorials of Beverley Minster*, 1:xxxvi.

51. Horrox, "The Later Medieval Minster," 39.

52. Barnwell and Horrox, introduction, 9.

53. Leach, *Memorials of Beverley Minster*, 1:xciv–xcv; the documents edited in Leach's two volumes include numerous references to collectors for the fabric fund in the years 1305–28. See also Horrox, "The Later Medieval Minster," 37–39.

54. Poulson, *Beverlac*, 723; Miller, *Beverley*, 47; Palliser, "The Early Medieval Minster," 32; W.C.B. Smith, *St Mary's Church, Beverley: An Account of its Building over Four Hundred Years from 1120 to 1524* (Beverley: Friends of St Mary's Church, 2001) (Smith's book was written in 1978 but published and copyrighted in 2001); Allison, *History of the County*, 238–40.

55. The ordinance of Archbishop Melton establishing Saint Mary's as a vicarage in 1325 is given in Poulson, *Beverlac*, 725.

56. See D.R. Dendy, *The Use of Lights in Christian Worship*, Alcuin Club Collections 41 (London: SPCK, 1959), 38: "By 1300 candles around the altar had in large measure given way to candles on the altar. The English references suggest that, as far as parish churches were concerned, the minimum was not easily obtainable." Dendy also comments (p. 42) that wills of around the fifteenth century "show an almost morbid desire for the increase of lights."

57. Leach, *Memorials of Beverley Minster*, 1:lxxvi–lxxxv; Smith, *St Mary's Church*, 21–2. Smith points out (p. 22) that the priest of another parish, that of Saint Nicholas,

was also threatened with excommunication in 1309 for failure to attend Minster processions.

58. Smith, *St Mary's Church*, 22.

59. F.E. Howard and F.H. Crossley, *English Church Woodwork: A Study in Craftsmanship During the Mediaeval Period, A.D. 1250–1550*, 2nd ed. (New York: Scribner, 1927), 147–62. For a particularly good discussion of the circumstances in which parishes in Germany adopted institutions of greater churches, see Klaus Jan Philipp, *Pfarrkirchen: Funktion, Motivation, Architektur: Eine Studie am Beispiel der Pfarrkirchen der schwäbischen Reichsstädte im Spätmittelalter* (Marburg, Germany: Jonas, 1987), 32.

60. On chantries at the Minster, see Poulson, *Beverlac*, 604. The subject of chapels is complex; for three rather different types of chapel in England, see especially Nicholas Orme, "Church and Chapel in Medieval England," *Transactions of the Royal Historical Society*, ser. 6, vol. 6 (1996), 75–102; G.H. Cook, *Mediaeval Chantries and Chantry Chapels*, rev. and enl. ed. (London: Dent, 1963; reprint, London: J. Baker, 1968), and, on Lady chapels, Peter Draper, " 'Seeing That It Was Done in All the Noble Churches in England,' " in Eric Fernie and Paul Crossley, eds., *Medieval Architecture and Its Intellectual Context* (London: Hambledon, 1990), 137–42.

61. Smith, *St Mary's Church*, 23–24, 29.

62. Survivals—and presumably also the variety of original production—are richer in East Anglia and the West Country than in the North. For the iconography and its significance, see in particular Eamon Duffy, "The Parish, Piety, and Patronage in Late Medieval East Anglia: The Evidence of Rood Screens," in Katherine L. French, Gary G. Gibbs, and Beat A. Kumin, eds., *The Parish in English Life, 1400–1600* (Manchester: Manchester University Press, 1997), 133–62.

63. Nicholas Dawton, "The Medieval Monuments," in Horrox, *Beverley Minster*, 131–55. For monuments generally, see Fred H. Crossley, *English Church Monuments, A.D. 1150–1550: An Introduction to the Study of Tombs and Effigies of the Medieval Period* (London: Batsford, 1933), Jerome Bertram, ed., *Monumental Brasses as Art and History* (Stroud: Sutton, 1996), and for a local study, Robert Dinn, " 'Monuments Answerable to Mens Worth': Burial Patterns, Social Status and Gender in Late Medieval Bury St Edmunds," *Journal of Ecclesiastical History* 46 (1995), 237–55.

64. Horrox, "The Later Medieval Minster," 39, and Nicholas Dawton, "The Percy Tomb at Beverley Minster: The Style of the Sculpture," in F.H. Thompson, ed., *Studies in Medieval Sculpture* (London: Society of Antiquaries of London, 1983), 122–50.

65. Poulson, *Beverlac*, 708–09, 754.

66. Ibid., 708 n. 1.

67. Davies, *Secular Use of Church Buildings*.

68. Steven J. Schloeder, *Architecture in Communion: Implementing the Second Vatican Council Through Liturgy and Architecture* (San Francisco: Ignatius, 1998), 58.

69. Horrox, "The Later Medieval Minster," 44–45. See also Poulson, *Beverlac*, 654 (on the feast of fools) and 657 (on the boy bishop). Davies, *The Secular Use of Church Buildings*, 81–82, refers to the Feast of Fools observed at Beverley—and also, p. 85, to a thirteenth-century play in the churchyard that drew so large an audience that some could not see, and went into the church "either to pray or to look at the pictures or to beguile the weariness of the day by some kind of recreation and solace."

70. Christa Grössinger, "The Misericords in Beverley Minster: Their Relationship to Other Misericords and Fifteenth-Century Prints," in Wilson, *Medieval Art and*

Architecture, 186–94; Malcolm Jones, "The Misericords," in Horrox, *Beverley Minster*, 157–69; and T. Tindall Wildridge, *The Misereres of Beverley Minster: A Complete Series of Drawings of the Seat Carving in the Choir of St John's, Beverley, Yorkshire* (Hull, 1879; reprint, Hutton Driffield, Yorkshire: Honeyfields, 1982). See, more generally, Christa Grössinger, *The World Upside Down: English Misericords* (London: Harvey Miller, 1997), and G.L. Remnant, *A Catalogue of Misericords in Great Britain* (Oxford: Clarendon, 1969; Oxford: Clarendon Press, and New York: Oxford University Press, 1998).

71. On a misericord with a hoopoe, see Edward G. Tasker, *Encyclopedia of Medieval Church Art*, ed. John Beaumont (London: Batsford, 1993), 239; for hoopoes elsewhere in churches, see W.B. Yapp, *Birds in Medieval Manuscripts* (London: British Library, 1981), 53. For the phallic misericord, see Christa Grössinger, "Bristol Misericords and Their Sources," in Laurence Keen, ed., *"Almost the Richest City": Bristol in the Middle Ages* (n.p.: British Archaeological Association, 1997), 85-86 and plates XXVIIA–B. The taste for whimsy persists: visitors to Yorkshire churches eventually discover the work of Robert Thompson of Kilburn, a twentieth-century woodworker whose furnishings are marked with a signature figure: a small mouse, sometimes clearly on display but often discreetly placed. If a pew, a lectern, a rood screen, or a communion rail has a mouse carved into the wood, one knows Thompson has been at work. The church at Hemingborough has stalls on which a Thompson cat stares across at a Thompson mouse in perpetual fascination or frustration. The mouse on a stall at York Minster may be easy enough to see, but finding the signature carving on the Paschal candle at Adel or the crucifix in the Mouseman Center at Kilburn is more of a challenge.

72. Dell Upton, *Holy Things and Profane: Anglican Parish Churches in Colonial Virginia* (Cambridge, Mass.: MIT Press, 1986), xxi.

73. Poulson, *Beverlac*, 764, 771, 772 n. 1; Miller, *Beverley*, 51–52; Allison, *History of the County*, 181–82; Michael Robson, *The Franciscans in the Medieval Custody of York* (York, England: Borthwick Institute, 1997).

74. Poulson, *Beverlac*, 774; Miller, *Beverley*, 52; Allison, *History of the County*, 182.

75. Poulson, *Beverlac*, 720; Miller, *Beverley*, 47–48; Allison, *History of the County*, 240–41.

76. Miller, *Beverley*, 48.

77. Poulson, *Beverlac*, 769; Miller, *Beverley*, 48–51; Allison, *History of the County*, 181; and Martin Foreman, *Further Excavations at the Dominican Priory, Beverley, 1986–89* (Sheffield, Yorkshire: Sheffield Academic Press, 1996).

78. Martin Foreman, *Beverley Friary: The History and Archaeology of an Urban Monastery* (Beverley: Hutton Press, 1998).

79. Foreman, *Beverley Friary*, 35–36.

80. Duffy, *The Stripping of the Altars*, especially 347–48.

81. Allison, *History of the County*, 182–83.

82. Miller, *Beverley*, 53–54.

83. Poulson, *Beverlac*, 730, 785, 788–89; Allison, *History of the County*,183.

84. On this point see my article "Convention and Conversion: Patterns in Late Medieval Piety," *Church History* 67 (1998), 32–51. On Norwich and King's Lynn see Norman P. Tanner, *The Church in Late Medieval Norwich, 1370–1532* (Toronto: Pontifical Institute, 1984), 2–3.

85. John Neal Dalton, ed., *The Collegiate Church of Ottery St Mary: The "Ordina-*

cio et Statuta Ecclesie Sancte Marie de Otery Exon. Diocesis," A.D. 1338, 1339 (Cambridge: Cambridge University Press, 1917); John A. Whitham, *The Church of St. Mary of Ottery in the County of Devon: A Short History and Guide,* 8th ed. (Gloucester, England: British, 1982). The phenomenon of urban parish adaptation of cathedral design is discussed in Aart J.J. Mekking, "Traditie als maatstaf voor vernieuwing in de kerkelijke architectuur van de middeleeuwen: de rol van oud en nieuw in het proces van bevestiging en doorbreking van maatschappelijke structuren," *Bulletin KNOB* 97 (1998), 205–23, with specific reference to Utrecht, Cologne, and Liège.

86. Nikolaus Pevsner, *Yorkshire: The West Riding* (Harmondsworth: Penguin, 1959), 206; A.R. Martin, *Franciscan Architecture in England* (Manchester: Manchester University Press, 1937; reprint, Farnborough: Greg, 1966), 18.

87. Virginia Chieffo Raguin, Kathryn L. Brush, and Peter Draper, eds., *Artistic Integration in Gothic Buildings* (Toronto: University of Toronto Press, 1995), is exceptional in attending as much as it does to a holistic understanding of churches (including their liturgical use), although specific articles in the collection tend to focus more on special and extraordinary factors than on the ordinary liturgical and devotional functions that would have been of primary significance for most worshipers.

88. In a town with multiple parish churches, the relationship between guilds and parishes could become yet more complex, with individuals belonging to guilds connected with more than one parish, or to parishes other than their own. See, for example, Andrew D. Brown, *Popualr Piety in Late Medieval England: The Diocese of Salisbury, 1250–1550* (Oxford: Oxford University Press, 1995), 132–80; Norman P. Tanner, *The Church in Late Medieval Norwich, 1370–1532* (Toronto: Pontifical Institute of Mediaeval Studies, 1984), 67–82; and G. Rosser, "Communities of Parish and Guild in the Later Middle Ages," in S.J. Wright, ed., *Parish, Church and People: Local Studies in Lay Religion, 1350–1750* (London, 1988), 29–55.

89. Edouard Dumoutet, *Le désir de voir l'hostie et les origines de la dévotion au Saint-Sacrement* (Paris: Beauchesne, 1926), and *Corpus Domini: Aux sources de la piété eucharistique médiévale* (Paris: Beauchesne, 1942); also Peter Browe, *Die Verehrung der Eucharistie im Mittelalter* (Munich, 1933; reprint, Sinzig: St. Meinrad Verlag und Antiquariat, 1990); P. Camporesi, "The Consecrated Host: A Wondrous Excess," in Michel Feher, Ramona Naddaff, and Nadia Tazi, eds., *Fragments for a History of the Human Body* (New York: Zone, 1989), 220–37 (a rather breathless account); and Miri Rubin, *Corpus Christi: The Eucharist in Late Medieval Culture* (Cambridge: Cambridge University Press, 1990) (full of useful material).

90. I do very much mean to imply here the kind of businesslike mentality that Eamon Duffy ascribes to his subjects in *The Stripping of the Altars,* chap. 10. To speak of people as being deeply invested in the piety of the era is to use an altogether appropriate metaphor.

CHAPTER 6

1. George A. Lane, *Chicago Churches and Synagogues: An Architectural Pilgrimage* (Chicago: Loyola University Press, 1981). For American church architecture overall, see Peter W. Williams, *Houses of God: Region, Religion, and Architecture in the United States* (Urbana: University of Illinois Press, 1997); Peter W. Williams, "Religious Architecture and Landscape," in Charles H. Lippy and Peter W. Williams, eds., *Encyclo-*

pedia of the American Religious Experience (New York: Scribners, 1988), 1325–40, and "Sacred Space in America," *Journal of the American Academy of Religion* 70, (2002), 593–609.

2. Harry Lorin Binsse, "Looking-Backwards Architecture," *Liturgical Arts* 7 (1938–39), p. 58.

3. Emile Mâle, *The Early Churches of Rome*, trans. David Buston (London: Benn, 1960), especially 137–38; Richard Krautheimer and Slobodan Curcic, *Early Christian and Byzantine Architecture*, 4th ed. (Harmondsworth: Penguin, 1992), 87–92.

4. Daniel M. Bluestone, *Constructing Chicago* (New Haven: Yale University Press, 1991), 84.

5. Saint John's Church at Leeds is a classic example; Christopher Wren used the Gothic idiom at Saint Mary Aldermary in London (1681–1704), and less prominent architects employed it at Upton Lovell in Wiltshire, Great Houghton in Yorkshire, Great Dalby in Leicestershire, and elsewhere. See the essays on Devon and Saint Mary Aldermary and "Gothic Survival and Gothic Revival," in Howard Montagu Colvin, *Essays in English Architectural History* (New Haven: Yale University Press, 1999). For America, see Stephen P. Dorsey, *Early English Churches in America, 1607–1807* (New York: Oxford University Press, 1952), 53–55. For the tradition generally see now also Michael Hall, ed., *Gothic Architecture and Its Meanings, 1550–1830* (Reading: Spire, 2002).

6. Terry Friedman, *James Gibbs* (New Haven: Yale University Press, 1984).

7. Robin Middleton and David Watkin, *Neoclassical and ninteenth-Century Architecture* (New York: Abrams, 1980); Damie Stillman, *English Neo-Classical Architecture* (London: Zwemmer, 1988); William Harvey Pierson, *American Buildings and Their Architects: The Colonial and Neoclassical Styles* (Garden City, N.Y.: Doubleday, 1970).

8. The literature on Victorian church-building is extensive; one can begin with Chris Brooks and Andrew Saint, eds., *Building the Victorian Church* (New York: St. Martin's Press, 1995); Roger Dixon and Stefan Muthesius, *Victorian Architecture* (London: Thames and Hudson, 1978), 182–235; Peter Howell and Ian Sutton, eds., *The Faber Guide to Victorian Churches* (London: Faber, 1989); James F. White, *The Cambridge Movement: The Ecclesiologists and the Gothic Revival* (Cambridge: Cambridge University Press, 1962); Phoebe Stanton, *The Gothic Revival and American Church Architecture* (Baltimore: Johns Hopkins Press, 1968).

9. A. Welby Pugin, *Contrasts: Or, a Parallel Between the Noble Edifices of the Fourteenth and Fifteenth Centuries, and Similar Buildings of the Present Day, Showing the Present Decay of Taste, Accompanied by Appropriate Text* (London: Pugin, 1836; reprint, Edinburgh: Grant, 1898; reprint, New York: Humanities, 1969), *An Apology for the Revival of Christian Architecture in England* (London: Weale, 1843), and *The True Principles of Pointed or Christian Architecture* (London: Bohn, 1853). See M. Belcher, *A.W.N. Pugin: An Annotated Critical Bibliography* (London: Cassell Academic, 1984).

10. E. Brooks Holifield, "The Architect and the Congregation," *Faith and Form* 19 (spring 1986), 39.

11. Dell Upton, *Holy Things and Profane: Anglican Parish Churches in Colonial Virginia* (Cambridge, Mass.: MIT Press, 1986), 229.

12. David Cole, *The Work of Sir Gilbert Scott* (London: Architectural Press, 1980).

13. Butterfield "set himself to build without affectation or antiquarianism a Gothic architecture for the Victorian age, using the ordinary thin pit-sawn timbers,

the common bricks and tiles which were the builder's stock-in-trade. Out of these he made churches whose curious proportions and fierce ornamentation are often extremely moving." John Summerson, *Architecture in England since Wren* (London: Longmans, Green, 1948), 13, quoted in Keith Murray, "Material Fabric and Symbolic Pattern," in Peter Hammond, ed., *Towards a Church Architecture* (London: Architectural Press, 1962), 82.

14. James F. White, "From Protestant to Catholic Plain Style," in Paul Corby Finney, ed., *Seeing Beyond the Word: Visual Arts and the Calvinist Tradition* (Grand Rapids, Mich.: Eerdmans, 1999), 457–76, on Greek and Gothic revivals in America.

15. Designed by Ithiel Town; see Susan B. Matheson and Derek D. Churchill, *Modern Gothic: The Revival of Medieval Art* (New Haven: Yale University Art Gallery, 2000), 60.

16. See Lamia Doumato, *James Renwick* (Monticello, Ill.: Vance Bibliographies, 1981).

17. The first designed by John Dillenburg and Gerhard Zucher for the exterior, John Mills Van Osdel for the interior (1857–60); the second by Edward J. Burling (1856–57, and substantially rebuilt in 1875 after the fire); see Lane, *Chicago Churches and Synagogues*, 24–25, and Michael A. Marcotte, "Holy Family Church," *Chicago History*, 22 (1993), 38–51.

18. The fame or notoriety of the city's water tower—"a castellated monstrosity with pepper boxes stuck all over it," as Oscar Wilde is often quoted—made early Chicago known for a more fanciful interpretation of the Gothic style.

19. Ralph Adams Cram, *The Substance of Gothic: Six Lectures on the Development of Architecture from Charlemagne to Henry VIII*, 2nd ed. (Boston: Marshall Jones, 1925), xviii–xxi.

20. Richard Upjohn, *Upjohn's Rural Architecture* (New York: Putnam, 1852; reprint, New York: Da Capo, 1975); William Gaddis, *Carpenter's Gothic* (New York: Viking, 1985).

21. Virginia Chieffo Raguin and Mary Ann Powers, eds., *Sacred Spaces: Building and Remembering Sites of Worship in the Nineteenth Century* (Worcester, Mass.: Iris and B. Gerald Cantor Art Gallery, College of the Holy Cross, 2002), 158.

22. The first by the firm of Peter Camburas and Theodore J. Theodore (1958), the second by that of William Pavlecic, Radoslav Kovacevic, and Radmilo Markovich (1968–69).

23. Designed by John Tomich (1968–71), Tasso Katselas (1970–71), and Radoslav Kovacevic (1973–75).

24. Henry Russell Hitchcock, *The Architecture of H. H. Richardson and His Times* (Cambridge: MIT Press, 1970).

25. Designed by Edward Burling and Francis M. Whitehouse (1885); see Lane, *Chicago Churches and Synagogues*, 50–51.

26. Francis William Wynn Kervick, *Patrick Charles Keely, Architect: A Record of His Life and Work* (South Bend, Ind.: private printing, 1953).

27. William McKenzie Woodward and Edward F. Sanderson, *Providence: A Citywide Survey of Historic Resources* (Providence: Rhode Island Historical Preservation Commission, 1986), 123.

28. Dixon and Muthesius, *Victorian Architecture*, 224–25.

29. Harry C. Koenig, ed., *A History of the Parishes of the Archdiocese of Chicago*

(Chicago: Archdiocese of Chicago, 1980), 2:578–88. According to tradition it was Native American women who prepared the church for its dedication. For the quotation, from Archbishop Peter Kenrick of Saint Louis, see Charles Shanabruch, *Chicago's Catholics: The Evolution of an American Identity* (Notre Dame, Ind.: University of Notre Dame Press, 1981), 12. A.T. Andreas, *History of Chicago from the Earliest Period to the Present Time* (Chicago: Andreas, 1884–86), is a rich source of information on the early churches.

30. For a cautionary note on the role of Saint Mary's in this development, see Walter Field, "A Reexamination into the Invention of the Balloon Frame," *Journal of the American Society of Architectural Historians* 2, no. 4 (1942), 3–29 (esp. 16–23); also Dell Upton, *Architecture in the United States* (New York: Oxford University Press, 1998), 153.

31. Bessie Louise Pierce, *A History of Chicago* (New York: Knopf, 1957), 3:225.

32. Ibid., 232.

33. A.D. Field, *Memorials of Methodism in the Bounds of the Rock River Conference* (Cincinnati: Cranston and Stowe, 1886), 286–87.

34. Edwin O. Gale, *Reminiscences of Early Chicago and Vicinity* (Chicago: Revell, 1902), 361.

35. Bluestone, *Constructing Chicago*. 62–103.

36. See George S. Philips, *Chicago and Her Churches* (Chicago: E.B. Myers & Chandler, 1868), 193, on Second Presbyterian.

37. Bluestone, *Constructing Chicago*, 65, 68, 84–85.

38. R.R. Langham-Carter, "South Africa's First Woman Architect," *Architect and Builder* 17 (Mar. 1967), 14–18.

39. Pierce, *History of Chicago*, 3, 355.

40. Philips, *Chicago and Her Churches*, 219–20.

41. The first by Charles Bulfinch (1816), the second by Benjamin Latrobe (1806–18).

42. Holifield, "The Architect and the Congregation," 39.

43. Elias Colbert and Everett Chamberlin, *Chicago and the Great Conflagration* (New York: Vent, 1871), 400–407, focuses on the experience of Robert Collyer at Unity Church and gives a series of plates between pp. 120 and 121 and between pp. 328 and 329 showing gutted churches (not in the order specified in the list of illustrations on p. viii). The cover of *Harper's Weekly* 15, no. 776 (Nov. 11, 1871), also gives these plates, and is reproduced in Carl Smith, *Urban Disorder and the Shape of Belief: The Great Chicago Fire, the Haymarket Bomb, and the Model Town of Pullman* (Chicago: University of Chicago Press, 1995), thirteenth plate in the gallery between pp. 126 and 127.

44. Lane, *Chicago Churches and Synagogues*, 26–27; Koenig, *History of the Parishes*, 1:367–82. For the story about the vow, see Joseph P. Conroy, *Arnold Damen, S.J.: A Chapter in the Making of Chicago* (New York: Benziger, 1930), 177–80. The fire actually began to the north and east of the church and spread further north-northeast from its point of inception; if instead it had spread southwest toward Holy Family, the heart of the city and far more churches would have been spared.

45. Bluestone, *Constructing Chicago*, 96.

46. Ibid., 95–96, 99–101.

47. Shanabruch, *Chicago's Catholics*, 39–53.

48. Raguin and Powers, *Sacred Spaces*, 70 and 161.

49. Shanabruch, *Chicago's Catholics*, 74 and 78–104.

50. Pierce, *History of Chicago*, 3, 424–25.

51. Ibid., 423.

52. Bluestone, *Constructing Chicago*, 90.

53. By 1902, sixty-two of the city's 132 churches were dominated by the Irish.

54. Shanabruch, *Chicago's Catholics*, 39–53. The figures in 1880 were nine German, three Polish, three Bohemian, one French; in 1902, nineteen German, fifteen Polish, five Bohemian, three French, three Lithuanian, three Italian, one Croatian, one Slovenian, one Slovak, one Dutch, and one African-American (referred to as "Negro").

55. Shanabruch, *Chicago's Catholics*, 155–98. Mundelein was made a cardinal in 1924.

56. Lane, *Chicago Churches*, 23–24.

57. Mary Ellen Young and Wayne Attoe, *Places of Worship—Milwaukee*, 2nd ed. (Milwaukee: [Department of Architecture, University of Wisconsin-Milwaukee], 1977), 60.

58. Designed by Giuseppe Beretta (1884–86); see Lane, *Chicago Churches and Synagogues*, 49.

59. For a popular statement of the usual assumption, see Susan Nelson, "Keeping Faith: Chicago's New Citizens Built Churches to Remind Them of Those They'd Left Behind," *Chicago*, Mar. 1980, pp. 144–49.

60. Joseph John Parot, *Polish Catholics in Chicago, 1850–1920: A Religious History* (DeKalb: Northern Illinois University Press, 1981); Edward R. Kantowicz, "To build the Catholic city," *Chicago History* 14, no. 3 (fall 1985), 14–15.

61. Lane, *Chicago Churches*, 42–43. According to a privately held, unpublished history of the Barzynski family (written by Mary Barzynski Smietanka, Chicago, 1942), Vincent Barzynski and his brother, both Resurrectionist priests, were immigrants who fled to America, with other members of their family, in the wake of the January Insurrection of 1863. After some time at a mission in Texas they were sent to Chicago, where the family became leaders in the early Polish church and in Polish journalism in Chicago. Their father, who accompanied them, was an amateur inventor: "Being of an inventive mind, he made many gadgets that were in use around the parish house and church. One of these inventions that I remember was a sort of moving platform which fitted over the tabernacle and which was lowered and raised when the Monstrance was placed upon it during benediction. It worked by a spring. He also contributed to work on the perpetual motion problem but never made much progress."

62. Kantowicz, "To Build the Catholic city," 4 and 8–12.

63. Kantowicz, "To Build the Catholic city," 18 and 21–23.

64. Koenig, *History of the Parishes*, 2:1071–91.

65. Information is from the album produced by the church, *Golden Jubilee of Holy Cross Lithuanian Roman Catholic Parish, Chicago, Illinois, 1904–1954;* the quotation is from p. 145. See also Koenig, *History of the Parishes*, vol. 1, pp. 363–67.

66. Koenig, *History of the Parishes*, 1:519–23. The church is now dedicated to Our Lady of Fatima, but the shrine is still in place. Mr. Lawrence Haptas tells me that the relic was brought from Apt in France.

67. Pierce, *History of Chicago*, 3, 367. On the history of the city's Lutherans, see Walter Kloetzli, ed., *Chicago Lutheran Planning Study*, vol. 2 (Chicago: National Lutheran Council, 1965).

68. As at St. Stephen's Lutheran Church on the south side of Chicago.

69. Information on Petterson is in Charles E. Gregersen, *A History of the Swedish Ev. Lutheran Bethany Church—Svenska Ev. Lutherska Bethania Kyrkan of South Chicago, Illinois, with a short biography of its architect, Erick Gustaf Petterson* (n.p., 1968).

70. Jeanne Halgren Kilde, "Architecture and Urban Revivalism in Nineteenth-Century America," in Peter W. Williams, ed., *Perspective on American Religion and Culture* (Malden, Mass.: Blackwell, 1999), 174–86.

71. Bluestone, *Constructing Chicago*, 96.

72. First Baptist was built in 1866; First Congregational was designed by Henry Gay (1866), and Union Park Congregational (now First Baptist Congregational) by Gurdon P. Randall (1867).

73. Both designed by Dankmar Adler (1873 and 1874).

74. Quoted in Bluestone, *Constructing Chicago*, 63.

75. Jeanne Halgren Kilde, *When Church Became Theatre: The Transformation of Evangelical Architecture and Worship in Nineteenth-Century America* (New York: Oxford University Press, 2002), 113; Bluestone, *Constructing Chicago*, 85–90.

76. Darrel M. Robertson, *The Chicago Revival, 1876: Society and Revivalism in a Nineteenth-Century City* (Metuchen, N.J.: Scarecrow Press, 1989), p. 50–1 (and 178 n. 33).

77. At roughly the same time, Kilde shows, the "cult of domesticity" led Evangelical churches to imitate another secular model, the home: Queen Anne and Shingle styles of design were used for churches as for houses, while parlors and domestic facilities were increasingly adopted by churches.

78. This is a theme in Kilde, "Architecture and Urban Revivalism in Nineteenth-Century America."

79. Donald J. Bruggink and Carl H. Droppers, *Christ and Architecture: Building Presbyterian/Reformed Churches* (Grand Rapids, Mich.: Eerdmans, 1965), 387–415.

80. See George C. Giles, Jr., *History of the Church of the Ascension, Chicago, Illinois (1857–1982)* (Aberdeen, S.D.: North Plains Press, 1984), especially iii–xii and 1–24. For further critique of Anglo-Catholicism, see Philips, *Chicago and Her Churches*, 478.

81. Bluestone, *Constructing Chicago*, 90–91; and Roderic B. Dibbert, *Chicago's Cathedral, 1861–1976: A Symbol in the Heart of the Diocese, compiled from Diocesan Archives by the Historiographer* (Hackensack, N.J.: Custombook, 1976).

82. George Craig Stewart, *A Little Journey through Saint Luke's, Evanston, Illinois* ([Evanston]: [St. Luke's Church]: 1928).

83. Julius Melton, *Presbyterian Worship in America: Changing Patterns since 1787* (Richmond, Va.: John Knox, 1967), 65 (and see, more generally, pp. 59–78). See also John Hall on the exodus of Presbyterians to Episcopal churches, 1851, in Kilde, *When Church Became Theatre*, 80–81.

84. Kilde, *When Church Became Theatre*, 70.

85. Melton, *Presbyterian Worship in America*, 68.

86. Erne R. Frueh and Florence Frueh, *The Second Presbyterian Church of Chi-*

cago: Art and Architecture (Chicago: Second Presbyterian Church, 1978), on the church as it was rebuilt in the 1870s.

87. Ibid., 69.

88. E.F. Jansson, "Church Building in Chicago since 1833," in *The Place of the Church in a Century of Progress, 1833 to 1933* (Chicago: Chicago Church Federation, 1933), 28; on chancels in various denominations, see Charles W. Bolton, *Fifty Years of Church Building and a Study Concerning the Future* (Philadelphia: Bolton, 1928), 34–41.

89. Lane, *Chicago Churches and Synagogues*, 106–07; Theodore Turak, "A Celt among Slavs: Louis Sullivan's Holy Trinity Cathedral," *Prairie School Review* 9 (1972), 5–22; Robert Twombly, *Louis Sullivan: His Life and Work* (New York: Viking, 1986), 369–70; and Suzan von Lengerke Kehoe, *Holy Trinity Orthodox Cathedral and Rectory* (Chicago: Commission on Chicago Historical and Architectural Landmarks, 1978).

90. Lane, *Chicago Churches and Synagogues*, 121.

91. Designed by N. Dokas (1910); see Lane, *Chicago Churches and Synagogues*, 120; on Greek churches elsewhere, see Anthony Cutler, "The Tyranny of Hagia Sophia: Notes on Greek Orthodox Church Design in the United States," *Journal of the American Society of Architectural Historians* 31 (1972), 38–50.

92. David T. Van Zanten, "The Early Work of Marion Mahony Griffin," *Prairie School Review* 3, no. 2 (1966), 5–23; James Weirick, "Spirituality and Symbolism in the Work of the Griffins," in Anne Watson, ed., *Beyond Architecture: Marion Mahony and Walter Burley Griffin: America, Australia, India* (Sydney, Australia: Powerhouse, 1998), 56–85.

93. Koenig, *History of the Parishes*, 2:1204.

94. Robert Muccigrosso, *American Gothic: The Mind and Art of Ralph Adams Cram* (Washington, D.C.: University Press of America, 1979); Douglass Shand-Tucci, *Ralph Adams Cram: American Medievalist* (Boston: Boston Public Library, 1975); Douglass Shand-Tucci, *Ralph Adams Cram: Life and Architecture* (Amherst: University of Massachusetts Press, 1994–); Richard Oliver, *Bertram Grosvenor Goodhue* (Cambridge, Mass.: MIT Press, 1983).

95. Jean F. Block, *The Uses of Gothic: Planning and Building the Campus of the University of Chicago, 1892–1932* (Chicago: University of Chicago Library, 1983).

96. Katherine Solomonson, *The Chicago Tribune Tower Competition: Skyscraper Design and Cultural Change in the 1920s* (Cambridge: Cambridge University Press, 2001), especially chap. 5.

97. Elam Davies, *Fourth Presbyterian Church of Chicago, Illinois: One Hundred Years, 1871–1971* (Chicago: [The Church], 1971), and Marilee Munger Scroggs, "Making a Difference: Fourth Presbyterian Church of Chicago," in James P. Wind and James Welborn Lewis, eds., *Portraits of Twelve Religious Communities* (Chicago: University of Chicago Press, 1994), 1:464–519.

98. Designed by Coolidge and Hodgdon (1925–16).

99. Designed by Denison B. Hull (1929–31); see Lane, *Chicago Churches and Synagogues*, 188.

100. Bluestone, *Constructing Chicago*, 96–99.

101. Cram, *The Substance of Gothic*, 210.

102. Ralph Adams Cram, *Church Building: A Study of the Principles of Architecture in Their Relation to the Church*, 3rd ed. (Boston: Marshall Jones, 1924), 10–11.

103. Cram, *Church Building*, 6–10.

104. Robert W. Jenson, "God, Space, and Architecture," in *Essays in Theology of Culture* (Grand Rapids, Mich.: Eerdmans, 1995), 12.

105. Marcia B. Hall, *Renovation and Counter-Reformation: Vasari and Duke Cosimo in Sta Maria Novella and Sta Croce, 1565–1577* (Oxford: Clarendon, 1979), 1–15.

106. J. J. Burke, *Reasonableness of Catholic Ceremonies and Practices*, 2nd ed. (New York: Benzinger, 1894), 17–18. Originally published as a pamphlet in 1892.

107. John Henry Newman, *Loss and Gain* (London: Burns, 1848), reprinted as *Loss and Gain: The Story of a Convert*, ed. Alan G. Hill (New York: Oxford University Press, 1986), chap. 20, pp. 226–27.

108. On Eastern Orthodox liturgy, see Timothy Ware, *The Orthodox Church*, new ed. (Harmondsworth: Penguin, 1997), 264–73.

CHAPTER 7

1. On all this see William J. R. Curtis, *Le Corbusier: Ideas and Forms* (New York: Rizzoli, 1986), 178–79. Among recent books on the architect see Kenneth Frampton, *Le Corbusier: Architect and Visionary* (London: Thames and Hudson, 2001), and Giuliano Gresleri, Glauco Gresleri, and Valerio Casali, *Le Corbusier: il programma liturgico* (Bologna: Compositori, 2001). On Le Corbusier's response to the question whether the designer of Ronchamp needed to be a Catholic, and on differences between him and Schwarz, see Edwin Heathcote and Iona Spens, *Church Builders* (Chichester, Sussex: Academy, 1997), 46.

2. J. M. Neale and B. Webb, introduction to their translation of Guillelmus Durandus, *The Symbolism of Churches and Church Ornaments*, 3rd ed. (London: Gibbings, 1906), xxi–xxv; see J. G. Davies, *The Secular Use of Church Buildings* (New York: Seabury, 1968), 110–11.

3. Laura Burns Carroll, "Revisiting a Church of Radical Design—and Its Visionary Priest," *Faith and Form* 28 (fall 1994), 13; Michael J. Crosbie, "Urban Religious Spaces: Designing for Liturgy," *Faith and Form* 31 no. 2 (1998), 16. See the comment of Michelucci, in Roberto de Alba and Alan W. Organschi, "A Conversation with Giovanni Michelucci," *Perspecta* 27 (1992), 118: "Look, the important thing is to know nothing. There is a danger of applying a preconceived form to the object that we're studying, and this is already a problem, because we don't give ourselves the time to understand the demands or the needs of what we're studying."

4. Richared Lacayo, "To the Lighthouse: What Should a Church Look Like Today? One Bold Answer: Rafael Moneo's L.A. cathedral," *Time*, Sept. 2, 2002, p. 66.

5. George A. Larson and Jay Pridmore, *Chicago Architecture and Design* (New York: Abrams, 1993), 193.

6. Oskar Söhngen, "Die Wallfahrtskirche von Ronchamp: Zum Problem des Sakralen im modernen Kirchenbau," in *Reich Gottes und Wirklichkeit: Festgabe für Alfred Dedo Müller zum 70. Geburtstag* (Berlin: Evangelische Verlagsanstalt, 1961), 179. All German-language books cited in this chapter were published in Germany.

7. Meredith L. Clausen, *Spiritual Space: The Religious Architecture of Pietro Belluschi* (Seattle: University of Washington Press, 1992), and *Pietro Belluschi, Modern American Architect* (Cambridge, Mass.: MIT Press, 1994), 134–61. Also "First Presbyterian Church, Cottage Grove, Oregon, Pietro Belluschi," *Progressive Architecture* 33, no. 3

(Mar. 1952), 64 ("Belluschi . . . believes in respecting and preserving 'that feeling of emotional continuity which is the very essence of religion' ").

8. F.W., "Does Architectural Design Shape liturgy?" *Progressive Architecture* 47, no. 3 (Mar. 1966), 138–39.

9. The best general study is Wolfgang Pehnt, *Rudolf Schwarz (1897–1961): Architekt einer anderen Moderne* (Stuttgart: Verlag Gerd Hatje, 1997), with an index by Hilde Strohl of Schwarz's architectural and written work, 227–305. Thomas Hasler, *Architektur als Ausdruck: Rudolf Schwarz* (Berlin: Mann, 2000), is good particularly on the formal qualities of Schwarz's design. Rudolf Stegers, *Räume der Wandlung, Wände und Wege: Studien zum Werk von Rudolf Schwarz* (Wiesbaden: Vieweg, 2000), places Schwarz in his cultural context, with commentary that is sometimes desultory and perhaps at times idiosyncratic. Other books on Schwarz and his work include *Rudolf Schwarz: Gedächtnisausstellung des BDA Köln, gefördert von der Akademie der Künste, Berlin* (Heidelberg: Kerle, 1963); Manfred Sundermann, Claudia Lang, and Maria Schwarz, eds., *Rudolf Schwarz* (Bonn: Deutsche UNESCO-Kommission, 1981); Conrad Lienhardt, ed., *Rudolf Schwarz (1897–1961): Werk, Theorie, Rezeption* (Regensburg: Schnell and Steiner, 1997). See also Edward H. Teague, *Rudolf Schwarz: Bibliography and Building List* (Monticello, Ill.: Vance Bibliographies, 1985).

10. Ludwig Neundörfer, quoted in Stegers, *Räume der Wandlung*, 179.

11. *Vom Bau der Kirche* (Würzburg: Werkbundverlag, 1938) was most recently reissued in German in 1998 (Salzburg and Munich: Puset) and translated into English as *The Church Incarnate: The Sacred Function of Christian Architecture*, trans. Cynthia Harris (Chicago: Regnery, 1958). The later book is *Kirchenbau: Welt vor der Schwelle* (Heidelberg: Kerle, 1960). Less well known but also important are his many articles, including "Geistliche Übung: Gedanken zu einer Werklehre des Gebets," *Die Schildgenossen* 8 (1928), 193–98, and "Liturgie und Kirchenbau," in Erich Endrich, ed., *Heilige Kunst* (Stuttgart: Schwabenverlag, 1953), 35–41.

12. Pehnt, *Rudolf Schwarz*, 191–96; Schwarz, *The Church Incarnate*, vii; Walter Zahner, "Rudolf Schwarz: Leben, Werk und Wirkung," in Lienhardt, *Rudolf Schwarz*, 37.

13. Frédéric Debuyst, *Modern Architecture and Christian Celebration* (Richmond, Va.: John Knox Press, 1968), 45–46.

14. Stegers, *Räume der Wandlung*, 7.

15. Steven J. Schloeder, *Architecture in Communion: Implementing the Second Vatican Council through Liturgy and Architecture* (San Francisco: Ignatius, 1998), 234–38, gives an altogether puzzling interpretation of Schwarz. He takes Schwarz's "Cathedral of All Times" as suspiciously similar to Saint Peter's Basilica, and the resemblance seems to him facile and problematic. But in fact he has reproduced the wrong image: what he takes to be Schwarz's drawing of the "Cathedral of All Times" is in fact Schwarz's rendering of Saint Peter's. (To be sure, the preliminary sketches reproduced in the 1998 edition of *Vom Bau der Kirche* suggest that at one point Schwarz viewed the design of Saint Peter's as one variation on what was then his eighth and final plan, but in the published book it had been shifted to the chapter on the sixth plan and there received rather unsympathetic treatment). More serious distortion, oddly inquisitorial in its character, occurs when Schloeder claims to have found various Christological heresies in Schwarz's work, at which point his critique becomes confused and bears little connection to what Schwarz actually says. And when he con-

cludes that "Schwarz denied that church architecture was about theology or liturgical practice and therefore could not concern himself with the ecclesiological nature of the parish community or with the liturgical ramifications of the Mass," one can only wonder what he could possibly mean, since these matters were of deep and central concern to Schwarz. The remarks on Schwarz in Heathcote and Spens, *Church Builders*, 33–36 ("The Church Incarnate: Modernism and the Church") and 41–46 ("Postwar Germany"), are perfunctory.

16. Walter Zahner, *Rudolf Schwarz: Baumeister der neuen Gemeinde: Ein Beitrag zum Gespräch zwischen Liturgietheologie und Architektur in der liturgischen Bewegung* (Altenberge: Oros, 1992), gives all the information one could want about the connections between Schwarz and liturgical reform, particularly in the period between the world wars. See also Pehnt, *Rudolf Schwarz*, 44–49. On the history of the movement, see John R.K. Fenwick and Bryan D. Spinks, *Worship in Transition: The Liturgical Movement in the Twentieth Century* (New York: Continuum, 1995), and for the early phase especially pp. 23–28.

17. Odo Casel, *Die Liturgie als Mysterienfeier* (Freiburg: Herder, 1922); *Das christliche Kultmysterium* (Regensburg: Pustet, 1932); the latter was translated into English as *The Mystery of Christian Worship*, ed. Burkhard Neunheuser (London: Darton, Longman, 1962).

18. Romano Guardini, *Von Geist Der Liturgie* (Freiburg: Herder, 1918), in English as *The Spirit of the Liturgy*, trans. Ada Lane (New York: Crossroad, 1998).

19. Guardini, *The Spirit of the Liturgy*, 94.

20. Ibid., 66.

21. Romano Guardini, *Von heiligen Zeichen* (Rothenfels am Main: Quickbornhaus, 1922), in English as *Sacred Signs*, trans. Grace Branham, rev. ed. (Wilmington, Dela.: Michael Glazer, 1979).

22. *Sacred Signs*, 73–75.

23. Schwarz, *Kirchenbau*, 36–46; Zahner, "Rudolf Schwarz," 13–15.

24. Pehnt, *Rudolf Schwarz*, 46.

25. *The Church Incarnate*, 68 (1998 German ed., 54).

26. *The Church Incarnate*, 154, 160 (1998 German ed., 126, 130–31).

27. *The Church Incarnate*, 180–81 (1998 German ed., 148). The reference to a *Strahlenmonstranz* calls to mind a Baroque monstrance with the sun's rays shown surrounding the consecrated host. (The tone is somewhat more romantic in the English translation than in Schwarz's original German.)

28. *The Church Incarnate*, 195 (1998 German ed., 157).

29. *The Church Incarnate*, 219 (1998 German ed., 172–73): the "instructions" ("Weisungen") are not model designs (Musterentwürfe), specifications (Bauprogramme), elements of an architectural "canon," or "formulas."

30. Alfred Döblin, "Impressionen von einer Rheinreise," *Frankfurter Allgemeine Zeitung*, Feb. 1 and 8, 1931, reprinted in Peter Müllenborn, et al., *St. Fronleichnam, Aachen, 1930–1980* ([Aachen: The Church, 1980]), 24–25.

31. *The Church Incarnate*, 191–93 (1998 German ed., 153–55).

32. *The Church Incarnate*, 76–78 (1998 German ed., 62–63). The translator makes minor changes in the ordering of material in this passage but does not alter its substance.

33. Romano Guardini, "Die Neuerbaute Fronleichnamskirche in Aachen," *Die*

Schildgenossen 11 (1931), 266–68; reprinted in Müllenborn, et al., *St. Fronleichnam*, 16–18.

34. *The Church Incarnate*, 107 (1998 German ed., 88).

35. *The Church Incarnate*, 172 (1998 German ed., 140).

36. *The Church Incarnate*, 52–53 (1998 German ed., 41): "Bauen . . . heißt, vor Gott große gemeinschaftliche Formen darlegen."

37. Rudolf Schwarz, " 'The Eucharistic Building,' " trans. V. Hoecke, *Faith and Form* 2 (Jan. 1969), 21; see *The Church Incarnate*, 202 (1998 German ed., 161).

38. *The Church Incarnate*, 88 (1998 German ed., 72).

39. Martin Dudley, "Honesty and Consecration: Paul Tillich's Criteria for a Religious Architecture," in Diana Wood, ed., *The Church and the Arts* (Oxford: Blackwell, 1995), 515–22.

40. *The Church Incarnate*, 198–99 (1998 German ed., 159): "sie soll verzehrt werden, so wie die Gestalten der Wegzehrung Nahrung werden."

41. *The Church Incarnate*, 202 (1998 German ed., 162).

42. On the familiarity with Rilke, and with Guardini's study of the *Duino Elegies*, see Pehnt, *Rudolf Schwarz*, 86

43. Schwarz, *Kirchenbau*, 12–14; Pehnt, *Rudolf Schwarz*, 52–55; Zahner, *Rudolf Schwarz*, 189–92.

44. See also *The Church Incarnate*, 172 (1998 German ed., 140).

45. Schwarz, *Kirchenbau*, 30.

46. Evelyn Underhill, *Worship* (New York: Harper, 1937; reprint, Guildford, Surrey: Eagle, 1991), 30.

47. *The Church Incarnate*, 115 (1998 German ed., 94).

48. *The Church Incarnate*, 116 (1998 German ed., 94).

49. *The Church Incarnate*, 126–27 (1998 German ed., 103).

50. *The Church Incarnate*, 132 (1998 German ed., 107).

51. *The Church Incarnate*, 147 (1998 German ed., 120–21).

52. *The Church Incarnate*, 132–33 (1998 German ed., 108).

53. *The Church Incarnate*, 119, 135 (1998 German ed., 97, 109).

54. *The Church Incarnate*, 177 (1998 German ed., 144–45).

55. *The Church Incarnate*, 148–49 (1998 German ed., 121–22). The term *überirdisch*, here rendered as "wonderfully," is difficult to convey in English; "supernaturally" would be too strong, and "in an otherworldly way" too cumbersome.

56. *The Church Incarnate*, 65 (1998 German ed., 52).

57. David Perkins, *A History of Modern Poetry* (Cambridge, Mass: Harvard University Press, 1976), 1:502 (*The Waste Land* "struck readers as aggressively modern and bewildering"), 514 ("Eliot's reviews and critical essays . . . were a shock for many of their readers"). Perkins also notes (544–45) that poets such as William Carlos Williams, with their accessibility, their charm, their concern with familiar circumstances, their lack of romantically intense emotions, and their "deliberately scaled down" tone, were little recognized in the twenties but rose in recognition during the fifties.

58. See the comments in Peter Hammond, *Liturgy and Architecture* (New York: Columbia University Press, 1960), 55–62: Hammond went so far as to suggest that with a few exceptions the renewal of church design up to around 1933 was largely restricted to Germany. Among the important works on the subject are *German Church*

Architecture of the twentieth Century: Exhibition (Munich: 1964); Hans A. Maurer, *Moderner Kirchenbau in Deutschland*, 2nd ed. (Ostern: Fritz Lometsch, 1964); Sep Ruf, *German Church Architecture of the Twentieth Century* (Munich: Schnell and Steiner, 1964); *Kirchenbau in der Diskussion: Wanderausstellung der Deutschen Gesellschaft für Christliche Kunst* (Munich: Deutsche Gesellschaft für Christliche Kunst, 1973); Hugo Schnell, *Twentieth Century Church Architecture in Germany: Documentation, Presentation, Interpretation*, trans. Paul J. Dine (Munich: Schnell and Steiner, 1974); *Kirchenbau in der Diskussion: Neue Textbeiträge* (Munich: Deutsche Gesellschaft für Christliche Kunst, 1975); Barbara Kahle, *Deutsche Kirchenbaukunst des 20. Jahrhunderts* (Darmstadt: Wissenschaftliche Buchgesellschaft, 1990).

59. Jean Badovici, "Entretiens sur l'Architecture vivante," *Architecture vivante* 1, no. 1 (autumn 1923), 11–20 (and plates 1–13); *Notre-Dame du Raincy* ([Paris: The Church], 1989); John Ely Burchard, "A Pilgrimage: Ronchamp, Raincy, Vézelay," *Architectural Record* 123, no. 3 (Mar. 1958), 171–78; Peter Collins, "The Doctrine of Auguste Perret," *Architectural Review* 114 (Aug. 1953), 90–98; and Peter Collins, *Concrete: The Vision of a New Architecture: A Study of Auguste Perret and His Precursors* (New York: Horizon, 1959), 163, 202–04, and 212; Heathcote and Spens, *Church Builders*, 28–31. Adriano Cornoldi, ed., *L'architettura dell'edificio sacro*, 3rd ed. (Rome: Officina, 2000), particularly pp. 169–273, is an exceptionally rich source of plans and drawings for modern churches, including many of the ones discussed here.

60. Dorothea Eimert, *St. Engelbert in Köln-Riehl* (Munich: Schnell and Steiner, 1977); Heathcote and Spens, *Church Builders*, 26–27.

61. H.A. Reinhold, "A Revolution in Church Architecture," *Liturgical Arts* 6 (1937–38), 123–33.

62. Bernard A. Miller, "Modern Church Architecture: The English Contribution," *Church Quarterly Review* 122 (1936), 292–303.

63. The first by Andrew Rebori (1938–39), the second by Charles Nagel and Frederick W. Dunn (1939); see James J. Mertz, *Madonna della Strada Chapel, Loyola University: An Apostolate of Love* (Chicago: Loyola University Press, 1975); Walter A. Taylor, "A Survey: Protestant Church Design in America," *Architectural Record* 86 no. 1 (Jul. 1939), 66.

64. Under the Nazis more than 270 churches were built or rebuilt in Bavaria, and twenty-eight were built in Munich alone in the years 1932–40, but only three in Cologne under the Third Reich; see Pehnt, *Rudolf Schwarz*, 91.

65. See the buildings surveyed in Rienhard Gieselmann, *Contemporary Church Architecture* (London: Thames and Hudson, 1972); note p. 14: "The inspiration to church architecture derived from the Second World War was not as profound as after the First World War. On the contrary: Despite all the good will to create something new, despite all the idealistic notions of a new church and a new society, no lasting idea emerged, at least in German church architecture."

66. On Assy, William Stanley Rubin, *Modern Sacred Art and the Church of Assy* (New York: Columbia University Press, 1961); Albert Christ-Janer and Mary Mix Foley, *Modern Church Architecture: A Guide to the Form and Spirit of Twentieth-Century Religious Buildings* (New York: McGraw-Hill, 1962), 84–87; John Dillenberger, "Artists and Church Commissions: Rubin's *The Church at Assy* Revisited," *Art Criticism* 1, no. 1 (spring 1979), 72–82, reprinted in Diane Apostolos-Cappadona, ed., *Art, Creativity, and the Sacred: An Anthology in Religion and Art* (New York: Continuum, 1984), 193–

204. On Vence, see Sœur Jacques-Marie, *Henri Matisse: La Chapelle de Vence* ([Nice]: Gardette, 1992), and Henri Matisse, Marie-Alain Couturier, and L.-B. Rayssiguier, *The Vence Chapel: The Archive of a Creation*, trans. Michael Taylor (Houston: Menil Foundation, 1999). On Las Condes, see Francisco Bullrich, *New Directions in Latin American Architecture* (New York: Braziller, 1969), 87–89, and Damián Bayón and Paolo Gasparini, *The Changing Shape of Latin American Architecture: Conversations with Ten Leading Architects*, trans. Galen D. Greaser (Chichester, Sussex: Wiley, 1979), 115–17. On Collegeville, see Ronald Roloff, *Abbey and University Church of Saint John the Baptist*, 5th ed. (n.p.: North Central, 1980); and *Marcel Breuer: The Buildings at St. John's Abbey, Collegeville, Minnesota, Design Quarterly* 53 (special issue) (1961).

67. Stamo Papadaki, *The Work of Oscar Niemeyer* (New York: Reinhold, 1950), 92–103, and Henry-Russell Hitchcock, *Latin American Architecture since 1945* (New York: Museum of Modern Art, 1955), 66–67. See also the comment in "The Horizontal Cathedral: A Discussion with Mario Salvadori on Today's Structural Potentials," *Architectural Record* 119, no. 6 (Jun. 1956), 185. The design for Saint Clement's Episcopal Church in Alexandria, Virginia (1948), met with a great deal of resistance, and the rector judged that it gained approval only because many parishioners were from military families who did not expect to remain long in the parish anyway; see Carroll, "Revisiting a Church of Radical Design," 14.

68. Bernard A. Miller, "Modern Church Architecture: The English Contribution," *Church Quarterly Review* 122 (1936), 292–303.

69. Barry Byrne, "A German city church," *Liturgical Arts* 6 (1937–38), 137–38.

70. Designed by Joseph D. Murphy and Eugene J. Mackey (1952–54); see *Architectural Record*, 110, no. 2 (Aug. 1951), 132–5, and *Architectural Forum*, 101 (Dec. 1954), 124–7.

71. "Meeting House of the First Unitarian Society of Madison, Wis.," *Architectural Forum* 97, no. 6 (Dec. 1952), 85–91; John Gurda, *New World Odyssey: Annunciation Greek Orthodox Church and Frank Lloyd Wright* (Milwaukee: Milwaukee Hellenic Community, 1986); "Spirit of Byzantium: FLLW's Last Church," *Architectural Forum* 115, no. 6 (Dec. 1961), 83–87. There is perennial interest in Frank Lloyd Wright's Unity Temple; see Joseph Siry, *Unity Temple: Frank Lloyd Wright and Architecture for Liberal Religion* (New York: Cambridge University Press, 1996), and Robert McCarter, *Unity Temple: Frank Lloyd Wright* (London: Phaidon, 1997); Anthony Cutler, "The Tyranny of Hagia Sophia: Notes on Greek Orthodox Church Design in the United States," *Journal of the American Society of Architectural Historians* 31 (1972), 38–50 (esp. 41–44).

72. For Schwarz's aversion to Ronchamp, see Pehnt, *Rudolf Schwarz*, 160, and Stegers, *Räume der Wandlung*, 121–22, 173. Some of the earlier criticism of Ronchamp is cited in Curtis, *Le Corbusier*, 178.

73. Burchard, "A Pilgrimage," 171–78.

74. Debuyst, *Modern Architecture and Christian Celebration*, 48.

75. On the distinction between *admiratio* and *imitatio*, see especially Caroline Walker Bynum, "Wonder," *American Historical Review* 102 (1997), 1–16.

76. Designed by Hans Schilling (1957–58); see the photograph in Hiltrud Kier, *Kirchen in Köln* (Cologne: Bachem, 2000), 203. On churches inspired by Ronchamp, see Gieselmann, *Contemporary Church Architecture*, 18; Stegers, *Räume der Wandlung*, 161 (pilgrimage church of Hennef-Süchterscheid); Pehnt, *Rudolf Schwarz*, 160 (Hans

Schilling's Kapelle im Oberbergischen Feld, Rudolf Steinbach's Gnadenkapelle in Süchterscheid).

77. George Pace, "Architecture and Architect in the Service of the Church," in William Lockett, ed., *The Modern Architectural Setting of the Liturgy* (London: SPCK, 1962), 78, cited with further commentary by Elain Harwood, "Liturgy and Architecture: The Development of the Centralised Eucharistic Space," in *Twentieth-Century Architecture: The Journal of the Twentieth Century Society* 3 (1998), 57. On the contrary tendency toward formulaism, see the scathing remark in "Anarchy in Our Churches," *Architectural Forum* 97, no. 6 (Dec. 1952), 93, that already in the years 1949–52 "the most nearly typical US church has been a cheaper imitation of an earlier perfection, in a vain attempt to keep pace with building costs rising faster than church budgets."

78. Schwarz, "'The Eucharistic Building'," 22.

79. Schwarz, *Kirchenbau*, 16–30; Rudolf Schwarz, "Fronleichnamskirche in Aachen," *Zentralblatt der Bauverwaltung* 51 (1931), 441–45, and "Die Fronleichnamskirche in Aachen," *Der Baumeister* 30 (1932), 35–40; Pehnt, *Rudolf Schwarz*, 70–77; Zahner, "Rudolf Schwarz," 18–20; Hasler, *Architektur als Ausdruck*, 134–43; Zahner, *Rudolf Schwarz*, 198–220; Müllenborn, et al., *St. Fronleichnam*; Hammond, *Liturgy and Architecture*, 8, 33, 55–57, 68; Debuyst, *Modern Architecture and Christian Celebration*, 45–46.

80. In a letter of December 19, 1930, to Guardini, cited in Pehnt, *Rudolf Schwarz*, 70.

81. Peter F. Smith, *Third Millennium Churches* (New York: Galaxy Music Corporation, 1972), 1, 89.

82. See the comments of Söhngen, "Die Wallfahrtskirche von Ronchamp," 177, referring to Schwarz's Darmstadt speech of 1951, "Mensch und Raum."

83. For a much later parallel see the work of Alvaro Siza, such as his Santa Maria in Marco de Canavezes, Portugal (1994–97); Judith Dupré, *Churches* (New York: HarperCollins, 2001), 151, comments, "Siza's trademark white walls rise, blazingly pure, above the granite."

84. Edward Maufe, *Modern Church Architecture, with fifty Illustrations of Modern Foreign Churches* (London: Incorporated Church Building Society, [1948]), 29.

85. Ibid., 4–5.

86. Schwarz, *The Church Incarnate*, 200 (1998 German ed., 160), with scathing reference to Le Corbusier's notion of a house as a "machine for living."

87. Schwarz claimed a later church like Sankt Christophorus had no connection with factories and warehouses, although Rudolf Stegers, *Räume der Wandlung*, 175, suggests that in fact the design owes much to industrial precedent.

88. Guardini, "Die neuerbaute Fronleichnamskirche in Aachen."

89. Schwarz, *Kirchenbau*, 20,

90. Barbara Kahle, *Rheinische Kirchen des 20. Jahrhunderts: Ein Beitrag zum Kirchenbauschaffen zwischen Tradition und Moderne* (Cologne: Rheinland-Verlag, 1985); and Harald Blondiau, *Glaube und Raum: Neue Kirchen im Rheinland, 1945–1995* (Cologne: Erzbischöfliches Generalvikariat, 1995). On the general project of reconstruction in Cologne, see Stegers, *Räume der Wandlung*, 139–40.

91. Harwood, "Liturgy and Architecture," 59; Pehnt, *Rudolf Schwarz*, 144 (in the archdiocese of Cologne, between the end of the war and 1956 there were 367 new or renovated churches).

92. Pehnt, *Rudolf Schwarz*, 144.

93. Ibid., 143: while Schwarz was recognized as an avant-garde church designer around 1930, after 1945 he was renowned as an established master of the art.

94. Monika Schmelzer, Carsten Schmalstieg, and Wolf-Rüdiger Spieler, *Kirchen in Köln* (Munich: Verwaltungsverlag, 2000), 177.

95. Schwarz, *Kirchenbau*, 207–23; G.E. Kidder Smith, *The New Churches of Europe* (New York: Holt, Rinehart & Winston, 1964), 160–63; Christ-Janer and Foley, *Modern Church Architecture*, 67–69; Zahner, "Rudolf Schwarz," 27.

96. Dorothea Eimert, *St. Engelbert in Köln-Riehl* (Munich: Schnell and Steiner, 1977), 10.

97. Schwarz, *Kirchenbau*, 254–61; Zahner, "Rudolf Schwarz," 28.

98. Schwarz, *Kirchenbau*, 276–84; Kidder-Smith, *New Churches*, 176–81; Zahner, "Rudolf Schwarz," 29.

99. Kidder-Smith, *New Churches*, 176; Wolfgang Götz, *Katholische Pfarrkirche Maria Königin in Saarbrücken* (Cologne: Rheinischer Verein für Denkmalpflege und Landschaftsschutz, 1988), 10.

100. Ibid., 18, quoting Hugo Schnell.

101. Schwarz, *Kirchenbau*, 235–46; Pehnt, *Rudolf Schwarz*, 152; Kidder-Smith, *New Churches*, 172–75; Zahner, "Rudolf Schwarz," 26; Adalbert Dabrowski, Erika Hülder, and Helmut Jurgasz, *Heilig Kreuz Bottrop: Kleiner Kirchenführer* (Bottrop: Katholische Kirchengemeinde Heilig Kreuz, [1999]).

102. For the comment on the "Eye of God" window see Kidder-Smith, *New Churches*, 174. On the "Infinity" window, see Georg Meistermann, *Die Kirchenfenster* (Freiburg: Herder, 1986), quoted in Dabrowski, Hülder, and Jurgasz, *Heilig Kreuz Bottrop*, 30: "The parabola is a form that continues to infinity, always expanding, without reaching closure. Or: it clasps the entire universe and brings it back to the altar. This was the liturgical idea of Schwarz. It occurred to me spontaneously, that only one form corresponds to such a such an out-going and at the same time in-bringing form seen in the [architectural] elevation: that of the spiral."

103. Pehnt, *Rudolf Schwarz*, 152; Stegers, *Räume der Wandlung*, 168; on use of the parabolic form elsewhere, see 170–72.

104. Schwarz, *Kirchenbau*, 269–75; Zahner, "Rudolf Schwarz," 30.

105. Schwarz, *Kirchenbau*, 296–303; Hasler, *Architektur als Ausdruck*, 143–51 and 154–64.

106. Debuyst, *Modern Architecture and Christian Celebration*, 45–46; Edward Anders Sövik, "Tea and Sincerity," *Liturgical Arts* 37, no. 1 (Nov. 1968), 7.

107. Schwarz, *Kirchenbau*, 179–90; Pehnt, *Rudolf Schwarz*, 146; Hasler, *Architektur als Ausdruck*, 190–99. For those who might wonder how such differential height might function if used symmetrically on the two sides of a rectilinear nave, Schwarz's Sankt Antonius in Essen gives one answer: the altar is toward the west side, there are exceptionally wide areas with markedly lower ceilings both in the northeast corner (where the main entrance is located) and in the southeast corner, and the effect is to create an interior space that begins at a modest level, then opens up dramatically in the nave and across the west side, but then closes down just as dramatically, creating what some might perceive as a needlessly confusing complexity of design. On this church see Schwarz, *Kirchenbau*, 286–96, and Hasler, *Architektur als Ausdruck*, 244–54.

108. Schwarz, *Kirchenbau*, 223–35; Pehnt, *Rudolf Schwarz*, 146–49; Kidder-Smith, *New Churches*, 164–71; Christ-Janer and Foley, *Modern Church Architecture*, 62–66; Zahner, "Rudolf Schwarz," 25; *St. Anna in Düren* ([Düren: The Church], n.d.); Hasler, *Architektur als Ausdruck*, 223–43.

109. On the L-form in churches, see Stegers, *Räume der Wandlung*, 159.

110. Pehnt, *Rudolf Schwarz*, 143–44.

111. Schmelzer, Schmalstieg, and Spieler, *Kirchen in Köln*, 202.

112. Ibid., 177. Photographs of this church before and after the alteration are in Kier, *Kirchen in Köln*, 194.

113. "Ein neuer Altar für die Fronleichnamskirche in Aachen? Ein Bericht des Arbeitskreises 'Architektur und Denkmalschutz' des Bundes Deutscher Architekten, BDA in Nordrhein-Westfalen," *Kunst und Kirche* 44 (1981), 100.

114. Karl Rörlich, "Gemeinde und Kirche im Wandel," in Müllenborn, *St. Fronleichnam*, 40–43.

115. *The Church Incarnate*, 64–65 (1998 German ed., 51–52).

116. Stegers, *Räume der Wandlung*, 177–79: he now thought of such celebration as bringing the entire plan of the church "into confusion."

117. Again, *The Church Incarnate*, 64–65 (1998 German ed., 51–52).

118. The allusion is to Paul Ricoeur's "second naiveté," a notion developed in *The Symbolism of Evil*, trans. Emerson Buchanan (New York: Harper and Row, 1967).

CHAPTER 8

1. *Directives for the Building of a Church, by the Liturgical Commission of the German Hierarchy*, English trans. (Collegeville, Minn.: Liturgical Press, 1949); "Diocesan Building Directives: Diocesan Liturgical Commission, Superior, Wisconsin," *Liturgical Arts* 26, no. 2 (Feb. 1957), 7–9.

2. Peter Hammond, *Liturgy and Architecture* (New York: Columbia University Press, 1960); Peter Hammond, ed., *Towards a Church Architecture* (London: Architectural Press, 1962).

3. Theodor Filthaut, *Kirchenbau und Liturgiereform* (Mainz: Matthias-Grünewald-Verlag, 1965); in English as *Church Architecture and Liturgical Reform*, trans. Gregory Roettger (Baltimore: Helicon, 1968).

4. The Council's only direct instruction for church architecture says only that church buildings should be appropriate for the celebration of liturgical actions and for the active participation of the faithful ("In aedificandis vero sacris aedibus, diligenter curetur ut ad liturgicas actiones exsequendas et ad fidelium actuosam participationem obtinendam idoneae sint"); see Vatican Council II, *Constitutio de Sacra Liturgia*, "*Sacrosanctum concilium*," *Acta Apostolicae Sedis*, 56 (1964), 97–138, 7.124.

5. Steven J. Schloeder, *Architecture in Communion: Implementing the Second Vatican Council Through Liturgy and Architecture* (San Francisco: Ignatius, 1998), 9, 42 (see 242), 29.

6. Michael Davies, *The Catholic Sanctuary and the Second Vatican Council* (Rockford, Ill.: Tan, 1997); Michael S. Rose, *The Renovation Manipulation: The Church Counter-Renovation Handbook* (Cincinnati: Aquinas, 2000).

7. Michael S. Rose, *Ugly as Sin: Why They Changed Our Churches from Sacred*

Places to Meeting Spaces and How We Can Change Them Back Again (Manchester, N.H.: Sophia Institute Press, 2001).

8. Ibid., 141; also Abbot Boniface Luykx, "Liturgical Architecture: *Domus Dei* or *domus ecclesiae?*" *Catholic Dossier*, May/Jun. 1997, cited by Rose.

9. Rose, *Ugly as Sin*, 173–74.

10. Cristiano Rosponi and Giampaolo Rossi, eds., *Reconquering Sacred Space: New Catholic Architecture for the New Millennium* (Rome: Il Bosco e la nave, 1999). Reviewed by Denis McNamara in *Adoremus Bulletin* 6, no. 5 (Aug. 2000),pp. 3 and 11.

11. Ethan Antony, "Neo-Gothic Architecture Today," *Sacred Architecture*, spring 2001, p. 30.

12. Ludwig Feuerbach, *The Essence of Christianity* (New York: Harper, 1957), 20, quoted in Harold W. Turner, *From Temple to Meeting House: The Phenomenology and Theology of Places of Worship* (The Hague: Mouton, 1979), 331. For a more pungent statement of the point, see Joseph L. Price, "The Quest for the Historical Bibfeldt," in Martin E. Marty and Jerald C. Brauer, eds., *The Unrelieved Paradox: Studies in the Theology of Franz Bibfeldt* (Grand Rapids, Mich.: Eerdmans, 1994), 33: "Blessed are the rich in money, for they can build bigger and better churches. Who cares about the Kingdom of God?"

13. Letter 58.7, in Saint Jérôme, *Lettres*, ed. and trans. Jérôme Labourt (Paris: Les Belles Lettres, 1949–63), 3:81.

14. J.G. Davies, *The Secular Use of Church Buildings* (New York: Seabury, 1968), 206 and 211. Reinhold Niebuhr commented on the Cathedral of Saint John the Divine: "Perhaps we ought not try to symbolize the truths of our religion in stone and steel. The result is usually some unhappy combination of the sense of divine majesty and human pride." See Reinhold Niebuhr, *Essays in Applied Christianity*, 43, as quoted in James A. Whyte, "The Theological Basis of Church Architecture," in Hammond, *Towards a Church Architecture*, 190.

15. Michael M. Winter, *Mission or Maintenance: A Study in New Pastoral Structures* (London: Darton, Longman, and Todd, 1973), 24, quoted in Turner, *From Temple to Meeting House*, 323.

16. Giovanni Catti, "Le chiese nell'educazione dei cristiani," in *Nuove Chiese* (Bologna: Natale, 1969), 3, quoted in Giacomo Grasso, *Tra teologia e architettura: analisi dei problemi soggiacenti all'edilizia per il culto* (Rome: Borla, 1988), 76.

17. "Anarchy in Our Churches," *Architectural Forum* 97, no. 6 (Dec. 1952), 94, regarding Warren Weber's Cedar Hills Congregational Church, near Portland, Oregon.

18. Edward A. Sövik, "Living on the High Wire," *Faith and Form* 26 (fall 1993), 11.

19. Designed by Jozsef Kerényi (1984–91); see the IFRAA International Architectural Design Awards in *Faith and Form* 26 (winter 1992–93), 11.

20. Horst Schwebel, "Liturgical Space and Human Experience, Exemplified by the Issue of the 'Multi-Purpose' Church Building," *Studia liturgica* 24 (1994), 16–20. See Manfred Ludes, *Sakralbauten: Projekte, 1964–1998* (Wuppertal, Germany: Müller und Busmann, 2001), 58–61, for reflections on multiuse spaces (*Mehrzweckräume*) and for an example of a church where peripheral areas can serve purposes other than worship but can be opened when necessary for congregations too large for the core church.

21. Damián Bayón and Paolo Gasparini, *The Changing Shape of Latin American Architecture: Conversations with Ten Leading Architects*, trans. Galen D. Greaser (Chichester, Sussex: Wiley, 1979), 194.

22. This is not to say that such a movement was typical for Anglo-Catholic priests; it was not. See the discussion in Kenneth Leech, "The End of the Dolling era? Fr Joe Williamson in Stepney," in *The Anglo-Catholic Social Conscience: Two Critical Essays*, (Croydon, Surrey: Jubilee Group [1991]).

23. To take a sampling from the Roman Catholic Archdiocese of Chicago: Our Lady of Perpetual Help in Glenview (1949–53, Colonial); Saint Anne in Barrington (1950–51, Gothic); Saint Leonard in Berwyn (1950–51, Gothic); Saint James in Arlington Heights (1950–52, Colonial); Saint Mary Magdalene in Chicago (1952–54, Romanesque); Saint George in Tinley Park (1953, Colonial); Saint Vincent Ferrer in River Forest (1954–56, Gothic); Queen of All Saints in Chicago (1956–60, Gothic); Saint John the Baptist in Harvey (1956–59, Romanesque); Saints Faith, Hope and Charity in Winnetka (1961–62, modernized Colonial). See the listings in Harry C. Koenig, ed., *A History of the Parishes of the Archdiocese of Chicago* (Chicago: Archdiocese of Chicago, 1980). See also E. Brooks Holifield, "The Architect and the Congregation," *Faith and Form* 19 (spring 1986), 40: "Period architecture did not disappear, but by the 1950s a host of architects could declare that the older colonial and antebellum styles for churches and synagogues were 'artistically archaic.'"

24. Turner, *From Temple to Meeting House*, 335.

25. Edward Maufe, *Modern Church Architecture, with fifty Illustrations of Modern Foreign Churches* (London: Incorporated Church Building Society, [1948]), 3; see the comment in "Anarchy in Our Churches," 102, "Now it is true that in the past people always built in the style of their time. But Maufe's bright remark does not face the issue altogether—for while it is traditional to be modern, it is not modern (or polite) to ignore tradition." See also the comment of Edward A. Sövik, "A Portfolio of Reflections on the Design of Northfield Methodist Church," *Your Church* 13, no. 5 (Sept./Oct. 1967), 48, that "in the history of church building, all those buildings out of the past which we now consider to be great architecture, were to some degree a surprise and often a very disturbing surprise to the people for whom they were built." In "The Horizontal Cathedral: A Discussion with Mario Salvadori on Today's Structural Potentials," *Architectural Record* 119, no. 6 (Jun. 1956), 185, the church designer is compared to a lover who praises his beloved with a *new* song.

26. Hammond, *Liturgy and Architecture*, 157.

27. Laura Burns Carroll, "Revisiting a Church of Radical Design—and Its Visionary Priest," *Faith and Form* 28 (fall 1994), 13.

28. "Diocesan Building Directives," 7–9; Hammond, *Liturgy and Architecture*, 3.

29. Charles Davis, "Church Architecture and the Liturgy," in Hammond, *Towards a Church Architecture*, 109–10.

30. Sövik, "A Portfolio of Reflections," 46.

31. Donald J. Bruggink and Carl H. Droppers, *When Faith Takes Form: Contemporary Churches of Architectural Integrity in America* (Grand Rapids, Mich.: Eerdmans, 1971), 9–10. On concern with style in the initial phases of planning at a Presbyterian church, see Meredith L. Clausen, *Pietro Belluschi, Modern American Architect* (Cambridge, Mass.: MIT Press, 1994), 155.

32. Rudolf Schwarz, *Vom Bau der Kirche*, new ed. (Salzburg: Pustet, 1998), 5, in

English as *The Church Incarnate: The Sacred Function of Christian Architecture*, trans. Cynthia Harris (Chicago: Regnery, 1958), 9. E.A. Sövik, *Architecture for Worship* (Minneapolis: Augsburg, 1973), 25 (concealment of steel or concrete skeletons in masonry or wood "gave the illusion of ancient forms, but the result is more like stage scenery than authentic architecture").

33. Paul Tillich, *On Art and Architecture*, ed. John and Jane Dillenberger, trans. Robert P. Scharlemann (New York: Crossroad, 1989), 216, 221–28.

34. Lance Wright, "Architectural Seriousness," in Hammond, *Towards a Church Architecture*, 221–22. See also Mildred Schmertz, "Liturgy and Tradition Shape Designs for Three Faiths," *Architectural Record* 138, no. 11 (Nov. 1965), 134: "Vestigial historicism, unfortunately, with time can become less vestigial"—the community that commissions a church with minimal historical reference is likely to go further in its historicism with decorations.

35. "A Baptist Church by Weese," *Architectural Record* 138, no. 12 (Dec. 1965), 114, quoted in the context of an article on Harry Weese's First Baptist Church of Columbus, Indiana.

36. Rudolf Arnheim, *The Dynamics of Architectural Form* (Berkeley: University of California Press, 1977), 206.

37. Wright, "Architectural Seriousness," 229; see also Sövik, *Architecture for Worship*, 42

38. Wright, "Architectural Seriousness," 229, 240. See the contrary argument in *Directives for the Building of a Church*, 5: "It would be a mistake to plan the exterior structure in its outlines and spatial proportions, in its structural members and its decoration, according to the style of the profane architecture of the time and of the surroundings: lest the attractiveness of the church building be merely that of this world."

39. Davies, *Secular Use of Church Buildings*, was a major stimulus for this development, but both the concept and the term "multipurpose" (or "multiuse") antedated Davies by several years. See, for example, "Meeting House of the First Unitarian Society of Madison, Wis.," *Architectural Forum* 97, no. 6 (Dec. 1952), 90, and "Anarchy in Our Churches" (with reference to Paul Schweikher and Winston Elting's First Methodist Church at Plainfield, Iowa).

40. *The Church for Others and The Church for the World: A Quest for Structures for Missionary Congregations: Final Report of the Western European Working Group and North American Working Group of the Department on Studies in Evangelism* (Geneva: World Council of Churches, 1968), 28.

41. Sövik, *Architecture for Worship*, 38.

42. Clausen, *Pietro Belluschi*, 159: First Presbyterian Church, Cottage Grove (1948–51).

43. Designed by Hugh Stubbins (1977); see "Saint Peter's Church, New York, N.Y., 1977; Architects: Hugh Stubbins and Associates," *Process: Architecture*, 10 (1979), 38–41; Patricia M. Snibbe and Richard W. Snibbe, *The New Modernist in World Architecture* (New York: McGraw-Hill, 1999), 80–81.

44. Designed by Holabird and Roche (1922–24); see George A. Lane, *Chicago Churches and Synagogues: An Architectural Pilgrimage* (Chicago: Loyola University Press, 1981), 163.

45. Paul Goldberger, *The City Observed: New York: A Guide to the Architecture of Manhattan* (New York: Random House, 1979), 159.

46. Francis Morrone, *The Architectural Guidebook to New York City* (Salt Lake City: Gibbs Smith, 1994), 172.

47. Robert Campbell, "A Church Struggles to Look Like One," *Faith and Form* 26 (spring 1993), 34–35 (with relevant correspondence on pp. 35 and 37), reprinted from *Boston Globe*, Sept. 8, 1992, "Living" Sect., p. 49.

48. Vida D. Scudder, "A Plea for Social Intercession," in *The Church and the Hour: Papers by a Socialist Churchwoman* (New York: Dutton, 1917).

49. Richared Lacayo, "To the Lighthouse: What Should a Church Look Like Today? One Bold Answer: Rafael Moneo's L.A. Cathedral," *Time*, Sept. 2, 2002, p. 64.

50. See Edwin Heathcote and Iona Spens, *Church Builders* (Chichester, England: Academy, 1997), 14, for statements by W. R. Lethaby and Adolf Loos in opposition to ornament; for the latter see Adolf Loos, *Ornament and Crime: Selected Essays*, ed. Adolf Opel, trans. Michael Mitchell (Riverside, Calif.: Ariadne Press, 1998).

51. Ninian Comper, *Of the Atmosphere of a Church* (London: Sheldon Press, 1947), 31, quoted in Hammond, *Liturgy and Architecture*, 28.

52. Albert Christ-Janer and Mary Mix Foley, *Modern Church Architecture: A Guide to the Form and Spirit of Twentieth-Century Religious Buildings* (New York: McGraw-Hill, 1962), 184–90.

53. Schloeder, *Architecture in Communion*, 44, cf. 170.

54. Karl Barth, "The Architectural Problem of Protestant Places of Worship," in André Biéler, *Architecture in Worship: The Christian Place of Worship: A Sketch of the Relationships between the Theology of Worship and the Architectural Conception of Christian Churches from the Beginnings to Our Day*, trans. Odette and Donald Elliott (Philadelphia: Westminster, 1965), 92–93.

55. Gregory Wolfe, *Sacred Passion: The Art of William Schickel* (Notre Dame, Ind.: University of Notre Dame Press, 1998), 54–74; the chapel before and after the remodeling is shown also in Sövik, *Architecture for Worship*, 120. On Cistercian churches generally see Anselme Dimier, *Stones Laid Before the Lord*. trans. Gilchrist Lavigne (Kalamazoo: Cistercian Publications, 1999), especially 111–23 and 137–58.

56. Tillich, *On Art and Architecture*, 193, 227–28; Martin Dudley, "Honesty and Consecration: Paul Tillich's Criteria for a Religious Architecture," in Diana Wood, ed., *The Church and the Arts* (Oxford: Blackwell, 1995), 515–22. Oskar Söhngen said in 1962 that his age had recovered a sense not for the merely simple but for a "filled" (we might say "pregnant") simplicity, for an "articulate" emptiness; see his article "Der Begriff des Sakralen im Kirchenbau," in *Kirchenbau und Ökumene: Evangelische Kirchenbautagung in Hamburg 1961* (Hamburg: Friedrich Wittig Verlag, 1962), 197–99. The German *"erfüllte"* means "filled," but in other contexts *erfüllte* could also mean "fulfilled," and here too it conveys a sense of purposive plenitude.

57. Romana Schneider and Wilfried Wang, eds., *Moderne Architektur in Deutschland 1900 bis 2000: Macht und Monument* (Ostfildern-Ruit, Germany: Gerd Hatje, 1998), is the catalogue for an exhibition at the Deutsches Architektur-Museum in Frankfurt am Main; none of the articles, however, focuses on church architecture per se. The exhibition is reviewed by Peter M. Bode, "Power and Monumentalism," *Kultur Chronik* 3 (1998), 41–42.

58. Davies, *Secular Use of Church Buildings*, 207.

59. The Most Reverend Robert J. Dwyer, Bishop of Reno, Nevada, "Art and Architecture for the Church in Our Age," *Liturgical Arts* 27, no. 1 (Nov. 1958), 2–6.

60. Davis, "Church Architecture and the Liturgy," 107–8, 126–27; see also Sövik, *Architecture for Worship*, 63–64 ("The end of the cathedral?"); Bruggink and Droppers, *When Faith Takes Form*, 116; and Whyte, "The Theological Basis of Church Architecture," especially 185.

61. Frédéric Debuyst, *Modern Architecture and Christian Celebration* (Richmond, Va.: John Knox Press, 1968), 9–10, 53–55; see Hammond, *Liturgy and Architecture*, 48. Michael E. DeSanctis, *Renewing the City of God: The Reform of Catholic Architecture in the United States* (Chicago: Liturgy Training, 1993), 12, quotes one undated diocesan newsletter that put the point bluntly: "We are not concerned with building monuments." In more recent years one architect has echoed these themes in theologically puzzling terms, saying that a massive and ornate church "may be in scale with God, but it is out of scale with man"; see Ken Sidey, "So Long to Sacred Space: Consumer-Minded, User-Friendly Buildings—Not Glorified Monuments—Are Driving Church Designs," *Christianity Today* 37, no. 13 (Nov. 8, 1993), p. 46. But see the opposing view of Dennis McNally, *Sacred Space: An Aesthetic for the Liturgical Environment* (Bristol, Ind.: Wyndham Hall, 1985), 80: "Monumentality is the sense that the building gives of the power of the community, the power of the divinity, the power of life. In other words, the sense of lasting strength that the house-of-God, house-of-His-people, is a kratophany. The power of God, the power of the Church, is a healing manifestation in such buildings as Bourges or Durham."

62. Wright, "Architectural Seriousness," 233–37.

63. Günter Rombold, "Vom Purismus zum Schwulst," *Kunst und Kirche* 49 (1986), 110–13. For a somewhat analogous case in America, see Campbell, "A Church Struggles to Look Like One."

64. Schwebel, "Liturgical Space and Human Experience." See Ludes, *Sakralbauten*, 58–61, for reflections on multiuse spaces (*Mehrzweckräume*) and for an example of a church where peripheral areas can serve purposes other than worship but can be opened when necessary for congregations too large for the core church.

65. Willem Gerard Overbosch, "Kirchenbau in Holland," in *Kirchenbau und Ökumene: Evangelische Kirchenbautagung in Hamburg 1961* (Hamburg: Friedrich Wittig Verlag, 1962), 55.

66. Mark Allen Torgerson, "Edward Anders Sövik and His Return to the 'Non-Church'" (Ph.D. diss., University of Notre Dame, 1995), 337–47, 348–56, 357–67.

67. See two issues of *Kunst und Kirche*: vol. 42, no. 3 (1979), dedicated to the concept of postmodernism and its relevance to church architecture, and vol. 48, no. 1 (1985), on the theme of living with history and what that can mean in a "postmodern" situation (although neither issue deals so directly with ecclesiastical architecture as one might have expected).

68. Duncan G. Stroik, "Modernist Church Architecture," *Catholic Dossier*, vol. 3 May/Jun. 1997, pp. 6–10.

69. Designed by the firm of Dick Hammel, Curt Green, and Bruce Abrahamson (1987–89); see *Inland Architect*, Nov./Dec. 1989, pp. 44–46.

70. Designed by Clovis Heimsath (1988); see DeSanctis, *Renewing the City of God*, 39–41, citing Donald Canty, "Little Palazzo on the Prairie: An Italianate Texas Church," *Architecture* 78 (1989), 78–79.

71. Chambers Chapel at Boys Town, Nebraska (designed by Dennis Raynor, 1989), and Saint Andrew Presbyterian Church in Sonoma, California (designed by

William Turnbull Associates); see the listings of IFRAA International Architectural Design Awards in *Faith and Form* 26 (winter 1992–93), 17, and 27 (winter 1993–94), 36. See Antony, "Neo-Gothic Architecture Today," 30.

72. Other takeoffs on Tom Wolfe's *From Bauhaus to Our House* (New York: Farrar Straus Giroux, 1981) did appear, notably Leslie Garisto, *From Bauhaus to Birdhouse* (New York: HarperCollins, 1992).

73. K.L. Sijmons, *Protestantsche kerkbouw* ('s-Gravenhage: D A Daamen, 1946), 10. When I was discussing with one colleague the categories sacramental, evangelical, and communal church he proposed substituting "the good, the bad, and the ugly."

74. Schloeder, *Architecture in Communion*, 9; see Thomas Gordon Smith, "An architecture to Honor the Church's Vision," *Adoremus Bulletin* 3, no. 8 (Nov. 1997); Rose, *Ugly as Sin*, 171.

75. Duncan G. Stroik, "Possiamo permetterci di non costruire belle chiese? / Can We Afford Not to Build Beautiful Churches?" in Cristiano Rosponi, Giampaolo Rossi, and Duncan G. Stroik, ed., *Riconquistare lo spazio sacro 2000: la chiesa nella città del terzo millennio / Reconquering Sacred Space 2000: The Church in the City of the Third Millennium* (Rome: Il Bosco e la Nave, 2000), 86.

76. Jack Barnett, "Our Buildings Need to Be Far More Friendly," *Architect and Builder*, Feb. 1995, p. 16, taken from the *Cape Times*, Jan. 31, 1995.

77. Campbell, "A Church Struggles to Look Like One," 35.

78. Daniel Lee, "Architecture's Role in Christianity," *Sacred Architecture* 2 (fall 1998), 15.

79. Schloeder, *Architecture in Communion*, 40, 44, 170, 242; see Gretchen T. Buggeln, "Architecture as Community Service: West Presbyterian Church in Wilmington, Delaware," in David Morgan and Sally M. Promey, eds., *The Visual Culture of American Religion* (Berkeley: University of California Press, 2001), 95, on expectations within the neighborhood of a new church building.

80. Camilian Demetrescu, "Simbolo nell'architettura e iconografia sacra / Symbols in Sacred Architecture and Iconography," in Rosponi and Rossi, *Riconquistare lo spazio sacro* (1999), 53.

81. Giampaolo Rossi, "Il cristiano e l'arte: per una cultura della speranza / The Christian and the Art: Towards a Culture of Hope," in Rosponi and Rossi, *Riconquistare lo spazio sacro* (1999), 9–15.

82. Schloeder, *Architecture in Communion*, 42, "Above All, a Catholic Church Ought to Look Like a Catholic Church"; see 242.

83. For example, Paul Likoudis, "Is *Domus Dei* D.O.A.?", *The Wanderer*, 2 Dec. 1999, pp. 1 and 7.

84. Schloeder, *Architecture in Communion*, 29.

85. Evelyn Underhill, *Worship* (New York: Harper, 1937).

86. *Environment and Art in Catholic Worship*, issued by the Bishops' Committee on the Liturgy, National Conference of Catholic Bishops (Chicago: Liturgy Training Publications, 1978).

87. The most important passage (1.14) says all the faithful should be led "ad plenam . . . consciam atque actuosam liturgicarum celebrationum participationem." In parallel passages the most consistently used adjective is *actuosa*: the document refers simply to "actuosa participatio" (1.19, 1.27, 1.30, 6.114, 6.121, 7.124); to "plenaria et actuosa participatio totius plebis" (1.41); to "pia et actuosa fidelium participatio"

(2.50); or to "conscia, actuosa et facilis participatio" (3.79). Only occasionally is the term omitted or replaced: "perfectior Missae participatio" (2.55); "actualis participatio" (1.26).

88. John R.K. Fenwick and Bryan D. Spinks, *Worship in Transition: The Liturgical Movement in the Twentieth Century* (New York: Continuum, 1995), discuss liturgical reform in these and other denominations. See especially Gregory Dix, *The Shape of the Liturgy* (London: Black, 1945), 12–13.

89. J.J. Burke, *Reasonableness of Catholic Ceremonies and Practices*, 2nd ed. (New York: Benzinger, 1894), 17, was already writing that "when a priest says Mass the people, by the English Missals or other prayer-books, are able to follow him from beginning to end."

90. Holifield, "The Architect and the Congregation," 41.

91. This is one of the respects in which Auguste Perret's Notre Dame du Raincy is recognized as innovative: the sanctuary is elevated high above the nave, but with no structural division between the two.

92. "Diocesan Building Directives," 7–9; Davis, "Church Architecture and the Liturgy," 117; see also Hammond, *Liturgy and Architecture*, 43–44; and *Environment and Art in Catholic Worship*, 29: "special attention must be given to the unity of the entire liturgical space. . . . Within that one space there are different areas corresponding to different roles and functions, but the wholeness of the total space should be strikingly evident."

93. Frederick Gibberd, *Metropolitan Cathedral of Christ the King, Liverpool* (London: Architectural Press, 1968), 20–28; Gyo Obata, "Design of Saint Louis Priory and School," *Liturgical Arts* 26, no. 2 (Feb. 1957), 50–61 (specifically 50 and 59–60).

94. Hammond, *Liturgy and Architecture*, 41.

95. James Fitzsimmons, "Prototype of an Organic Modern Church," *Art Digest* 26, no. 6 (Dec. 15, 1951), 11 and 23, shows a model by Jean Labatut (with the muralist André Girard) for a round Church of the Four Evangelists in which a wall covered with murals occupies the position behind the altar.

96. DeSanctis, *Renewing the City of God*, 29–41.

97. Theodor Filthaut, *Church Architecture and Liturgical Reform*, trans. Gregory Roettger (Baltimore: Helicon, 1968), 47–49. Filthaut's use of the term "confrontation" provoked some misunderstanding, for example by Debuyst, *Modern Architecture and Christian Celebration*, 65; what he clearly means is simply a *facing* of priest and people.

98. Designed by Claudio Caveri and Eduardo Ellis (1957); see Francisco Bullrich, *Arquitectura argentina contemporanea: Panorama de la arquitectura argentina, 1950–63* (Buenos Aires: Ediciones Nueva Visión, 1963), 143–45; Damián Bayón and Paolo Gasparini, *The Changing Shape of Latin American Architecture: Conversations with Ten Leading Architects*, trans. Galen D. Greaser (Chichester, England: Wiley, 1979), 19; and Francisco Bullrich, *New Directions in Latin American Architecture* (New York: Braziller, 1969), 62 and 68. Two further possibilities, less common, were the centralized transeptal arrangement and "antiphonal choir" seating. The first had distinct blocks of seating on three sides of the focal point, each of them arranged as rectangular blocks—something like the arrangement in a traditional cruciform church, but with the seats in the transepts facing inward. Some early examples of modern church design used this arrangement, but it quickly became clear that it resulted in segmentation of the

congregation into distinct and detached groups. Antiphonal choir seating has pews arranged like choir stalls on either side of an aisle or of the central liturgical space, giving the congregation something of the role assigned to the choir in a medieval church.

99. Edward Anders Sövik, "An Architect's View: Architecture for Hymn Singing," in Dennis Fleisher, et al., *Acoustics for Liturgy: A Collection of Articles of The Hymn Society in the U.S. and Canada* (Chicago: Liturgy Training, 1991), 17–24.

100. Robert Maguire and Keith Murray, "Anglican Church in Stepney," *Churchbuilding* 7 (Oct. 1962), 15.

101. Schloeder, *Architecture in Communion*, 30.

102. C.S. Lewis, *Surprised by Joy: The Shape of My Earthly Life* (London: Bles, 1955), 160.

103. Terry K. Boggs, "A Pastor's View: Acoustics and Meaningful Places for Worship," in *Acoustics for Liturgy*, 51–59.

104. The German *Directives for the Building of a Church*, 10–11, had warned, "It would be a mistake to arrange and decorate the interior of the church in such way as to create the atmosphere of a comfortable and cozy bourgeois residence: and a mistake also to wish to imitate the poverty of a proletarian dwelling." One might be reminded of an experiment in teaching carried out at an American university. Someone had the idea that seminars might be taught in dormitory lounges, within the students' own living space, so they would be all the more relaxed and forthcoming. The result in at least some cases was quite the opposite. In large part because the environment was a casual one meant for relaxation, it seemed difficult for the students to sustain the kind of energy they might have had elsewhere.

105. On the complexities of this issue, see Boggs, "A Pastor's View," 51–59.

106. Giles Dimock, "Will Beauty Look after Herself?" *Sacred Music*, 117, no. 3 (fall 1990), 16.

107. Duncan Stroik, "Ten Myths of Contemporary Church Architecture," *Sacred Architecture* 2 (fall 1998), 10–11.

108. Louis Bouyer, *Liturgy and Architecture* (Notre Dame, Ind.: University of Notre Dame Press, 1967); see also Josef Andreas Jungmann, "The New Altar," trans. John J. Galvani, *Liturgical Arts*, 37, no. 2 (Feb. 1969), 36–40, where other voices of caution are cited (including, in a nuanced way, Jungmann's own).

109. Rose, *Ugly as Sin*, 141 n. 78.

110. In Christian usage (perhaps most importantly in Augustine) the adjective *actuosus* can be fully synonymous with *activus*, and *vita actuosa* can be a synonym for *vita activa*, as distinguished from the *vita otiosa* or *contemplativa*. Elsewhere *actuosus* refers to energetic action or to extravagant bodily motion or gesture, such as that of actors and dancers, who are thus sometimes called *actuosi*. For examples of usage (including Christian) see the *Oxford Latin Dictionary* (Oxford: Clarendon, 1968), 30, and *Thesaurus linguae Latinae, editus auctoritate et consilio Academiarum quinque Germanicarum Berolinensis, Gottingensis, Lipsiensis, Monacensis, Vindobonensis*, vol. 1 (Leipzig: Teubner, 1900), 449.

111. At one point (1.19) the Constitution on Liturgy refers explicitly to active participation that is both inward and outward ("actuosam fidelium participationem, internam et externam . . . animarum"), and while this participation is ascribed specifically to souls, the adjective *externam* makes clear that the inward disposition is to be ex-

pressed in outward behavior. Elsewhere (6.114) the Constitution says choirs should be encouraged, especially in cathedrals, but that bishops and other clergy should stive zealously for active participation of all the faithful, in a manner fitting for them, in every sung liturgical observance.

112. Quoted in Söhngen, "Der Begriff des Sakralen," 183–85.

113. Oskar Söhngen, "Die Wallfahrtskirche von Ronchamp: Zum Problem des Sakralen im modernen Kirchenbau," in *Reich Gottes und Wirklichkeit: Festgabe für Alfred Dedo Müller zum 70. Geburtstag* (Berlin: Evangelische Verlagsanstalt, 1961), 177, 185–86.

114. Harvey Gallagher Cox, *The Secular City: Secularization and Urbanization in Theological Perspective* (New York: Macmillan, 1965).

115. Ignazio M. Calabuig, "The Rite of Dedication of a Church," trans. Matthew J. O'Connell, in Anscar J. Chupungco, ed., *Liturgical Time and Space* (Collegeville, Minn.: Liturgical Press, 2000), 346. A popular and practical version of the argument appears in Sidey, "So Long to Sacred Space." See also the statement of Eduard Schweizer, quoted in Horst Schwebel, "Liturgical Space and Human Experience, Exemplified by the Issue of the 'Multipurpose' Church Building," *Studia liturgica* 24 (1994), 14: "Everything is holy, nothing any longer is profane, because the world belongs to God, and because the world is the place where God is to be praised and thanked." Peter W. Williams, "Metamorphoses of the Meetinghouse: Three Case Studies," in Paul Corby Finney, ed., *Seeing beyond the Word: Visual Arts and the Calvinist Tradition* (Grand Rapids, Mich.: Eerdmans, 1999), 503–4, distinguishes usefully between *overt* rejection of the category of *positive* sacred space and *covert* affirmation of a *negative* sacred space.

116. Davies, *Secular Use of Church Buildings*, 16, 36, 39–40, and 96–97. The point might have been broadened: Yves Congar, "The Sacralization of Western Society in the Middle Ages," *Concilium* 47 (1969), 55–71, shows how in the early Middle Ages the Old Testament provided models for conception of Christian society and social order generally.

117. Davies, *Secular Use of Church Buildings*, 17.

118. Jacqueline Jung, "Beyond the Barrier: The Unifying Role of the Choir Screen in Gothic Churches," *Art Bulletin* 82 (2000), 629, suggests (drawing on records from Chartres) that the bays of the *jubé* could have been put to yet more unconventional purposes.

119. Davies, *Secular Use of Church Buildings*, 95.

120. Ibid., 107.

121. Ibid., 97.

122. Ibid., 98–99.

123. Ibid., 102, 113.

124. Ibid., 16.

125. Ibid., 223–24, expanded pp. 224–36.

126. Ibid., 213, 222–23.

127. Turner, *From Temple to Meeting House*, 342, 12. For a compatible position, see J.C. Hoekendijk, *The Church Inside Out*, ed. L.A. Hoedemaker and Pieter Tijmes, trans. Isaac C. Rottenberg (Philadelphia: Westminster, 1966), as quoted in Davies, *Secular Use of Church Buildings*, 212–13: "In church building a shift ought to take place from *sacral architecture* to the designing of a *fellowship house*."

128. For discussion of Turner and others, see Paul Corby Finney, "Early Christian Architecture: The beginnings (a Review Article)," *Harvard Theological Review* 81 (1988), 319–39.

129. Roberto do Alba and Alan W. Organschi, "A Conversation with Giovanni Michelucci," *Perspecta* 27 (1992), 122.

130. Christof Martin Werner, *Das Ende des Kirchen-Baus: Rückblick auf moderne Kirchenbaudiskussion* (Zürich: Theologischer Verlag, 1971), and *Sakralität: Ergebnisse neuzeitlicher Architekturästhetik* (Zürich: Theologischer Verlag, 1979). See also Söhngen, "Der Begriff des Sakralen im Kirchenbau," 185, quoting Kurt Marti, "Christus, die Befreiung der bildenden Künste zur Profanität," *Evangelische Theologie* 8 (1958), 372–73: "Jesus Christus ist das prinzipielle, das heißt theologische Ende jedes Sakralraums und jeder Möglichkeit dazu. . . . Es gibt nur noch profane Orte und Räume."

131. Patrick J. Quinn, "The Church in the Future City: House-Church or Parish Place?" *Liturgical Arts* 35, no. 2 (Feb. 1967), 88–90.

132. The classic instance is that of Uzzah, in 2 Samuel 6:6–7 and 1 Chronicles 13:7–10.

133. Schloeder, *Architecture in Communion*, 45.

134. Marilyn J. Chiat, "Form and Function in the Early Synagogue and Church," *Worship* 69 (1995), 406–26, suggests the possibility that early synagogues served as precedent for early Christian basilicas; if they did, their function would have been to pave the way for Christian adoption of Roman rather than specifically Jewish architectural forms, although Chiat also argues that attitudes toward early churches combined Roman architecture with Jewish conceptions of the Temple. Biblical references to early Christian worship in the Temple and in synagogues (sometimes but not always with proselytizing in mind) no doubt reflect only one of several options; Christians also worshiped in homes, and (as Richard Krautheimer suggested) wherever it was practical for them to assemble. In any case, that they continued at all to use the Temple for worship gave biblical warrant for continuity with the cultic practice of ancient Israel. The extent and the forms of that continuity could of course be debated, but the extreme position—that Christian faith is antithetical to the use of sacred space—would be hard to justify in strictly biblical terms.

135. Cettina Militello, "A Theology of Liturgical Space," trans. Matthew J. O'Connell, in Chupungco, *Liturgical Time and Space*, 405–6.

136. For a nuanced statement, see Yves M.-J. Congar, *The Mystery of the Temple, or The Manner of God's Presence to His Creatures from Genesis to the Apocalypse*, trans. Reginald F. Trevett (Westminster, Md.: Newman, 1962), especially 112–50. See Militello, "A Theology of Liturgical Space," 401–2.

137. On relations between Christianity and rabbinic Judaism, both as heirs to ancient Israelite tradition, see Alan F. Segal, *Rebecca's Children: Judaism and Christianity in the Roman World* (Cambridge, Mass.: Harvard University Press, 1986).

138. Tillich, *On Art and Architecture*, 213.

139. Edward A. Sövik, "Remembrance and Hope," *Faith and Form* 30 no. 2 (1997), p. 9.

Index